YOUNG QUEER AMERICA

YOUNG QUEER AMERICA

Real Stories and Faces of LGBTQ+ Youth

By Maxwell Poth
Foreword by Isis King

CHRONICLE BOOKS

SAN FRANCISCO

Copyright © 2023 by Maxwell Poth.
All rights reserved. No part of this book may be reproduced in any form without
written permission from the publisher.

Library of Congress Cataloging-in-Publication Data

Names: Poth, Maxwell, author.
Title: Young queer America : real stories and faces of LGBTQ+ youth /
by Maxwell Poth ; foreword by Isis King.
Description: San Francisco : Chronicle Books, [2023]
Identifiers: LCCN 2022048149 | ISBN 9781797214412 (paperback)
Subjects: LCSH: Gay youth—United States.
Classification: LCC HQ76.27.Y68 P68 2023 | DDC
306.76/60835—dc23/eng/20221021
LC record available at https://lccn.loc.gov/2022048149

Manufactured in China.

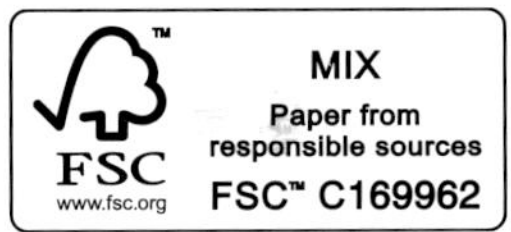

Design by Howsem Huang.

10 9 8 7 6 5 4 3 2 1

Chronicle books and gifts are available at special quantity
discounts to corporations, professional associations, literacy programs,
and other organizations. For details and discount information, please
contact our premiums department at corporatesales@chroniclebooks.com
or at 1-800-759-0190.

Chronicle Books LLC
680 Second Street
San Francisco, California 94107
www.chroniclebooks.com

CONTENTS

Introduction   6

Project Contrast   7

Foreword by Isis King   8

Stories from Young Queer America   10

Stockton's Story   280

Conclusion   285

State Resources   286

Acknowledgments   288

INTRODUCTION

All queer coming out stories have their similarities: Revealing your true self to friends and family after living in hiding is a nearly universal experience for LGBTQ+ folks. Some people come out at fifty, some in their first decade of life, but there is no singular queer experience for all that we have in common. Some of us are lucky enough to have supportive families and communities, but it's still extremely dangerous to be queer in many parts of the country.

I came out ten years ago, when I was seventeen years old. I'd fallen in love with a boy named Alexander at a Backstreet Boys reunion concert (cliché, I know), and he made me realize that I didn't want to hide who I was becoming in my small Utah town. We are still close to this day. As liberating as it was to tell my friends and family, I felt isolated in my small Mormon town of Bountiful, Utah. My own community ignored that I was gay. The ones who did choose to recognize it bullied and tormented me. As soon as I graduated, I moved to Salt Lake City in search of a queer community. I live in Los Angeles now as a photographer and photojournalist, representing my queer family, but I always look back to my Utah roots and remember what made me the gay man I am today.

There are still places in America where no one is out. Places where being queer just isn't an option. The media prominently shows queer culture in areas where it thrives: New York City, Los Angeles, Miami, San Francisco. Fifty years ago you couldn't be openly LGBTQ+ anywhere in America, and now our biggest cities are the safest places to be gay. Gay liberation was born in these cities, and it's wonderful to see that part of queer culture take center stage for all of America.

These cities are beacons of promise for queers everywhere, but they don't reflect the experiences of the queer community everywhere else. What's it like to be gay in Rapid City, South Dakota? Have you ever seen the infamous drag kings and queens at Mad Myrna's in Anchorage, Alaska? What is it like to live in Lincoln, Nebraska, where, until recently, there wasn't a single gay bar because the last one had been burned down? (I'm sure you can guess why.)

Even though gay liberation has transformed American culture, there are places where queers are still fighting for basic human rights. Our beautiful transgender community has always faced discrimination, and now conservative political parties and transphobic leaders are pushing more anti-trans legislation than ever before. Republican-run states are trying to reverse the progress that we've fought for, rejecting and endangering our trans community. And while the gay liberation movement was once led by LGBTQ+ adults, now the battles are being joined by the younger generations.

Sadly, many do not make it out alive.

Almost everyone I know has lost someone to suicide. It isn't something we prepare for, nor does it always happen to the people we'd expect.

Through my work with Project Contrast, I meet young, beautiful queer people who often feel alone and helpless, not knowing that there is another kid just like them only miles away. Some of the kids I work with have never met another queer person before. They need community *now*. They need a way to see that leaving your home isn't the only way to achieve happiness, love, and acceptance.

I started Project Contrast to amplify the voices of queer youth living across America. Their stories matter. Their advice can save lives. Creating opportunities for queer youth to support one another is priceless and can help other struggling LGBTQ+ kids understand that they are not alone.

PROJECT CONTRAST

Four years ago I started a photo project that had no name, just a simple goal. I wanted to call attention to the fact that my homestate of Utah was doing a horrible job of protecting its young queer residents—the leading cause of death in Utah for those between the ages of ten and seventeen is suicide.

This statistic was brought to my attention when two boys took their own lives over the same weekend in Utah. Both of them were gay.

One of the boys went to Bountiful High School, just like me, and when he died he was the same age that I was when I came out. His name was Stockton. The similarities threw me. Surrounded by acceptance and love in my adult life, I had forgotten what it felt like to be out and alone in a small town. Statistically, queer kids are coming out younger and younger each year, but in spite of all the supposed progress, young queer people are still taking their own lives.

In December 2016 I flew back to Utah for the holidays. I had met a sixteen-year-old gay boy going to high school in Murray, Utah. He was out, proud, and loved his life. I was impressed and inspired by his confidence and ability to thrive in such a conservative community. There were queer kids only miles away who felt alone and unsupported. What might it mean to them to hear his story?

And so Project Contrast was born.

I photographed three young queer kids and asked them to write about growing up in Utah. The series went on to run in both *The Advocate* and *OUT* magazine.

The four-part series debuted online on February 14, 2017, with a new story released each day, starting with my own. The stories made a huge impact, and not long after they were published, I started receiving messages from queer youth all over America. My life was changed forever.

Following the success of the articles, I decided to go back to Utah to work with local queer advocates to highlight more queer youth. So, with the help of my dear friend, Jacob Dunford, I created Project Contrast to amplify queer youth all over America and work toward lowering the number of teen suicides within the LGBTQ+ community.

Since I turned Project Contrast into a nonprofit, I have been traveling the country documenting queer youth. I have interviewed and worked with more than two hundred queer kids and teens from twenty different states. And in this book I've compiled stories and photographs of seventy-three young queer folks living in areas where being LGBTQ+ is still difficult.

The stories of queer people and queer youth that we see in the media have unimaginable reach, but there are also millions of other stories—devastating, inspiring, relatable, *real* stories—that have yet to be shared. In these pages you will find kids and teens sharing their journeys toward happier lives. Some of these kids have faced challenges no young person should ever have to endure: homelessness, homophobia, transphobia, grief, and loss. Some of them have been subjected to violence or sexual assault, while others started self-harming to deal with feelings of dysphoria. But theirs are also tales of strength and happiness in the face of hardship.

I hope that this book leaves you with a better understanding of what it is like to be queer in America. I hope that you are compelled to share these stories. I hope that these words help struggling teens realize that there are so many kids just like them out there, still standing and doing their best to get through each day.

If I save even one life, this book was worth it all.

FOREWORD

By Isis King

Navigating life can and will come with many challenges when you find the courage to live out loud. This is something that you can do on your own, but finding your tribe—and getting insight from those who came before you—can be vital in navigating a world that discriminates against, and unfairly disadvantages, members of the LGBTQIA community, especially when they are people of color or visibly queer.

I remember feeling completely alone and isolated in college when I discovered Octavia St. Laurent in *Paris Is Burning*, the incredible documentary about New York's underground ballroom scene. I was in my second year of college, battling depression while juggling being in school on a full scholarship. Coming from a low-income household, I knew that failure wasn't an option because my family's resources were already being stretched to help me attend school. I was also living with a lover who was physically and verbally abusive to me. All of my friends were lovely cishet women who were in my fashion design program. They all accepted me as the "token gay kid" of the group, but I always knew I was different. The day I watched Octavia St. Laurent in *Paris Is Burning* was the first time I felt seen, truly seen. Octavia shared stories in such a confident and poetic way that you had no reason not to believe the words that came out of her mouth. She was going to be a star, and her being trans wasn't going to stop that. Before I watched *Paris Is Burning*, the only images of trans women I had seen were on television shows that exploited them as the punch line. Seeing Octavia was a light bulb moment for me, one that single-handedly changed the

trajectory of my life. She gave me hope, as well as the confidence I needed to blossom into who I was meant to be.

I soon found myself out of that abusive relationship and back home in Maryland, regrouping and in therapy for survivors of domestic abuse, when I had the epiphany that I needed to live in my truth! My journey to New York City to follow in Octavia's footsteps was a rocky one. My family didn't understand me wanting to transition, but I had just turned twenty-one and found the courage to finally put myself first. After six months in the New York area, my funds were low. I found myself moving into an LGBT shelter, regrouping once again, and then, in what felt like an instant, I was thrust onto the TV screen as a contestant on *America's Next Top Model* only ten months after starting hormone replacement therapy. I didn't realize at the time that this attempt to finally escape poverty and make something of myself would lead me to expose my insecurities to millions of people, and then have to emotionally regroup again. The show wasn't the end of my journey, but my appearance on it did have a ripple effect, as many people learned that there was someone out there in the world like them, or perhaps saw a vision of what they wanted to become. My journey is a testament to perseverance and having faith not only in the universe, but also in who you truly are inside.

A month after I was on *America's Next Top Model*, a young gay teen sent me a detailed message explaining how my story saved him from suicide by helping him realize that there was a light at the end of that dark tunnel. That was the moment that the responsibility of who I was and the weight of what I was doing hit me. I knew my mission was to help others, and I always knew I was a fighter, but sometimes things manifest differently than you expect. Since then, I've tried to be aware of the things I do and always look for opportunities to elevate others. I wanted to make things easier for those after me, especially trans youth out there thinking that their lives don't matter. This is why sharing our stories is so important. Our youth are impressionable, so why not fill their hearts and spirits with truthful stories that could inspire them and help them feel supported? My story is unique in the details, but there are countless others like me who are surviving—and thriving—in their self-knowledge. Their stories need to be heard!

Maxwell's book is so special. It takes only one story. One story can change the entire trajectory of a life. It's like discovering a cheat sheet or a treasure map, something that can connect you to so many others who are just like you. A key that opens the door to a world so many choose to misinterpret. A world where you can truly be free to live out loud. The stories will not always be pretty, but they will be true. We all deserve to be happy, and safe, and successful, but some young people live in a world where they rarely see people like themselves thrive on the same level as everyone else. These stories have the power not only to save lives, but also to help so many thrive.

We deserve it.

YOUNG QUEER AMERICA

Abby

18 years old, she/her, Kansas
CW: This story contains references to suicide.

Let me introduce myself. My name is Abby, but my birth mom called me Etta. Sometimes I wish I was Etta, because no one knows who Etta is. I can make Etta whoever I want her to be. She could love who she wants and be who she wants to be. Abby, unfortunately, isn't as lucky. Let me start from the beginning.

I was born on April 29, 2003, in Florida, but a couple of weeks after I was born I was given up for adoption. Every day since I was separated from my family, I absolutely resented them. I couldn't process how two people could just give me up like that. I thought I would learn to understand as time passed, but that never seemed to be the case. I went to live with a family soon after and we moved to Dodge City, Kansas, but I went to school in a tiny town called Minneola, Kansas. Fast-forward to elementary and middle school, or as I call them, the worst years of my life. I was the only Black girl at the entire school. When I was younger it didn't affect me as much, but the older I grew the more I learned.

Suddenly the racist jokes became more apparent to me. I learned that people who I thought of as friends were really just making fun of me. Not long after this I discovered more about my sexuality. Now, being a queer in Kansas you are basically guaranteed to get bullied or worse. There is very little support for queers

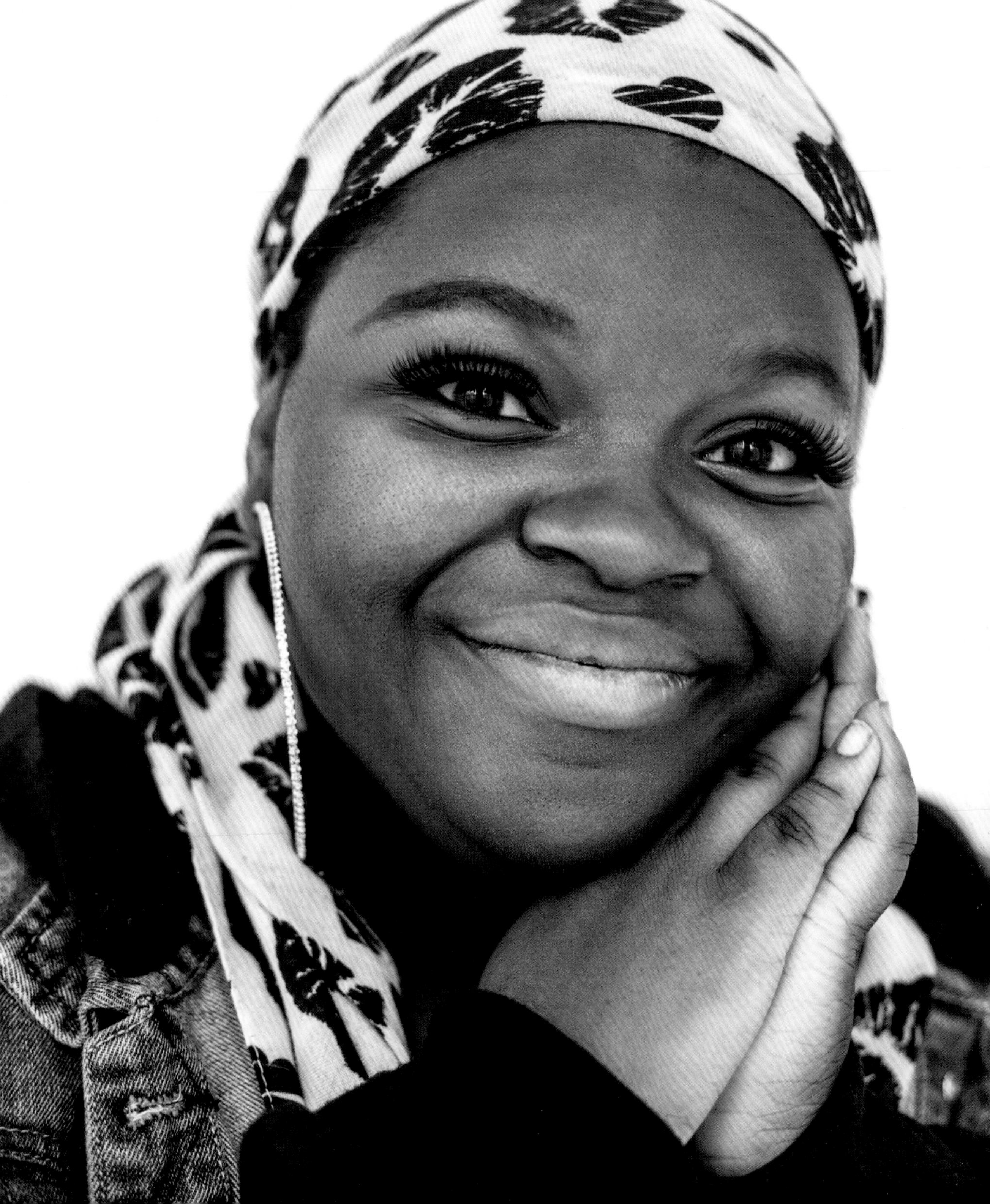

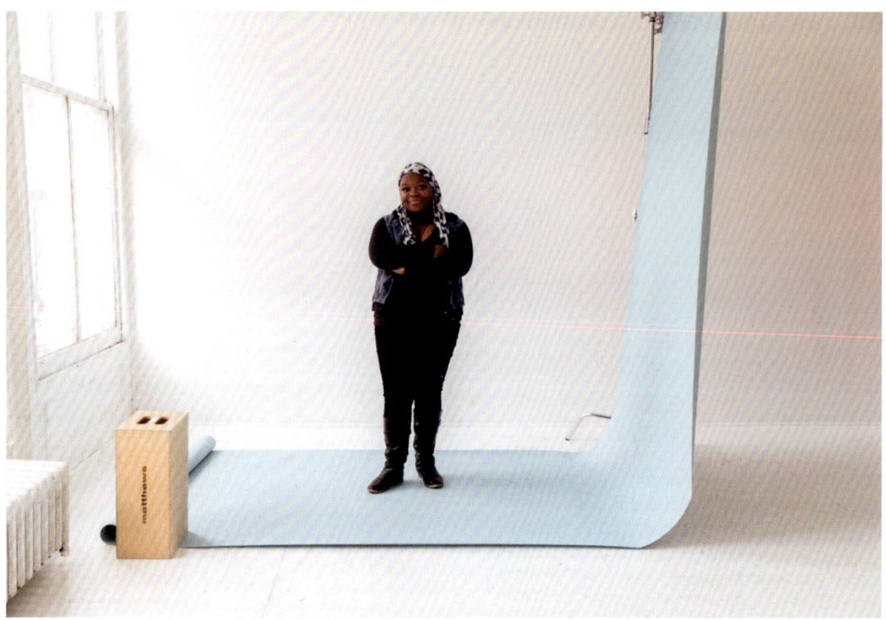

in Kansas, which is the sad thing about that state. I grew up in a white Republican Christian home where we were taught that being straight is the only sexuality. My dad was the pastor of a church, so that was what I was solely taught. All our family friends were Christians, and it was like the word *homosexual* was banned in my home. These old-school Christian households were against things like premarital sex, abortions, gay marriage, masturbation, etc. I grew up thinking that what my parents taught us was always right and that any other way of thinking was wrong. I was scared to even imagine myself with another girl. When I got to seventh grade I was still getting bullied for being Black. I had about two really good friends who loved me for me, but their love could only go so far. Halfway through my seventh grade year I attempted suicide. I didn't want to live in a world where not only would I get bullied for being Black, but I would also get bullied for being queer. It was safer for me to stay closeted. Thankfully my suicide attempt failed, and I was sent to see a therapist. My therapist didn't help me at all. It's hard to explain to someone how it feels to be Black and queer when they aren't. She blamed my outbursts on sexual frustration and told me she gave me "permission to masturbate," which confused the hell out of me.

At the end of my eighth grade year my parents told me we were moving to South Dakota. I was sad to leave my friends, but I was excited to escape most of the other kids. My first couple years of high school were great in the friend department but weak in my mental health department. I felt like every single day was a struggle to get out of bed, much less go to school. But something life changing happened my sophomore year. I was a little bit of an investigator, so I went digging through my personal papers. I ended up finding my birth mom's and birth dad's names. I found my birth mom's Instagram and sent her a DM. It wasn't ideal, or how I wanted to meet her, but at that point in my life I would have given anything to just know who she was and to get some answers about my life.

The next day she messaged me back confirming she was my mother. We spent months talking in secret, and she helped me understand more of who I am. Sadly, I found out my father had died when I was eight years old. I knew I would have to tell my adoptive parents about me reuniting with my birth mom, and eventually they learned to accept that she was back in my life for good.

Senior year started, and I was at the best point in my life. I had lots of friends who loved me. I was able to be a leader in my community, not just for Black Lives Matter but for many other things. My greatest moment of my senior year was getting my school's dress code changed so it was inclusive of the Black population. This was the year that changed my life for the better. This was the year I met my mother for the first time. She was there to watch me graduate and give the graduation speech. I am now a first-semester college student at the American Musical and Dramatic Academy in New York City, and I couldn't be happier.

So now let me reintroduce myself. My name is Etta. I am a bisexual, Black, Christian woman and I am damn proud of it. I have been through hell and back and it has only made me stronger. Even now I have not come out as bisexual to my parents, but that is okay. I think it is just going to take them longer to accept it. At least I have a supportive birth mother who loves me regardless. I hope my story has inspired you, and if you are going through something similar, let me be the first to tell you it gets easier. The road there might be a pain in the ass, and you are going to have so many moments when you are ready to give up, but you listen to the voice in the back of your head that says to keep going. You are stronger than you realize, and once you realize that, you are gonna be unstoppable. I never expected to get as far as I did, and look at me now. I am studying at my dream school with big plans for my future. Thank you for listening to my story and I hope one day I will get to listen to yours.

Addison

14 years old, she/her, Oklahoma

My name is Addison. I am a Lesbian, I go by She/Her, I am fourteen, and I live in Norman, Oklahoma.

I figured out I was a Lesbian when I was in the fourth or fifth grade, when I learned what LGBTQ+ was and what the labels meant. I had many friends who were also in the LGBTQ+ community, which also helped me figure out who I was. I have been very confident in my identity for as long as I can remember, and I have always known to ignore anyone trying to ruin that.

The older I get, the fewer people there are who don't accept my identity. This has helped me gain confidence and tell anyone who has a problem with it to buzz off. Initially, I came out to my mom, who accepted me the most and made me feel comfortable sharing my identity. Since then, I am very open with my identity to anyone who will listen, in school or elsewhere.

There has been a lot of acceptance and recognition from others outside our community, but we still have a long way to go. I believe it will come in time, but those of us within the community have to stand strong and be proud of who we are. We are who we are, regardless of who we choose to love, and I wish people would see that more.

We should all stand tall in our identities and we must not be ashamed. I feel like the only thing in our community that I would change would be more willingness to understand that we are all different, but we are all fighting the same fight. No one has all of the answers; be a light to those in the community that may be struggling. My identity has helped me because I believe in myself and know that it isn't weird, gross, or anything else that others may label it.

My focus is not on what others have to say about my community or my identity, because I know I am valid and no one else has a say in who I am, what I do, or how I represent myself. Since coming out and figuring out who I am, my confidence in my identity has helped me greatly in my life. As a result, I am free to be who I am without worrying about anyone who dislikes it, and I can avoid those people once they become a problem in my life. To anyone reading this who is having trouble being confident in their identity, your community will stand by you when you need it, and you are who you are.

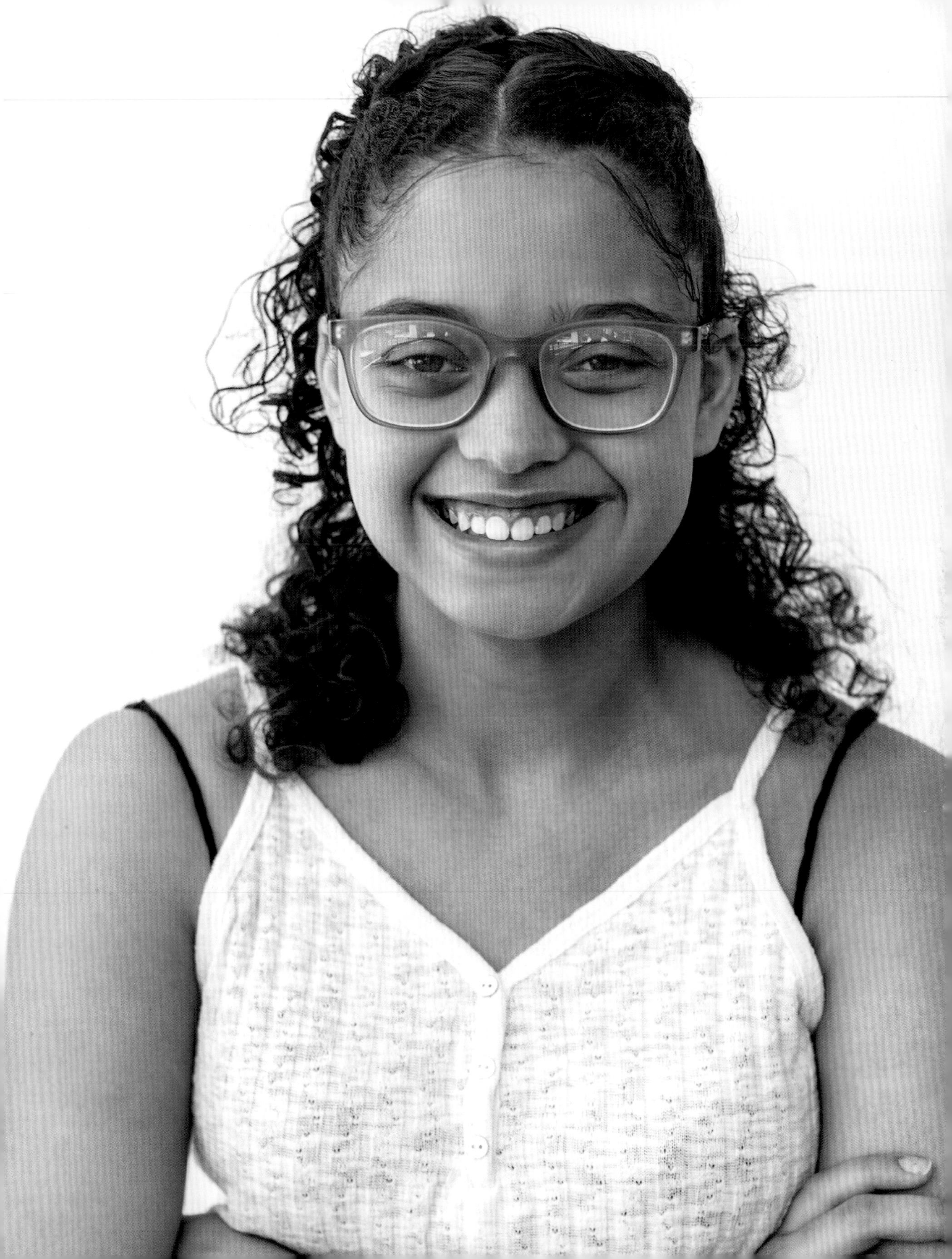

Adrian

17 years old, he/they, Alabama

My name's Adrian, I go by he/they pronouns, and I'm from the port city of Mobile, Alabama.

Growing up in the South is honestly a different experience depending on where you are. Here in Mobile, I feel lucky enough to have found a wonderful community of people like myself. Before that, however, it was a lot harder. I grew up in a religious household, where I put on my little Sunday dresses and went with my mom to church like clockwork. It was a really nice community, everyone loved each other, and we enjoyed service every day. At the time, I didn't even know I was trans.

In elementary school I was always the loud kid. I got in trouble constantly, and I almost always had to sit out of recess because I was in some sort of trouble. Later on, in around fourth grade, I learned what it meant to be gay, and I was taught it was a negative thing. I forced myself into being like all the other girls, and I said I had a crush on some guy just to fit in. Learning that being gay was bad was ingrained into me pretty early on in my childhood.

I really noticed my own differences in middle school, when I transferred to a performing arts school a good drive away from my previous school. Here I realized that there was more than being straight, and even more than being cisgender. At the time I didn't know what it meant to be trans. I hadn't heard the word at all—I had just been told that being gay was wrong and nothing else. At this performing arts school I not only learned that I was a trans man, but I also learned that I had a love for music and a passion for it that I hadn't discovered before.

For me, coming out was a very long process. I never had the opportunity to come out to my mom. Sadly, we lost her years ago. I remember coming out to my dad, down to the date. At that point I had wanted to tell him for months that I was trans, but I didn't know how. I knew he would accept me, but I was still so scared. I remember picking out a book to give him first, to try and ease the way, and to provide him with some information other than me just telling him I was trans. I walked up to him and just blurted out to him that I was trans, and I gave him a book to read about what it meant to have a trans kid.

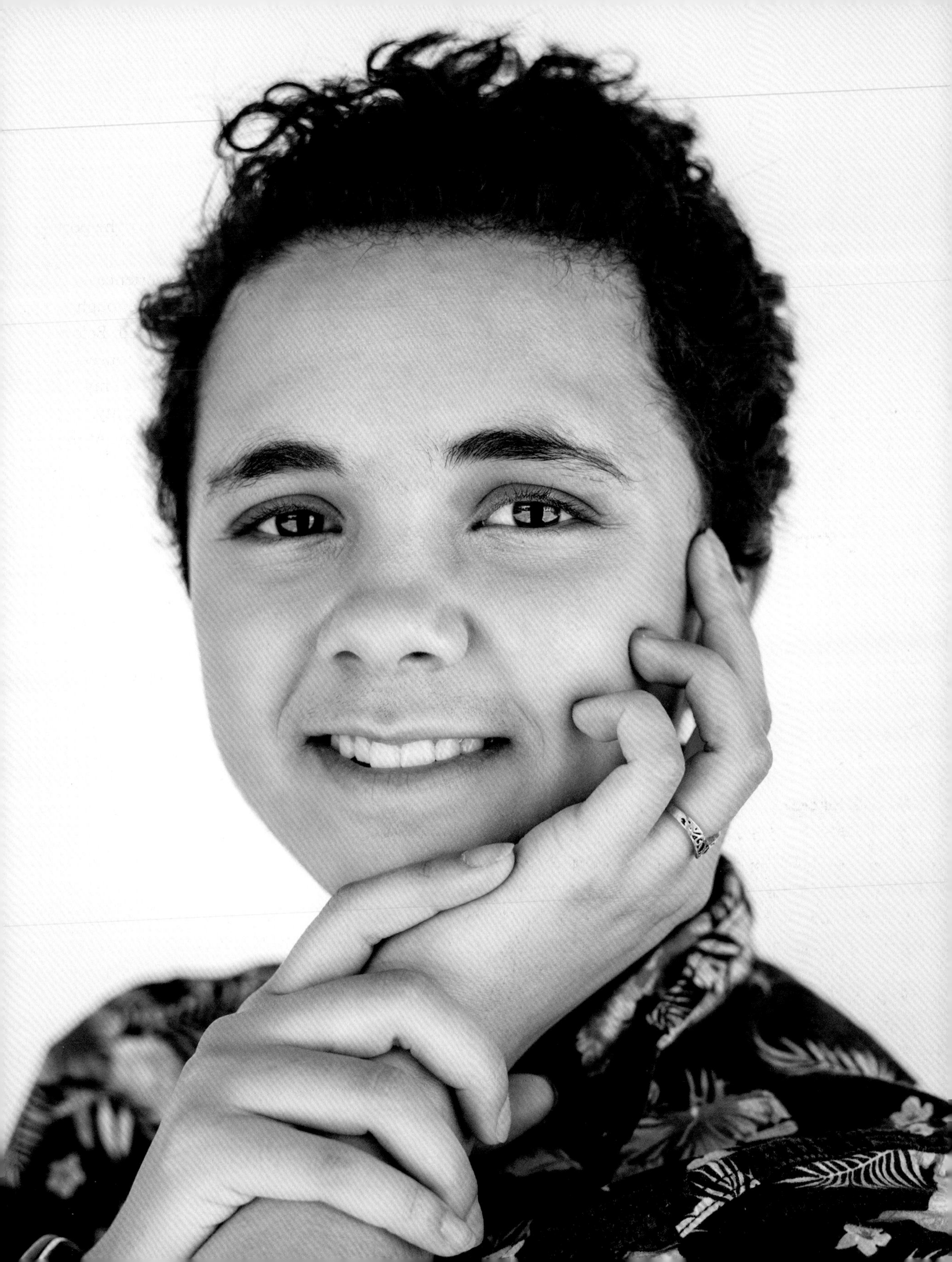

After his initial shock passed, he accepted me without a thought. It took him a lot of time to get used to my new name and pronouns. But he really did try. The hardest part, though, was yet to come. Unlike my father, a lot of my relatives were not so happy about my new name and pronouns. We lost touch with a couple of people over it, actually. Honestly, though, it doesn't really bother me. To me, those people were never my family to begin with if they weren't going to accept me.

After I came out, I very quickly started advocating for LGBT people in my local area. Currently I help at Prism United, our local LGBT+ youth group. I also got to attend a protest in favor of Drag Queen Story Hour, which was actually the first time that event was held in Alabama.

The message I want to leave people with is this: Anything is possible. People are so cruel sometimes, but as a community, we can get through it. People will yell and spit and say slurs to your face sometimes, but we are so much more than they'll ever be. I promise you that. Live, and live to show them how amazing we all can be.

Alex

15 years old, he/him, South Dakota
CW: This story contains brief references to suicide.

Hi, my name is Alex. I am from Watertown, South Dakota. My pronouns are he/him/his, and I identify as a transgender demisexual bi-romantic man. My story doesn't start off easy, but then again, whose story does? It began the day I was born. I came out of my mom and said, "This isn't me!" Just kidding.

My story about discovering myself begins not long after I entered preschool. I began as a "normal" kid in my small South Dakota farm town. I had always felt different, but I didn't know how to express myself. I just knew something was wrong.

As a child I had severe anger issues and problems with my emotions because I didn't know what to do or how to say anything. I didn't speak and I was shy. I didn't understand what I was feeling or what these emotions were.

Once my emotions became too strong for me to handle, my parents began sending me to a facility in Sioux Falls to learn how to deal with them. There I began to understand where these feelings might have been coming from, and I began to feel less angry. Even though I was still quiet at my sessions, and I didn't talk to anyone like I do now, I was allowed to play with "boy toys" while I was there, which made me feel like I could do stuff on my own and I didn't have to worry about people telling me I couldn't play with cars or action figures. Even though now I know nothing about cars (I'm not a car guy), being able to finally try things that made me feel comfortable helped me start my journey to discovering who I am today.

As I got older I discovered the power of the Internet and a website called YouTube. There I was able to find all these different LGBTQ+ people. I saw them all as people that I could relate to, and I liked their content.

I learned the word *transgender*. Then it hit me like a train! I understood what this meant, and then I knew that this is what I was. I knew I wasn't normal, but I didn't want to say anything about it because I didn't fully understand it at the time. All those years prior, when I was getting angry and emotional, and now I finally had an understanding as to why I was feeling the way I was.

But while I was still discovering that I was trans, I already knew I was in the LGBTQ+ community, and this is when I came out

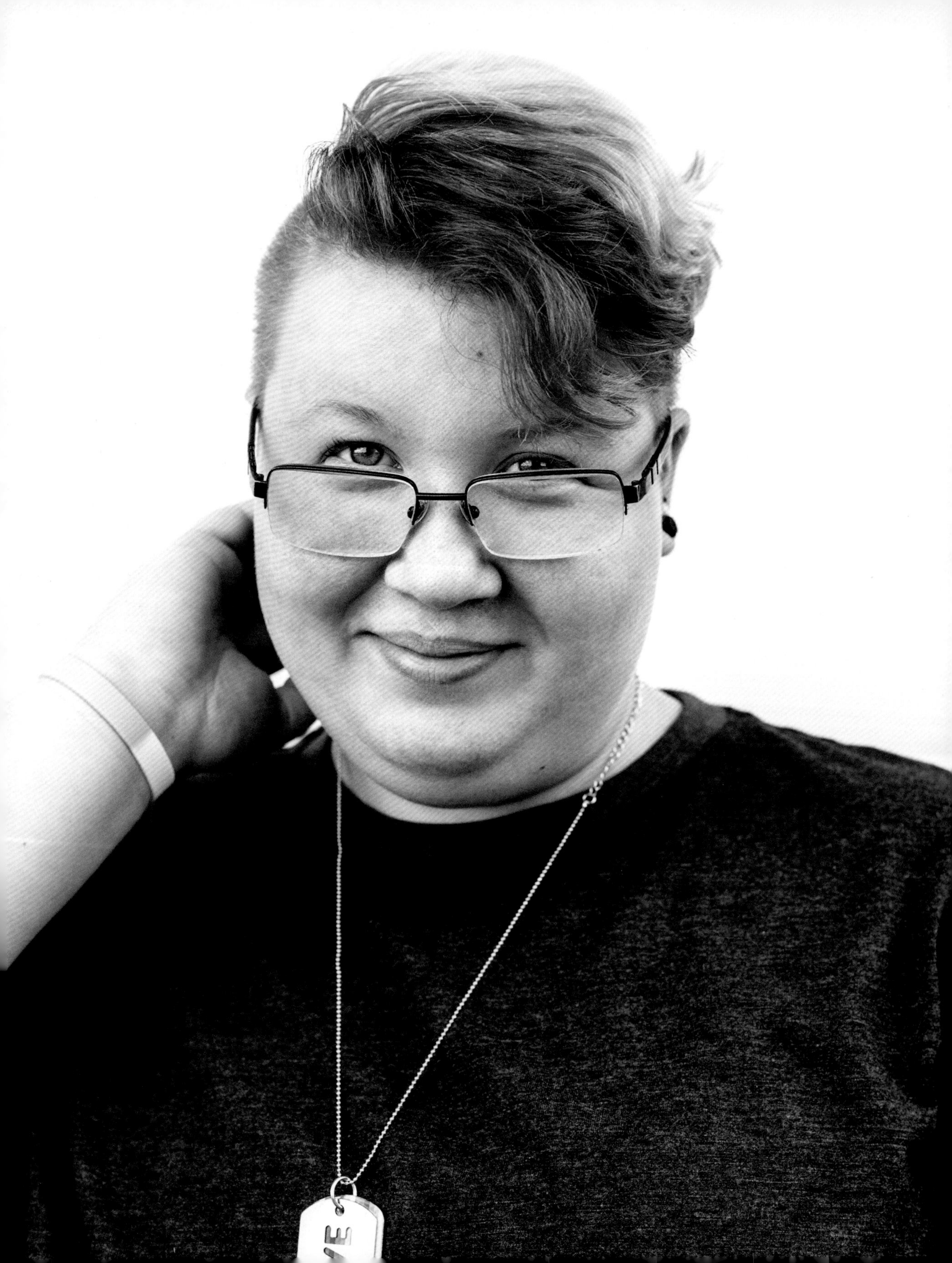

the first time as a lesbian. I first came out to my mom. She just said that she loved and accepted me, I was still her child, and that wasn't going to change.

Knowing I had the support of my mom made me feel great. She has always been such a supporter. That same night I told my dad. Not long after, I told the rest of my family, and they all took it just as well. I am very lucky to have the family I have. They have always been so supportive of my journey.

Then came my second coming out. At first I began playing with different labels to see how I felt, and it started to feel right. But I didn't tell my mom about this at all. She knew me as a lesbian, but I knew it still wasn't who I was. I knew that I had to tell her eventually, so I had a sit-down with my mom and ended up just telling her how I felt. I told her everything. How I was not a lesbian. How I was still discovering, that I had no answers, but that being transgender is where I was heading.

Then I ended up telling my dad and he was okay with it too! He is still learning, but he will always have my back!

Coming out to the rest of the world was my next step, and I did it in the most teenage way possible . . . in a Facebook post. It was mostly good. A lot of people didn't understand, but as long as they were respecting me, that is all I cared about.

When I started middle school I began to come out and transition at school. This took a huge toll on my mental health, and I am still recovering from it today. When I came out as transgender, I lost a lot of people at school who I thought were my friends. It was hurtful because I was still the same person; I had just finally shared something that I'd kept hidden. My teachers also ignored it and continued to call me by my birth name, which only made it harder for me. This is when my mental health really took a downfall. I didn't feel safe at school—or really anywhere in my South Dakota town.

My mom noticed me not being what I would call "normal." I shut down. I was reclusive and I stopped talking to people, just like when I was a little kid. Around this time my mom took me to a doctor and I started my antidepressants. They did not end up working at all, but I still didn't know what to say, so I was quiet about it. But I was starting to become more accepted as middle school went on.

I began to educate my new friends on what the word *transgender* meant, that I was still me, and that they should love me for who I am. They told me that they accepted me no matter what, which is what friends should do.

I started to show interest in my hobbies again, and I talked to my mom about how I was feeling. This was the start of my journey toward accepting myself.

Not long after this, I lost a friend of mine to suicide. They were nonbinary and pansexual. This was very hard for me, and because of this my mom started Watertown Love, a group for LGBTQ+ youth, adults, and their allies. I am the current youth ambassador for the board. Together my mom and I work toward making South Dakota a more accepting place for queer people like me.

My advice to other queer youth like me would be don't be afraid to speak your mind because your mental health matters more than what other people think. Because I didn't speak up for myself, I ended up a thousand times worse than I could have been. Even though I did struggle, and I still have some struggles today with my peers and teachers, I am confident in who I am and excited for my future!

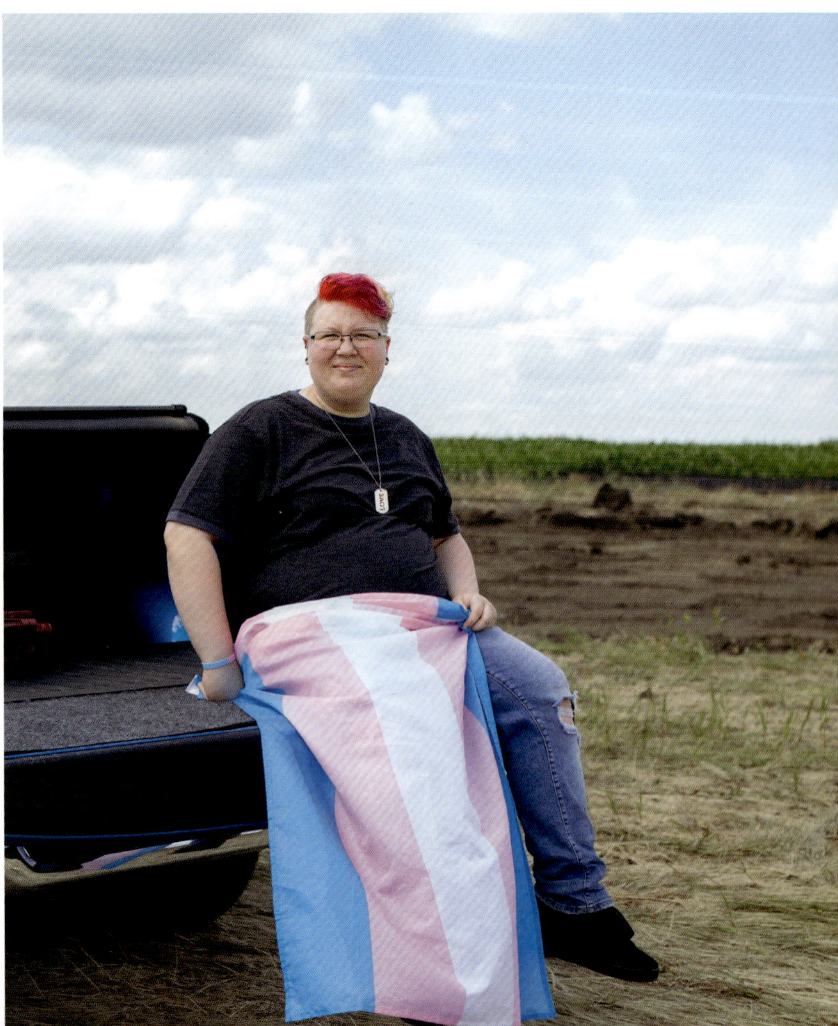

22

Anavera

14 years old, she/her, Alaska

Well, I have a lot to say, so I guess to start out I'd like to say hi! My name is Anavera, my favorite color is blue, my favorite animal is a buffalo, and I live in Wasilla, Alaska. No, I do not ride a polar bear to school; and no, I don't live in an igloo; but yes, it is cold sometimes. Now that we have that out of the way, wc can get down to the more interesting stuff.

When I was too young to remember, my parents split up, but that's okay because my father married someone who soon gave birth to my amazing little sister, Samantha. Now, before we continue, I'd like you to know that my two homes are *very* different, and that's because my parents are two *very* different people. At my dad's house my stepmom says a prayer before we have dinner and we go to church on Sundays (though mostly I protest), and at my mom's house we eat food while it's being cooked. If you haven't already guessed, my stepmother is very religious, to the point where I could say "I like bacon" and that somehow turns into her saying something about how we should always be thankful that God has let us find our way through life. I'm not so sure those two ideas correlate, but okay, I guess. My father isn't as religious, but he goes along with what she says until he gets either bored or annoyed. Now onto the exciting part (I'm not sure whether I'm being sarcastic or not myself, so bear with me, please): coming out!

Around fourth grade or so, crushes became a big deal. And if you said you didn't have one, you were either lying or boring. It made things confusing for me, because I didn't get what was so fascinating with these weird boys in my class. I figured at this point that a crush must mean that you think a boy is funny or more tolerable than others. It took a couple more years to figure out why. It wasn't until sixth grade that I began to explore my sexuality, not that that's what I would have called it. I just started to look at my girl friends and think, "Wow, they are so pretty! I wish I could hold their hand. Maybe they would give me a hug if I helped them with their homework." I guess it hit me that that's not how people normally think about friends; I finally had a crush! After finally admitting to myself I was gay, it began to overwhelm me. I started pulling away from people I cared about for fear that they would hate me or think that I

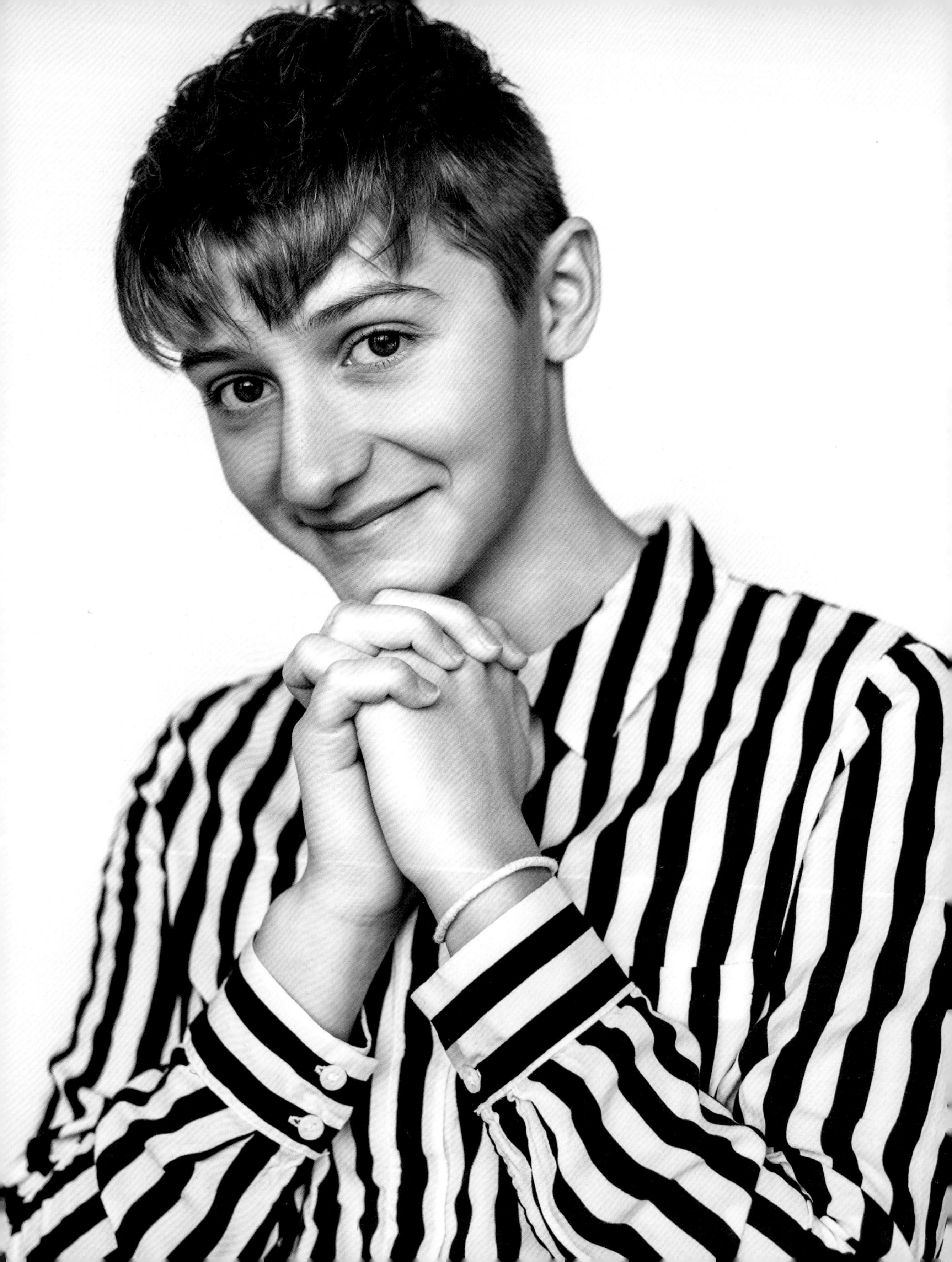

was disgusting. I was scared, and conversations with my friends and family gave me a lot of anxiety. I had struggled with the idea for a bit, but I decided to come out in seventh grade. By "decided," I mean that I couldn't keep carrying all the weight of not being able to be myself around other people. I didn't have anyone I felt I could really talk to about it, so it was just bottled up inside me. So, I was eleven years old, sitting in the truck with my mom on our way to the dump (isn't that lovely?). She was talking, something to do with marriage, and said, "Well, when you get a husband . . ." I kind of stopped her. "Mom, what if I don't want to marry a man?" And then it was out there—I had said it! In short, her response was, "Oh, you're gay! That makes so much more sense!" And of course on hearing this I began to cry. "Oh, baby, it's okay! Now I don't have to worry about you accidentally getting pregnant!" Which didn't stop me from crying, but thanks anyway, Mom!

After that happened I just felt so relieved. But I couldn't just say it once and be done with it; no, life's not that easy. Next I started with my close friends—"okay, cool"—and that was that! Maybe a hug or something, but I think they already knew. It all went down-hill from there. I told a friend I had something to tell her. Standing in the hallway, she said, "Just tell me already!" So I took a deep breath: "I'm gay." And when she heard this her face contorted into what can only be described as pure disgust. "For who?" she asked me. This was very confusing. Sure, I liked someone, but I'm not gay *for her*, so I said, "For me?" And she just looked me up and down and said, "Ew, you're joking right? That's disgusting." So I laughed nervously and sadly replied with "yes." But it was obvious that she didn't believe me. From that day forward, I was the gay kid at school. Not the only one, but the only one that would say it out loud.

So all that was left to do was to come out to my dad and my extremely religious stepmother. I'm sitting in a drive-through with my stepmom, listening to a segment on the radio that happened to include a gay man. She turned off the radio and angrily said, "I can't believe they would put something like that on the radio!" I started to become anxious, and I asked her why, even though I knew the answer. Her reply was something about him being gay. And of course I thought this was the best opportunity I would get and said, "Oh, well, I'm gay." She just looked at me. "No, you're not." Which eventually became yelling at me, even pulling over on the side of the road to continue yelling, I suppose so she wouldn't accidentally crash while screaming at me. Isn't that thought-ful! Once we got home, she decided to tell my father about the "conversation." Then my dad is asking me to hop in the car for a ride. Why are the conversations on this topic always in a car? Anyway, now he is yelling at me because I told my stepmom and not him, suggesting I could've just pulled him aside and said, "Hey Dad! Guess what? I'm a lesbian!" Well, actually, he couldn't even bring himself to say the word "gay," much less "lesbian." I tried to explain that it wasn't so easy. Then he brought up religion, and I honestly wasn't paying attention because I was crying. Note: Me coming out is basically just a giant crying session for me.

Anyway, after all of that my dad and stepmom decided to start sending me to youth groups on Wednesdays and church on Sundays. I didn't enjoy going. It seemed like all they would talk about is split homes and how being gay and trans was against God's will. And even more suspiciously, though it was a group "discussion," they would stop, look at me, and say, "Anavera, do you have any questions?" Not that that didn't suck, but it wasn't the worst part. I went to see my therapist and she looked . . . not so much worried, but I can't really explain it. Anyway, she told me that my stepmom had talked to her before I came in that day and said that I was having troubles with thinking that I was gay and she was hoping my therapist could fix me. Yes, "fix" me. I couldn't do anything but cry. She asked if she could hug me and said it was okay, that I wasn't broken so there was nothing to fix. It's not like I'm a clock or something. After I finally calmed down, she asked how I figured out I was gay. Then we talked about me coming out and what had happened. It was not the only coming out talk we would have; my gender identity was something I would put off.

A few summers later I cut all of my hair off because it made me feel, on the outside, a little more like myself on the inside. I became involved in a queer youth group in Alaska that met via Zoom. I appreciated being able to meet other people who I could relate to, but I was only able to do that on my mom's time because I knew I couldn't do things like that with my dad. In fact, we hadn't talked about me being gay since the day I came out. I got a girlfriend. We would hang out at my mom's place, who was the one parent I felt comfortable talking to about that sort of thing. She was 100 percent supportive of me and us. Well, except for one time, when she wished that I would only date someone that was out. You see, I was waiting on the couch, excited because my girlfriend was coming over. Then I suddenly got a weird text from her phone. "Hi, this is her mom. Are you in a lesbian relationship with my daughter?"

I'll spare you the details, but basically she had been outed to her mom and was in serious trouble. Later I found out she had gotten all forms of communication taken away, her door taken down, her room searched, and all of her texts read out loud to the entire family. And, after a couple of days, she was taken out of school with talk of conversion therapy. A lot has happened since then, and a lot I want to avoid. My mom tried to hang a Pride flag on our porch, but I asked her not to for the sake of my friends. Not all of my friends are out, and I definitely do not want them to be outed just by hanging out with me. Their parents might see the flag when they were being dropped off, or maybe someone who knew me would see it as they passed by, thus bringing up the possibility of my friend being queer because I am.

I don't think there is really much to say other than that. So thank you for taking the time to read this, even if it was very messy. And if you're going to take anything away from this, please let it be that no matter what anyone does or says, there isn't anything wrong with being you. You don't need to be fixed because you're not broken. And if no one else wants to admit that you're an amazing and wonderful human being, I will, because I think you're awesome.

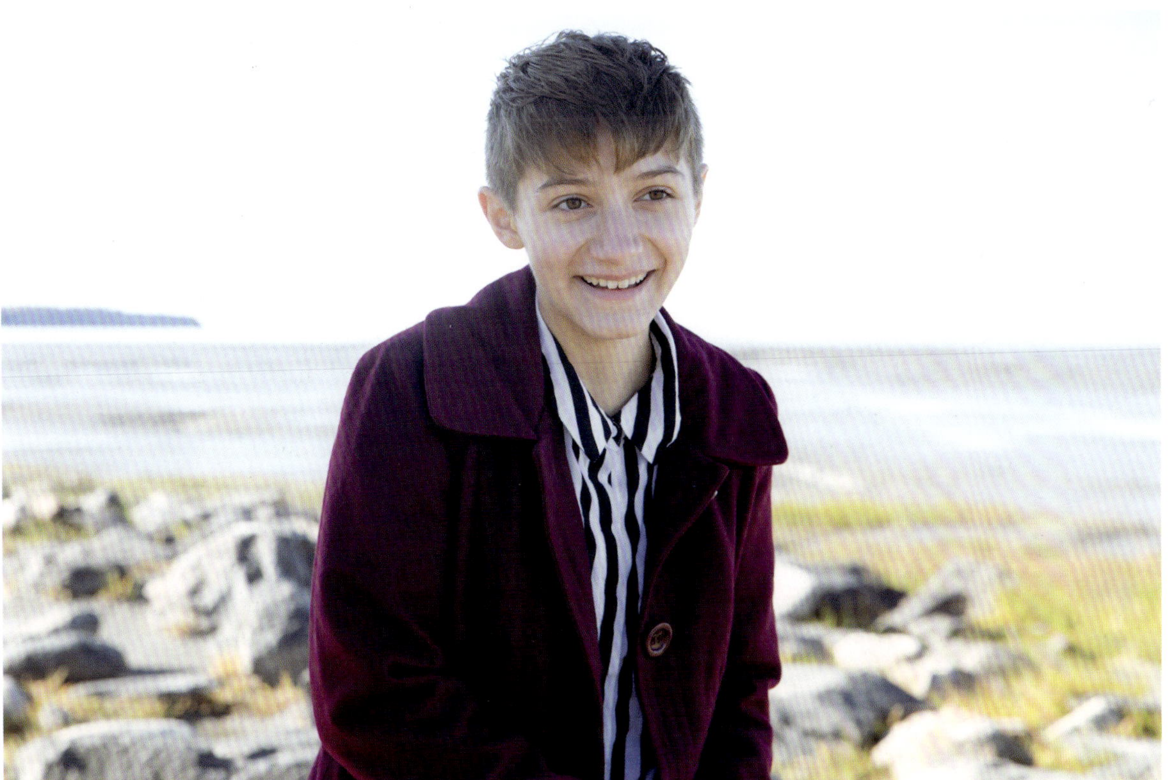

Andrew

16 years old, he/him, Arkansas

My name is Andrew, and I am a gay trans man. My pronouns are he/him. I am sixteen years old and live in Arkansas. Growing up in this community has had its ups and downs. You see a lot of infighting, but more than infighting there is love and acceptance, and you get to be around people who see you as you and not solely how you identify. Growing up in Arkansas, you don't see much acceptance from the older generation of cis people, but the newer generation is much more accepting and you are able to be open about yourself more.

I decided to come out to my aunt first, because if she didn't accept me then no one was going to; but she did accept me, so I came out to my mom through text. She took it well, so we started the steps to transition. I started going to the gender clinic, got my name legally changed, and then started testosterone. Recently I was able to have top surgery, and we are starting the process to get my gender marker changed. This has been my process, but not every transition journey looks like this. For one, not every trans person will bind their chest, not every trans person will go on hormones, and not every trans person has surgery. It is up to you what your journey looks like. And in part this is because not every trans person has a supportive family like I do, and not every trans person has the financial resources that I have. But even though you may not be supported now, you will find people who will care about you and love you for you. That is the wonderful thing about finding a chosen family. Even though you may be stuck in a conservative state, I promise that you will find people who will accept you for you, no matter if it is in a couple of weeks or in forty years. However, you don't need to focus on others' opinions all the time; focus on you and what is best for you, and never pressure yourself to come out until you believe the time is right.

In 2021 so many anti-trans laws were passed in many different states. My state was one that led the charge for a healthcare ban for transgender youth. My mom and other parents of trans kids testified against the bill, pleading with the representatives to vote no. They passed it anyway. Our governor vetoed the bill, but because Arkansas had a Republican supermajority it was passed into law

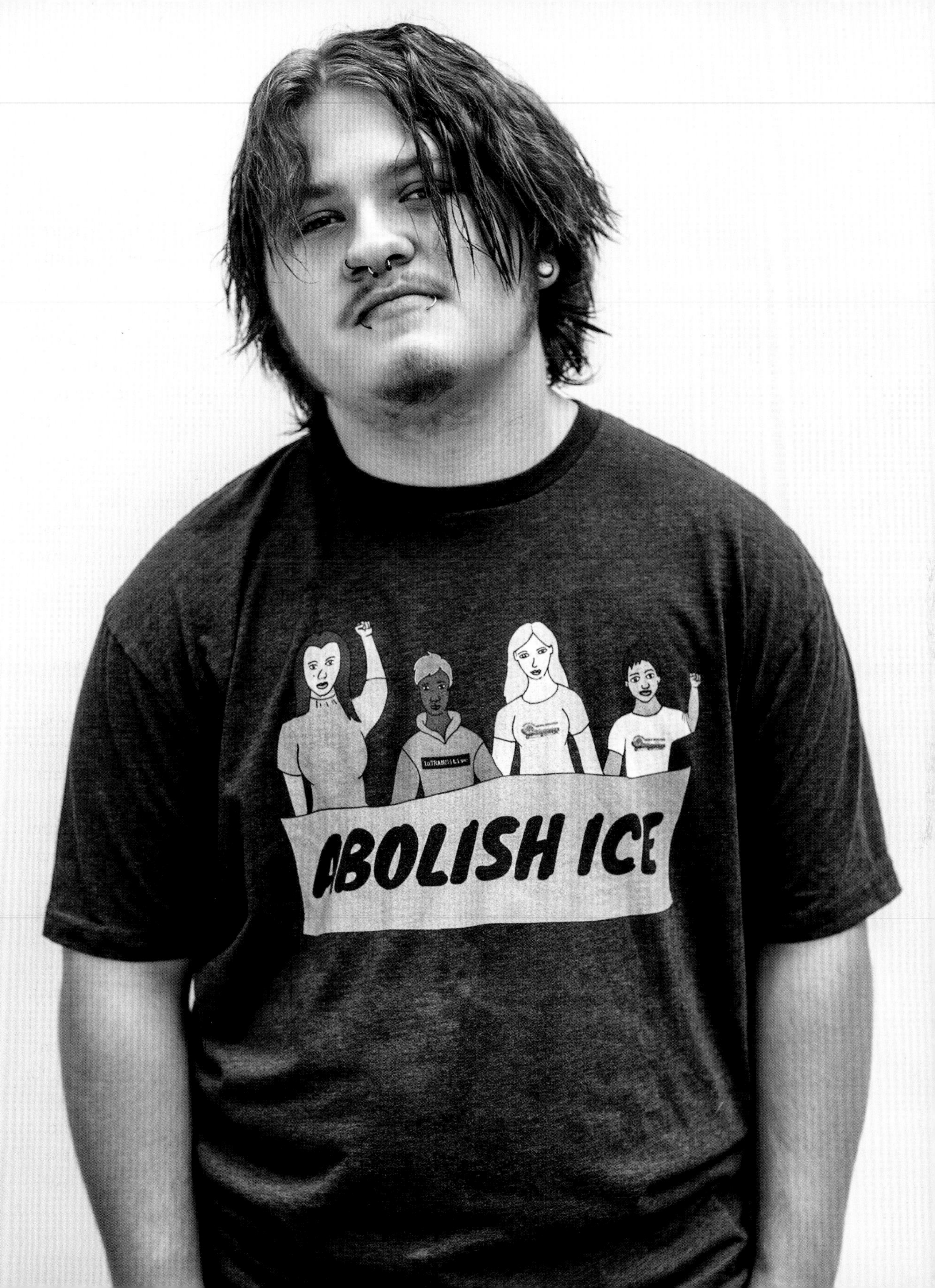
inTRANSitive
ABOLISH ICE

anyway. During this time my mom started getting requests for me to tell my story, to show there are real people with real names and faces attached to these bad bills. We did so many interviews with national and global news outlets. It was a crazy time in my life because I didn't expect to get so much attention for just being myself and for my mom allowing me to live authentically. But my one message to every trans kid out there was that even if you don't have support, there are trans people who are fighting for you and with you. You may not know us personally, but we are your allies, out here fighting for you to exist. We often were asked by reporters whether we ever thought of moving, and we always said no. If everyone picks up and moves, that would give the state their way, and who knows who they would come after next. Someone has to stay and fight no matter what they throw at us; there is still so much work to do.

There may be plenty of trans men, but there is only one of you. Each and every one of you is unique and has your own special qualities. There is no way to give advice to "trans men like me," and that is because there is no trans man exactly like me. So, what I want to tell you is just be uniquely you and don't spend your time living up to other people's expectations of how you should be.

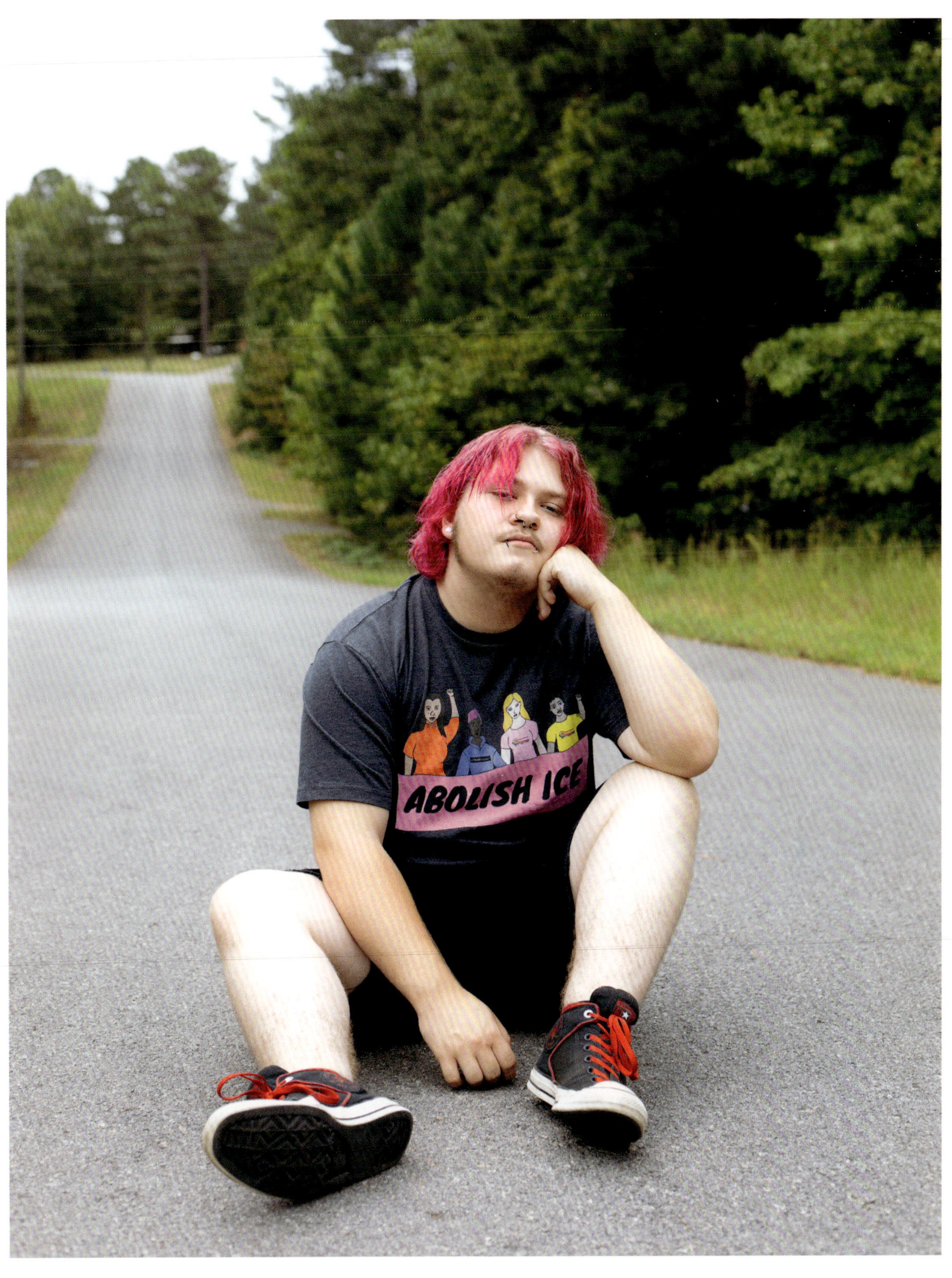

Andrew

Atlas

14 years old, he/it, Colorado

I am a fourteen-year-old trans male born in Colorado. I am a freshman in high school and live in a conservative community. Although we have an LGBTQ+ group in my town, most members of the community that I live in are not open-minded and not willing to understand what it's like to live as an openly queer person.

I dress in an alternative manner, and I do wear skirts and gender-neutral clothing, which can be confusing for others and is why I wear a pronoun pin. But many people at my school do not respect my pronouns or gender identity. I have some teachers who will not treat me with respect and kindness, but I also have teachers who are kind and willing to learn and assist me if an issue occurs. For example, my gym teacher gives me a private space to change since there are no gender-neutral locker rooms.

Being a trans student has been difficult because there are no safe bathrooms for me or my other non-gender-conforming friends. During the second week of school, when I walked out of the boys' bathroom, a group of older male students were waiting outside the bathroom and they called me a dog and barked at me. It made me feel scared to use the bathroom without a friend to watch the door and upset that there are no safe restroom options for me.

Because of COVID we haven't been out a lot since I came out. When I do go out, a few people read my pin or just ask what pronouns I use and how I identify, even though I live in a conservative community. It makes me feel happy, respected, and accepted.

In 2020 I came out to my family as pansexual by text; we got a cake and celebrated. My brother Jake also came out that evening and we got a second cake to celebrate him too. My family is really accepting of me, and later I felt comfortable enough to share that I was a trans male when I realized that I identified as male but could still dress the way I liked regardless of normal stereotypes for boys. My brother Jake also came out as a trans male when I was still questioning my own gender identity. I like growing up with a trans brother; it's nice to know there is someone else in my house going through similar experiences. I'm glad I can talk to him if I have questions or want opinions.

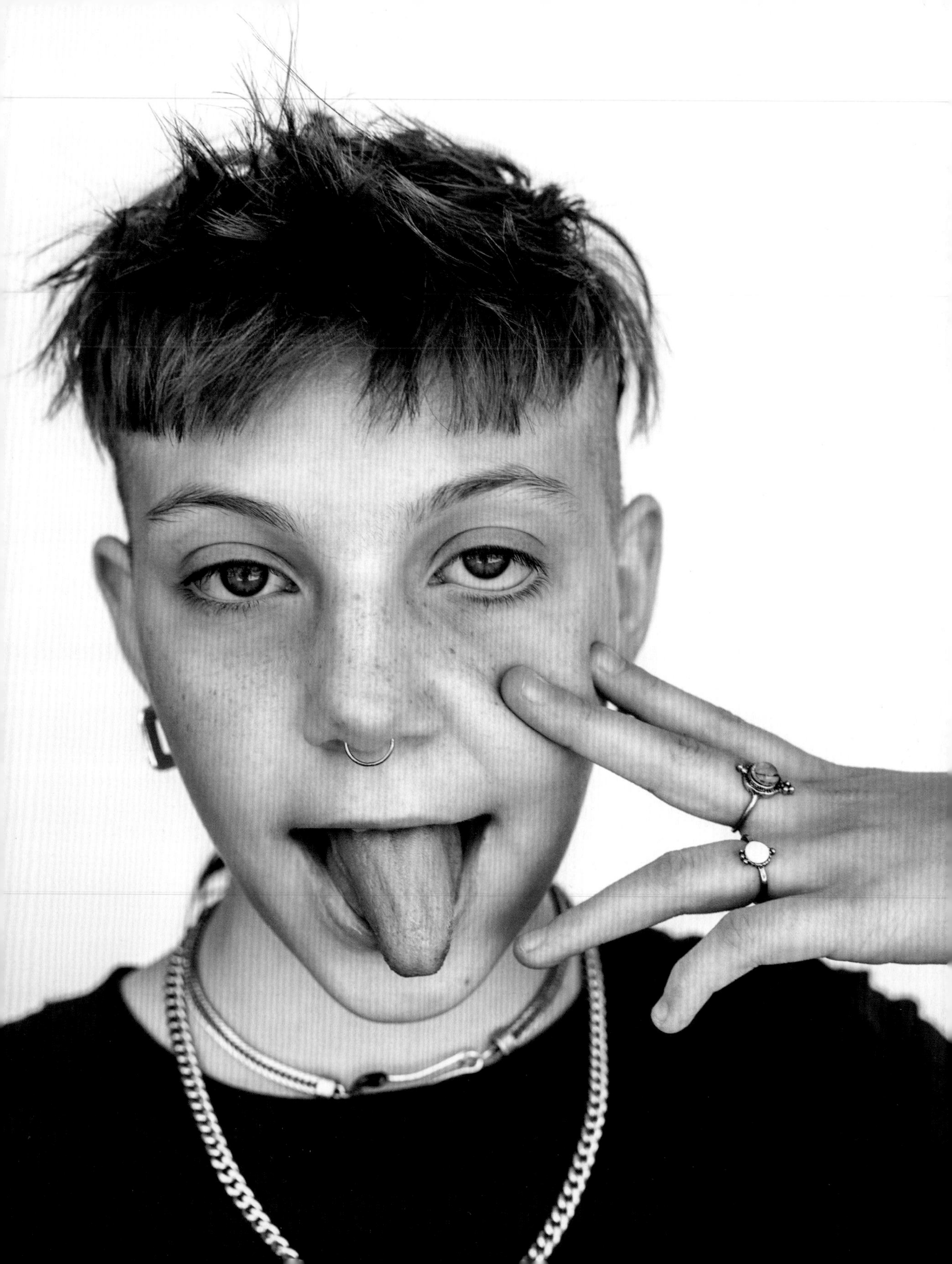

When I came out, some of my longtime friends were uncomfortable with my identity and became very distant from me. Some of them even make transphobic jokes around me. I am very social, and losing most of my close friends was difficult.

Soon after I started high school, I found a large group of alternative friends from all over the queer spectrum. Even though I'm one of the only freshmen in that group, they are still very nice to me. I have also become a support person for other kids who are questioning their identity.

I have learned that being trans doesn't mean you have to look or act a certain way. You can do, wear, and say anything that a cis person can do, wear, and say—regardless of how you identify. If a cisgender guy can wear a skirt, then so can I. Also, even though I lost some good friends, I found other friends who support me and care about me.

If I could speak to someone out there struggling with their identity, I would say to them that it doesn't matter what other people think of you. If you're passionate about yourself, your gender, what you're wearing, don't let some homophobic person stop you from feeling good about yourself. You will find people who will accept and love you for you, but you have to be true to yourself first.

Also, if you don't have a good support system at home, try to find good friends to talk to, or a school counselor, or someone else you can trust. You're important to so many people, and I'm glad you're still here. Just know that I and so many more people are here for you.

Jake

18 years old, he/him, Colorado

When I was very young, I always wanted to be a boy; however, I didn't know about transgender people, so I just lived my life wanting to be a boy. I didn't have extreme body dysphoria, and I accepted who I was as a person.

In middle school I had a crush on a female friend, but I didn't know what to say or do as there were not a lot of queer examples in my community, particularly when I was young. I wasn't angry or upset; I just didn't understand since I had no models of same-sex

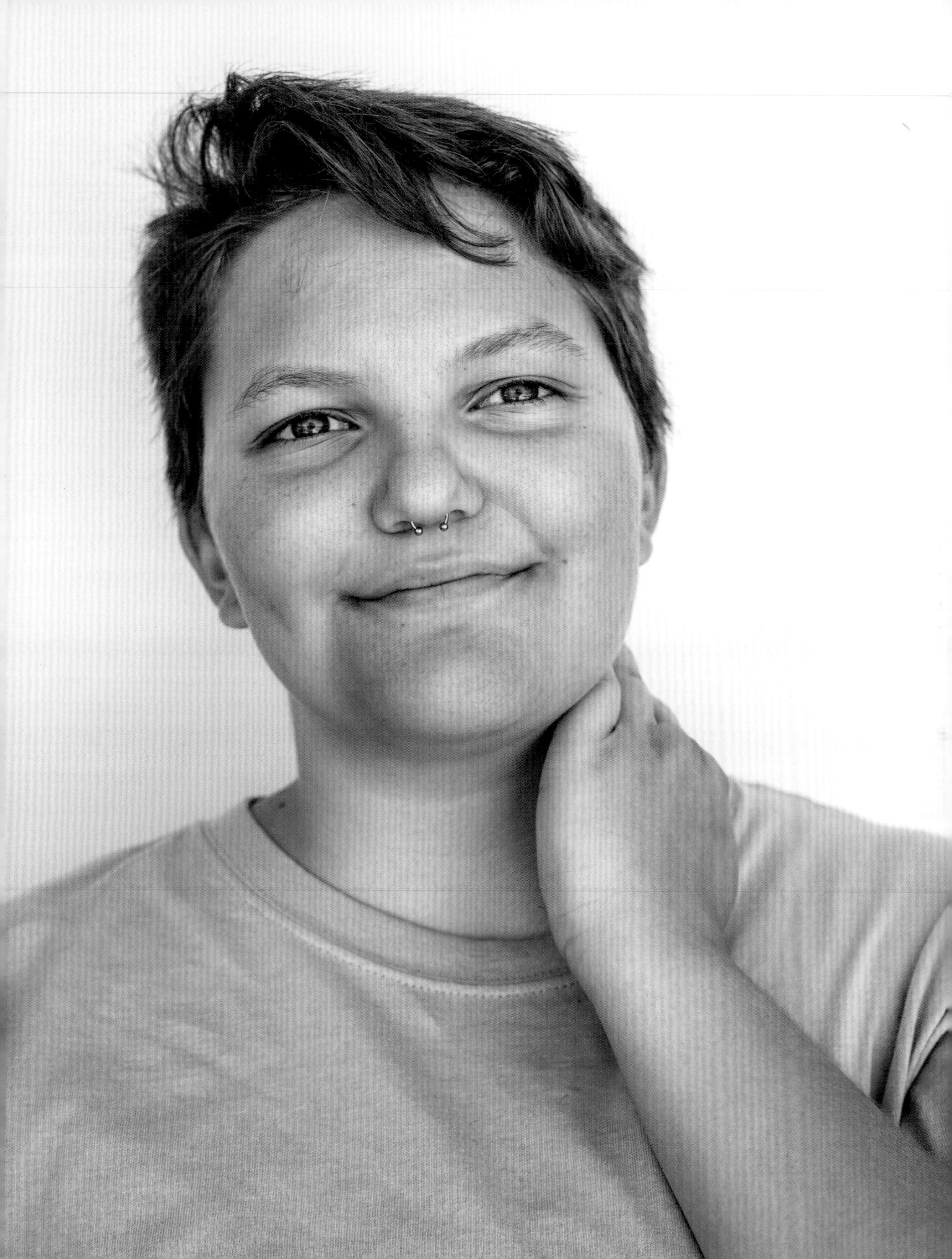

relationships. A similar situation occurred my first year of high school. At the time I thought I just really, really wanted to be friends with this person, but now I realize I had a serious crush.

I always accepted dating boys as "normal" and had a few boyfriends, but I was more attracted to girls, even though I wasn't dating them. I figured out I was bisexual in my sophomore year, when I came out to close friends. I had a queer community at my school, but we didn't really go out or do group events; we just knew we were there for each other.

I also used to be kind of transphobic. I thought that most trans people were "transtrenders," meaning they just did it for attention. I thought this because, although I wanted to be a boy, I didn't fit into the mold of a stereotypical self-hating pretransition transperson model, and I was scared I was a transtrender too.

I came out to my family as bisexual when my sibling came out as pansexual, because they got a cake to celebrate and I also wanted a cake. The cake was pretty good.

I haven't had many challenges; no one has been really homophobic to me. I do tend to keep to myself and not attract attention. I always dressed like a tomboy so no one knew I was bi unless I shared it with them.

One night when I was up late, I realized that I shouldn't judge people for being transtrenders, and I realized that I am transgender masculine myself. The next morning I woke up and shared my realization with my mother, who was very confused and didn't know anything about the trans lifestyle or community. I told my dad too, but I don't think either one believed me.

Later, my sibling Atlas also came out as trans male. It's interesting to have two kids in the same family identify as transgender. No other family members are trans that we are aware of. All of us are getting more knowledgeable about the community and support for transitioning socially and physically.

I never really experienced any transphobic comments since I came out at an alternative school in Castle Rock, Colorado. The support of the faculty and students has really helped me become who I want to be. I also have a therapist who has helped me have confidence in my gender and sexuality.

However, at my summer job I had many rude customers who didn't respect my pronouns and made it apparent they were being transphobic. They would use the wrong pronouns even though I wore a pronoun pin, and they would make rude comments about how I was dressing, saying my outfit was only for men. Luckily,

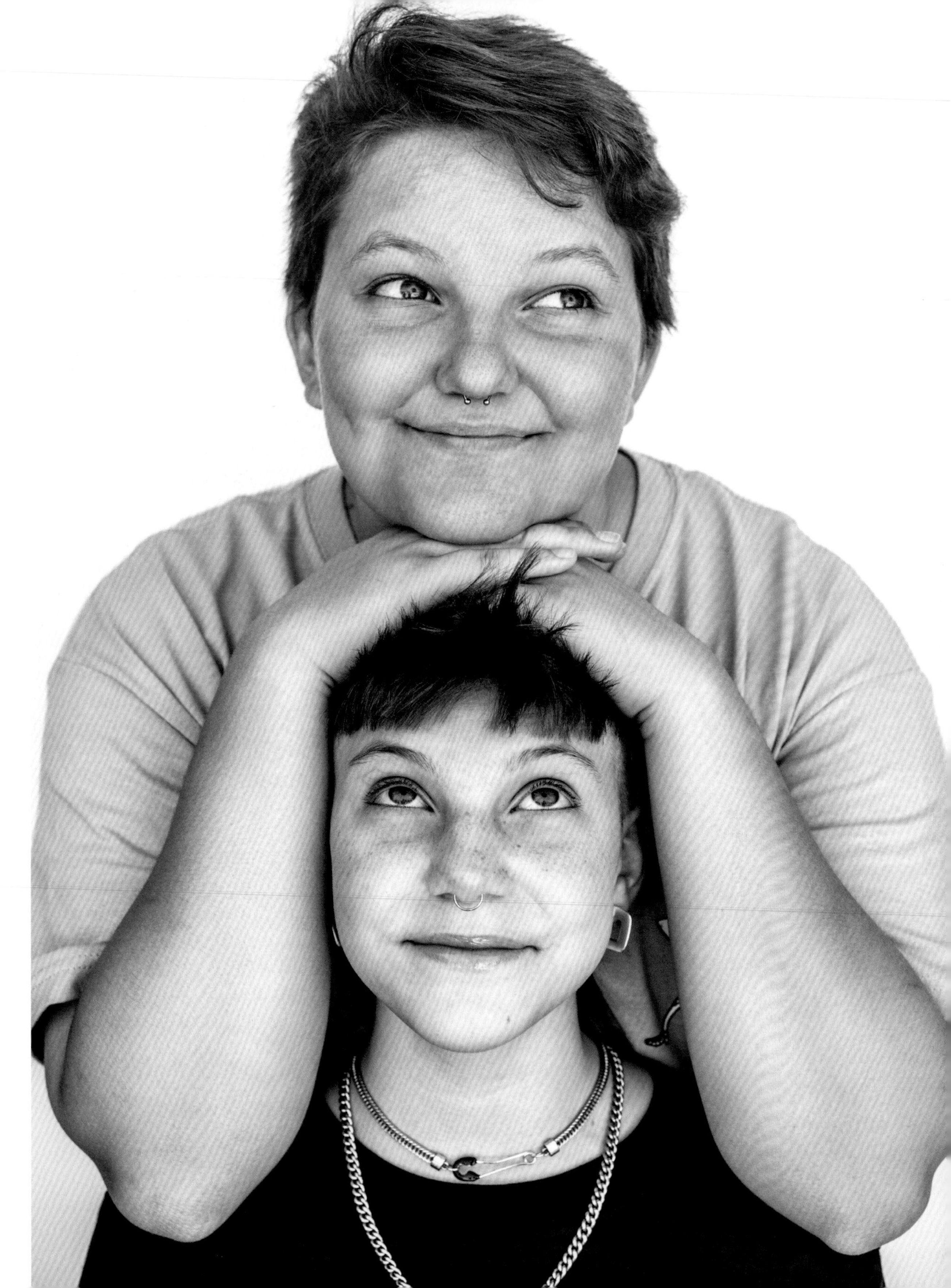

though, all of my coworkers were very supportive and all let me vent and talk through my feelings about the matter.

For those of you questioning your gender or sexuality, you don't always have to be the extreme version of something to be it. I spent my whole life thinking that because I accepted myself and my body I couldn't be male, or that since I dated boys I wasn't queer. Find someone you trust who has experience and talk to them about your feelings and questions. Don't spend your life wanting to be something and not living it!

Atlas

17 years old, he/him, Oklahoma
CW: This story contains references to suicide.

Growing up queer and trans in Oklahoma is . . . less than ideal. My name is Atlas, I am seventeen years old, and I am a neurodivergent and physically disabled advocate. I make jokes a lot of the time that I'm the "diversity hire" or a "triple threat" because I feel like I have "too many things wrong with me." I came out as transgender when I was twelve, before I got sick and before I began receiving help for my mental disorders. Living in the small town of Sapulpa, Oklahoma, this alone was enough for me to be called slurs and be bullied physically. It happened enough that my vice principal sent me to an alternative school my freshman year because, he said, "People have their opinions, and maybe traditional schools just aren't for someone like you." I seriously believed everyone. I thought I was the problem. I attempted suicide for the first time when I was thirteen, and during high school I was in inpatient treatment for suicidal ideation eight times; several of those times were residential stints where I spent more than a month in treatment. I switched schools too many times to fit on my permanent record.

I found my real home in advocacy. I hated what I was going through, and I knew I wouldn't be able to change it until I was an adult, but I didn't want anyone else to go through it either. I was lucky enough to be able to join an LGBTQ+ youth group at Oklahomans for Equality and realized that there were other kids like me and opportunities for people who struggled in the same ways I struggled. I kind of see it as my backstory now, I guess?

Once this new world opened up to me, I knew that as long as I kept pushing through everything at home and at school, one day I would find my place in the world. I became president of my school's Gender Sexuality Alliance (GSA) and ran a secret LGBTQ+ library out of a locker I rented near the classroom it was hosted in. I had saved money for months to buy books, and my friends contributed their LGBTQ+ books as well. It didn't last long because, unfortunately, I had to switch schools again due to family issues. But the number of times someone called me something awful because I was openly queer at that school was horrific. I once had

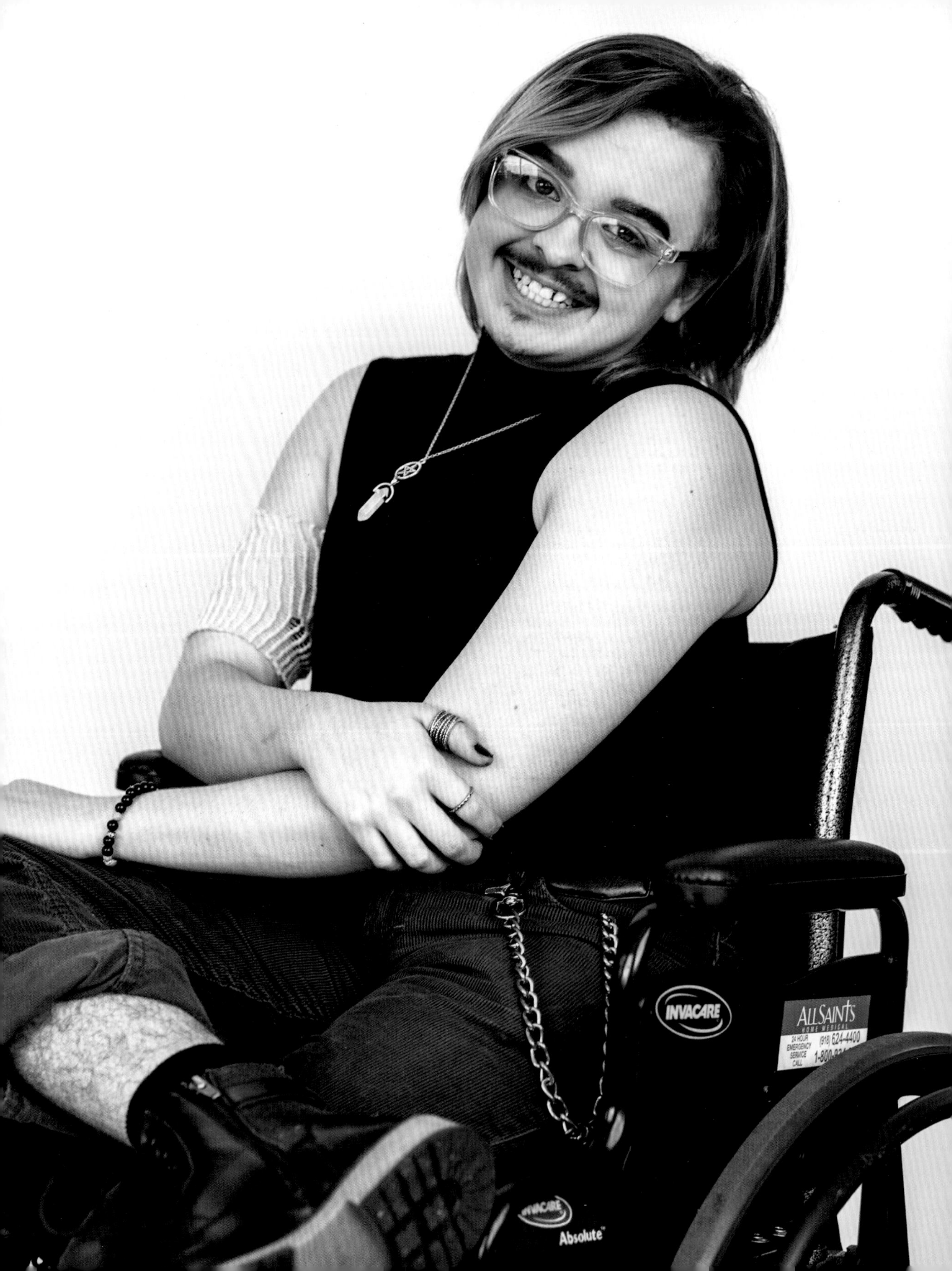

INVACARE
ALLSAINTS
HOME MEDICAL
24 HOUR
EMERGENCY
SERVICE
CALL
(918) 624-4400
1-800-
INVACARE
Absolute

my backpack stolen and was called slurs for taking it back. When I reported the situation I was told it was my fault for "getting physical" (taking my bag back). There's still a video on YouTube of the assembly where I spoke to my school about the GSA. The video is called "Welcome to the 2019–2020 SHS Howdy Assembly!" Honestly, I use it a lot as an example to show people who do not believe me about how bad it was. At 24:48 you can see the weird transition into my speech, which I'm sure was because they turned off the crowd mic. I went all out and dressed as queer as possible, putting a rainbow Ziggy Stardust bolt on my face and a GSA flag around my shoulders, but you can hear the fear and uncertainty in my voice. At 25:55 you can barely hear me over the angry crowd after I made a joke about how no one should be closeted.

I never want anyone else to go through what I went through. I never want anyone else to feel like they aren't good enough to justify their existence. In my junior year, very shortly before COVID, I fell ill and was practically bedridden for a year. My new school refused me an IEP (Individualized Education Program) and I broke my spine on campus, after which they told me to find a new school that was accessible. I dropped out of school, but once I had the money I got my high school equivalency. I already felt like a failure, and so many people told me I should have made it work to get my traditional diploma. So many people have pushed this idealized version of how they think I should exist, and it has been absolutely destroying my self-image since I was twelve. "Well maybe if you weren't ______ then that wouldn't have happened." Not everybody has the opportunity to grow up in a nice school with a healthy family, not everyone has access to a good education, not everybody is middle class, not everybody has the ability to be the "ideal" LGBTQ+ person that cishet folks want to see; so that's why I chose advocacy. It would be unrealistic to say it always gets easier, but eventually existing unapologetically starts to happen more naturally. It does get better, and I want to be the kind of change I believe kids like me need in this world.

Bex

14 years old, they/them, Michigan

Hi, my name is Bex, my pronouns are they/them, and I am a fourteen-year-old from Oak Park, Michigan. Growing up queer in Michigan, especially in two different places, has made my life somewhat of a struggle. My parents got divorced when I was about a year old, and I have stayed generally in the same two places all of my life.

Detroit is one of the most accepting places in Michigan to be queer, which is ironic because just outside of it, where I grew up on my dad's side of the hill, is very conservative. It's filled with old, rich white people who all know each other and are very religious. My dad was raised this way too, and even now he is still trying to push those values and ideas on me just like his community did to him.

As many closeted queer people are, I was forced into religion at a very young age, and I truly never enjoyed it or got anything out of it. My experience with Catholicism and Christianity has been that it is not worth it for me. It felt almost cultish to have rules and regulations on who you are as a person. Having to attend services and meetings to show that I am a good person didn't feel right.

Realizing that I was queer was a revelation for me. It wasn't an answer to all of my problems, but it was definitely an answer to most of them. When I was beginning to figure out that I was queer, I didn't know exactly who or what I was, but I knew I was not straight. I really came to terms with it in the fourth grade, when I had my first crush on a girl. Like most pansexual people, I originally thought I was bisexual, but when I got to thinking about it, I was like, "Oh, I like this label better." I sadly haven't had the same experience with my gender, though, as I am still figuring out how I want to identify myself. I've had a huge struggle for the past couple of years over what label I want to go by, as I know I am not cisgender, but I also don't feel that I am fully transmasculine and I don't like the label of nonbinary.

My mom raised me in a completely different way than my dad did. My mom listened, and she tried to encourage me to be who I wanted. She grew up in a very large household with three brothers, and she was always overlooked. Raised with the idea of discipline, and being the only girl in a family of boys, she was raised to be

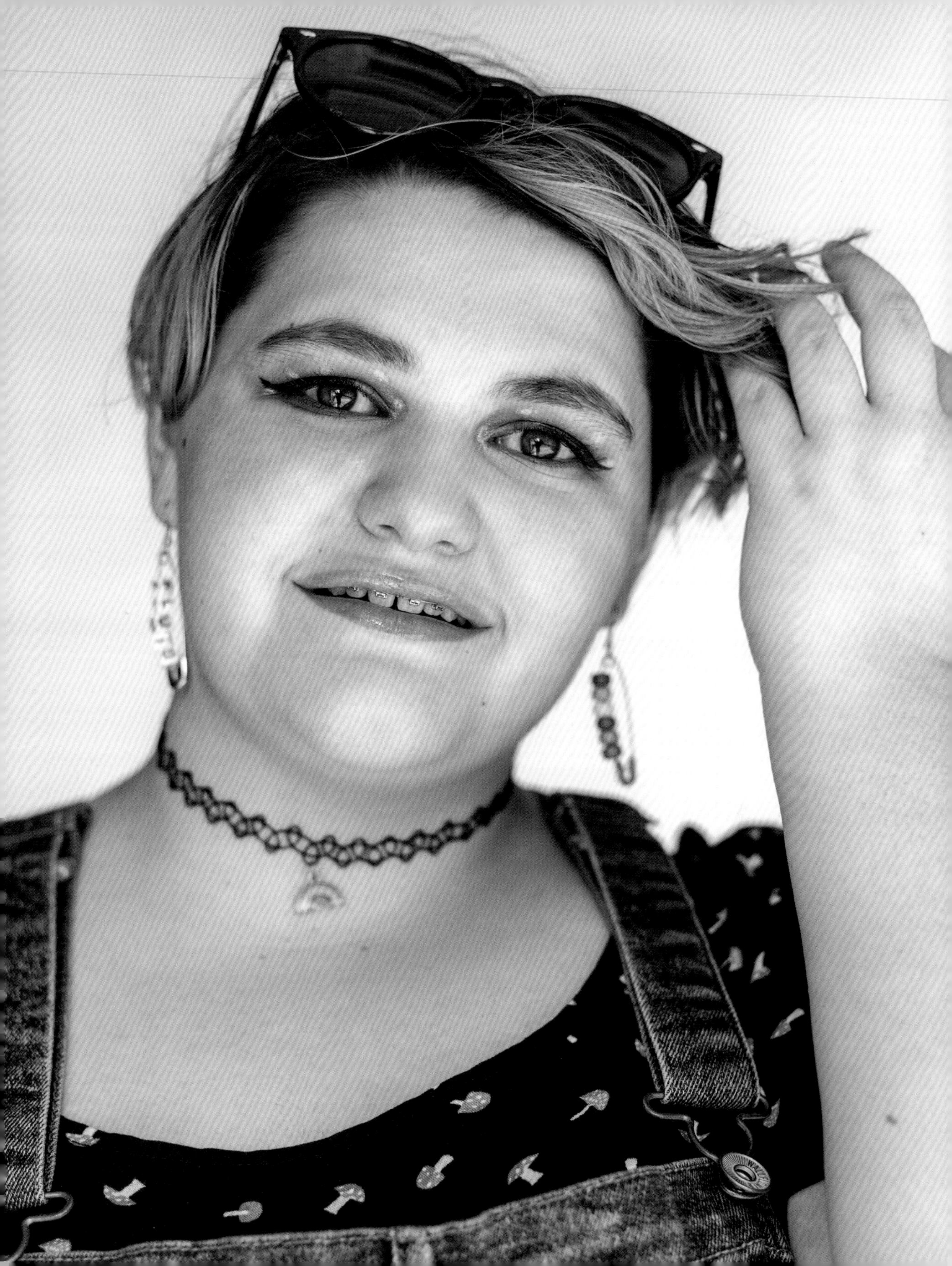

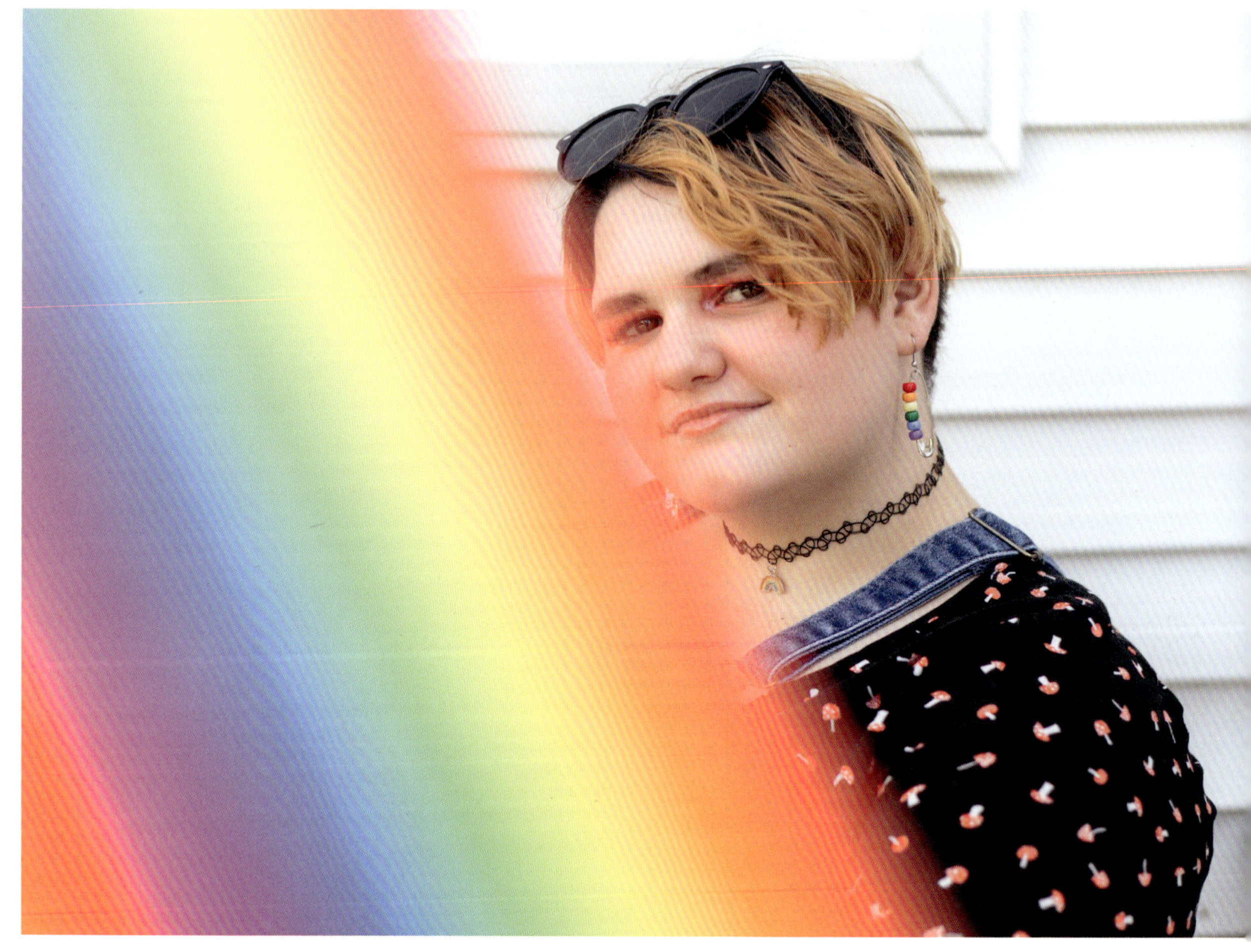

tough, without any room for empathy. She understood my struggles around feeling alone in my family.

In Michigan there's not a lot of queer representation outside of Ferndale. I feel like Michigan is a place where there are a lot of gay people, but everyone is too quiet or scared to talk about it because there are quite a lot of churches here.

Along with the struggle of being raised Catholic and struggling with my identity, I didn't know how my family was going to react when I came out. I also didn't know how my friends were going to react. I was really one of the only queer people I knew of at the time. Being still partly in the closet, there's always that uncertainty of not knowing how someone is going to react.

I was forced out of the closet when I was twelve years old, and even writing about this now really brings back a lot of horrible memories. I didn't have a healthy outlet for talking about my identity, so I turned to people I thought I could trust online. My family found out that I was doing this and read through every text message between me and my friends and found out that I was queer. Most of my family didn't take it well.

When I started to find a community online, I thought I had finally found my place, but I didn't realize that some of the people I'd met were encouraging unhealthy ideas and actions. They were not there for me like I thought they were, and I discovered that some people online weren't good friends.

I understand that finding community online may be your only option, so make sure it's a healthy community and not encouraging bad behavior. I eventually found my community through an organization, and it was the healthiest option.

The big turning point for me was finding Affirmations, where people did have the same experiences as me, or something very similar, and it was a healthier environment. I still don't know how my family would react if I told them that I was trans or gender-fluid, but overall they have been more accepting of the community than most adults are. Except for my dad.

A really big impact on my struggle with who I am as a person is my anxiety, as well as body dysmorphia and gender dysphoria. Dealing with something like body dysmorphia, and coupling that with crippling anxiety, made me feel like, "Why should I even try and label myself if no one is even going to care or know?" I see now that that kind of idea is not good because it's absolutely not true, especially now that I am finding my people. But those thoughts still creep up on me every so often, and it can be very, very hard to deal with them.

My advice to anybody who is struggling with these thoughts is to talk them out with somebody you're very close to and get support for yourself. It's something that's really helped me with these negative thoughts. Something else that has helped is finding a style of clothing that I really like and just being me and not caring about what anybody thinks. If somebody calls you out and says, "You shouldn't be wearing that," remember that how you look, what you wear, and what you do are *your* choices. So just don't give a crap and be happy with yourself.

My last bit of advice is to find like-minded people who you can relate to, and who you know are going to be there for you. It is so important to find those people because they're going to stick around.

Cam

14 years old, they/them, California

My name is Cam. I am nonbinary, my pronouns are they/them, and I am fourteen years old and living in the Central Valley, California. Since I was little, my mom always knew I was not like other girls. I remember that when I turned four years old, my mom let me pick my cake and I wanted a dinosaur cake so badly. I got my blue dinosaur and I was happy. For my fifth birthday I wanted a Spider-Man party, which my mom gave me, but she was asked by the other kids' parents why she allowed me to have a "boy's" party. I remember that in preschool and elementary school most of my friends were boys, and in a few instances I was the only "girl" invited to some of my preschool friends' birthday parties. I never fit into the girls' clique at all.

One day I was scrolling through Netflix and I found the PBS documentary *9 Months That Made You*. I was very curious and asked my mom if we could watch it. I was around eight years old. It was a three-part documentary, and in the last episode there was the story of Maddie, a seven-year-old transgender girl. I asked my mom if we could rewatch that episode over and over. I related to Maddie's story. I saw myself in her shoes.

A few weeks later I told my mom, "I think I am like Maddie." She said, "Just the opposite, right?" After that we went to see my pediatrician, looking for help so I could truly be me. Unfortunately, the response from the pediatrician was not a friendly one. That pediatrician told my mom and I that it was normal for me to feel that way because "girls usually don't want to go through puberty." After that visit we stopped going to that doctor, and we still have not found a trusted healthcare provider in the city where we live that is LGBTQ+ friendly or that is knowledgeable in transgender care for kids or teens like me.

After the visit with the pediatrician, I didn't bring up that "I was like Maddie" to my mom again until about two years later. During those two years, I tried to fit into the girl stereotype that I was supposed to be according to society. I even asked my mom to get me some dresses and a girly bedroom set. All this was because of those hurtful words I heard from that pediatrician who dismissed me as the kid who I truly was. But that pediatrician's narrow view of me was not who I was. I struggled internally. I struggled in school.

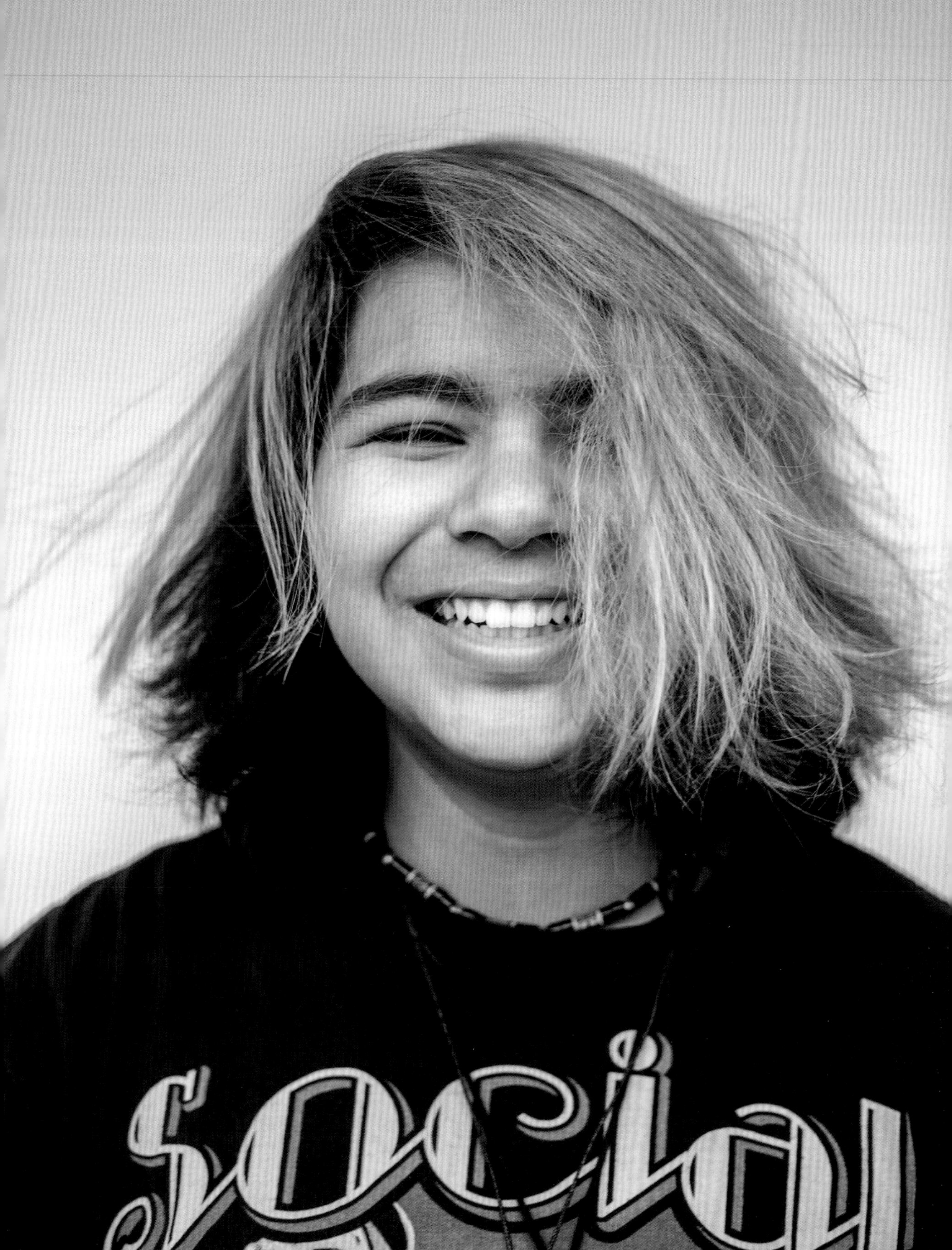
social

I could not concentrate and my studies suffered. I got teased at school. When it got to be too much for me to handle, I would have meltdowns and tell my mom that I did not fit into this world, that nobody understood me. I felt the world would be better off without me. I was suffering silently from anxiety and depression.

When I was ten years old and in fifth grade, to my surprise, my mom showed me some information about this organization called The Source coming into our city to do a pop-up meeting for LGBTQ people. We both attended the very first meeting, and my mom was able to get some information about the transgender support group the organization offered in the area, as well as learn where to go for transgender healthcare for me. Unfortunately, those transgender healthcare resources were three to four hours away, either in the Bay Area or in Southern California.

Since the very first meeting hosted by The Source in my town back in 2018, this organization has been part of my journey, giving me support. The Source has become an extended family to me and my mom.

My road as a transgender/gender-fluid kid in my town has not been easy, even though I've had the full support of my mom since I came out. I finished the few months left of fifth grade as the gender I was assigned at birth, but I was no longer comfortable using the girls' restroom. At the same time, I did not feel safe using the boys' restroom either, so I started using the school office restroom. Many times I even waited to get home to use the restroom. I also went back to wearing the items of clothing that I felt comfortable in, like when I was younger.

In 2018 I came out to my entire immediate family and they had my back and I felt their love. I also came out to my friends and my family's friends in the town I live in. I still remember the words my mom told me while we were sitting at the dining room table, that my road as a transgender kid was not going to be an easy one and that there would be people who would not accept me and would not want to be friends with our family anymore. Unfortunately, those words came true. There were people who did not accept me and stopped being our friends. Their loss.

On the bright side, my mom was able to get an appointment in Southern California for transgender healthcare for me. The appointment was scheduled for the day of my birthday. I was excited because I was turning eleven and it felt like I was being reborn. A few months later I was able to start on blockers.

The first year of my transition at school was not very smooth, as some of the school staff and my classmates continued to use my deadname or used the wrong pronouns. It was very stressful for me, especially when we had substitute teachers because I was more worried that they would deadname me or misgender me. It wasn't until I was in seventh grade that we were able to have my name and gender changed in the school system. However, there were a few classmates who would misgender and deadname me on purpose. That didn't help with my anxiety and depression.

One positive thing that happened to me during the COVID-19 pandemic in 2020 was that I was able to start on testosterone shots while I was in eighth grade, and it's been a year since that milestone.

Being out has not only changed my life but has also improved it, including my mental health. Now that I have just started high school, I am more comfortable with who I am. I am more comfortable dressing in the items of clothing that make me feel like myself. However, because of the area where I live, I do continue to worry about being a victim of a hate crime, which still gives me a lot of anxiety.

If I had to give my eight-year-old self some advice, or even advise other youth my age, I would tell them it takes some patience but you will get there. Whether it takes a year or ten, don't give up, and surround yourself with people who truly support you and love you for who you are.

Cam

Carson

18 years old, they/them, Kansas

My name is Carson. I identify as panromantic and demisexual, use any pronouns (with a preference for they/them), am eighteen years old, and reside in Lindsborg, Kansas.

Originally I'm from the very small town of Minneola, Kansas, just south of Dodge City, and it is home to fewer than eight hundred people. Overall, I never had many people who were LGBTQ+ that I got to see or interact with. There was no representation that I saw anywhere, and I never truly knew what being "gay" was until I got into junior high. There had been very few shows on TV that I saw that showed LGBTQ+ couples, one being *Say Yes to the Dress*, which I remember watching with my grandmother. I also remember her saying out loud that two women getting married was "disgusting." I felt really uncomfortable after she had said that, and I don't know if it was because of how she said it, or because I didn't feel the same as her, but I knew that I didn't agree with her.

The summer before my freshman year of high school, I realized that I was not straight. And that was one of the happiest days of my life. I remember texting one of my best friends who had told me beforehand that they were pansexual and telling them all about it. I was crying while texting them. When I got into high school, I self-identified as bisexual. I was only out to my closest friends. High school was where things changed quite a bit for me, and I felt more aligned with the terms *panromantic* and *demisexual*.

Growing up in such a small town in Kansas, I never felt like I could come out to my community. I remember first coming out to my friends, and then to my mother while we were at dinner together. At first she wasn't very receptive to it and she said to wait until I was in college so that I could "experiment." It made me very upset to hear her say that, and I just didn't bring it up again until I got up to either my sophomore or junior year of high school, when I told her that I still felt the same. Throughout the time between, I would periodically talk to her about LGBTQ+ topics and, although she didn't understand all of it, she did take time to learn. My senior year of high school, in October and on National Coming Out Day, I remember coming out to my dad. I was so scared to come out to him because of how he tends to say things, but he took it really well. Even now, he will ask questions when he's confused about something.

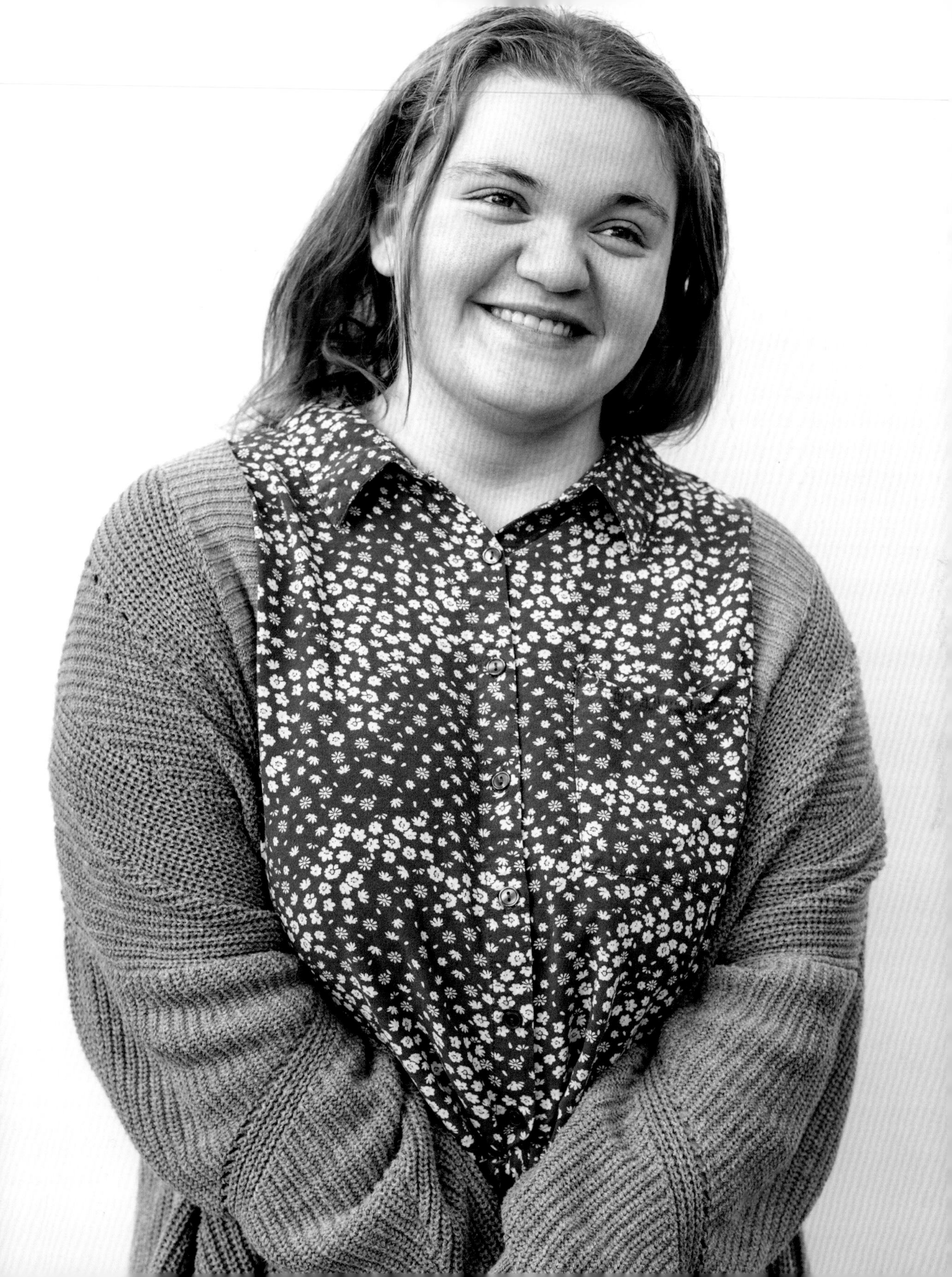

Being LGBTQ+ in Kansas, in my experience, is difficult. However, there are so many LGBTQ+ individuals, and I'm proud to be one of them. While I was in junior high and high school, no one identified as a part of the community for fear of being bullied or teased or worse. Minneola is one of those small communities where word spreads fast if you tell the wrong person, and while the "small-town" aspect can be nice, it can also be hell. I have heard the f-slur thrown around by painfully straight white cisgendered boys, and threats have been made against friends of mine.

Since moving to Lindsborg for college, I've had a much more pleasant experience than I did in high school, and I'm surrounded by so much diversity and a welcoming environment. I don't feel pressured to hide who I am, and I can finally be myself without fear. I can only imagine what others have to go through, and I know my story is one of many. I don't want to be that broken record, and I won't. Your path is your path alone. Someone else may have similar experiences, but you perceive what happens to you differently than them. Sometimes it feels like you're hanging on by a singular thread, and I as well as many others know how that feels. But it is your thread and yours alone. You weave your own story; you decide what you do. No one else can make the choice to come out for you, nor should they.

Many get sick and tired of hearing "it will get better." In a single moment in time, or for a week or more, life can be absolute crap. You are allowed to feel how you feel. You are allowed to be upset, frustrated, and angry. You're allowed to be happy and excited. Depending on where you live and where you grow up, circumstances can vary, and I'm not qualified to tell you what you should do with your life. I'm only a freshman majoring in psychology in college. However, when you feel ready, come out to yourself first. Become familiar with who you are and get to know yourself. You don't have to come out to your friends or family first. Figuring things out on your own (or even procrastinating on defining your sexuality and identity) takes time.

As you continue to read past this, take your time and make sure to take a deep breath. You are not alone, and the individuals who are in this book are all here for you. You will not walk alone on this journey, and though we may not know each other, you are loved and cared for. We as the LGBTQ+ community are all cared for. The road is long up ahead. Just remember to always keep fighting, for yourself and for what you believe in. You will fly high. Please take care of yourself day after day and pick yourself back up again when you fall. Remember to drink water, take deep breaths, and take your medications (if you take any). We have your back, 100 percent of the way. You are loved, beautiful, handsome, stunning, whatever you feel comfortable with. Thank you for being you, and for taking the time to read this section, as unorganized as it is.

You're going to go so far, and we all look forward to seeing you on the other side of this wild and crazy road trip down the winding hill that is known as life.

Cecil

16 years old, he/they, Alabama
CW: This story contains references to disordered eating.

My name is Cecil, I am seventeen, I use he/they pronouns, and I live in Spanish Fort, Alabama. I grew up playing with mud and dolls, I wore dresses without hesitation, and I was always falling for boys; I was even a massive Justin Bieber fan back then. I was happy. A happy little girl who had a loving family and who would have never imagined that over a span of ten years I would endure so many changes.

It was fifth grade when I started to realize I was different from all of the other girls my age. While they were head over heels for the new boys in our grade, I was interested in a girl. I thought I really just wanted to be her friend, but over time I could not get her out of my mind. I told my friend all about what I was feeling the whole year, and then at the end of the year he asked if I knew what *gay* meant, and for the rest of recess we talked all about it. I instantly was conflicted, yet I accepted this as what I was. I was just a girl, who still liked being a girl, who liked girls. I never thought it was weird, 'cause at that time I was not exposed to what it really meant to be LGBTQ+. I just lived life as normal, not telling anyone yet.

It is now 2016, and I am in sixth grade at Spanish Fort Middle. The election is on everyone's mind, politicians giving speeches and people getting in arguments about who should win. Despite not looking Mexican much, I am. Not only that, I was a natural-born activist, so with both combined I decided to tell the girls I was assigned to sit with at lunch about how I felt about it all. For the rest of the year I would be bullied mentally, in various ways, by these girls, never thinking I could tell the faculty there. Besides that, I came out indirectly to my mom. I had come home one day and she asked how school was. I said that I sat by my crush, she asked me the name of the boy, and I proceeded to tell her, "Her name is XXXXX" and then went and played Minecraft or did my homework. She accepted me: That was all that mattered.

Middle school was a hard time in my life. I struggled with the need to be the perfect daughter to make up for being gay, which led to an eating disorder; I got dysphoria from the smallest things, like wearing dresses; I was outed; and my anxiety spiked. I had happy parts then too, but alas the bad outweighed the good for me

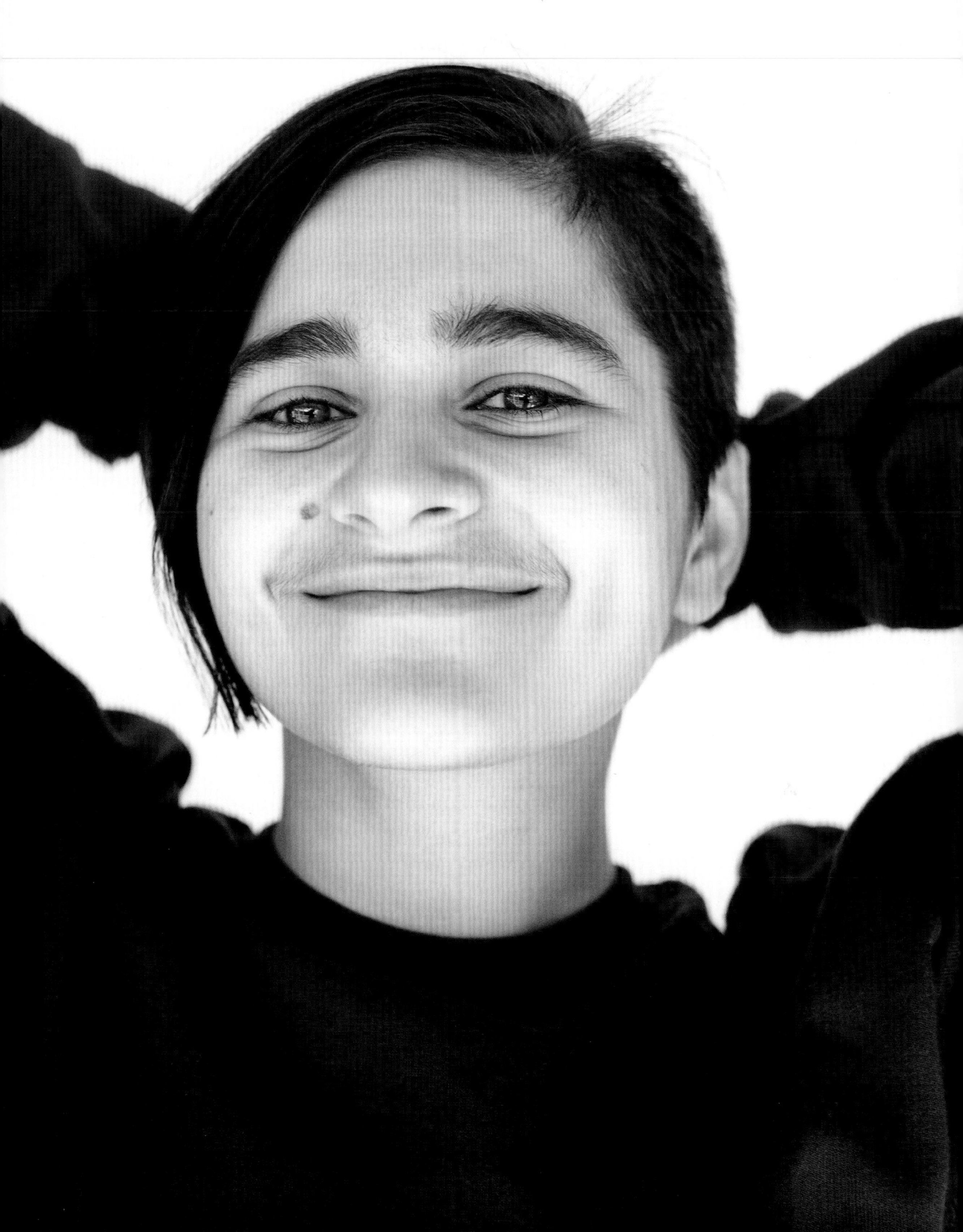

mentally. My mom had a hard time understanding that I am not her daughter anymore, but she has gotten better with my name/pronouns while my other family members still think I am their little perfect daughter/caring sister.

Things started to get better in 2020. I joined Prism (an LGBTQ+ group in the area) and met some of the best people of my life. I went through a lot of self-growth during quarantine, which led to me getting rid of my gender crisis, and I got into Dungeons & Dragons, or "D&D," which helped me pick out my chosen name, get some weird form of closure, and cope with my trauma. I started a Gender-Sexuality Alliance (GSA) at my school and came out as trans to my school; students and faculty started to address me by my chosen name. I started to finally feel good about how I dressed, even if I still got dysphoria from body features. I started to express my emotions through art and poetry, and I was slowly making my way to a big step of eating disorder recovery by becoming many months clean. One last thing that happened recently was that I started to wear the boys' uniform at my school.

If you told young me about the person they would become, and that in the last months of 2021 that he would start the legal name change process, he would not believe you and would just continue to play Minecraft. Sometimes I wish I could go back in time and warn young me, but at the same time I know that all of these challenges were worth it because it's the scars that help you grow.

For anyone reading this that is struggling, I want you to keep in mind these things: It is a tough fight, and a lot of people will never understand what you are going through; people over time will get more accepting; you are stronger than you think; there are people who are in your life or that you will meet who will help lead you through your journey; experimenting is a good thing to do throughout your journey; this journey can be long but you gotta stick through it; and finally, I am so proud of you.

Clay

14 years old, they/he, California

The world sees my non-androgynous-presenting body and assumes
I am like everybody else. But they do not see this: I am a Trans,
Nonbinary, Queer, Jewish, Disabled, creative person. There will
always be people who don't understand me, my identities, and my
pronouns, but I find community with those who do. I find community with those who ask, with those who make space for me to be
unapologetically me. My story isn't all unicorns and rainbows, but
I have been blessed with a safe home and amazing support systems
as well as opportunities.

As a Nonbinary teen, I have struggled to define what makes me
Nonbinary. Was I always Nonbinary, just without the terminology
at first, or was I at one point my "assigned gender"? You see, the
issue is that there isn't a correct answer. It's a question that I, as
well as many Queer people, will ponder for the rest of our lives.
One question I can answer with more ease is: Am I Transgender?
The short answer is yes.

Being Nonbinary is being all genders and none at the same
time. It's defying standards set in place to keep the systems happy.
It's defying what I was taught as a child: that there are only two
genders, male or female. Being Nonbinary means teaching my
family and friends how to use my pronouns. It is teaching my inner
circle how to dismantle the sociopolitical patriarchy of a spiderweb
that we have all woven ourselves into.

Everyone has pronouns (including neopronouns), your pronouns are not directly linked to your gender, and your presentation
to the world does not dictate your identity. Be yourself, live freely,
and have fun. Using the right name and pronouns for someone
is directly linked to suicide prevention. There has been so much
historical erasure when it comes to Trans and Nonbinary people in
BIPOC communities and cultures. They were always here (actually,
they were here first), just underrepresented in mainstream media
and largely erased. Queerness exists in nature and it is beautiful. We are not alone in our experiences. They are what bind us
together, connecting one person to the next.

Our Queer ancestors (Trans POC) taught us how to first march
for equality. Being "out" today always makes you a target. Our
Queer ancestors gave us hope. They gave me hope for a better

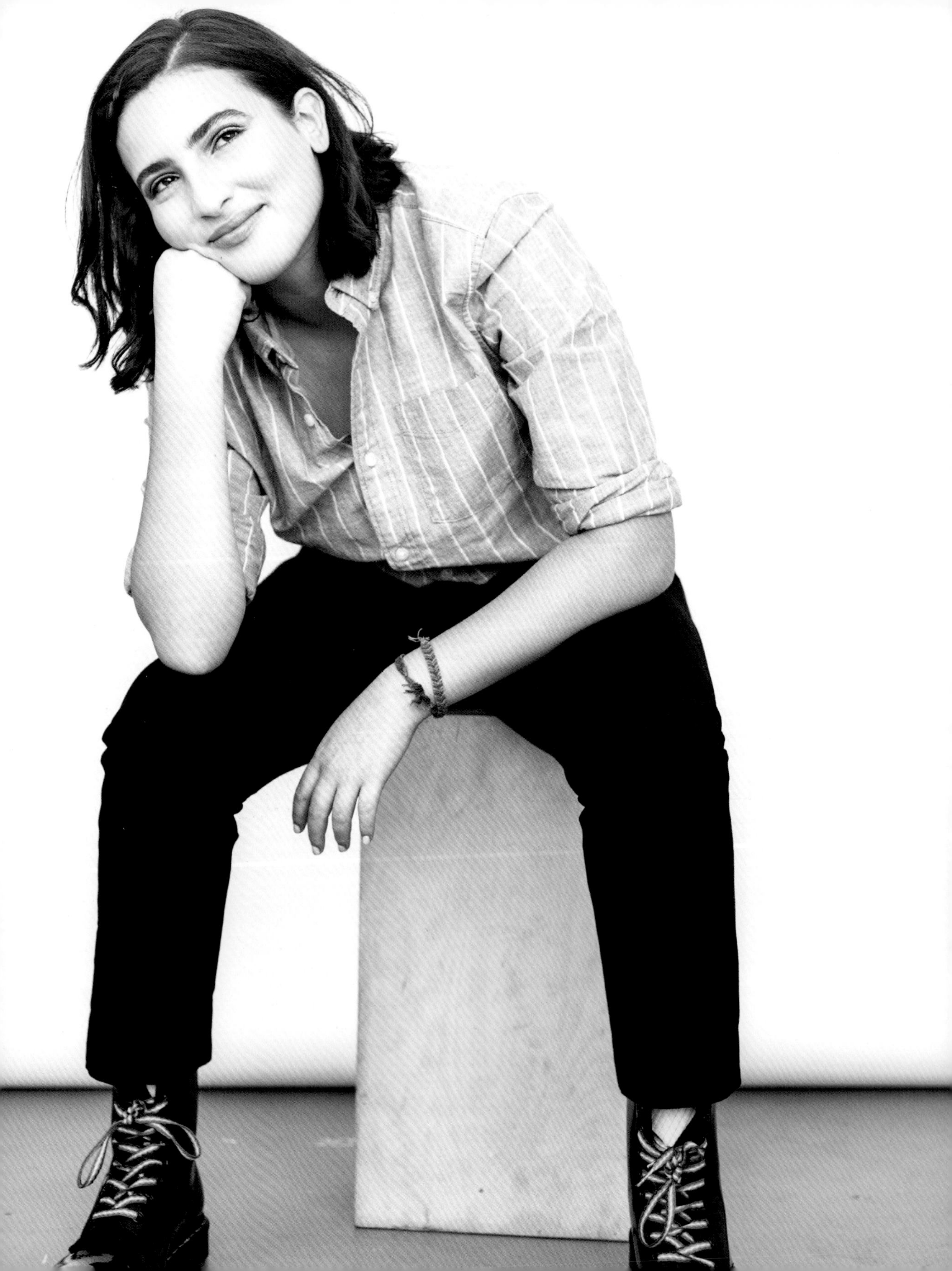

future. A world in which I am not a target, a world where no one's identity makes them othered. They gave us the strength to unapologetically be ourselves.

Struggling is okay. As a person with anxiety, depression, sensory processing disorder (SPD), and obsessive compulsive disorder (OCD), my experience with mental health has been difficult. There is a stigma surrounding talking about SH (self-harm) and suicide and mental health in general that has directly affected me and my friends. As teens struggling with mental health, we can relate to one another and aid each other and keep each other accountable. We also have our own professionally trained adults who aid us in our mental health journeys.

Before getting into my relationship with disability and how I have come to embrace that label, I need to address ableism. Ableism is discrimination in favor of able-bodied people. It's harmful because it reinforces the idea that Disabled people are "lesser" than able-bodied/minded people. Reinforcing the belief that there is a "right way" when it comes to what disability looks like is a form of systemic ableism.

I've struggled with invisible disabilities for a while—about six years to be exact. Some may say they're just not there, or they're all in my head, and that's okay. I have struggled with countless doctors, friends and family members, and even society to figure out where I fit in. Long story short, the answer is both everywhere and nowhere. Sometimes it feels as though my community is so large and the representation is truly there. Other times I feel isolated from the world.

Having invisible disabilities means living with constant self-doubt and disbelief. It means constant doctor's appointments with inconclusive results. It means feeling a constant pain that the world can't see. It means struggling with my mental health. Being a Disabled teenager is a lot of work in a world where we have to be perfect all of the time to avoid judgment and gossip. Disabled teens fear using mobility aids in school environments for fear of being teased or bullied. This inherently makes our experience more difficult in what is a pretty inaccessible environment to begin with.

In struggling with my mental health, I founded my initiative, Q.T. Wellness, in November of 2020. Q.T. Wellness focuses on helping LGBTQ2SIA+ teens (and questioning teens) develop tools to aid themselves and others relating to mental, physical, emotional, and social health and wellness. If I had this system to support me growing up, it definitely would have helped me to feel seen and heard in my trials and tribulations. There is power in shared experiences or even sharing your experience in a brave space! Q.T. Wellness focuses on connecting people to resources and is a constant reminder that we are not alone.

To learn more about Q.T. Wellness, follow us on Instagram @Q.T.Wellness, email us at q.t.wellness2020@gmail.com, and check out our website, qtwellness.org. We always love to hear from our community!

If there is anything to take away from my story, it is that intersectionality is your gift. No matter how you identify, your intersectionality is what connects you to other humans in this world. You are never alone. Even when you are not aware of it, there is support all around you. Even though our existence lies on a fluid spectrum, we are all different. Your experience is unique to you, but the fluidity of it means that change is constant and your labels and pronouns may change, and that's okay. Everyone has both visible and invisible identities, most being invisible. Try to remember this: *Fu** the boxes.* You don't need to fit in; it's better to be different.

Understanding and knowing parts of your identity at any age is a blessing. Learning and growing are constants, which both tie into fluidity. Everyone is moving at their own pace with their healing, Queer journey, and mental health journey. Coloring outside the lines is the beauty—but it's hated because it's different. There's support all around you, even if you don't know it's there or can't see it. Queer people are not the enemy; we are here to heal the world and make it a better, more inclusive place for everyone. This isn't new, it's just breaking the binaries. What binary are you going to break today?

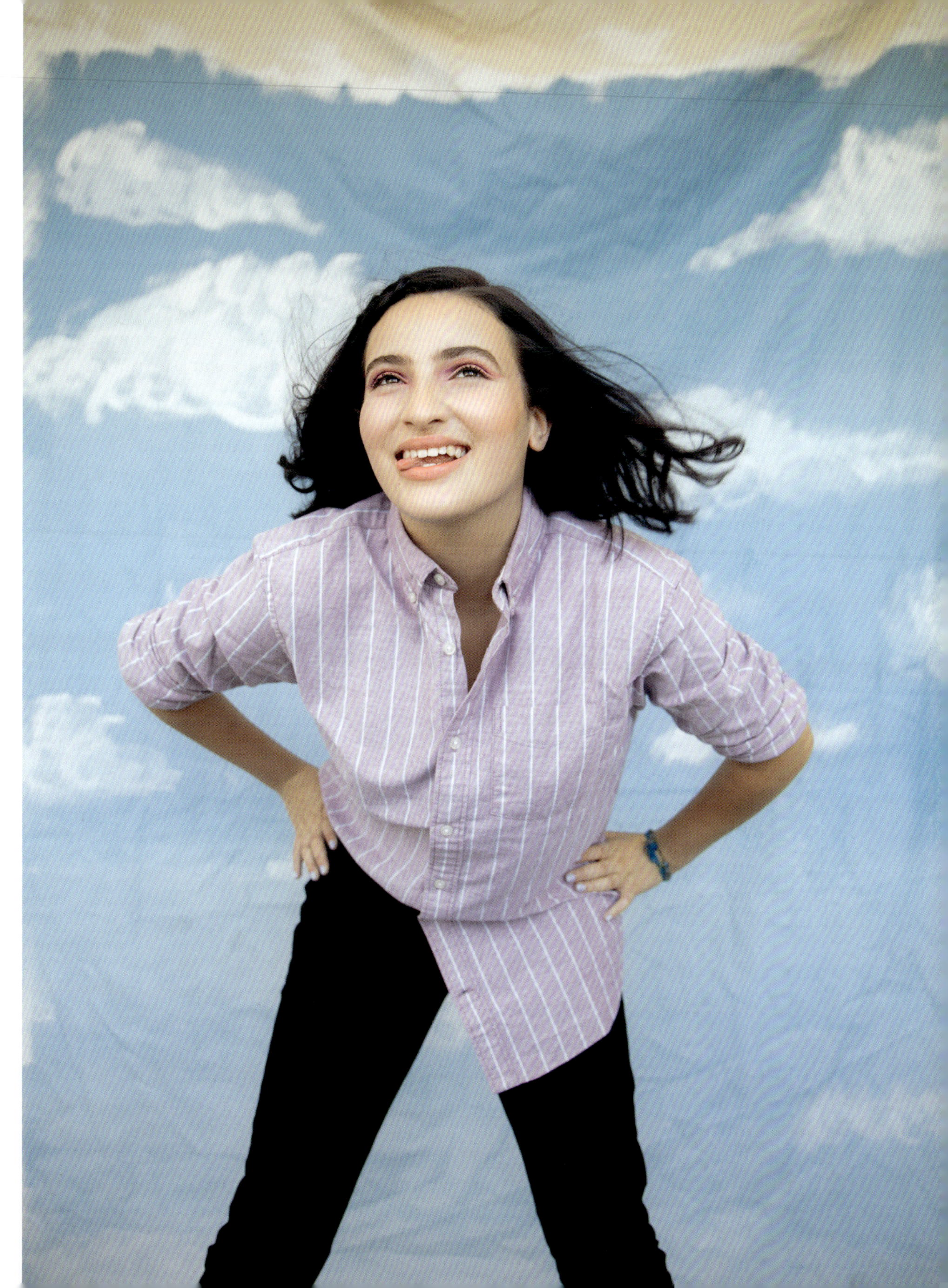

De'Onyae Dior Valentina

17 years old, she/her, Indiana
CW: This story contains references to self-harm and
suicide ideation.

Hello readers, I'm De'Onyae Dior Valentina, or Dede for short. I am from Indiana. My preferred pronouns are she/her, but anything works as long as it's used with respect.

Growing up was never easy for me. I had a hard time with my mental health and being a foster care youth. I have always struggled to fit in with the world around me. When I was four I was diagnosed with bipolar disorder, oppositional defiant disorder, ADHD, and ADD. I never, ever had a father figure. It was hard for me to not have a person to look up to, and never really having parents made it harder to navigate my mental health.

My bio mom has never been the best mother. She put me in the foster system at a young age. At the age of eight, I was sent to my first mental hospital for attempting self-harm. At that point in time I realized something was different about me and that something had to give. I started to explore the ideas of my gender and sexuality. By the time I was twelve, I realized I was gay. At the time my mom was making me see a gender identity doctor because, according to her, I never acted the way I was supposed to. The doctor helped me discover that I am gender-fluid on top of being gay. It felt good knowing who I was, but it didn't feel good that I had to hide it from everyone around me. I was scared people weren't going to accept me, so I hid it. I didn't have a good support group and didn't know who to go to at first.

So then my mental health started getting worse, and little did I know it was making an impact on how I functioned in this world and where I fit in. At this time I was in a secure residential facility because of my mental health. I was in about four of them starting at age thirteen until I was sixteen. This is where I started to discover myself more and come out to people in the facility who I thought would be accepting. There were other people like me there, and it made me feel more accepted and loved.

When I finally left the facilities, I came out to my therapist, my biological mom, and my brother. My mom was very accepting but still didn't feel comfortable when she was around me. Maybe she

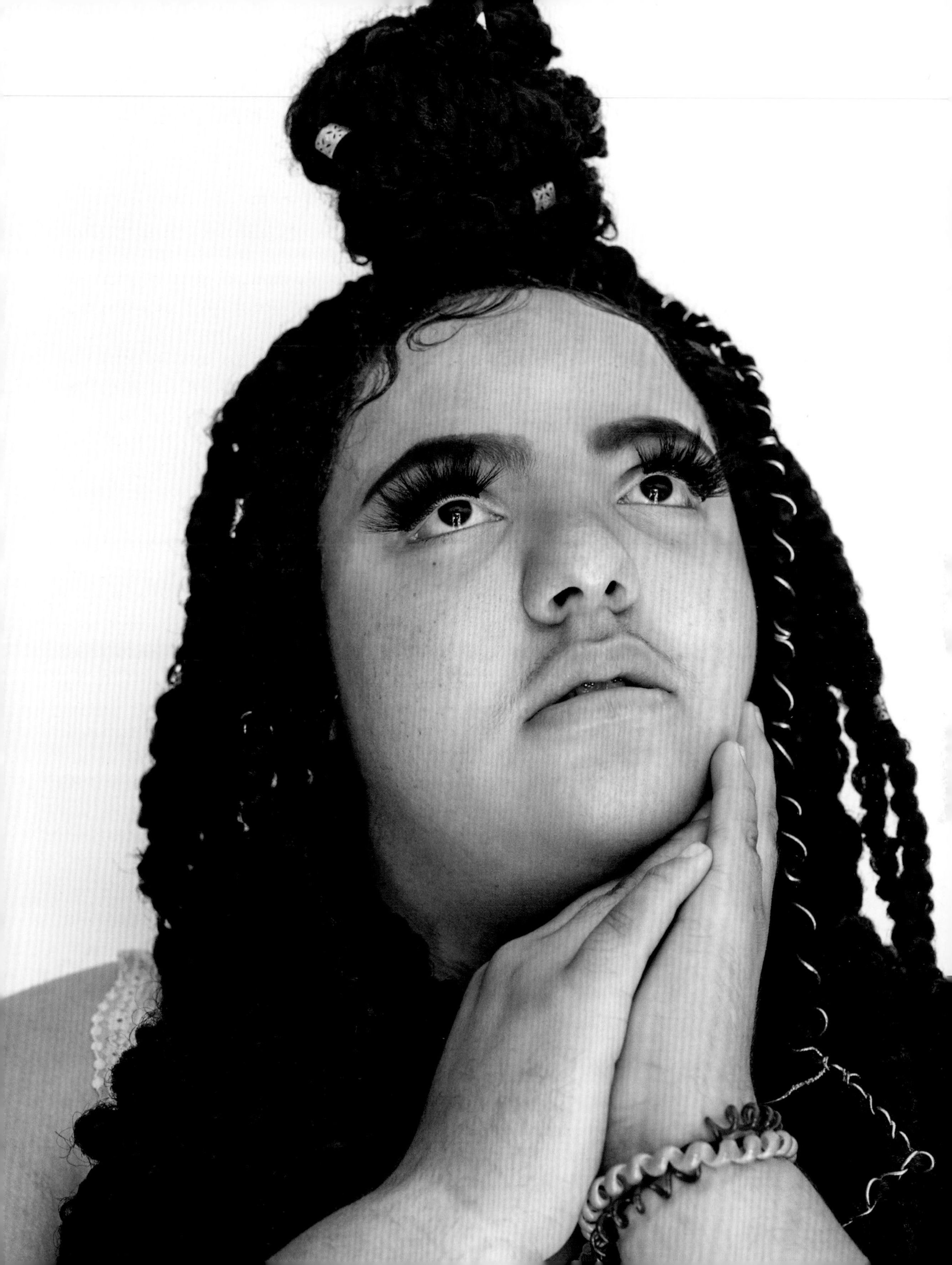

thought being gay was okay, but then having to deal with my gender was harder? My brother, on the other hand, was very accepting.

Once I left and started to get my footing again in society, I got my first job. I would hide who I was at work because I was scared that I would get fired or terminated because I am gay, which can still happen in Indiana. I started to come out slowly at work, and everyone was very accepting of me. I realized in 2019 that I could start being myself and forget what everyone else thinks. I wanted to be me.

Growing up in the foster care system, you had to stick to being either male or female to be able to get into a facility, and it always made me feel uncomfortable living in those situations because that isn't always what I identify as. There is not a lot of representation for queer people in the Indiana foster care system. I want to see more gender-affirming foster homes and more education on the LGBTQ+ community for the youth and parents. I've always felt belittled by the foster care system because of how I identified, and I would feel like I wasn't enough. Eventually I started to be myself 100 percent of the time, and I felt happier with myself and the confidence I was finding.

Indiana was not the best place to grow up and be gay, or anything outside of the norm. The people in this state tend to be unaccepting because of the way they live, due to both their religious and political lifestyles. At times I was bullied and judged for being me. It made me feel very negative about who I am because of the way people viewed me. People called me names. I was always known as the "little faggot" at school. Because of this I started to have suicidal ideations and thoughts. The kids in the neighborhood would always push me around and use me as a doormat. But I am not a doormat, I am a human being. Eventually I started standing my ground and not letting people bully me or tell me bad things, because I am strong and can do anything I put my mind to. Being a member of the minority community does not define me or make me less of a person.

My advice to other kids like me: In the foster care system, if you are a minority or anything else I mentioned earlier, then don't let anyone bring you down. Just know that you are worth it. You are everything that you want yourself to be. Don't let anyone define who you are. Let yourself define who you are. You can do anything in this world you put your mind to. You are loved by more people than you know.

Find passion in what you wanna do. I am me, you are you. Let's live in harmony.

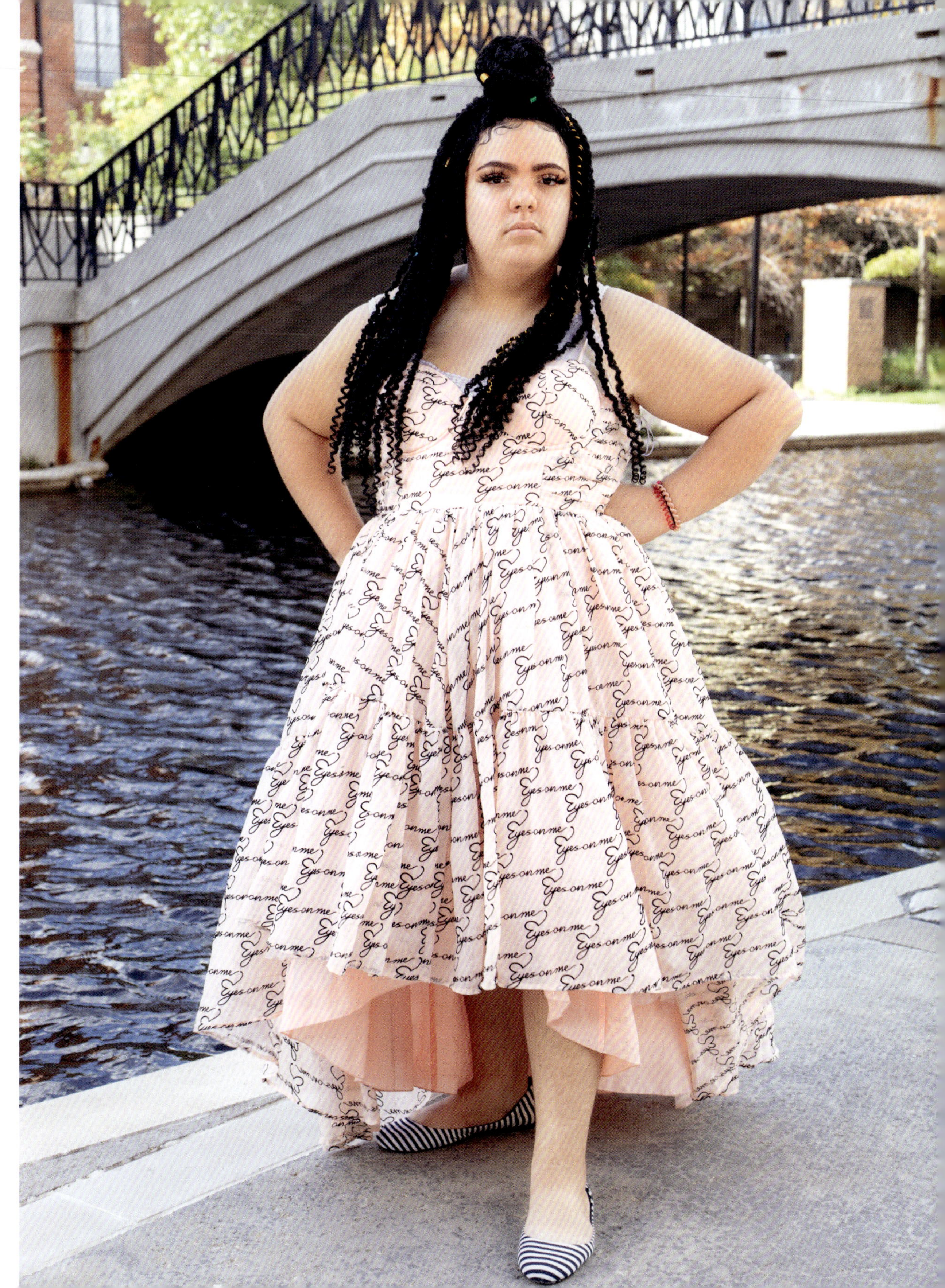

Eyes on me

Desmond is Amazing

13 years old, they/them, New York

Hey everyone! I'm known as Desmond is Amazing! I am from New York City. My pronouns are they/them. I am thirteen years old and I identify as gender-fluid! I am going to tell you how I found out who I am and why it is important to be yourself.

I was born and raised here in New York City with my beautiful mother and my father. We have several parrots and live in a cozy home. New York City has a wonderful vibe to it. It is filled with lots of things to do and unique people.

When I was about eleven or twelve years old I began to question my identity. I heard about nonbinary people through my friend, who at the time had recently come out as nonbinary. This began to help me find my identity. I went online and did a little research on nonbinary people. Then, I discovered the term *gender-fluid*. I realized there are no fixed genders, and I began to realize I was the same. Sometimes I feel like a boy, and sometimes I feel like a girl, and sometimes I feel like neither! I said to myself, "That sounds just like how I feel!" It felt very good and it just released this insecurity inside of me. I would always ask myself "What am I? Who am I? What do I identify myself as?"

When I discovered how I identify, I told my mother that I believe I am gender-fluid. She then replied, "Okay. I accept you and I understand."

Now I will tell you the tale of how I became Desmond is Amazing! In 2015, when I was eight years old, my parents and I went to the NYC Pride March. There was music playing and cheering while the floats would pass by and it made me want to dance. This is when everything changed for me! At the march I was voguing and a lot of people began to notice me in all my fabulousness. Then the next day I went viral! I was already doing drag at the time but I still didn't have a name for myself. A family friend of mine made a Facebook fan page titled "Desmond is Amazing." I loved the name so much that I decided to make it my official drag name. Thus, Desmond is Amazing was born!

As I was growing up in the city, I had always liked drag queens, so when I was around six or seven years old I started doing drag. Drag made me feel happy and it brought a positive light to my life because I was able to express myself and be me.

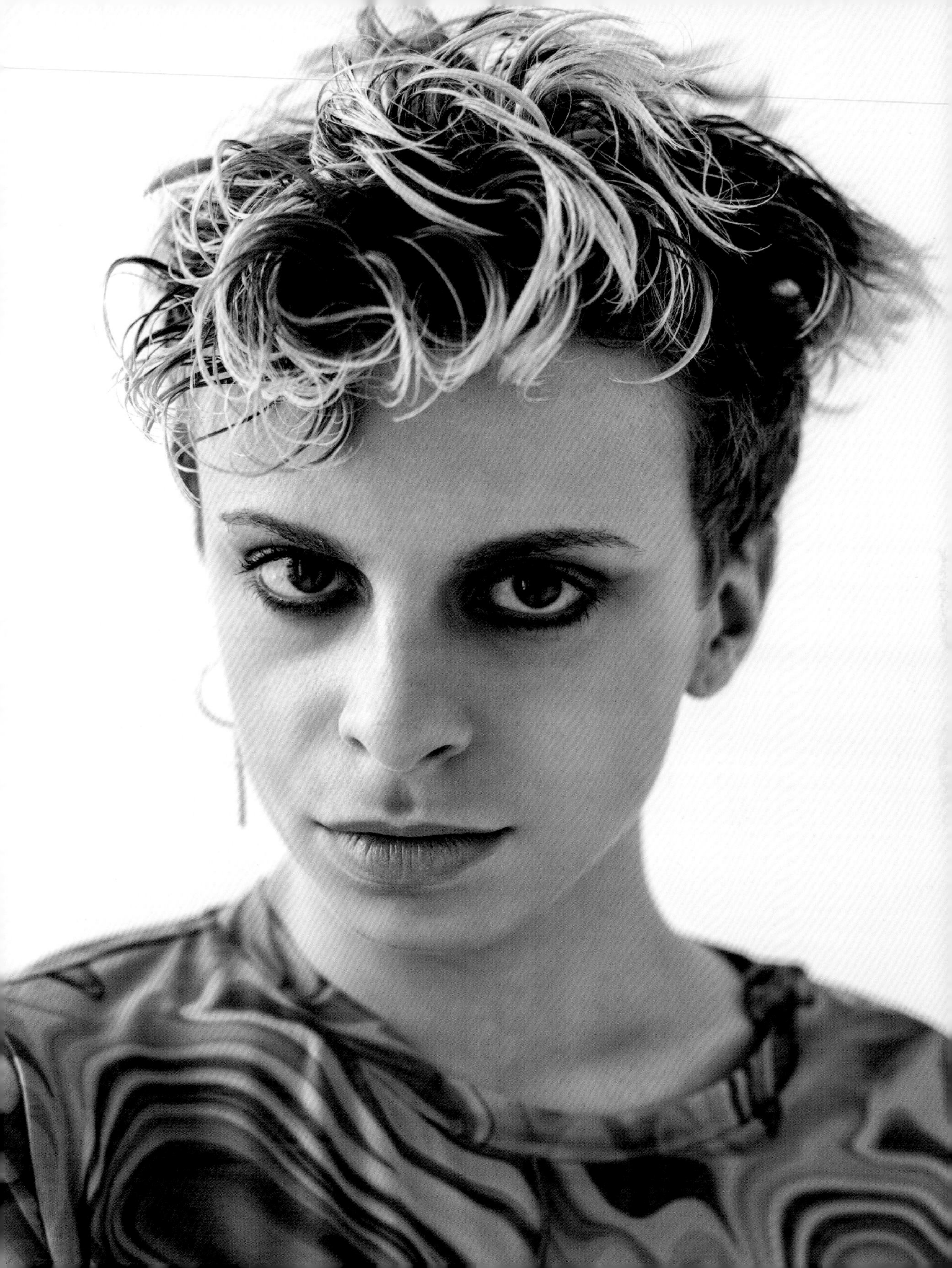

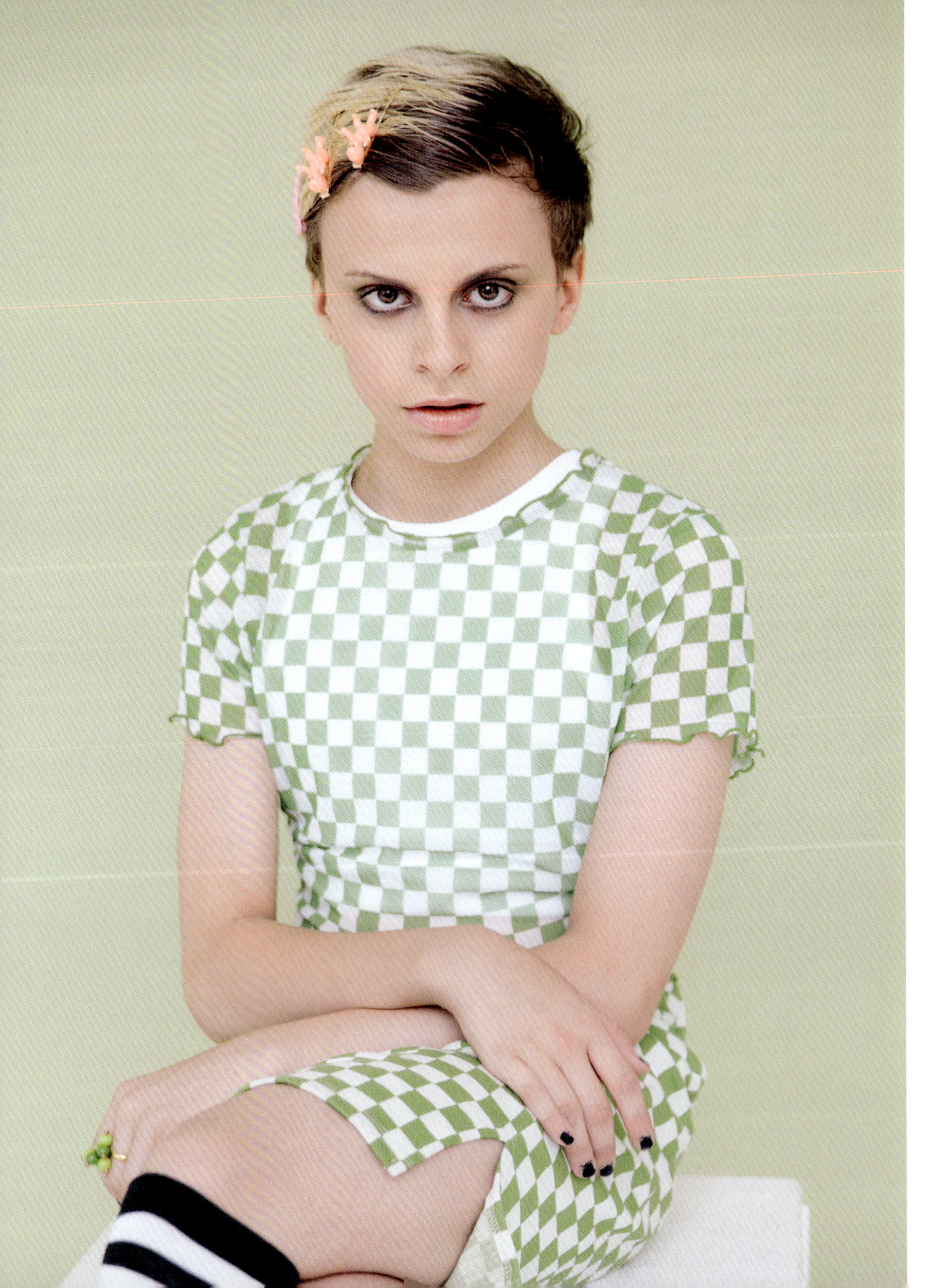

Ever since I went viral and found my drag name I have been able to perform more often for my community and the city. It was super unexpected but also cool! I am very happy to have the opportunity to spread my message and perform for my fans, which I call my "Amazie's." It is a blessing and I am so grateful for them. Becoming a drag queen has helped me find more confidence in myself and allowed me to spread positivity to the world.

It is important to be yourself because it makes you happy, and so you are not always sad. At least from my experience. Sometimes there are people in this world who do not agree with my fabulous lifestyle, but that is their opinion and I am going to pay it no mind!

My advice to other young drag queens or other young gender-fluid kids like me is "DO YOU!" Be who you are. Be fierce. You are just as amazing as Desmond is Amazing. So I'm going to vogue and death drop forever.

Diva

15 years old, he/they, Louisiana

Hi, my name is Diva, but you can call me Hime. This is the story of how I came out as transgender. Now I know a lot of people may say, "Oh, you're too young to know what you like or who you are. You aren't an adult; you'll change your mind when you get older." Well, yes, I'm not an adult—but I know who I am here and now. With that, let me tell you how it all started.

I think it was fifth grade when I first questioned my gender. I remember quite vividly asking my parents if they were sure I was born a female. Every time they answered yes, but that didn't convince me. I would go back to my room and question myself, "Am I a female?" All through school people would say I was a male in a female body, or that I should go to an all-boys school. These types of jokes made me question things often, but over time I stopped thinking about it. I started questioning again in eighth grade. I started to realize it was making me uncomfortable when people would call me a girl or even treat me like one. This is when I realized that I don't identify as female. With this, I started to identify as male, but only to myself. I was too scared to tell anyone, even my closest friends, because what if the whole school found out? Stuff there spreads like wildfire, and once one person knew, everyone else would too. So I continued through eighth grade hiding it from everyone and trying to find out other things about my identity.

When quarantine came around I was in a relationship. I wanted to try and see what type of people I liked, but it didn't come out the way I thought it would. The longer that relationship lasted, the more I wanted out. This is what led me to find out I was aromantic and asexual. Like, I still find all people attractive, but I wouldn't want to date anyone or do anything sexual with anyone. The thought of it now makes me uncomfortable.

My freshman year, since I had yet to come out to anyone about being trans, I, quite ironically, was put in an all-girls school. I felt out of place all day, every day. The teachers addressed the students as "ladies," which makes sense, since it's supposed to only be girls, but it just made things even more awkward for me. In the summer, after just ignoring it for the whole school year, I couldn't take it anymore. I had to tell someone. My camp counselor had planned a night for some of us camp kids to go bouldering. That car ride

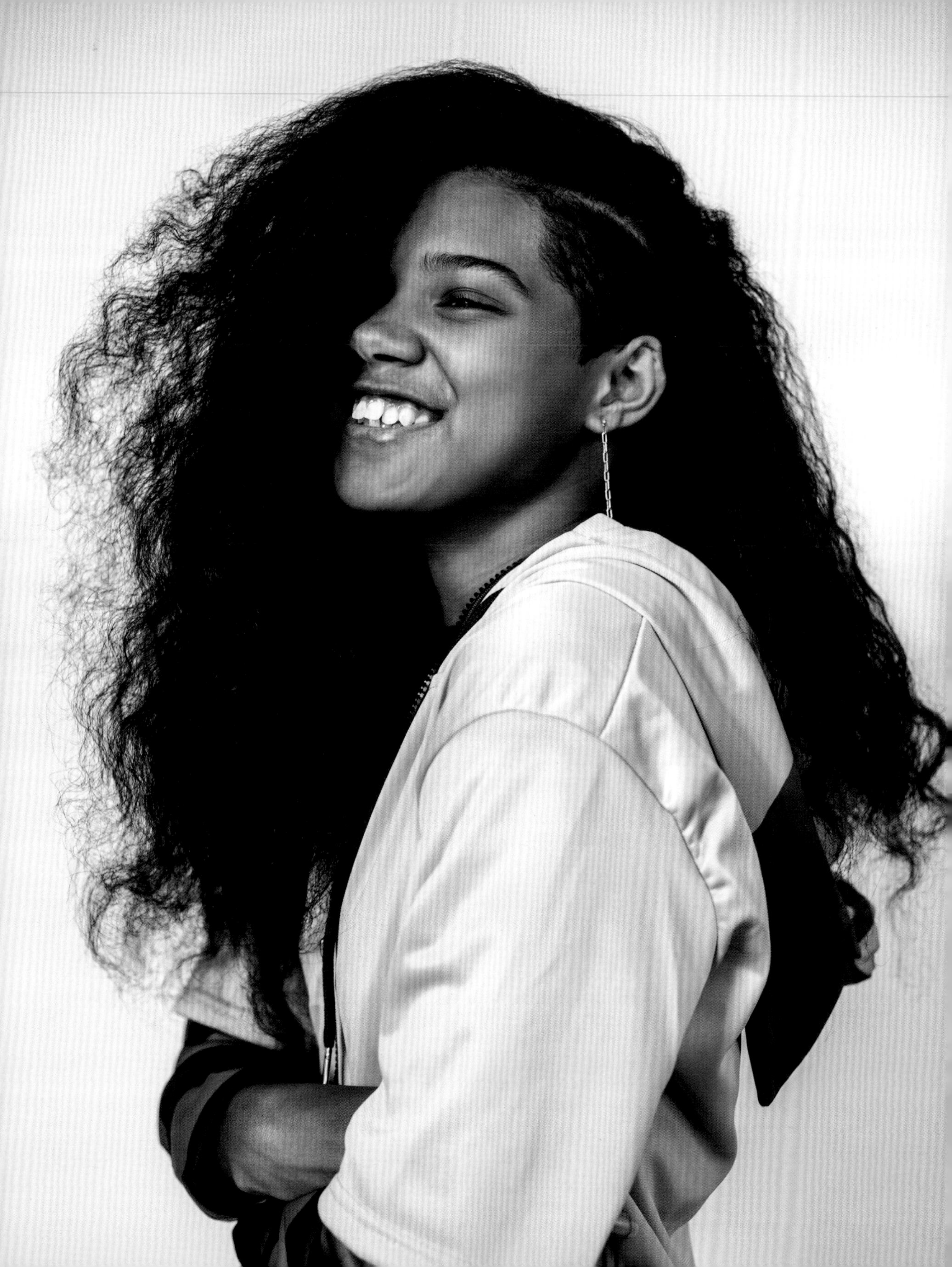

home was what changed me forever. As he was bringing me home, I came out to him. He was someone I saw as a guardian and who I felt comfortable around. We talked a lot, about all the different things we could do to help me feel more confident, and the people I could talk to that could help me with my transition. When I look back at it now, if it wasn't for that talk I would never have told my parents. About two weeks later I built up the confidence to tell my parents, after telling a decent number of other people I was fine telling. I ended up telling them everything, like what my pronouns were and how being in the school I was in made me extremely uncomfortable. They listened to everything I said and asked me questions to make sure this was my choice and not any outside influence. The conversation went way smoother than I thought. I actually enjoyed it as well. I mean, my dad even told me he just thought I was a lesbian before I came out to them, which I found quite funny.

That summer I went to camp and I felt accepted for who I was. No one said anything bad, and some helped correct people when they made a mistake with my pronouns. This all helped me be more confident in telling people what I would prefer to be called. When I finally went home, even though my parents weren't used to using my he/they pronouns, watching them try meant everything to me. Even though it is now my sophomore year and I am still stuck in the all-girls school with people who are calling me a sinner, I know who I am and who I want to be.

So now let me try introducing myself again. Hi, my name is Hime, and I am a normal guy who is still figuring things out. My advice to you is to always be who you are and who you want to be. Never let someone tell you otherwise, because what's the point of staying in the dark when you can be your best self all the time?

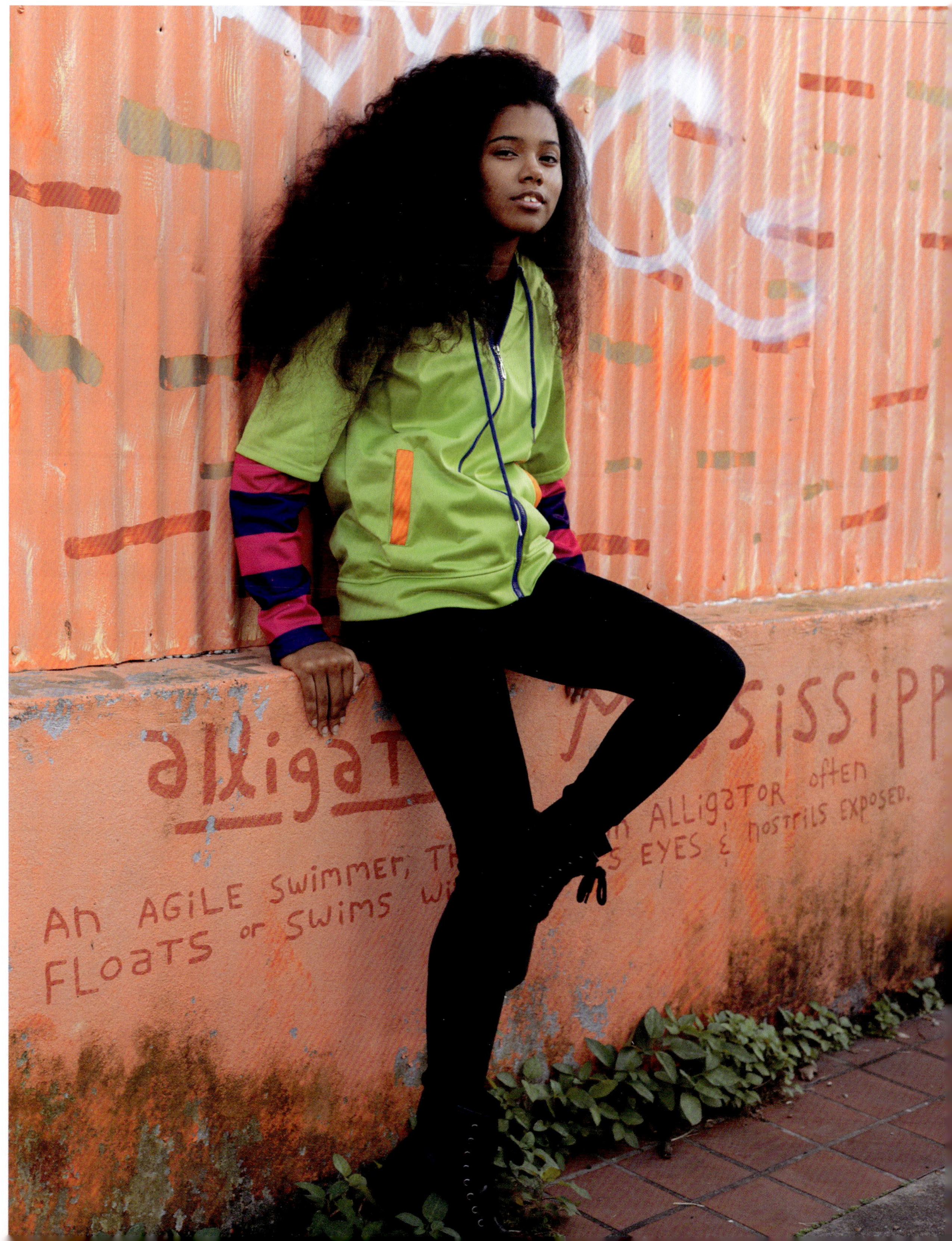

alligator
Mississipp
An AGILE SWIMMER, TH... ...n ALLIGATOR often
...S EYES & nostrils exposed.
FLOaTS or SWImS wi...

DJ

17 years old, he/him, Louisiana

Hello, I'm DJ. My pronouns are he/him/his. I'm seventeen years old and I currently live in Shreveport, Louisiana, but I am originally from Orlando. The cultural shift is crazy. If you imagine a unicorn in the middle of a rainforest, that's how I feel here. It is interesting but quite calming here—a little boring, but I am finding my way.

My story begins when I left one of my foster homes. I have been in the foster system since I was six years old. Once I left this particular home, I went to live with my relatives. Eventually I realized we had different views on life and life choices. My grandfather was a pastor. My grandmother was first lady at his church, and they already knew I was gay before I even knew. It wasn't long before we started fighting. I thought that if I spoke to them about whatever it was that bothered them, it would make them start to understand me more. At this time I was still in the foster care system. They were planning to adopt me, but because of their beliefs it was not going to work for me.

I went back into the foster system when I turned twelve years old. My thirteenth birthday was just around the corner, and I was excited because that meant I was able to join a foster group that only allowed boys thirteen years and up. This is where I began to feel more comfortable with myself. There were other gay kids there. I really looked up to one of them. He was three years older than me and he started to take me under his wing. We started going to groups together, which is where I learned about pronouns, about other queer people, and about boundaries. I learned how to make sure that everyone feels respected and how to create a safe space for other queer kids in the foster system.

Eventually I realized I was never alone. Even though I never felt fully alone, I needed that reassurance that I wasn't the only one. Once I aged out of the first group, it was time for me to be placed in a new home until I aged out when I turned eighteen. I was put up on a website for foster kids to find homes. That is where my dads found me.

I first met them right after school one day. The head of the house, the person who helps with the foster home, came up to me and said, "Two people want to meet you." I didn't say no, and he took me to meet Steven and Gerald. I hit it off with them very

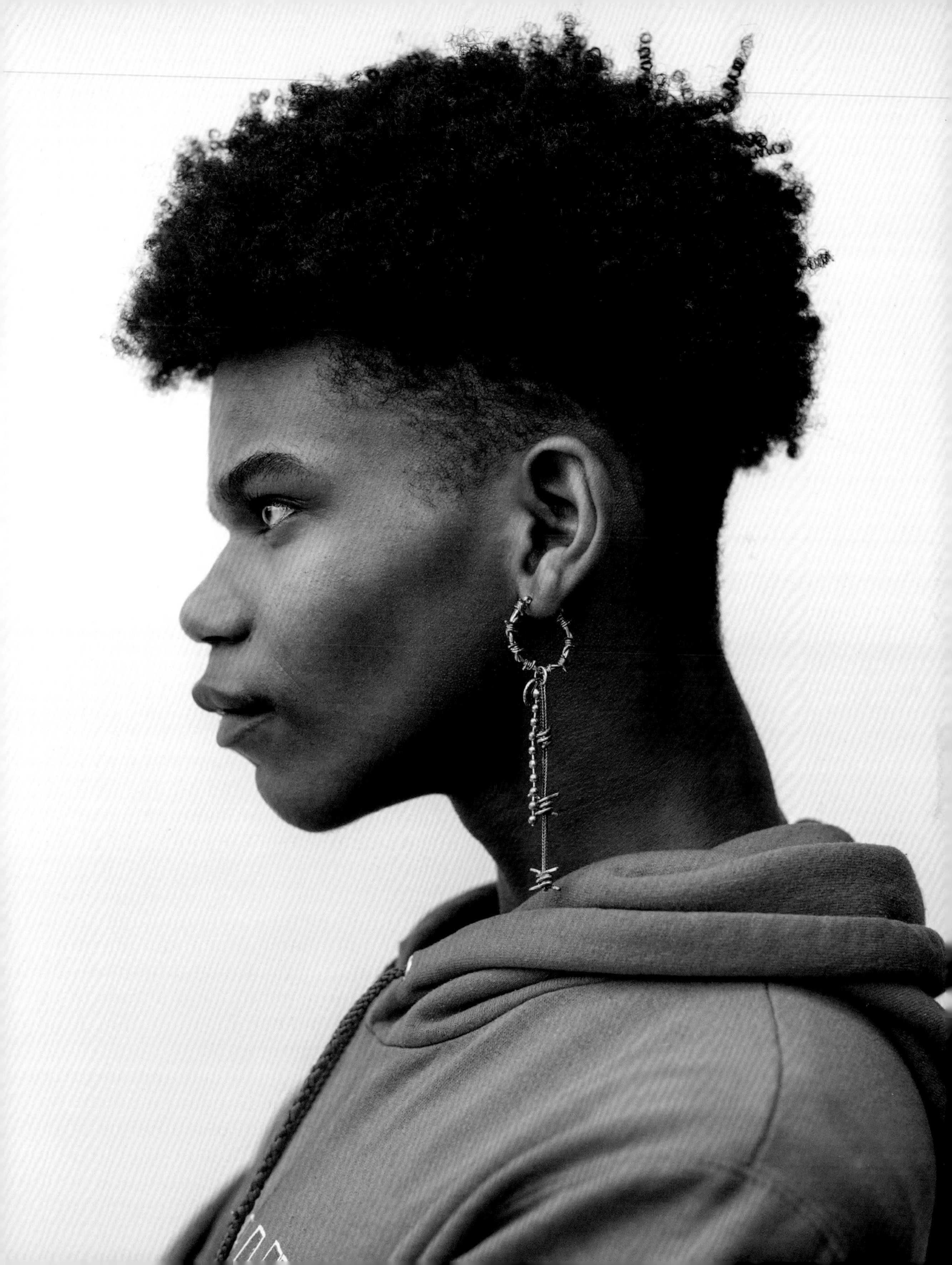

quickly. They made me feel like I was already a part of their family. I was really content with that and I wanted to meet them again. The second time I went to their house. It was warm and happy, and I even had a king-sized bed, which I jumped on right away! I stayed for the weekend. They took me to a lot of cool places—Disney World and more.

About two months later I was adopted by Steven and Gerald, my two dads. My dads have helped me be confident in myself and encouraged me to be who I am. They made me feel normal.

I always had a feeling that I was something else. I didn't know what *gay* was when I was younger, but I would always hear the word thrown around when my family would talk about my uncle. In my later years I learned the old meaning of the word *gay*: happy. I was like, "Well, I am happy." In middle school I started to embrace more things like painting my nails and liking jewelry, and I started to realize that I was not straight. When I was around fifteen years old is when I began my entrance into my gay life. Watching all my friends like girls, I started to feel lonely. Most of my friends were lesbians, and it seemed like everyone had a boyfriend or girlfriend except me.

Now I am almost eighteen years old. I'm finding my passions and figuring out my next steps. It could be modeling, dancing again . . . I could even sing. Who knows! But I am excited to see how I am going to turn out as a person.

My advice to other queer kids like me is to make sure you are heard. Speak up and be confident. Be a bad bitch! I heard a quote once that I will always remember: "Peace is never ending. It is always regrowing."

Ender

18 years old, rot/it/he, Alaska

My name is Ender. I am a transgender nonbinary-aligning person and my pronouns are rot/it. I am eighteen years old and I live in Anchorage, Alaska. I was born and raised as an Alaskan Native and I am Inupiaq. Growing up queer was both relatively easy and also challenging. I would be accepted by some and not accepted by others, and oftentimes I would have to correct other people.

My life in Alaska is pretty fun. When I was younger we would go fishing and camping a lot. I spent most of my childhood playing outside or cooking inside. My family is very close and did basically almost everything together.

My immediate family has always accepted me. Coming out at the age of twelve was an interesting experience. I had first come out to my mom, who was very accepting and loving but also had felt cautious around me. To this day I feel loved by and important to my mom. At first my biological dad and his wife struggled. He is a very Christian person, so when I came out to him he told me, "It is not what God wants." I was really frustrated with him. I stopped talking to him for about one year. After not talking for some time, I tried talking to him again. The conversation went a lot better. He apologized and started accepting me. He didn't want to lose his son and wanted to have a better connection. However, he said, "I love and accept you, but we will always know you as [deadname] and call you a girl." This had always been an issue, so I had talked to them a few years later about how it made me feel. The conversation was short, and they understood me. I would not be the same person I am now if things were different, and I'm grateful for such supportive parents.

My grandpa, however, had different things to say about me being trans. When I told him about me starting on testosterone, he said, "Testosterone will ruin your hormones; you won't be a girl anymore," and gave other excuses for me to not take testosterone. He never used my name and pronouns, and to this day I still correct him. But, he had always given me money for things and took me out to the stores, so I guess he isn't all that terrible. The rest of my family was pretty okay. My aunts were the most accepting, calling me their nephew and helping me get gender-affirming clothing. Sometimes they would even let me stay with them when I had gotten in trouble with my mom.

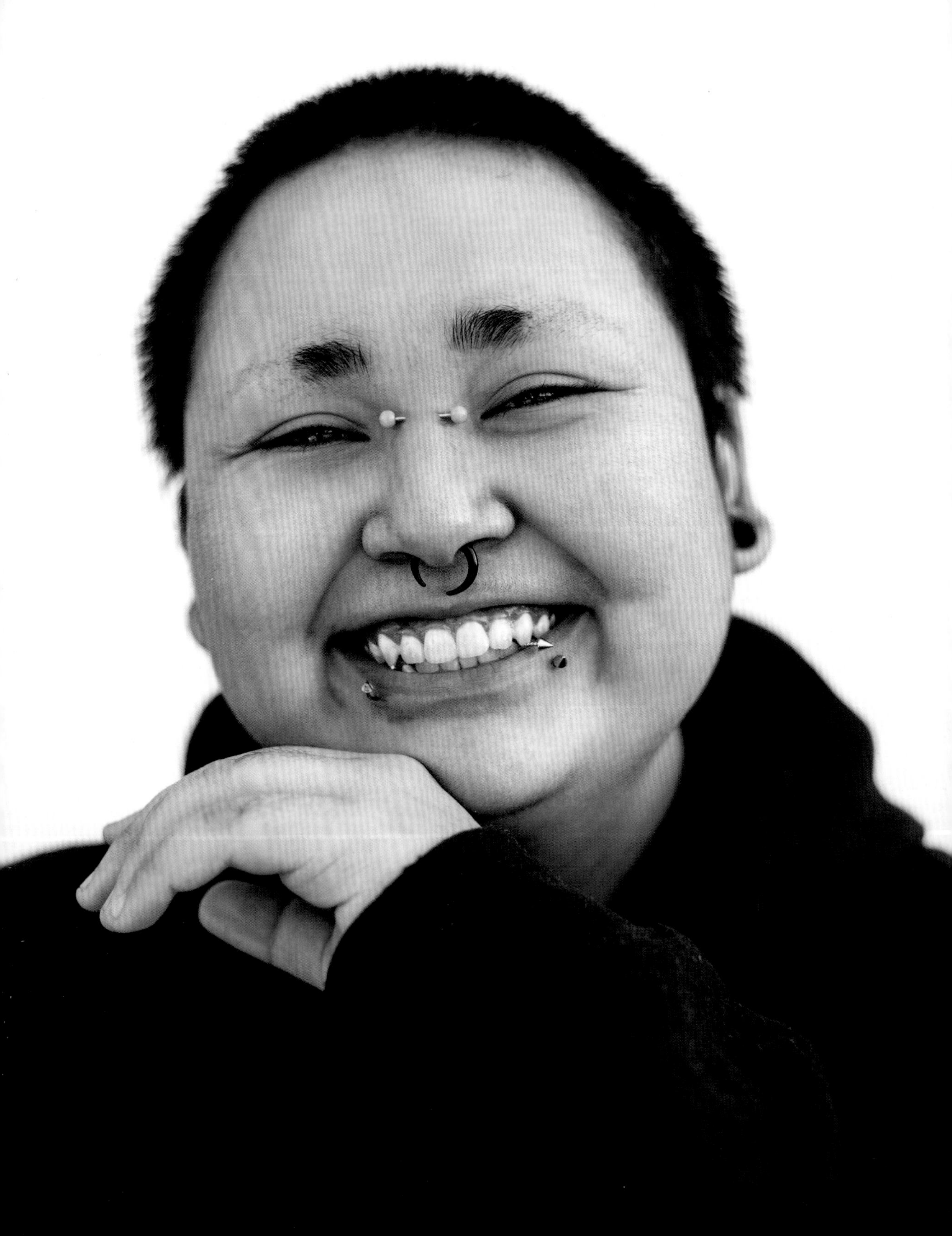

I started to realize that I was trans when I was around twelve years old. I had first learned about transgender people in middle school. When I heard the word I started to look into different genders. A transgender boy is what I felt closest to being. I was a little bit scared but also excited because although trans people aren't widely accepted in Alaska, there is a community of us here so I felt safe. The first time I met someone like me was my friend in middle school who introduced me to trans and LGBT identities. Meeting him and becoming his friend made me feel safer in school because he was very protective and I had felt very close to him.

The small group of friends I had then were really accepting and positive when I came out. They were my closest friends, and they helped me find community and self-acceptance. The other people in school around us were very homophobic. We usually ignored them, but at times we had to argue back and correct them. The best way to deal with bullies is to just ignore them. They are not worth your time, and it is going to make you feel worse if you feed into it.

In Alaska there are quite a lot of LGBT people, but most times it will feel lonely, seeing as they are so spread out. Most of the time you won't be able to tell who is trans or LGBT because they look like everyone else, so finding people in my community can be a little bit scary. The easiest way to find other people like me is at Pride or online Pride events. There are also centers like Identity or Choosing Our Roots here in Anchorage, which work toward community building to help us connect to each other.

I wish that LGBT identities were taught in school, because then it would be a lot easier to learn about yourself and accept yourself. If we all learned as kids then it would be so much easier for everyone at school to accept us. We wouldn't be dealing with as much bullying as we do, and we shouldn't be afraid to fight for that.

Now that I am eighteen and out of school, my next step and big goal is to work toward top surgery. I want to try and start working with other LGBT people and educate the younger LGBT people, to help them find the resources I wish I had when I was younger.

You don't have to come out right now if you're worried about your safety. If you come out to a homophobic family, you could get kicked out or much worse. Surround yourself with a safe community while you wait, and find resources nearby to help you with accepting yourself and your identity. Not everyone is going to accept you and that is okay. The most important thing is that you accept yourself.

Felanie

16 years old, they/them, Wyoming

I'm Felanie, I identify as Queer and Nonbinary, and I use They/
Them pronouns. I just turned sixteen, and I have lived in Lander,
Wyoming, my entire life.

Growing up, I never really had crushes on any of the guys at my
school. My friends would list names, "Oh, I love Blah Blah's hair."
"We are totally going to get married." "His eyes . . ." "His smile . . ."
I couldn't stand the way the other kids would look at me or the
things they'd say when I couldn't come up with an answer, so I
elected to stay quiet. It was unfathomable for a seven-year-old girl
to not be completely boy crazy. But I tried to not think too much of
it, until 2018.

When I was twelve I started noticing new feelings. I realized
I spent a little too long staring at Bella Swan in *Twilight* while
everyone else fawned over Edward or Jacob. I wasn't the only one
who noticed this. Eventually my mom asked me if I was gay. I'd
heard the word before, but I wasn't completely sure what it meant.
I did some research (and by that I mean I took the "Am I gay?" test
online about twenty million times) and eventually came to the conclusion that I was Bisexual. I still hadn't come out to the rest of my
family, and my mother was getting impatient, so she took matters
into her own hands. My family was accepting for the most part.
They never go out of their way to say or do anything intentionally
hurtful. Of course there are slipups, and jokes that don't always
land, but I know that there isn't hate behind what they say. The
whole thing was messy, complicated, and definitely not how I wish
things had gone, but there's really nothing I can do about it now.

Once I was more confident in my newfound identity, I decided
to come out to my closest friend at the time. She said she was
happy for me and made a joke about me having a crush on her. I
thought things were fine, but over the next few weeks a rumor had
spread around the school that I was gay. I confronted my friend,
and she admitted to me that she had told a few people. I was hurt
and scared, but I figured nothing bad would happen. But I was
wrong. I was so wrong. Things quickly spiraled. It started off with
a few homophobic remarks here and there. Kids told me I was a
freak, a weirdo, and I had slurs hurled at me from passing cars.
I was told I was a sinful disgrace, that I was going to hell. I had

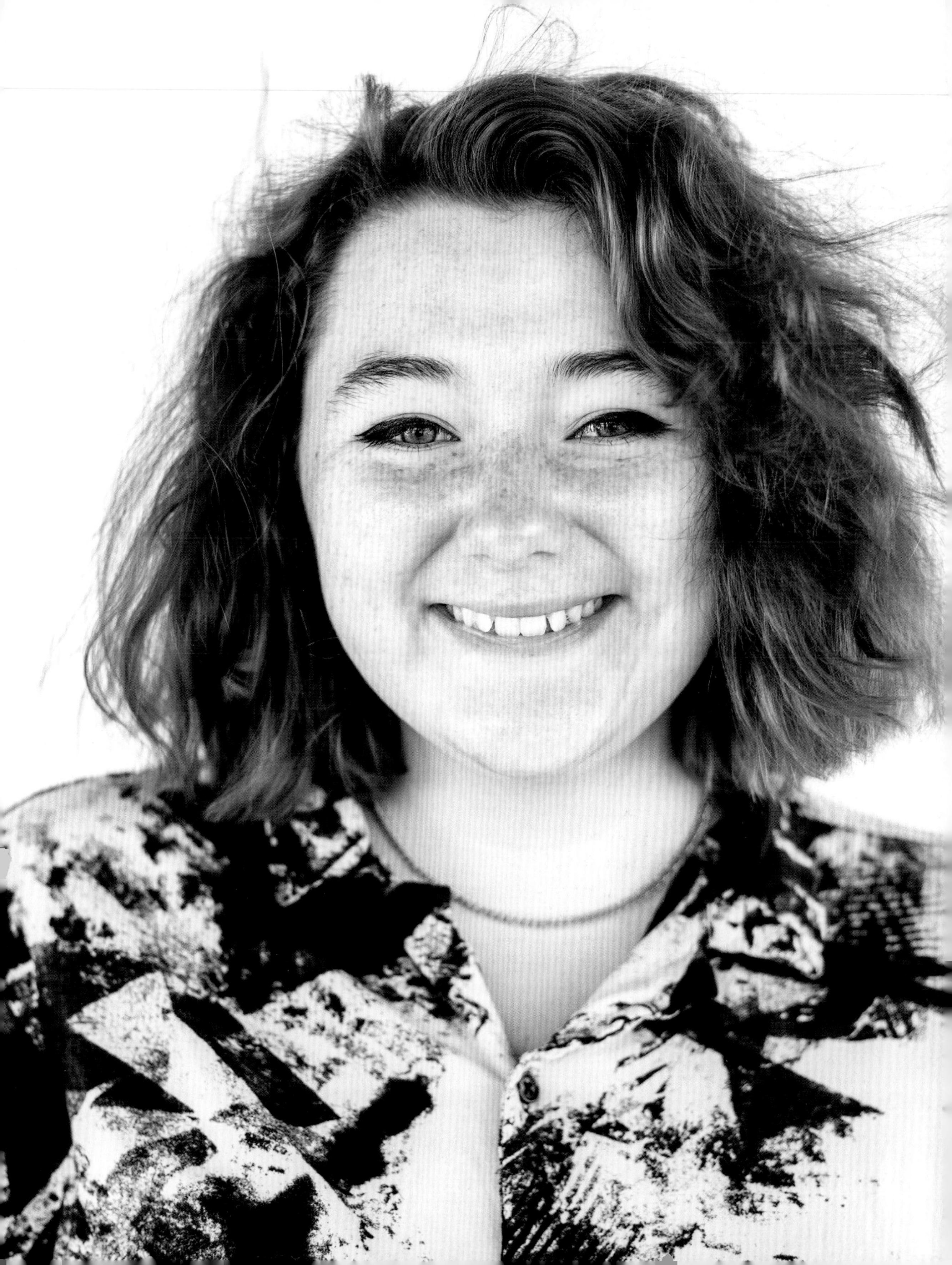

82

people tell me they could change me, fix me. It didn't stop there though. Things got violent. I was pushed and shoved in the halls, I had things thrown at me, and I was even jumped. I tried to reach out; I talked to teachers, counselors, anyone I thought could help me. But the adults were not much better. Many of the people I tried to reach out to blamed me for the assault and harassment. They told me I was too young to know for sure anyway, so why bother telling people. I felt like I was completely alone. I stayed home every chance I got, and my mom threatened to take me to the hospital on multiple occasions because of how many stomachaches I faked. I just couldn't stand to sit in a classroom full of people who hated me. I was having panic attacks daily, and I could barely bring myself to get out of bed most days. I was terrified. I just couldn't understand why someone would hate a person so much because of something they can't even change.

One good thing that came from this mess was my first non-male partner. We had bonded over our similar experiences and interests. They were confident and had this I-don't-care attitude about them. They made me feel comfortable and safe. We dated for a few months, and we were the only openly gay couple in our school. People either loved us or they hated us, but we didn't care either way. And even though it didn't work out, I will be forever grateful for them. They taught me that I don't have to pretend to be something I'm not, even if I didn't realize it at first.

When I was thirteen I started questioning my identity again. These thoughts terrified me so I tried my best to suppress my feelings. I did everything I could to be "normal." I got a boyfriend, and despite not being happy in the relationship, I stuck with it. I thought that if I was with a guy I could make everyone else happy. Honestly, that was the stupidest thing I've ever done. It took me eleven long months to realize that no matter what I do, I'll never be able to make everyone happy. Someone will always have a problem with what you do or how you live, but that doesn't matter. The only thing that should ever matter is how you feel about yourself.

Over the next year or so I took some time to focus on myself. I started experimenting with different labels, and when I was fourteen I came out as a lesbian. I struggled for a little bit, but I eventually came to terms with being nonbinary. I've never been completely comfortable with feminine or masculine labels, but I didn't think there were any other options until I learned more about trans identities. Basically what I learned is that trans is an umbrella term used for anyone who doesn't identify with their birth sex. Of course there are trans men and trans women, but there's another identity under the trans label: nonbinary. And under the nonbinary umbrella there's a bunch of other identities and labels such as gender-fluid and agender.

After a six-month quarantine I finally started my first year at Lander Valley High School. I met some pretty amazing people who are just like me, I came out to a few of my teachers, and I joined my school's SPEAK club. (The SPEAK club is a place for students just like me. It is our unofficial school GSA—unofficial because our school didn't want to approve an actual GSA because it would cause "exclusion.")

Now I'm a sophomore in high school. I'm an openly queer and nonbinary student, this time on my own terms. I'm still a part of the SPEAK club, and this year I'm working with the middle school to install a GSA so that queer students can finally have a place where they can feel safe. I've helped plan and put together a few Pride events in my town. People in my school see me as someone they can talk to, and I'm even telling my story. When I was thirteen I never thought I'd be able to do anything like this. But here I am, doing all that I can to try and make a difference and being unapologetically me.

Whether you have an accepting community or not, coming out, or even just being queer, is scary; it's vulnerable. There's a lot of pressure surrounding coming out and knowing exactly who you are. But really none of that even matters. It doesn't matter what labels you use (if any at all), how old you are, where you're from, or if you decide to tell people or not. The only thing that ever matters is that you are happy and safe.

You never have to explain yourself to anyone, and you never have to change to fit into anyone's box. You are perfect just the way you are.

Freedom

13 years old, he/him, South Dakota

Hello! My name is Freedom. I'm a thirteen-year-old, Two-Spirit, fabulous, gay young man from Brookings, South Dakota. My pronouns are he/him, but I also identify as nonbinary and don't care that much about pronouns or labels. I'm currently in seventh grade and am an enrolled member of the Sisseton-Wahpeton Oyate tribe, which is a Lakota Sioux Native American tribe in South Dakota.

Brookings is a small, conservative town. There is very little support for the LGBTQ+ community here and even less for queer youth. I wish there were more opportunities to meet other kids like me so we wouldn't feel so alone! I know more LGBTQ+ youth would feel comfortable coming out if they had more peer support. Unfortunately, many people in my town and my school have issues with racism and homophobia. Brookings needs a community space where LGBTQ+ youth like myself can feel safe, accepted, and just have fun being kids together!

Growing up here was great before I came out. I have a great childhood with a loving family who has always accepted me. I came out to my mom first, right before I turned eleven. I decided then that I didn't care who knew and I didn't want it to be a big secret, so I came out to everyone else after that.

My friends and family were very supportive. I was the first kid I knew of that wasn't straight in my town. I came out to everyone in fifth grade. A few other kids came out after I did and we became friends. It felt good to know that I might've helped them be courageous enough to come out later.

I am lucky to have so much support, especially from my mom. She's always been cool with dyeing my hair crazy colors and helping me express myself. She started educating herself about LGBTQ+ youth issues immediately after I came out. She accepted my friends when their parents didn't. She started going to PFLAG meetings and was on the board for an LGBTQ+ group that tried to get started here. We went to meetings together and planned a couple of youth activities. It was really fun, but then COVID hit and everything stopped. We are going to try and bring it back so hopefully we can have Pride events again.

I went to my first Pride parade right after I came out. It was my first time being open in public and it was the coolest thing

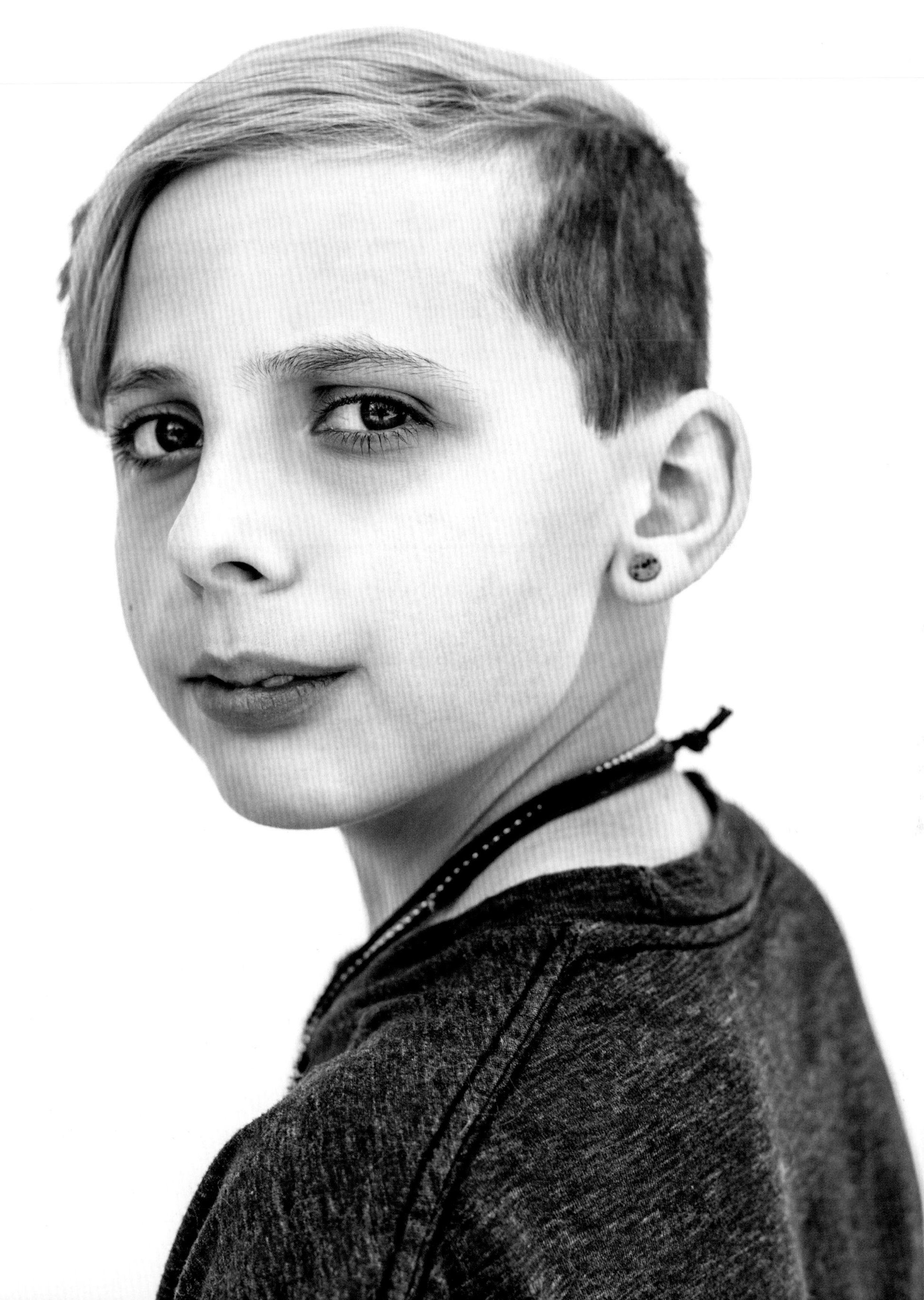

ever! When I got to the parade and saw so many beautiful people being confident in their differences, I said, "I feel like I'm home!" I couldn't wait to go to the next one and every one after that. This year I dressed up like Freddie Mercury and actually walked in the parade with my mom. People were smiling, waving, and wanted to take my picture! It felt so good to just be me and not deal with people making fun of me.

Although I'm confident with my sexuality, it hasn't always been easy. Once I began middle school, last year, I started getting bullied for being gay. A few kids called me names and threatened me in school. I had to move lockers in gym class to get away from one of them. They also bullied my friends who were LGBTQ+, and one who was from another country. They targeted us because we are different from them, and I guess that bothers some people. I was angry that they were hurting my friends' feelings because I care about my friends a lot! Seeing these bullies try to bring us down made me mad at first. Now I just laugh at them because I can't change what they think of me and I'm not changing myself for them! At first I didn't want to tell anyone about the bullying, but after we told the school, things got a little better. Eventually I just said, "It's 2021 and your jokes are old and not funny. Your words don't hurt me. Grow up already!" It's funny and strange when people judge you by how you look but they don't know anything about you!

I also feel bad for bullies sometimes. I think it's sad that they need to make others feel bad just to feel better about themselves. I think many of them have parents that didn't teach them about kindness and tolerance for people who are different. I hope that one day all parents will teach their kids to accept and respect everyone.

Being bullied also brought up some mental health issues for me. If you are struggling with negative thoughts, please know that there are great resources for you, even nationally, if you don't have any in your own town, like me. One great option is the Trevor Project national hotline and chat line. I also found one of my school counselors to be a great person to talk to when school days were extra tough. It's okay to be sad sometimes, but try to find one person you can trust and talk to if life gets too hard. I really think life is worth living and I can't wait to keep growing and discovering more about myself every day. I've found other outlets to help build up my confidence too. Jujitsu has been a great source of support. My coach is awesome. He knows that I'm gay and he's cool with it. He was also a smaller kid who was bullied, so he knows how hard it can be.

He's had a positive impact on my life. Jujitsu has taught me about self-respect, respect for others, self-discipline, and self-defense.

My heroes are Elton John and Freddy Mercury because they are gay and effing amazing! They also inspire me to be musical, and I'm teaching myself some of their songs on piano and guitar. I also look up to my dad because he is super supportive and hilarious and gives me great advice. He's also teaching me how to drive on dirt roads so I can get my license next year! Yes, you can get them that young when you live in a small place like Brookings.

My greatest hero is my papa, who was a Native American Vietnam vet who passed away from COVID last November. He was the wisest and kindest man I've ever met. He accepted my sexuality without even thinking about it, even though many elderly people don't. The last time I saw him, he said to me, "I don't care about any of that stuff. I will always love you just the way you are." He taught me to be proud of who I am. I miss him so much and would like to dedicate my story to him.

One thing I would like to mention is that if you don't feel safe coming out to your family, you do *not* have to! I have friends that came out to their parents and have not been accepted, which has made it really difficult for them. Some family members are emotionally, verbally, and even physically abusive when their child is different.

I wish all parents would be as accepting as mine, but that's not always the case. As I watch my friends struggle, I realize I need to be there for them. Finding others who accept you is so important. I accept you and others will too. Please don't give up: Your rainbow family is out there!

Growing up is hard and it feels like it's taking *forever* . . . but try to have fun in the meantime! Laugh at the bullies, find your true friends, and know that you aren't alone! Always remember the great words of Freddie Mercury and Queen: *"We are the champions of the world!"*

Gabi

9 years old, he/her, Arkansas

Hi! My name is Gabriel (pronouns he/her) and I am almost ten years old! I mostly go by Gabi (pronounced *GAH-bee*) for short. I am part Puerto Rican and I live in a small town called Morrilton, Arkansas.

At recess in third grade, I remember finally having the guts to tell my friends that I liked boys as well as girls. To my relief, they were completely surprised but very happy for me. I was really nervous: Before I told them, nobody else knew. For a while I was content with just my friends knowing who I am. I was still too scared to tell my parents or the rest of my family, though I never doubted they loved me.

A few months later my older brother, Jaiden, asked me outright if I liked boys or girls. I decided to put him in the loop. I told him I did like both genders. I thought that was the end of it, but he went and told my mom without my consent. I remember being upset that Jaiden betrayed my trust and outed me. I didn't know until my parents confronted me at the kitchen table. My nerves almost failed me, but somehow I found the courage to tell the truth. Yes, Mom and Dad, I liked both girls and boys. My little secret was out and I couldn't take it back even if I wanted to. My heart felt like it beat a mile a minute as I waited for their response. Luckily, my mom was cool with it.

One thing I really love to do is makeup. I love it. It makes me feel more like me and I feel beautiful with it on. My mom even let me start putting makeup on at home and get my nose pierced! I look so cool with it. My dad, however, struggles with it hard. He doesn't understand me. He grew up in a culture where having feelings for someone of the same gender wasn't discussed. Instead of dealing with the situation, for a while he just didn't want to think about it. Eventually, though, he came around. Dad went from not getting upset when I wore makeup to helping me put makeup on my mom. I did one side of my mom's face and my dad did the other. His side turned out pretty bad and I slayed, but it felt like we had turned a corner in our relationship. That made me happy, to see my dad doing something with me that made me feel confident and that is a part of who I am.

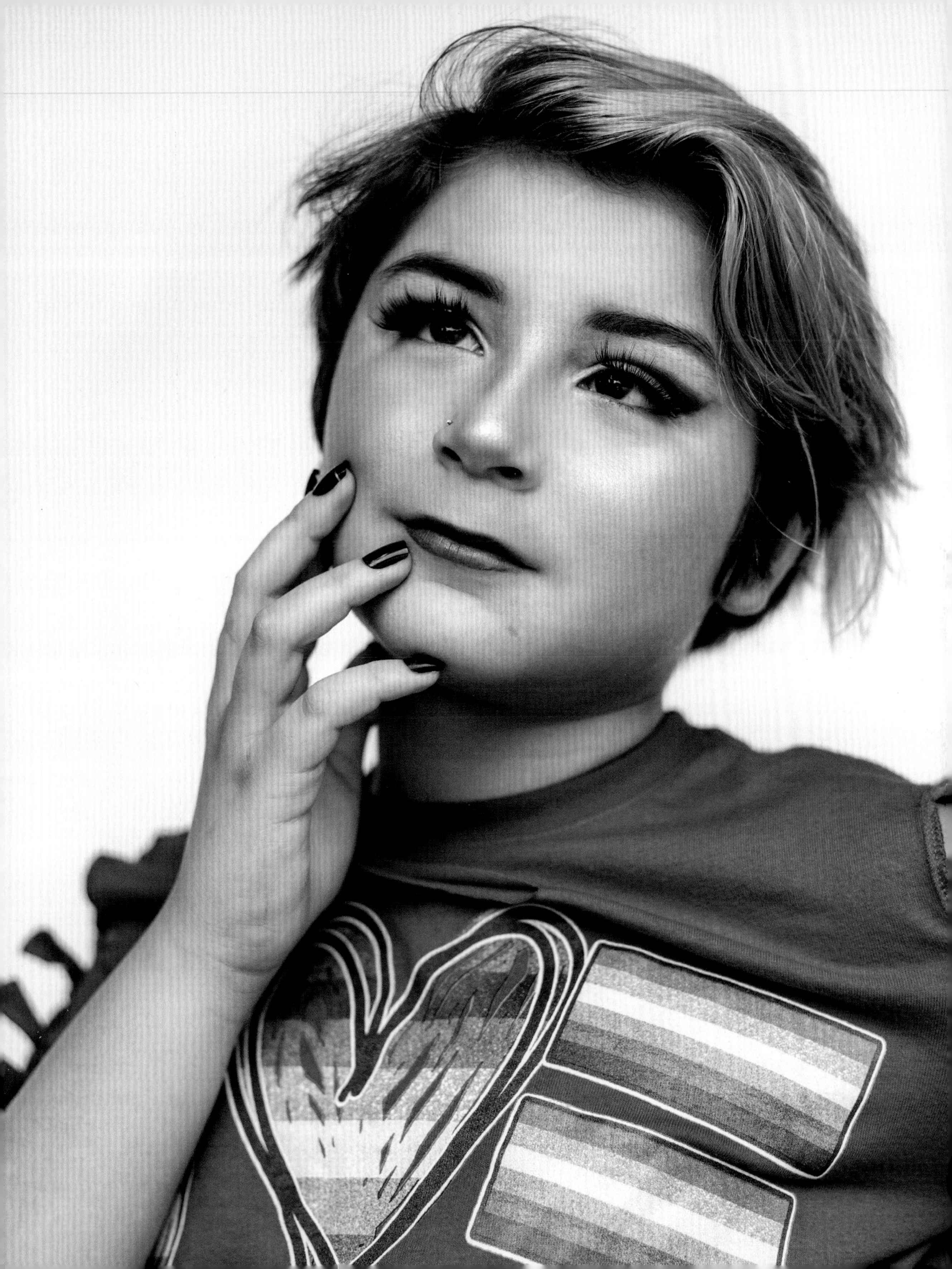

At first, mom wouldn't let me wear makeup outside of the house. She didn't want anyone to bully me or call me names. Then, eventually, she let me start wearing makeup out around town if she was with me. She only worries for my safety wearing makeup around in public.

I live in a small town here in Arkansas. It's fun sometimes and other times it can be weird when people stare at me because of my makeup or my hair and my clothing choices, but I don't really care anymore. I have gotten used to the staring and, as I gained more confidence in myself, I stopped caring what everyone around me thought.

School can be annoying too, just like the people in my town. The boys all make jokes about my makeup and how I am, teasing me. But once I stopped caring and showed them how fabulous I am they have all started to like me and tease me less. I find it interesting how so many people may feel weird around others who are different. From my experience, once I showed them my true colors and even normalized it, people in my community started to see the bigger picture—that everyone is equal and should be treated with love and kindness.

My advice for people like me is to be who you are. I may be the youngest in this book, but I know who I am just as much as the oldest one in this book. So do what you wanna do. Do what makes you happy and love yourself. I am happy to share my message with you.

The next stage is where I'm at now. I get to wear light makeup when I leave the house, even if my mom isn't with me. Most people put on makeup to cover up parts of themselves, but when I put makeup on, it's like I finally get to show people who I am.

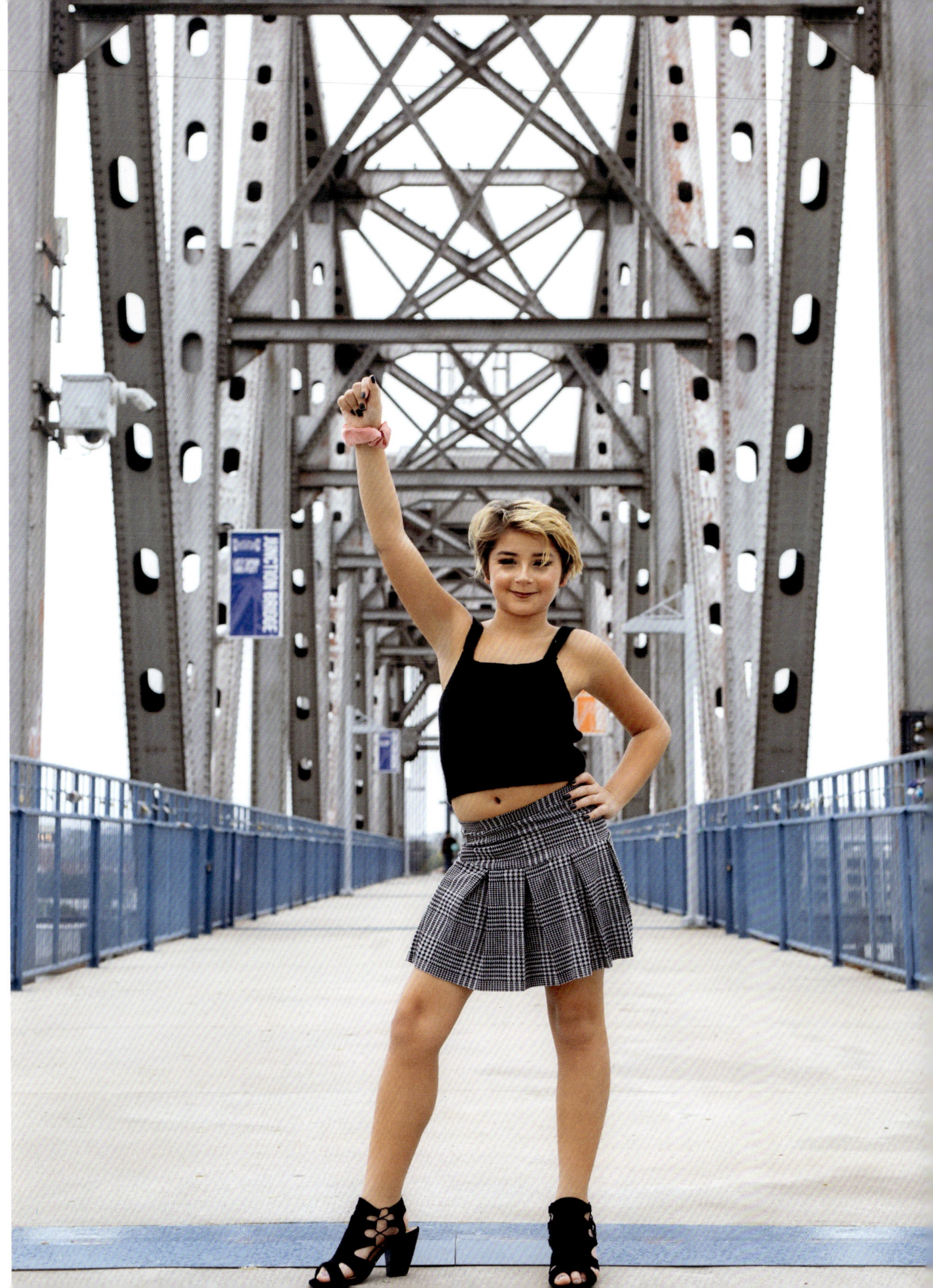

Gavin

17 years old, he/him, New York

Hello, my name is Gavin, and my pronouns are he/him. I am a transgender male. I realized who I was at the age of ten, in a town called Buffalo, in New York. The state is known to be Democratic, and there are many laws in New York that protect transgender people. I was lucky to be born and raised in a state where many are accepting, but there have been those who are not. I have recently found community with a nonprofit organization called Growing LGBTQ+ Youth Support (GLYS), and I am significantly thankful to have met those who participate in the program. It took seven years to meet those truly like me, and the relief is astounding. My journey is packed with many twists and turns, as well as ups and downs. However, I can only share a part of who I fully am, and I hope that this creates an impact on those who have the chance to indulge in my story.

"Say 'no' to the transgender agenda." That is what an ad on my social media account said when I was ten years old. I did not know what being transgender was, and the only agenda I knew of was the one I used for school to keep track of my homework. I recall being confused as to what this ad was talking about, but I ultimately kept scrolling through my feed and forgot about it. However, as the days passed the ad seemed to be the only thing I could think about. What was a transgender person? I ended up looking up what being transgender meant, and my initial reaction was fear.

My fear came from the realization that I was transgender. I had experienced feelings of gender dysphoria throughout my short life-time, and I never had the words to explain these feelings. I refused to bring up these emotions due to shame, and my belief that I was the only person who felt this way. Once I understood what being transgender was, and what having gender dysphoria meant, I was frightened. I was scared due to understanding the hate that transgender people faced, and the struggles they went through in life.

This led to a long year of refusing to show the world, and myself, who I truly was. I decided to hyperfeminize myself in every way that I knew how. I grew out my hair as long as I had ever grown it before, I wore dresses, I painted my nails, and I started to wear excessive amounts of makeup. I resented the way I looked, and every time I looked in the mirror I loathed what I saw looking

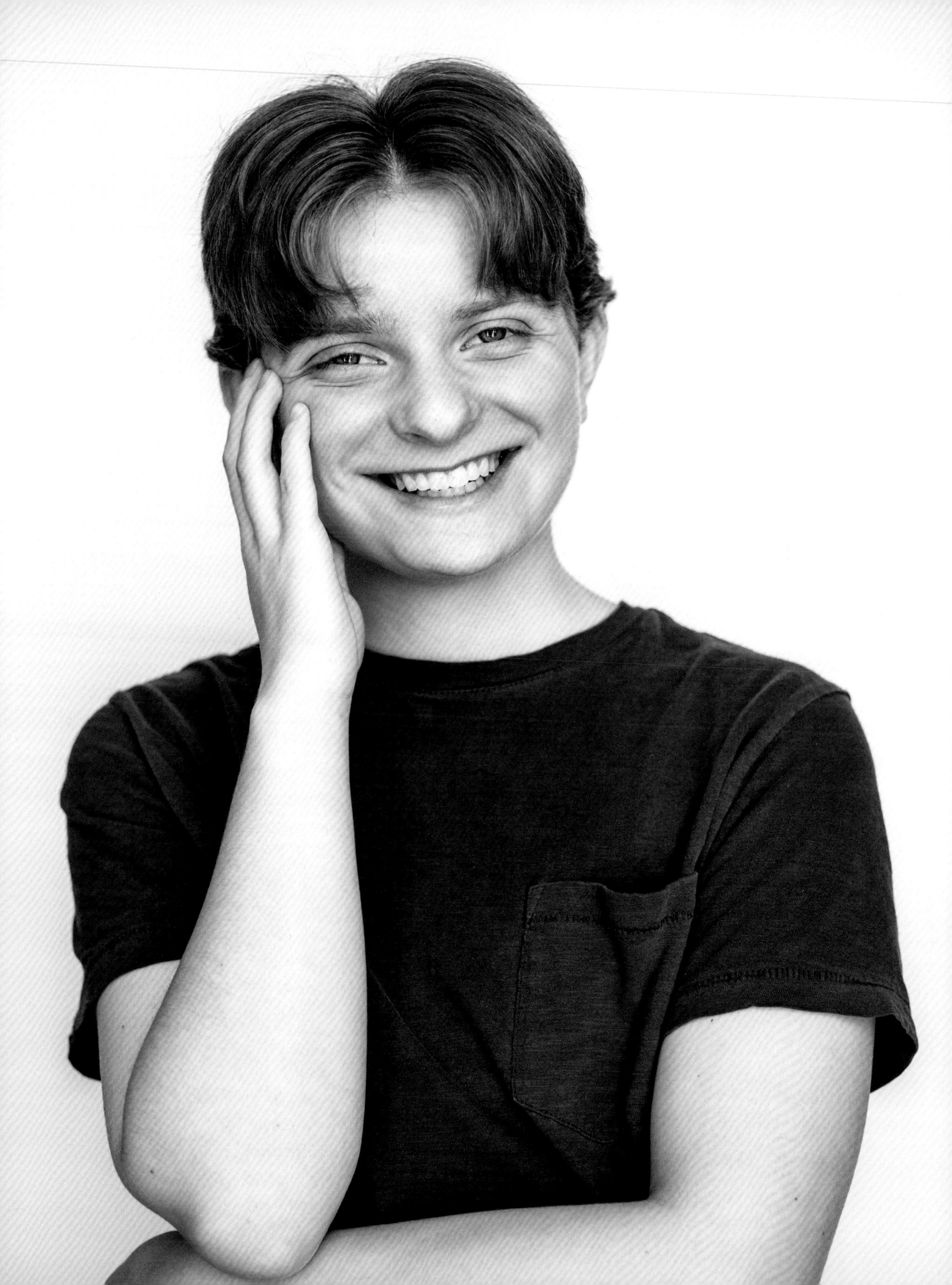

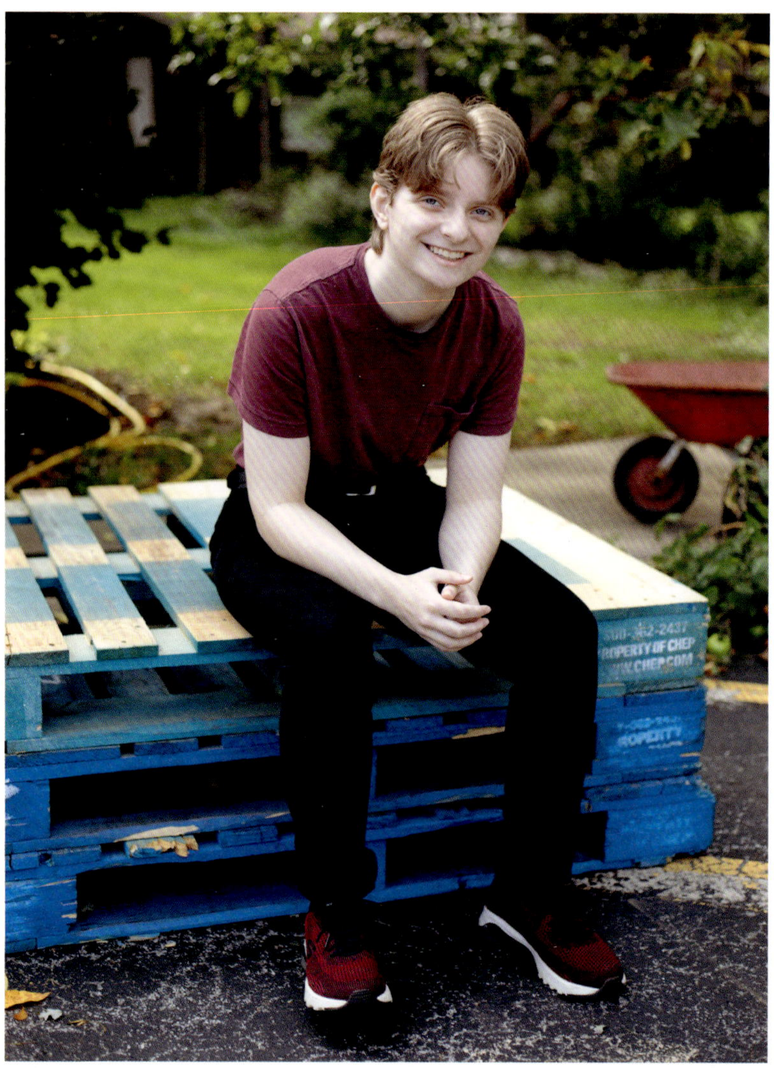

back, yet I received many compliments about how I presented, and it made me feel as though the way I looked was the right way to look, the only way to look. Nonetheless, I soon realized that I could not continue living a life full of wearing costumes and masks.

By hyperfeminizing my appearance, I put myself in a very dark place mentally. My mind despised everything about my appearance, and the days became more difficult. Every minute seemed excruciatingly long, and everything that occurred within this time period seemed dull. I found myself in a deep depression, and I could not find a way out on my own. I ended up reaching out to my parents, telling them that I was experiencing a tremendously depressed state of mind. They decided that I should see a therapist, and this was the best decision they have ever made for me.

By going to talk to a therapist for a few months, I realized that I needed to live my truth, and the only way I could be content and live to my full potential was by transitioning. My therapist helped me plan ways of coming out to my friends, and then eventually my parents. The first person I ever came out to was my best friend at the time. She and I did everything together and hung out as much as we possibly could. However, when I told her that I was a transgender boy, that my name was Gavin, and that I was going to start using he/him pronouns, she had a poor reaction.

Because she reacted in such a negative way, I feared that I would lose her as a friend and that I would lose all my friends if I continued to tell others. Nevertheless, I knew that I had to continue telling my truth because the alternative was to live a meaningless life, filled with agony and anguish. I eventually started to tell my other friends, and I had to explain to them what being transgender was. All of my other friends were very supportive.

I had to keep pushing myself, and the most important people to come out to were up next. My parents were very supportive of those in the LGBT+ community, and I knew that they would love me regardless of my identity, but I was still terrified to tell them. I delayed this process for months. One day, however, my parents asked me if I believed that I was a boy. I was shocked that they had asked me this, but I was also relieved. I had no idea how to bring up the conversation about my situation, and once they asked me this question, my life changed for the better.

My parents were as supportive as I believed that they would be. I told them that in the future I wanted to start hormone replacement therapy and get surgery in order to treat my gender dysphoria. Now, at seventeen years old, I have received both these treatments. I started HRT within the last year and had top surgery a few months ago. My journey for happiness has been long, but every minute has been worth it. I am so thankful to my friends, and my parents, for their constant love and support. I know that I would not be where I am today if it weren't for them.

If you're reading this and you're worried about what others might think of you, stop. You will never please everyone in your life. You will never change everyone's mind. All you can do is live the life you were meant to live, the life you were meant to achieve happiness with. If you feel as though you are trapped in a box, do something to break out of it. You are in control of your life because, at the end of the day, it's yours. Never live a life for other people—live yours.

Hammy

18 years old, they/them, Alabama

OUTside of Tradition

Hello all, my name is Hammy and I am Nonbinary and Bisexual! I am at the old age of eighteen and currently reside in Mobile, Alabama, for college. I basically grew up here and fell in love with the timeless look that remains. I know, the word *Alabama* doesn't seem ideal for any queer person, and I understand why. Alabama is constantly stuck in this loop of keeping things "traditional" and lags behind on the topic of equality. I never truly realized this until I went up North and saw items such as Pride flags publicly displayed. When I came back I noticed the same thing in Alabama, but with Confederate flags. It seemed like the town hated me, so I hated it back.

Growing up, I never was exposed to anything outside of tradition, specifically in school. I went to private schools my entire life. They were religious and *never* went outside of tradition; furthermore, they claimed that everything outside was "sinful." As a child I absorbed what they said because they were adults—they knew everything, right? It wasn't until around middle school that I knew that everything labeled as sinful, awful, and strange by my peers was who I am as a person. So, because of this, I hid a large part of myself from them and from myself. I never knew how harmful it was until the mental toll drained me and disconnected me from reality. Eventually I accepted myself before anyone else did. It was strange because I felt comfortable wearing feminine things. Before, I couldn't see myself painting my nails and enjoying it—or even wearing a dress. Slowly, I took my time with testing things and seeing what I personally enjoyed and what I simply did not. So, little by little, stepping outside my comfort zone helped me an immense amount.

When I came out to my family it was truly a breath of relief. They loved and accepted me as I was. My parents warned me that others will always judge, but if you love yourself it will always overpower hate. With this, I blossomed into who I always was. I didn't care what was "sinful" or outside of the tradition; it felt right to me, and that's all that mattered.

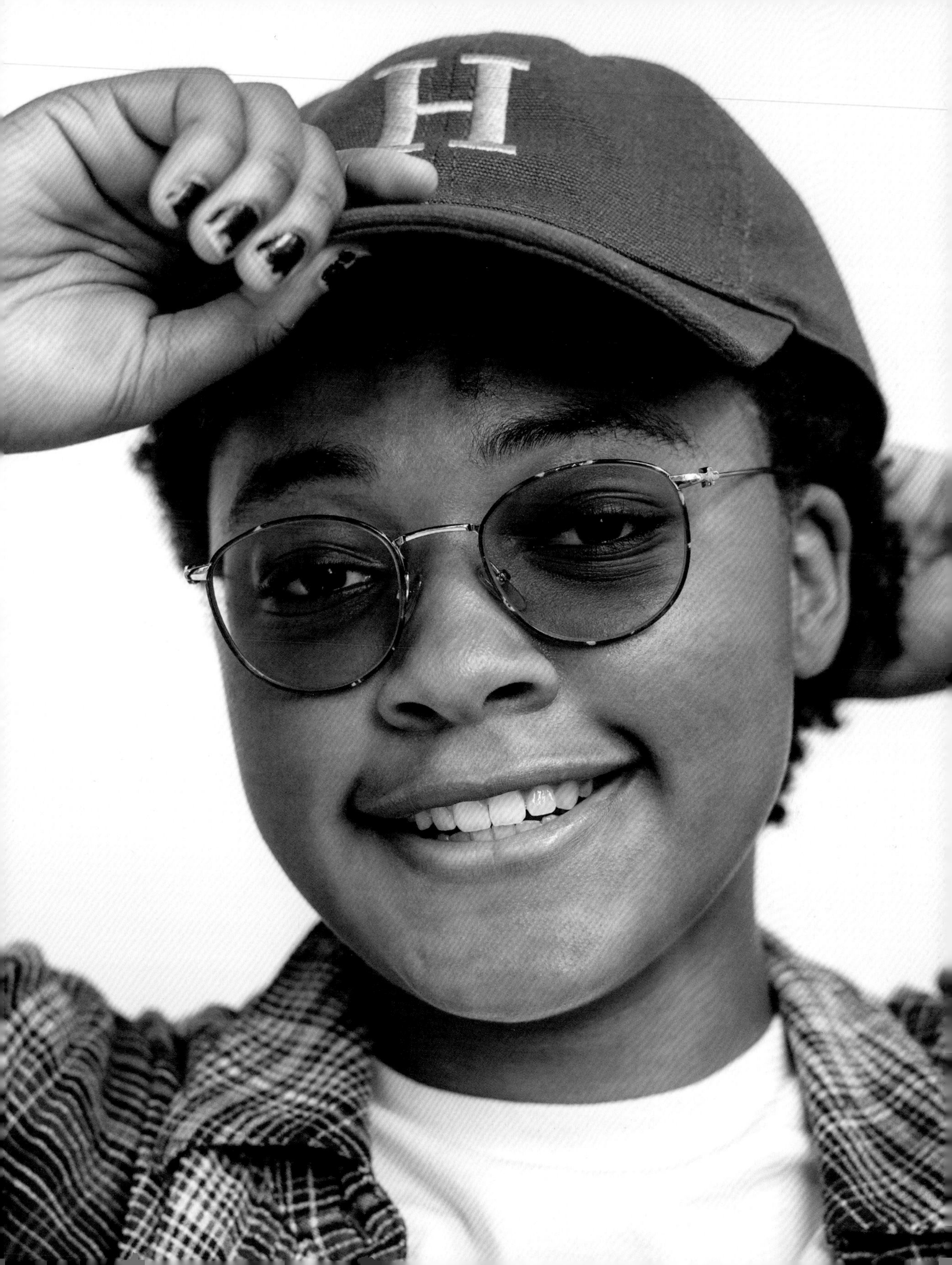

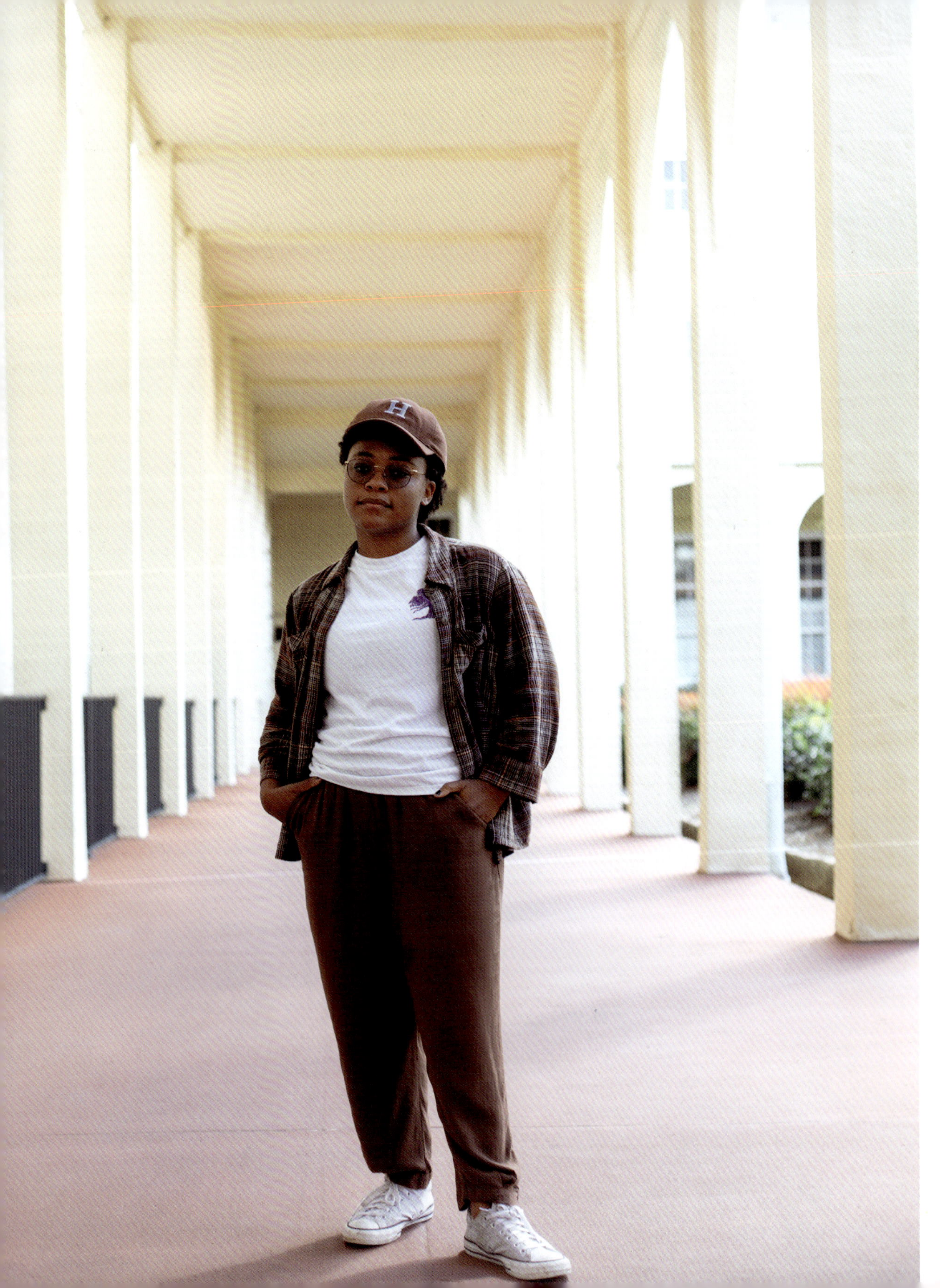

With my newfound love and acceptance, I started advocating for LGBTQ+ rights on TikTok. Quickly I grew an audience and noticed how much it was helping others with their situations. Positive comments about my activism quickly spread and companies started reaching out, including the It Gets Better Project. I started helping others on a much larger scale. Through It Gets Better I connected with people who craved to do the same; they are my friends for life. For my future, I want to continue working with the people I met along the way. My dream is to inspire people around me to advocate for LGBTQ+ rights, to make a movement that stretches globally. However, before I begin that journey I will not forget where I began. Alabama still lags behind on LGBTQ+ rights, and with a growing population of queer people it would be selfish of me to leave them feeling as I felt: hopeless. So, in response, I will continue to make the South an accepting and comfortable place for those outside of "tradition." Though the town didn't love me, I want it to love people like me before I go.

To sum up, if people dislike you for *you*, take their hatred and use it as power. Do not dwell within those bad thoughts. You are, well, *you*, and if people genuinely find an issue in that, it is their problem, not yours. Advocate not only for yourself but for the community that you are in, and through this you will build incredibly strong bonds. So, what I'm trying to say is be unapologetically you and love yourself and others as much as you can.

Han

18 years old, she/her, Arkansas

Hi! My name is Han. I'm a bisexual woman who uses she/her pronouns! I'm eighteen years old and I live in Arkansas.

My experience of being a member of the LGBTQ+ community in Arkansas has been very interesting, to say the least. I'm a Black bisexual woman in the Bible Belt, so most would expect it wouldn't be easy. Luckily for me, I spent most of my life in a more liberal city. I first realized that I was attracted to women when I was around fourteen years old. I had no label for it, and I thought this was how everyone felt. I had a friend tell me she wanted to confess her love to another woman. She told me that she was bisexual, and I was like, "Oh, cool! I'll help you!" I had zero idea what that meant. I ended up having a crush on the same woman as well. Fun fact: I had a crush on her boyfriend too! I ended up getting them together in the seventh grade instead of asking either of them out. They're still dating to this day!

Coming out was interesting for me too. I didn't really come out to my friends instantly. I just kinda casually let them know I like women too, and they didn't care. I eventually did say I was bisexual when we were all figuring our identities out. The more friends that I made, the easier it was for me to accept my identity. The majority of my friends are also a part of the LGBTQ+ community. I never felt a need to worry about my identity around them, which means I had a safety net in case anything went awry.

I remember coming out to my mother, which was a different story. She usually made homophobic jokes, which scared me from coming out to her. I was fifteen, and I had the bisexual flag around my shoulders. As she came up the stairs I started panicking and told her I was bi with tears running down my face. She gave me a hug and told me she was too, which was surprising! She told my dad about me and he didn't care about it at all. He was simply glad I wasn't hurt or in danger. Ever since then I've been telling my mom about my friends and such. She's become much more educated about the LGBTQ+ community ever since, and my father has as well. I was one of the few lucky people to have a safe way of coming out and being myself. However, everything wasn't always perfect.

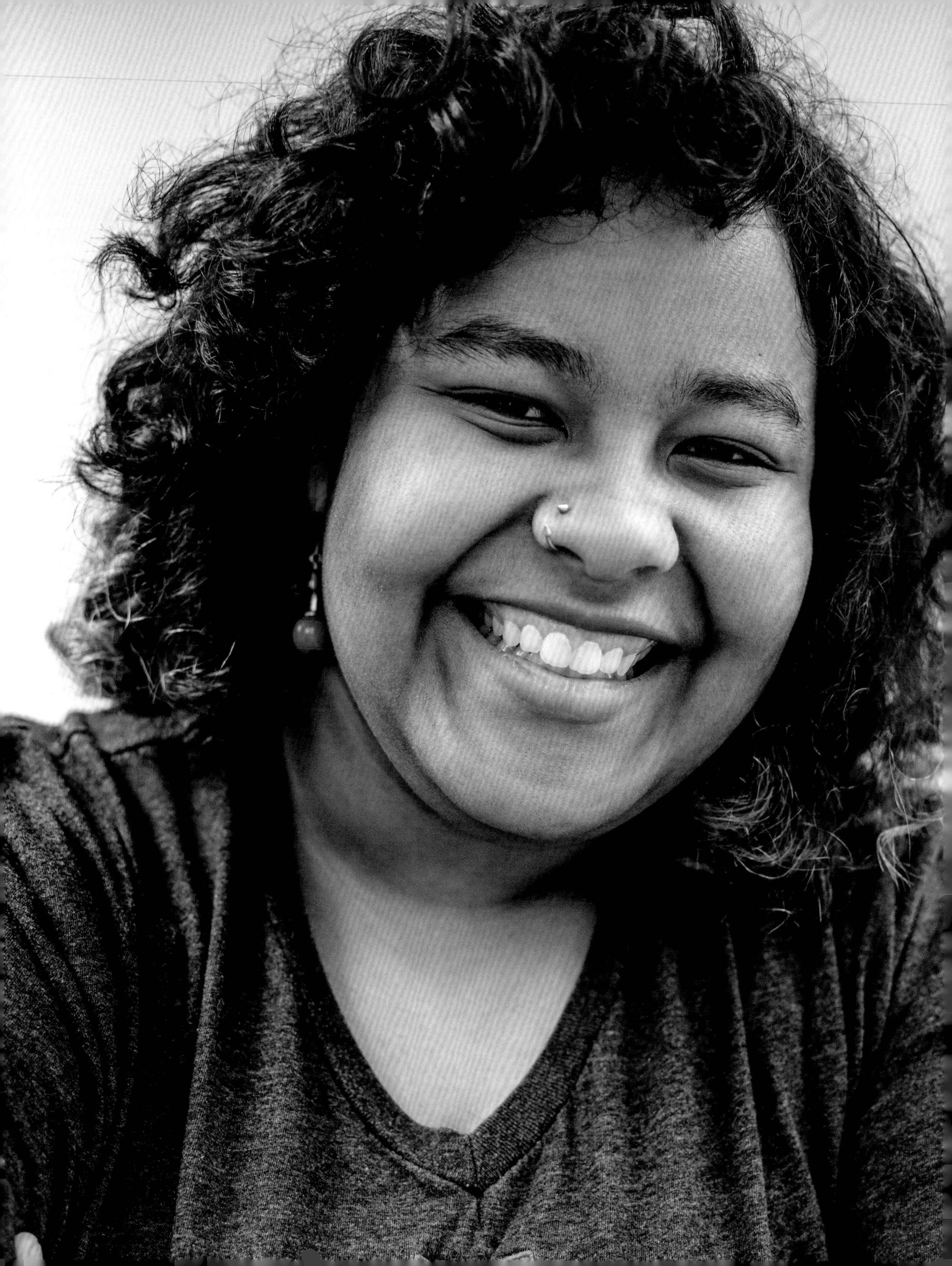

There was always some homophobia aimed at me online, ever since I was fifteen. I had grown-ass men telling me I would grow up to be a pedophile, threatening to rape me until I hate women, and that I was nothing but [insert so many slurs here]. I simply didn't care though. I actually found it funny, because my personal life outside this had been hell and back, so I could be considered a really strong person when it comes to insults. I won't deny that it hurt at least a bit, but I could still laugh it off. In high school the most homophobia I had experienced was someone calling me a dyke when I asked him to not boo homecoming girls for being Democrats.

So the advice I have to offer is based on helping my friends when they face any adversity. My advice? Do what *you* want. If you feel safe being out, be out and proud! If you don't feel safe, then you don't have to tell *anyone* about your identity. No one can force you to stay in the closet or push you out. There's no wrong choice, no matter what you do. Be confident in your identity. And, if you feel the need to change it, be confident with that too! We won't all instantly understand ourselves. I took a while to question my identity, whether I'm cis or trans, or whether I'm a lesbian or not. I feel that I have gotten my identity right, but questioning is always an important process. I'd say that if you've ever wondered what to do once you figure out your identity, introspection would be the best choice. Think about what it means for you to be yourself, what that would entail in the future, and the best way for you, personally, to deal with it. Because it gets better. It always gets better. Please, remember that one day, even if not today, you will be safe being yourself. There will always be people who love you for who you are. And you are you regardless of your identity. Regardless of whether you are gay, trans, nonbinary, cis, straight, or anything, do what you love, and love who you love. Most of all, love yourself.

Haniel

17 years old, he/him, Colorado

OMG hi! I'm Haniel, and I'm a Libra! I grew up in Boulder, Colorado, a beautiful city in the foothills of the Rocky Mountains. I had no idea how lucky I was to have grown up in such a liberal and accepting city. Oh, and I'm *gay* (duh)!

Let me set the scene for you: I was working as a lifeguard when I was sixteen years old. As I scanned the pool my thoughts would take me to a place where I didn't have to pretend. I watched the few swimmers that day from my lifeguard stand as I pondered the idea of being free, and true to myself. I remember that day being a quiet day, a slow day; it might have even rained, or not. I decided I would just ignore the idea that I would ever come out. That's when a couple came in. I've learned not to believe in signs, but this was a sign. A young couple came in, they looked so happy, with no shame, no guilt, but instead filled with love. I wanted that, I wanted what they shared. I had convinced myself that I didn't deserve that. I saw it as a privilege that only straight people could enjoy. I felt that God's punishment was for me to be forever alone. I was ready to live that life, but why? Why did I have to submit to the views of my parents, the church, and society? I was tired of spending night after night in my last waking moments hating who I was. I lost sight of who I was, out of fear. I hated myself. I'll be honest: I had no idea what I was thinking, but I came out that night, January 30, 2019, which I now consider my second birthday (gifts are appreciated). The thing is, I was over it, you know? I was over my closet; it was just too small. I find it funny that people always used to tell me how brave I was but, in reality I was just done caring what people thought of me. I came out not just to one person but to everyone I knew and who knew of me. I uploaded a video to social media, and immediately after that I turned off my phone. I was out.

I never doubted my parents' unconditional love for me, but I know that God will always be first for them. Though I do wish that they would have picked me, they didn't. Each of them would take turns blaming each other for my gayness. My mom would say my dad didn't spend enough time with me growing up and I lacked him in my life. My dad would say that my mom spent too much time with me and that she babied me. It was a never-ending back and forth. Regardless, they could agree on one thing: God was

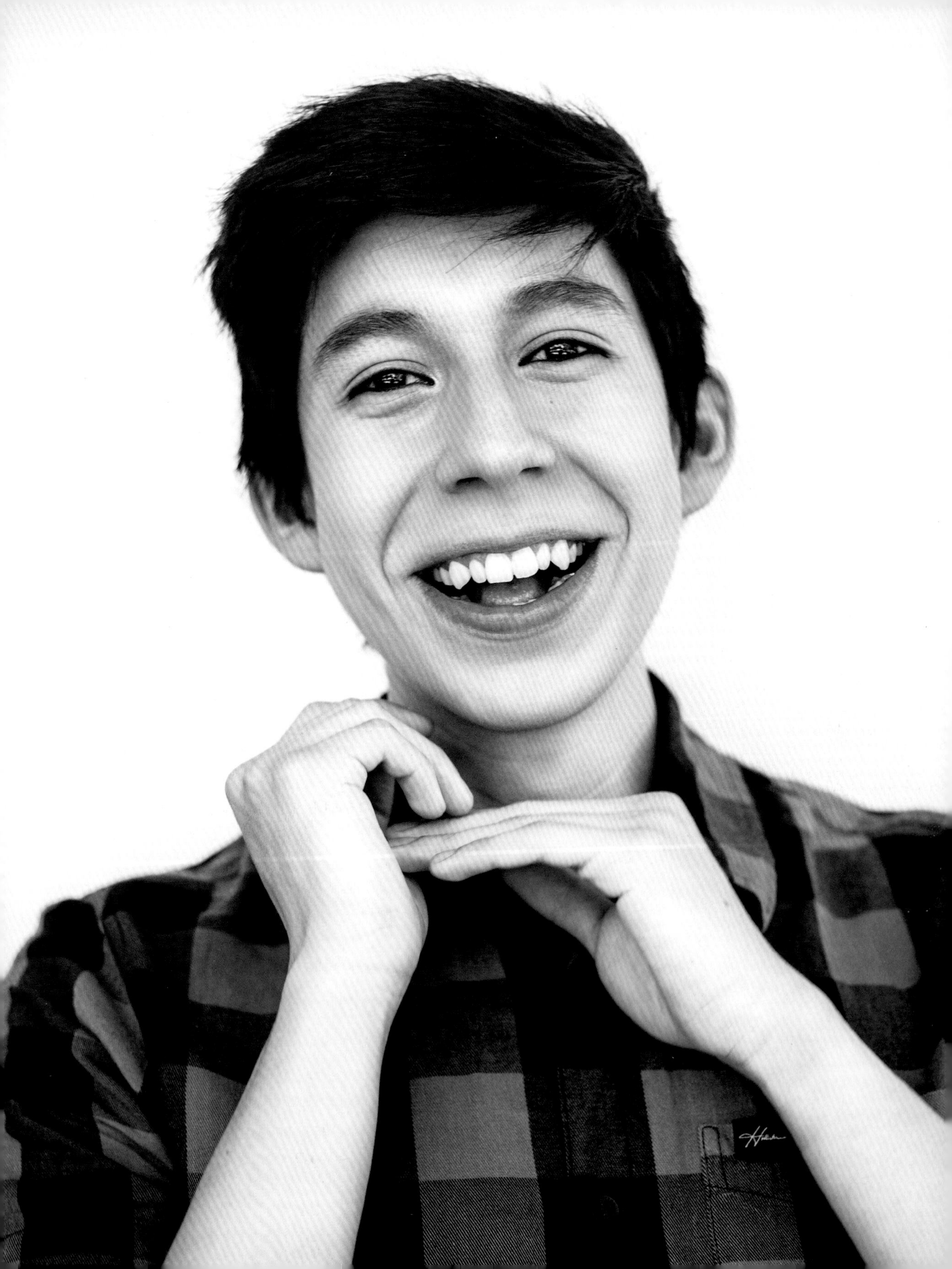

right and would be the one who would cure me and save me from my sins. They both cried as if I gave them the news of my passing. Worst of all, they would pray. My dad and mom would walk in and tell me to give them my undivided attention, and then they would each kneel by my bed and hold my hands. They took turns praying, asking God for "healing." I don't get emotional talking about my queer experience as much as I used to, yet that part right there, asking for "healing"—they saw my attraction to men as a disease. In their eyes, I was on my deathbed as they prayed for healing.

I wasn't asking them to jump for joy when I told them I wasn't into girls. I just wanted them to, well . . . I am not sure what I wanted them to do. I haven't thought about it very much, but I do know that I wanted them to deal with it away from me. I didn't need to see the disappointment I already knew was there. It hurt me because I'm not sick. I just needed them to be there for me.

But I'm an adult now, so I feel like I can be honest.

Dear Mom,

Anytime someone asks me what my favorite type of food is, I always say your cooking. And you know how my siblings would always say I was your favorite because you would make the food I was craving? I can go on and on about how inspirational you have been. How I'm in college because you were the one who pushed me to be here. I don't know if you remember, but I was there, I was there for you. I watched you cry when you found out about the truth you never wanted to hear. I was the first one you told. You confided in me. I was your rock. We cried together. Yet you weren't there for me. You made part of me feel like it would be better to have a dead son than a gay son. You broke me when you said you wouldn't go to my wedding if I married a man. I do hope one day you will apologize to me. I needed you to tell me that you loved me just the same.

Dear Dad,

You taught me that hard work pays off. I didn't believe you at first, but I'm starting to see it now. When people compliment me on my hard work, I say it's thanks to you. I know you wanted me to have a wife, have many kids running around calling you grampa. And when I shattered the idea you created of my future I broke you, and I saw you cry. That was the first time I ever saw you cry. How do you think that made me feel? Seeing your tears rolling down your cheeks, knowing that I was the cause of them? You were supposed to tell me that you would still love me, not that "We would find a solution" because me being gay was a problem in your eyes. *Los quiero mucho, ya sé que no fui y no soy lo que ustedes esperaban. Pero espero que algún día los haga orgulloso de tenerme como su hijo.*

Part of being a person in this world is understanding that the people who raise you are not perfect. They may try, and maybe in their world they may think they are. They are still human, and even God knows that no human is perfect. My heart is far too big to ever hold a grudge against them. I have forgiven them even though they never asked for forgiveness.

So now what? Great question. The answer: I left. Easier said than done, that's for sure, but I knew I couldn't stay. I'm now living my best life, and college is great! I've made so many unimaginable friends and have made some incredible memories. So this is the part where I give you a little pep talk before I send you off into the world, so here I go:

Don't give up! The number of times I wanted to call it quits is far too many. I sometimes think of everything I would have missed. Yeah, life sucks sometimes and people suck sometimes, but at the end of the day, you're the one living your life, so keep your head up! *And don't give up!*

I am gay! I am so thankful to be where I am today, and I am happy and have so much love for myself and who I am. However, when I look back, I still feel for the little boy who had no idea what to do with himself when he realized who he was. I remember all the pain he felt, and I wish I could hug him and show him all of the great things we did, we do, and are going to do.

Thank you for reading a glimpse of my story. Even though I'm in a better place, I'm still healing. But that's okay, because at the end of the day, in those last conscious moments before I fall asleep, I love being me, and that's the most important thing.

XOXO—H

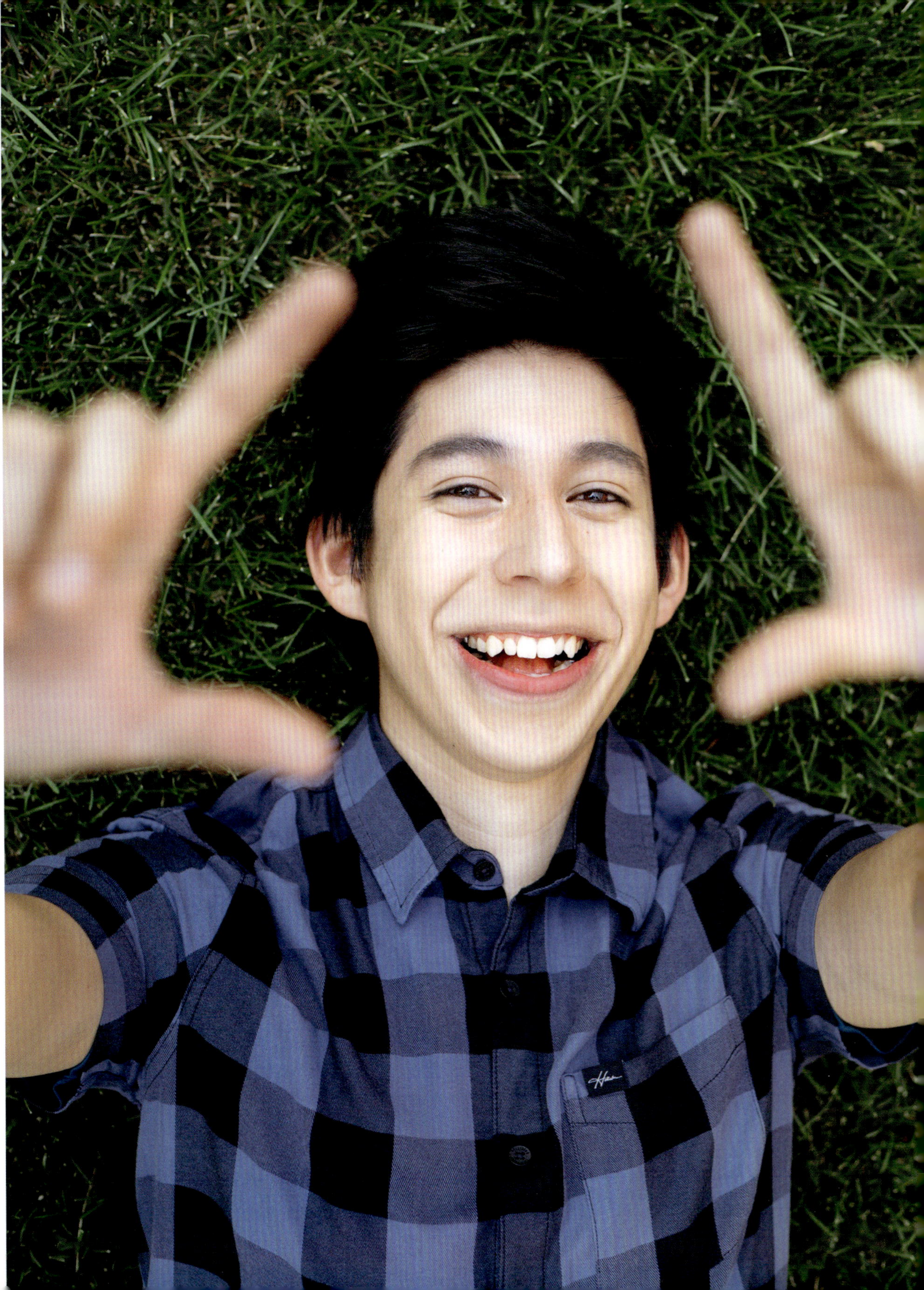

Hayden

17 years old, they/them, Texas

It was being at slumber parties in elementary school and never being able to name someone in the class I had a crush on when all the other girls were naming guys in the class. It was the reluctance to wear a skirt for Friday night dinners with my family. It was the urge to always put my hair up in a bun or tuck it in a beanie during freshman year of high school. This may sound familiar to many queer youth.

My identity consists of many intersecting components, some of which include: queer, asexual, nonbinary, Jewish, activist, student, Houstonian, Texan, and seventeen-year-old.

In Orthodox Judaism there's a phrase, "going off the *derech.*" *Derech* translates to "path" or "road." It's this idea that there's one religious path for an Orthodox Jewish person and that people can go off of this predetermined path and it's shameful to do so. I think that this idea can be applied even for non-Jewish people, in the sense that when we are born, those around us imagine a path that we should follow. When I was born my parents, family, friends, teachers—everyone that I was around in my early childhood— probably envisioned this hypothetical perfect path that I would take in life. I would grow up in an Orthodox Jewish household, go to the same Jewish school, go to college, date guys, marry one, have kids, work, etc. Obviously, life throws you curveballs, but for the most part I followed that path for a while and thought of it as my only option—until I got to about the age of twelve. That's when I realized this predetermined path was never going to be my reality, and I didn't want it to be. In fact, there are billions of paths with forks in the road to different decisions and events, because life isn't one narrow, predetermined thing. My parents understood this wholeheartedly, but there are a few things and ideas they didn't want to let go of. When I first came out to my father as gay, he responded with, "I don't care who you marry as long as they're Jewish and I get grandkids." My response was something along the lines of, "I can promise you it will be a nice person and you can have grandcats." Now that's changed even further because it turns out I'm allergic to cats, so grandcats for my dad may not happen.

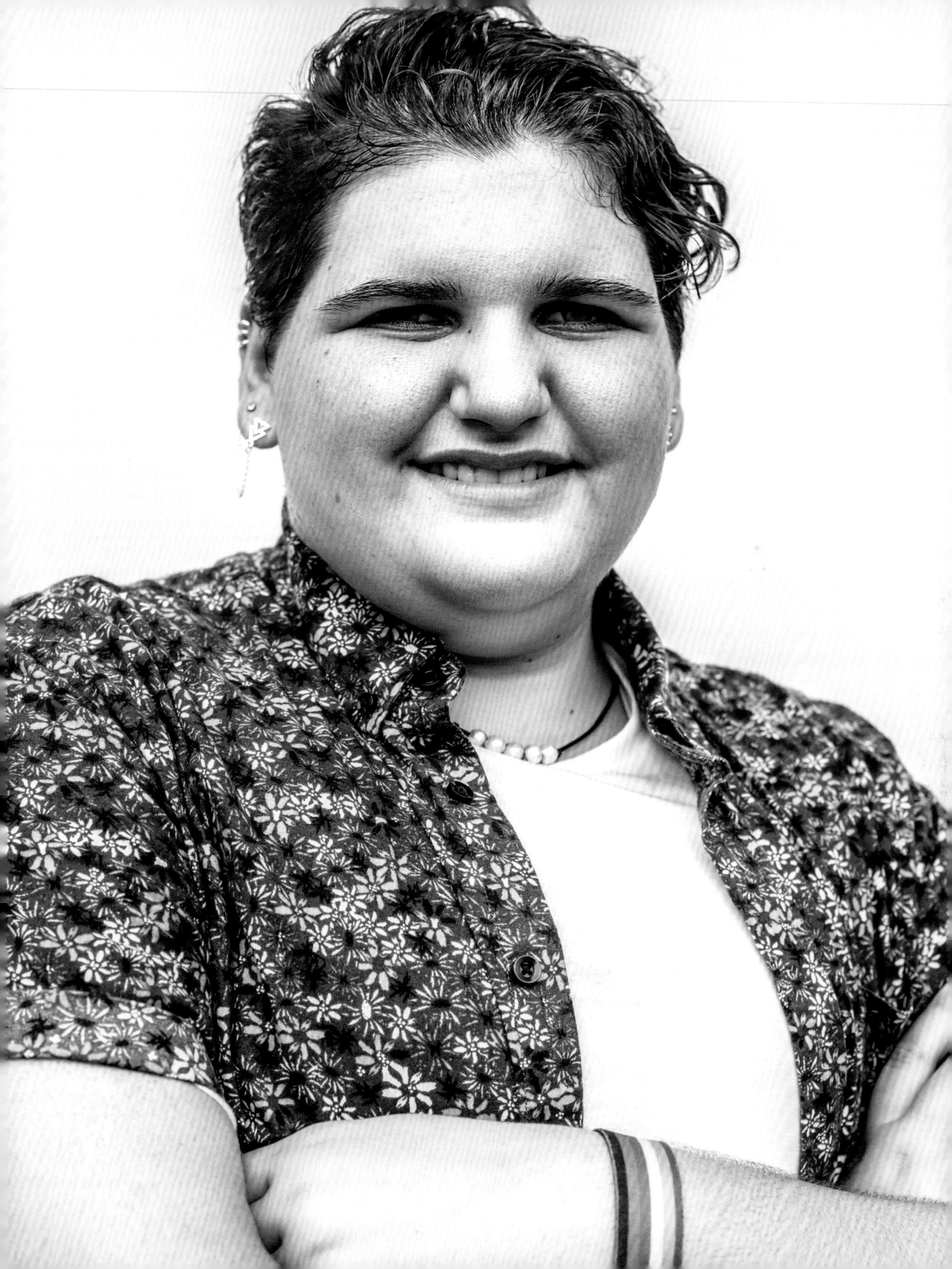

I came out to most people as gay the summer before starting
freshman year of high school, and I literally kicked down that
closet door. Went straight into my bowtie phase, joined my school's
Gender-Sexuality Alliance, and started attending a local LGBTQ+
youth group in Houston, which ended up being my favorite place to
be. Coming out as gay was probably the easiest thing I came out as
to my family. They were overall pretty accepting.

As I came out as gay, I started changing the way I dressed to fit
what was more me, which involved dressing more androgynously.
I was experimenting with my gender expression in the hopes that
this would clear up some things about my own sense of gender.
I knew I was different, and that I wasn't a guy—but I certainly
wasn't a girl. Fast-forward a bit of time and I learned gender existed
on a spectrum. But surely not every point on the spectrum could
be labeled, including wherever my identity lay, so I just stick with
the term *nonbinary* to make it easier for others around me to
understand. I know deep down my gender is probably too complex
to understand.

Being a queer androgynous-looking person in an Orthodox
Jewish community was definitely a unique experience. The entire
Jewish culture I was raised in was very gender oriented. I tried to
avoid going into a synagogue because that would mean having to
wear a skirt or dress, and, because I had short hair, I would get
stares anyway. I discovered an organization where I managed to find
a bunch of queer Jews my age who had very similar experiences.
Attending those events and talking to people just like me helped me
reconnect with Judaism and learn that religion isn't homophobic
and that there are accepting places within the community.

I live in Texas and always have, but it's not the "yeehaw" Texas
where we ride to school on horses and always wear cowboy boots.
I live in the fourth largest city and, yes, I did pass horses on the
way to school, but the rest of my daily life is spent on public buses
and hanging out in coffee shops in Houston's gayborhood. As soon
as I came out, I started realizing how accepting the environment I
grew up in was. My high school was relatively queer friendly, and
the city of Houston has a very vibrant queer history that I love
learning about. It isn't all sunshine and rainbows though. The
conservative-dominated government can be very homophobic, and
equality has always been an uphill climb. Gay sex and gender identity were never covered in my health education, but then again,
neither was consent. I tried to get it changed along with other
advocates, but it didn't happen, so the best we can do is educate

others around us. When the bills were filed for the 2021 Texas legislative session, I was shocked at what sorts of rights were on the line and how the bills would affect me and other queer youth around me. I soon learned that this happens all the time on the Capitol floor, and LGBTQ+ equality is fought over every two years.

Some days I wonder how I got from being the shy band kid to leading protests and constantly talking to anyone who will listen about LGBTQ+ students' rights and the need for change. I have worked toward trans-inclusive student bathroom policies in my school district, led GSA trainings, spoken on panels, created queer Jewish programming, taught sex ed, and ultimately worked to create safe spaces for queer youth wherever life takes me.

If there is one piece of advice I could give to anyone it's that "figuring out" your queer identity is not a linear, clear-cut process. You may not go through a questioning phase, figure out your identity, come out, and—yay—done. It's important to learn to embrace the idea of constantly experimenting and being open to the idea of your sense of queer identity changing. Most of your queer identity is going to be based on your environment and the social constructs around you, and because those things change and can be fluid, so will your idea of what words you may describe your identity with. It's okay to not have a definite sense of your queer identity, to change pronouns, to come out a million times during your lifetime. Just be comfortable with not always knowing.

Heiress

13 years old, she/they, New York

Yuurrrrr! My name is Heiress Destiny, I'm thirteen years old, and, yup, I'm from Brooklyn, New York. I am a model, an activist, an aspiring actress. I sing, dance . . . oh, and I just so happen to be a lesbian. I am ambivalent on whether or not I am nonbinary, so for now my pronouns are she/her and, depending on the day and how I feel, sometimes it's they/them. I wear so many different hats but *none* of these labels define me. For a few months I have been trying to pick a title. Trying to find an exact label to explain who I am. But there isn't one. There is no exact word, label, or title to define who I am. I just . . . am.

Sometimes I'm confused about this whole thing. For years I liked boys. I thought they were cute but I never really had a type. Which is why when I started to like girls I didn't say anything for a while. I was eleven years old when I realized I was attracted to girls. This was weird at the time because I knew I liked boys, but girls gave me a tingly feeling. It was difficult because a couple of months after realizing I was a lesbian the whole world shut down. I didn't get a chance to open up to my friends or even try to tell a girl I like her. I was secluded from everyone and no one knew my secret. I felt as if I had no one to talk to. Toward my twelfth birthday is when I finally said it out loud for the first time.

It was a few weeks before my twelfth birthday. I was a little nervous but not scared. I knew my parents would support me but I had never said it out loud. It was like a scene in a movie. I sat them both down, turned the TV off, and told them I had something important to tell them. After a pause that felt like an eternity, I just said, "I like girls. . . . I like, like girls." They looked at each other and then back at me. My mother broke the silence first. She responded with "That's it?" And my father said, "Ummm, okay. Where did that come from?" We talked for hours after that about labels and when I'll be old enough to date. I learned that my dad doesn't fully agree with homosexuality but he said he would support me no matter what because I'm his daughter. My parents being the first people I came out to made me feel good. It took me a while to tell the rest of my family and social media.

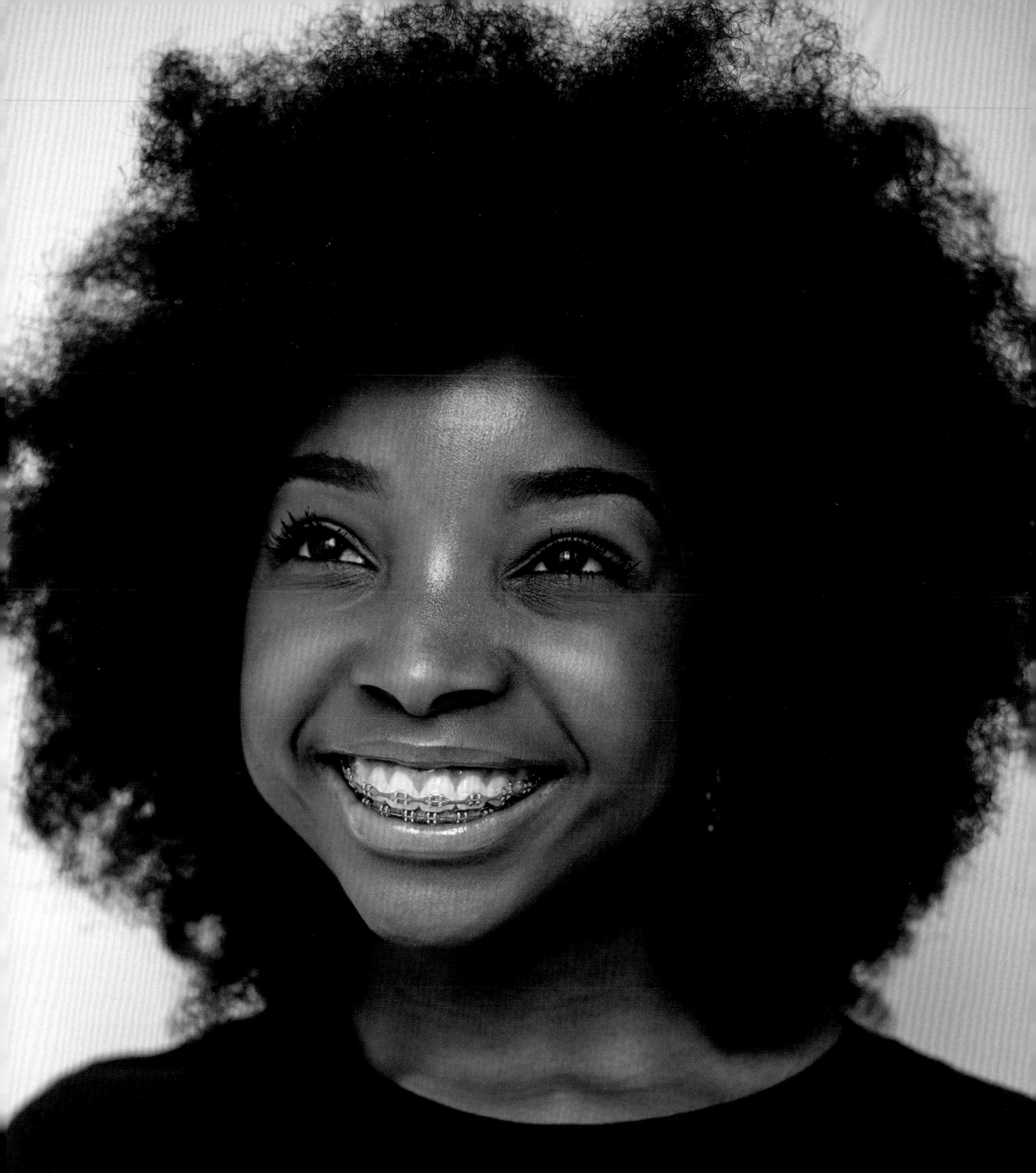

I AM THE

I have a tendency to care about what people think of me. That's something I'm still working on. I mentioned that I'm a model and an activist, but what I did not mention is that I have a pretty decent following on Instagram, Snapchat, and Facebook. A lot of my followers are other young models like myself, so naturally their pages are managed and overseen by their parents. I was very nervous about coming out on social media because I was afraid of being judged by the parents. I didn't want them to think I was coming for their daughters. Plus, the older generation tends to feel that my age group is too young to be thinking about sexuality, especially if it's same sex. My parents and I had huge discussions about how and when to come out. I manage all of my social media pages and just wanted to feel free. So this year during Pride Month I took to the social media streets and came out through a TikTok reel. Immediately after I started getting DMs from my followers supporting me. Some were coming out to me and saying they were afraid to tell their parents. If I had known that I would receive such positive feedback I would've *jumped* out of the closet. I realized that this was a perfect example of why I shouldn't care so much about what people may think or say.

Over the past couple of years I have used my social media platform to promote young people to use their voices. I have used my voice by giving speeches for the Black Lives Matter movement and by singing songs. Too many times young people are told to be seen and not heard by the older generations, or told that we don't know what it is that we are feeling. I want young people to know that they have a voice. Whether you're black, white, gay, pan, straight, or in-between, you are a voice in this world and you deserve to be heard. And it's okay to be afraid because that's the only way you can be brave.

Soon I am going to have to put my own bravery to the test. Yes, I am scared about going back to school for the first time as a lesbian. I don't know what's going to happen in a couple of weeks, but I do know that I intend to be *brave*. My parents and I have been preparing for this all summer. Even though I'm scared, I at least know that I have an army of support. So that part of my journey about being queer outside is still loading. I'll keep you posted.

When I think about what advice I could give to young LGBTQN+ people, I get stuck. Because how can I give advice to someone if I am still confused about my own journey? Or how can I give advice to someone without knowing their full story? Their living environment? Or if they even have the same support system like I have? But then I realized that, no matter the situation, no one should have to live a lie. First practice saying it out loud to yourself in the mirror. Write it down in your journal. Make yourself comfortable with who you are *first*, then the rest will follow. But you have to know, love, like, and accept who you are first before you can get others to accept who you are. And if they don't . . . *fuck them*! Seriously, they're not worthy of you. That's what my mother always says. As I give advice to you, whoever you are, please know I am also advising myself. So to myself and to you, love you and the rest will follow. And that's what I think about girls kissing girls!

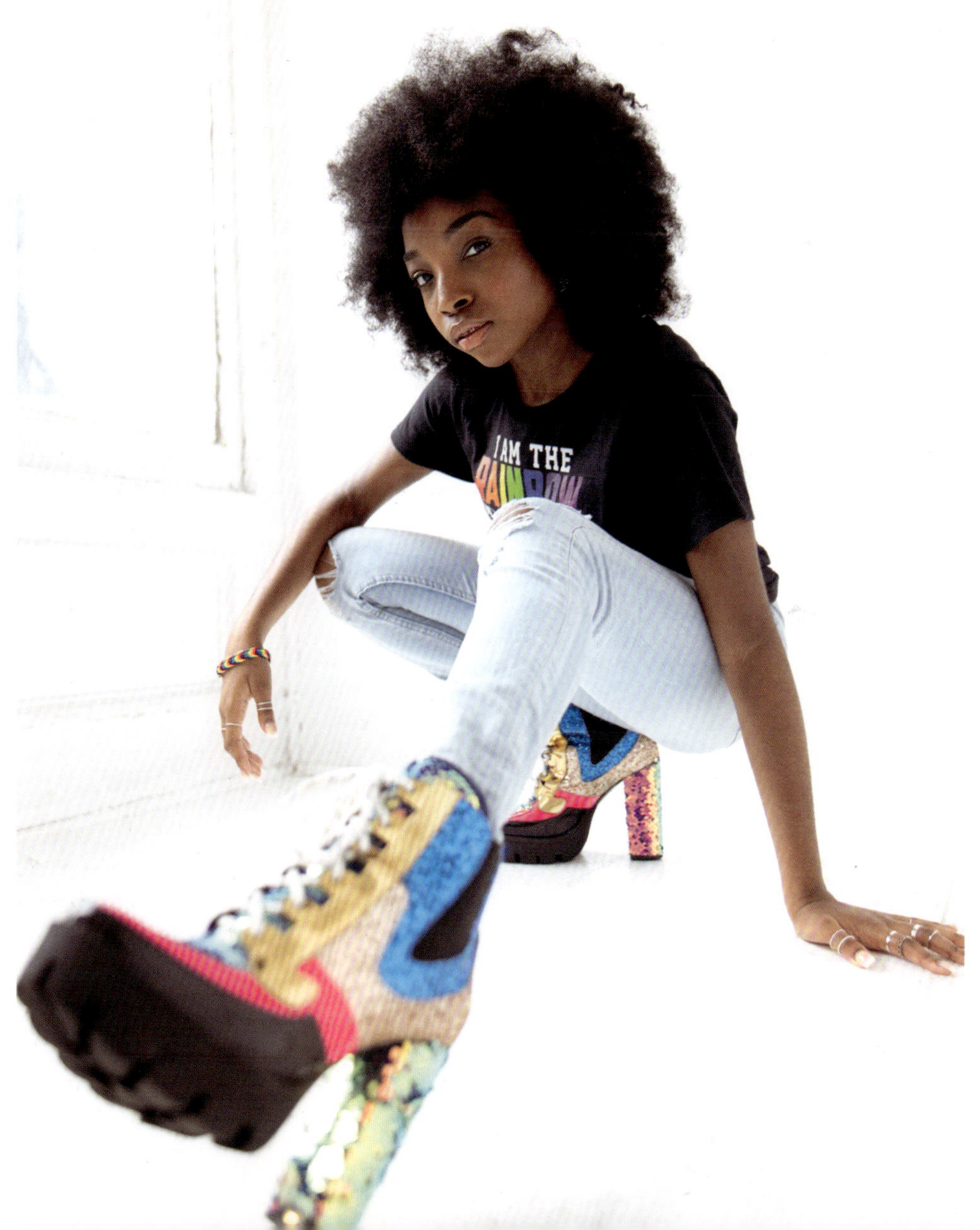

Ivy

11 years old, she/her, Michigan
CW: This story contains brief references to self-harm.

Hi! My name is Ivy. I'm eleven years old and in the sixth grade and I'm from Flint, Michigan. My pronouns are she/her. I am Jewish and I am third-generation Deaf. I speak with my hands (American Sign Language), I listen with my eyes . . . and I happen to be transgender.

I discovered my gender identity when I was in preschool. Shout out to Mrs. Gleeson for being the best teacher ever! Because of her I was able to discover who I was. During school we had daily activities, and one of those hours was free time. I would always pick the art table to put my creative artwork into play, or I'd go to the dress-up corner where I could pretend to be something like a doctor, a princess, a fairy, or anything in the world! It was the best ever because I could just be me as a whole person. During these free-time hours I knew I was feeling something different. I didn't know what the word for it was, and I was only in preschool at that time.

When I was younger, my dad said, "Good job, boy!" after my brothers and I did our chores. I didn't like it and it felt wrong. I found a way to speak up, "*No!* I'm a girl." Just like that. Within seconds my dad had no problem with changing my pronouns. When my dad told my mom, she didn't support it because she believed that gender identity was applied and assigned at birth based on your genitals. However, my dad didn't give up on my mom or me. He fought so hard for me by getting her to understand LGBTQIA2 people, because she's also a member of the LGBTQ+ community, but a different generation, meaning she only knows common terms and identities. Gender was never a thing she thought about.

Before me, my mom didn't know that transgender people existed. One day, gender dysphoria hit me so hard that it pushed me to attempt self-harm. My actions woke her up and made her realize that me being transgender was a real thing. She took a big leap from being in denial to being a determined mom. For months she educated herself, found resources, and networked with others to understand the transgender community better. She's also the reason I became an activist for my Deaf and Transgender communities due to lack of LGBTQIA2 resources within our Deaf community, where they are not 100 percent accessible to us.

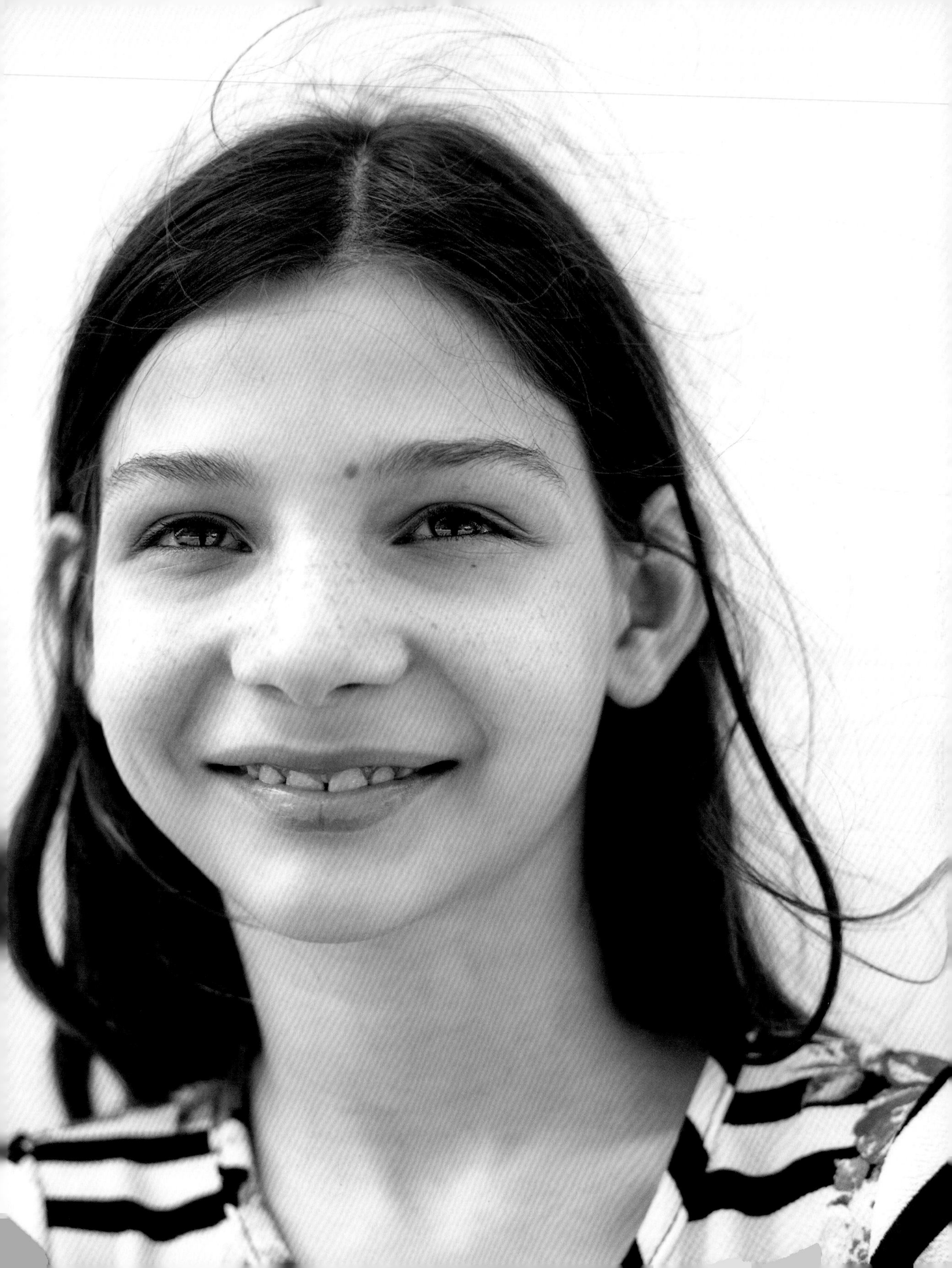

I transitioned at a young age, so I've experienced a few bullies and people misgendering me or criticizing my mom for how she allowed me to be myself and raised me. I've seen it all. It hurt me. I'm human and I have feelings because it affects me in so many ways as a person. People are afraid of learning something new that they might never have heard of, or that might be taboo to them. They shouldn't be. It takes time to grow and learn together, just like with me and my community, classmates, teachers, and family. You'll find kindness, love, and warmth in the LGBTQIA2 community.

I want to build the bridge between the Deaf and queer community. The Deaf community is incredibly small, and everyone is pretty familiar with everyone. The problem, however, is the Deaf community is incredibly difficult for everyone else; sometimes it feels like we are at the bottom of the food chain. It always takes time to catch up. So I am tired of looking for LGBTQIA2 locations that are Deaf friendly, and I want to help improve that access and help others understand that English isn't our first language; it is American Sign Language.

To those who are struggling: This is *your* journey. Not your family's. Not your friends'. It's all yours. There's only one person that knows you 100 percent and that is yourself. I always tell people and my friends: Be yourself! Don't follow what society expects you to be. Social expectations are very old and rusty. Change society from being old and rusty by being that shiny, polished, new-and-improved you. Whenever you leave something for a long time, it can get dirty and rusty. So you may be following the expectations of society being imposed on top of you. Break away from those expectations.

Izzy

17 years old, they/she, Alaska
CW: This story contains brief references to suicide ideation.

Hello. My name is Izzy. I am seventeen, I am bisexual, my pronouns are they/she, and I am from Alaska. I met Maxwell four years ago, when he first started this project, and I am so happy to be back to tell my story once again on a bigger platform.

Everyone has a story to tell. And everyone has different experiences. Growing up, my mom always told me that it was okay to be whoever I wanted. I grew up in a very friendly, positive household when it came to LGBTQIA+ and women's rights. I always knew that I was a little bit different from everybody growing up. I liked my best friends more than other people liked their best friends; my best friends were girls, and so was I. In my house it was normal and okay to be who you were and to like who you liked, and it didn't matter.

The first person I came out to was my best friend at the time and her immediate reaction was to ask if I had a crush on her. I was only twelve then and, looking at it now, I see that her response was a red flag. At that time, and when I came out to everyone else, it was a matter of me wanting to freely be myself. I then came out at school because rumors were getting spread. I accidentally came out to my mom, and then the rest of my family slowly found out, and I was incredibly lucky that for the most part everyone was accepting and my safety wasn't a concern.

I didn't officially identify myself until about my seventh grade year, and at the time I came out as bisexual. I have since also come out as more gender neutral and changed my pronouns to they/she. Growing up in Alaska I went to every single Pride parade and marched in every single one: I remember those as some of my most precious memories. Alaska sometimes seems very conservative, but there's this whole beautiful community up here full of people who will love and care about you and take care of you.

Sometimes, though, while being here and going to school, I encountered some not very friendly people. As I got older, the damage that other people caused became more emotional. People started saying things about me after I came out. They would call me names, tell people that I would fall in love with them if they became friends with me, that I was crazy and obsessive, that I would steal

your girlfriend. Which is a terrible feeling to have. It's a terrible feeling to experience, because at that point I didn't know what to do.

The transition from middle school to high school wasn't great either. I was officially diagnosed with major depression and general anxiety, and going into freshman year I was the most depressed that I've ever been, and I contemplated many times whether I should live or not. But I pushed through the summer. Coincidentally, that summer was also the summer that Project Contrast came up to Alaska, and I remember how nice it was to feel that I wasn't alone; there were other people in this community who were just like me. I remember Project Contrast being a turning point in my life when I finally felt okay with where I was and who I was. I realized that it doesn't matter about anybody else's opinion of me; it only matters what I think of myself—and I thought I was great. I rebuilt my confidence and I made more friends that were also in the community. They supported me and I supported them when people bullied us.

I am glad that I know who I am, because not everyone knows who they are, and it takes a long time to learn. I had to go through a lot to be where I am today—to be comfortable and confident in my skin and to figure out exactly how I wanted to present myself to other people. I'm still working on how I want to dress and present myself, but as I'm getting older it's getting easier to realize what I like and what fits me.

The LGBTQ+ community has always been a huge part of my life and a huge part of my character. Being bisexual and figuring out who I was at a young age helped in shaping me into the person I am today; and, despite all the things that I had to go through, I am happy and grateful that I figured out who I was because I couldn't be happier with the way I have turned out. I couldn't feel more accepted in a community than I do here. I'm glad that I get to share my story and maybe connect with someone who knows what it's like to grow up in a small town and be a part of the LGBTQ+ community.

In the end, it doesn't matter what other people think of you and it doesn't matter how other people view you. It only matters how you think and feel about yourself and if you're comfortable with who you are. If you aren't, then work toward changing it. Do whatever you want and be whatever you want to be. Be crazy, be funny, be happy, be smart, be gay, bi, trans. Speak up, because at the end of the day it is your identity and you get to choose who you are. You get to define who you want to be, and the only thing that I think anyone could ever ask for is to just be safe and happy with who they are. I am happy with who I am, and one day you will be too.

Jay

18 years old, they/them, South Dakota
CW: This story contains references to self-harm and suicide.

My name is Jay and, in 2021, I am a panromantic demisexual genderqueer person. I have no idea about the people my birth parents
were—just their addictions. I'm adopted by my grandparents, and
don't know much about my life before the age of eleven (trauma
tends to block out those hard times).

Overall I've lived a mostly mediocre life with no real hiccups. I
fear intimacy and genuine attraction. It takes a lot to get under my
skin, metaphorically and physically, and I've found that it's easier to
save face than it is to admit my deepest fear.

I grew up in South Dakota with a troubling family dynamic. If
that wasn't enough, I was also in a troubling dynamic with myself
and who I really was. I was always confused and frustrated but I
didn't know why, and it began to affect my mental health even more.

After my first suicide attempt, I was sent to a psychiatric facility
where I discovered a love for art and an appreciation for those
around me. When I returned to schooling after my discharge, I
aimed to keep my parents happy and passed my classes in school.
This is where my journey to discovering myself begins.

By sixth grade I had my first girl crush, and I discovered my
first taste of puppy love. Seventh grade was an entirely different
experience, and there I had my first male crush—funny, huh? I
left public school and was enrolled in a private Catholic school
in the state's center for seventh and eighth grade. My crush was
a taller boy, skinny, and had the worst sense of dry humor ever.
I loved him first as a best friend, and then as someone I would
willingly spend the rest of my life with if asked to. During this time
I thought I was bi. I was not.

When high school began I enrolled in a new public school. My
boy crush and I had split, and here I fell into a new depression. I
ended up snapping multiple times during the first year and began
harming myself. My family life and confusion over who I was really
began to take a toll on me.

It took failing freshman year twice for anyone to really notice.
So, on December 17, 2018—a few months into my third year as
a freshman in high school—I was admitted to a residential facility that would pave the way to a shaky recovery that I'm still not

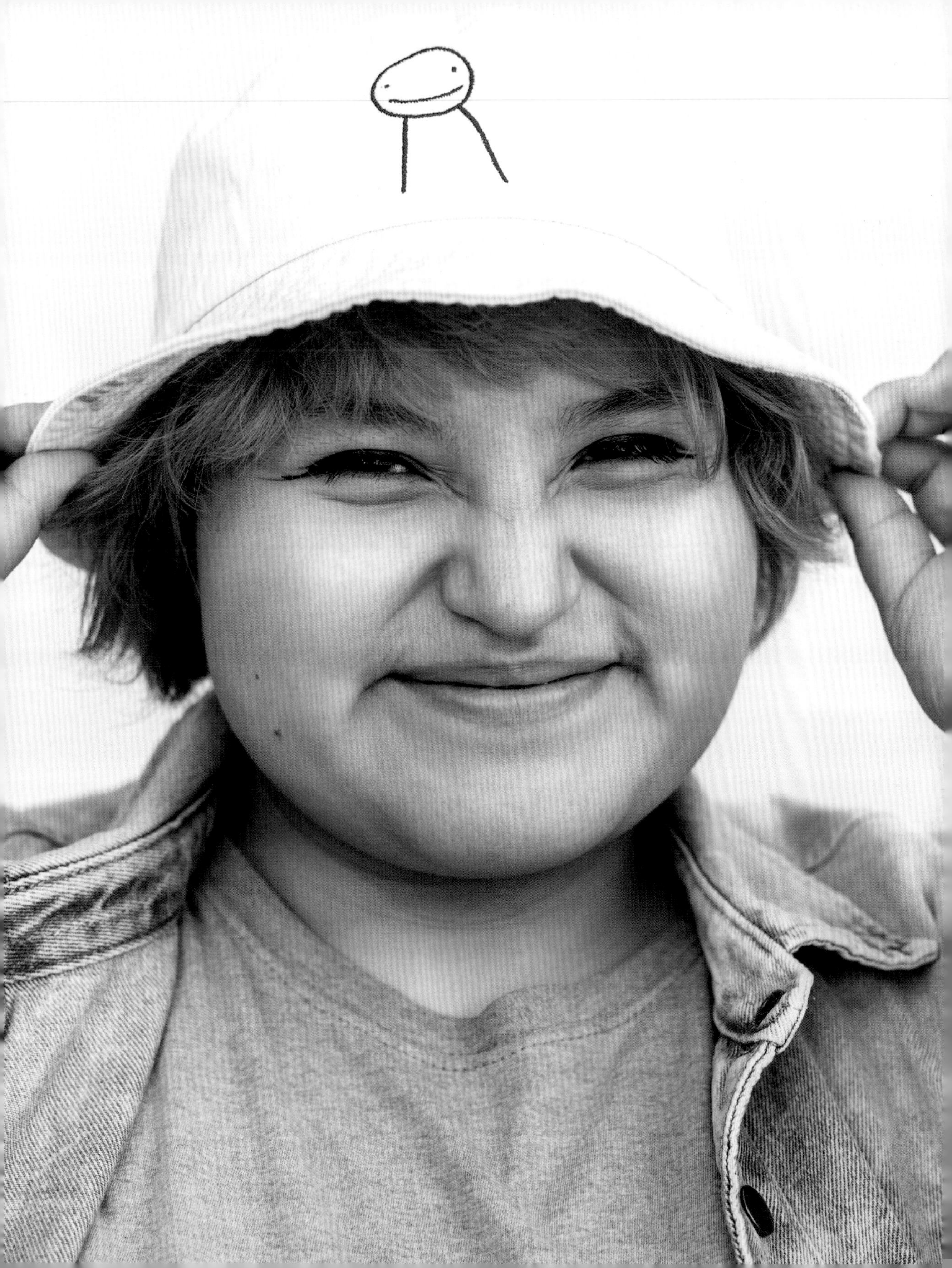

confident in. The first few months of the stay were the easiest, as they always are, and I went through the motions of faking recovery with a bland smile on my face while spewing empty promises. I wanted to go back to school and return to the easy life I lived as a husk. By July of 2019, it had been seven months—the program being a nine- to twelve-month program—and I was beginning to panic. I would spurn recovery and push against any help until I was flat-out resisting the program as a whole. Within those four months I would find myself questioning my gender identity. After my stay, I reached a final decision.

A group, run by one of my favorite staff members, would occur on either Tuesdays or Wednesdays—I don't quite remember—to educate residents about the LGBTQ+ community. There I was informed about sexualities and gender identities and the community's history as a whole. It was my favorite group, and I hold the teachings close to my heart still. I found myself through joining this group that helped educate me on who I am, and I will forever be grateful for being allowed that choice.

Turns out I was neither a lesbian nor bisexual. I'm a panromantic demisexual who identifies as genderqueer because I'm an enigma, and social norms are and always will be lame. Genderqueer is a spectrum of gender identities that are not exclusively masculine or feminine. I am neither and both at the same time. Panromantic demisexual: What does that mean? The panromantic part is all about a romantic connection but, with demisexuality, it needs to be a deeply emotional and trusting relationship.

January of 2020 I decided that I would stop being angry and let the past go. Two months later, in March 2020, I would be discharged from the facility successfully. After fifteen months of ripping myself from limb to limb within four walls, I emerged from the darkness with a brand-new outlook. I don't experience suicidal urges anymore, just a thought here and there about whether death would benefit those around me or if it would only make me angry. Turns out dying would only make me mad.

Driven by ambitions that somehow connect to proving people wrong, I'm doing a lot better. Sure, I did experience being kicked out and worried about money and shelter, but I'm doing okay now. Well, I'm as okay as I could be at eighteen and fresh out in the world with no prior knowledge of how to do it correctly. I have a steady income from the state and I am currently trying to find a job. It feels good.

No emotional boundaries are waiting on the other side if I ever choose to change who I am, identity-wise; I am a free person, and

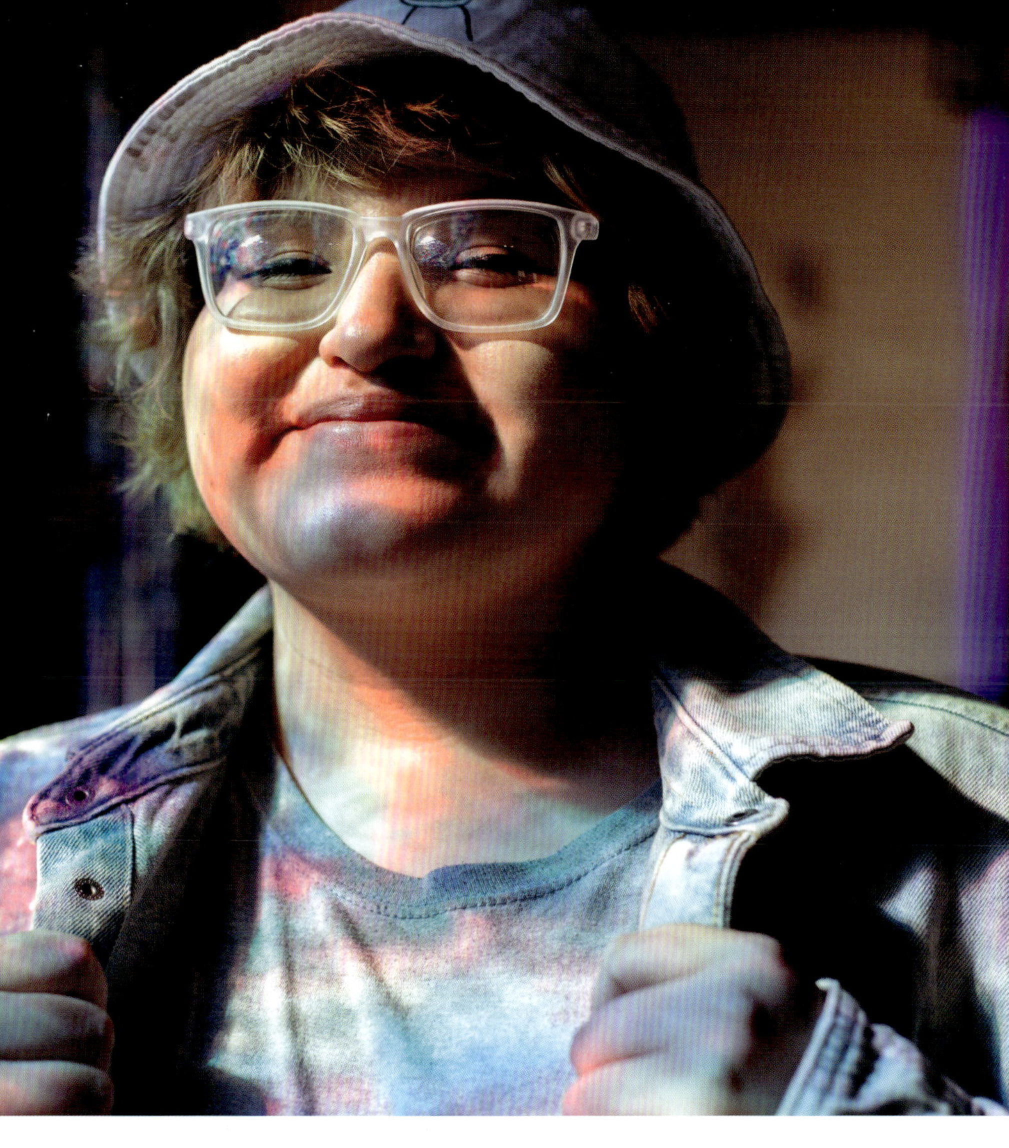

I've never felt more excited and scared at the same time. I wish that I could end this on a final note that would summarize all of my life stories, but I'm just getting started—I have a long life ahead of me, but things are looking up. Quite frankly, they're looking way up. I'm going to be successful and maybe famous for what I want to achieve—art, music, writing, and possibly streaming. I have all the time in the world, and so do you.

Honestly, getting kicked out was the best thing that could have happened to me; it forced me out of my comfort zone and into making the things I've always wanted a reality. I want to say that I know what's going to happen from here on out, but I don't, and that's the thrill of it, right?! You'll know when it's time to fly, trust me, okay?

Jayden

17 years old, they/them, Wyoming
CW: This story contains references to self-harm, suicide, abuse, and rape.

Growing up in my community has definitely been different from what a non-LGBTQ+ member may have experienced. A large majority where I live isn't fond of the LGBTQ+ community, and while I do have supportive people in my life, I've experienced a lot of hate. Personally, I wish I didn't have to be queer in Wyoming. Every so often I find myself thinking about leaving so I can feel at home, and I don't think anyone should have to feel that way! But there is a lot of hatred here. From abuse from my mother, to being raped, to being told to commit suicide for my identity—I don't view Wyoming as a safe space for LGBTQ+ youth.

Growing up, I lived with my mom for quite some time. She was an addict, and horribly unstable due to it. I always knew that I was different. I always felt a little uncomfortable in the dresses my mom put me in, and I never felt a bias between my love for men and women. Anytime I would mention these things, she'd get angry with me. She'd slam me into the wall, she'd throw my plastic toys at me, and she'd curse at me until her throat was sore. By fourth grade I left her house for good. By the time I was in fifth grade, I understood that I could be attracted to people no matter how they looked or identified, and I learned that I was uncomfortable being seen as a young lady. I didn't have a label for it, but I felt like I was wrong to feel that way. I began self-harming. I was only ten years old.

By the middle of my sixth grade year I had a label for my identity. I knew I was transgender and queer. However, I didn't come out until eighth grade. Most everyone assumed I was a lesbian up until this point. I was never comfortable with this label, but I never bothered to correct anyone. When I decided to go by my correct name, Jayden, I came out to some of my friends and my teachers at school. I'm not sure who decided it was okay, but fairly immediately my school contacted my parents. The school I went to asked my parents if it was okay for me to go by Jayden and use he/him pronouns. My parents said no. For the entirety of my final year of middle school I got deadnamed and misgendered. Students called me "it," which is dehumanizing when you don't use that pronoun. I had teachers tell me to get over myself when I felt uncomfortable

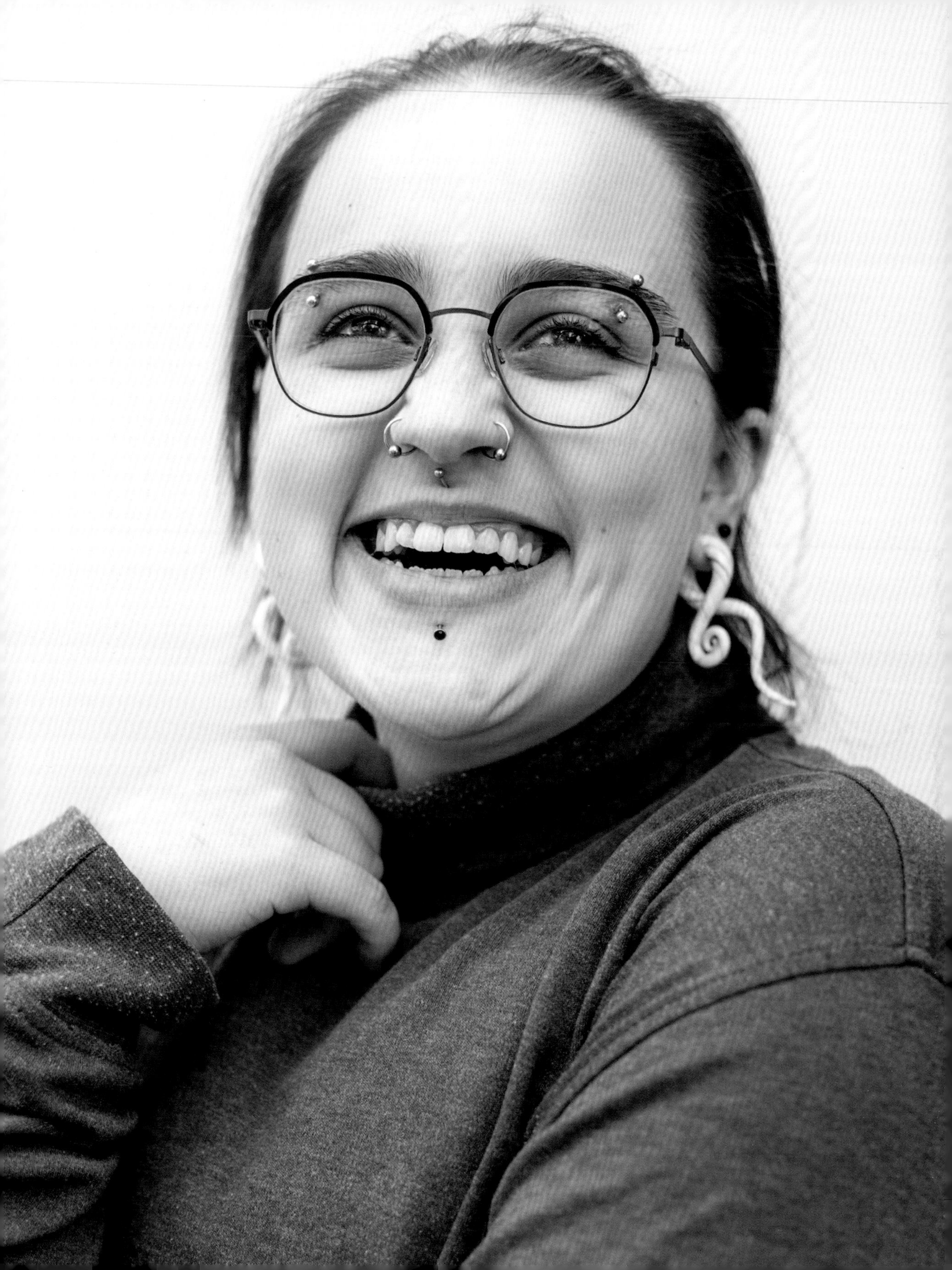

and complained. At one point, I was even raped so the man could "prove" that I was a "woman." My dad and I would get in arguments over how I identified all the time, and at one point he ended up telling me that his life would be a whole lot easier if I just killed myself. I became severely depressed. My self-harm became worse and worse until I eventually attempted suicide.

Thankfully, not much harm was done. I was placed on a seventy-two-hour suicide watch in the hospital. At no point did I feel safe as a member of the LGBTQ+ community, from others or myself. I felt that there was no place for someone like me.

I decided in high school I simply wouldn't come out. Up to this point, being LGBTQ+ had been traumatic. Within a week I shot down the idea of remaining closeted. I realized that I wouldn't be able to live as the person I had been forced to be for fourteen years. A kid's got to live their life at some point, and I decided that this is where I would start. This experience was much more positive! Every teacher was willing to use my name, a few were (and are) really good about using my pronouns, and there were no calls home. Unfortunately, my parents were highly unsupportive of me still. My mental health quickly began to decline. I had a plan to attempt suicide again. I had every intention of following through. The night I was going to attempt, I landed myself in the Wyoming Behavioral Institute (WBI). Did WBI help me? No. In fact, I would argue that I came out of WBI worse than when I went in. I was unable to talk, I was completely numb, and I didn't know how to handle anything around me. But WBI was a real wake-up call for me and a few teachers who I'm very close with to this day. I began being more open about my mental health issues and my feelings. I began expressing myself through art more and more. I told those two teachers about how negatively my parents treated me. I realized that avoiding home was healthier for me, so I did everything I could to avoid being home. I even slept in my car at times, not that I'd recommend it. It isn't safe, or healthy.

Obviously, the people I love could never fix my depression or my family, or even make me love myself. However, they made it possible to begin the journey of self-acceptance. I left my toxic home, and I now live in a homeless shelter that functions as a regular home. I've cut off contact with my parents completely. I've learned how to cope with suicidal thoughts, and I've begun the process of recovering from a seven-year-long addiction to self-harm that started because I felt wrong in my body. Is my journey done yet? No! But I've made a lot of progress along the way so far.

So, what do I think you should gather from this? Number one, if you have a good relationship with your parents as a member of the LGBTQ+ community, please don't take it for granted. For those of you who have a situation like mine, or even just an unhealthy environment in general, I want you to know that life will get better, and that you are allowed to heal. To heal from a situation, you need to start by removing the problem. If your parents—or any family member for that matter—are making you feel unsafe, unwelcome, or unloved, you are allowed to cut them out of your life. You don't need to feel any shame, or any guilt. You and your mental health should come first at all times. If you've been harmed more than helped, it is okay to leave. Leave as soon as possible. Remember that there is nothing wrong with you as a human. The people who have a problem with how you identify are the problem to begin with.

If you live in a toxic and/or abusive home environment, I want you to stay safe. Prioritize you! Do your best to get out of the house, and do your best to survive. Hang in there. Living is the most important thing for you right now. Maybe you don't see that right now. Maybe you don't want to live—and it's okay to have those feelings. However, it is not okay to act on them! I know you likely have heard it time and time again, but life will get better. Take it from me, someone who has hit rock bottom. Leaving is going to be the best thing for you. If you can't leave, avoid home. I hope you take the time to learn from my mistakes though. Don't sleep in your car. Sleep at a friend's house. Move out. Your state or town may have services for you as an unaccompanied minor. If you have options that aren't sleeping in your car or on the streets, take advantage of them! Remember that there is nothing wrong with you. You deserve to live your life to the fullest. The fullest may not come now, but it will soon. Do your best to save up money. Try to get a car. Try to go to school. Consider getting a job if you haven't yet. You deserve freedom. It sucks that you have to work a little bit harder to get it, but it's going to feel so much better when you do.

Jeremiah

15 years old, he/him, Alaska

Hey! I'm from the middle of nowhere! Just kidding, I'm from way up north, all the way in Nome, Alaska! Look it up! My name is Jeremiah, and I'm fifteen years old. This is my story and what it is like to be an LGBTQ+ kid up north.

I was born in Anchorage, Alaska, but have been raised in Nome all my life. I am Native Alaskan. In my region I am Inupiaq. I grew up knowing that I was different from who I was expected to be. I was always super close to my dad because I knew I wanted to be just like him. I wanted to walk like a man, talk like a man, and be a man. Even before I came out, my mom would always say, "You walk like your dad." Sadly, he passed away when I was seven. Losing him was very hard for me. It felt like I also lost a part of myself because I looked up to him. He was my role model.

Growing up I lived with my grandparents and went to the Lutheran church every Sunday. My mom has never really been in the picture, so I've always seen my grandparents as my parents. Early on they were very religious and homophobic, as was my mother. The first time I brought up to my mother that I might be trans, she told me I'd be "ugly." This made me begin to lose myself and hide who I was.

Not long after this is when my grandma passed away, and I had to live with my mom while my grandpa took time to grieve. It was pretty hard being back with my mom. She was verbally abusive and not able to care for me like most moms can. When we would get into arguments she would be rude to me and call me names. Even through all of this I was able to stay strong and patient and move back in with my grandfather.

So when I left her house and started to officially live with my grandpa again is when I started to have more confidence in myself. I didn't care anymore about what she thought or said about me. After I moved out I was able to come out to my grandfather. I told him I was not comfortable with the body I was born with and not comfortable with who he wanted me to be.

He learns more and more every day and accepts me more every day because I know my grandpa wants what is best for me and wants me to be happy. I would also like to mention my supportive friends and family, my two aunts who've been nothing but

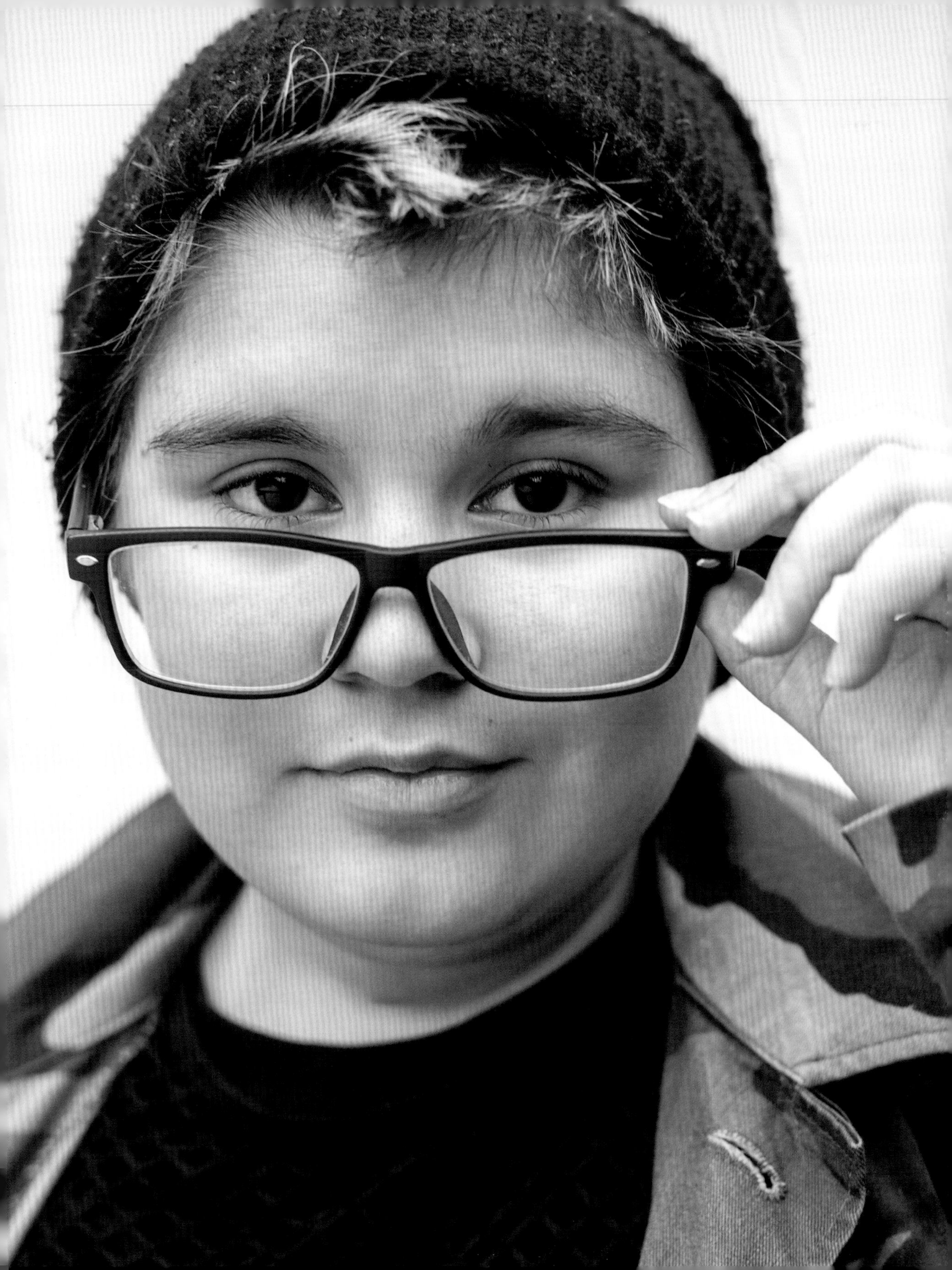

supportive, and the friends I grew up with or just recently met who are some of the best people I've ever known.

This year we had our first ever Pride float in our Midnight Sun Festival Parade, where we celebrate how we are the land of the midnight sun where the sun never goes down at all for the entire summer. Then, when it is winter, the sun comes out for only two to four hours. The Pride float even won best performance, and it was very cool. So many people had Pride flags. Usually people in Nome don't care, but it was so cool to see so many accepting people. It made my heart happy, and it made me feel safe to walk around with my Pride flag. Obviously there are people who are like "blah, go away," but we are going to do it anyway because it isn't their business in the first place. Sometimes we deal with it in school or other places around town.

We have the Pride Community Club at school. Sometimes our flags get ripped down, but we don't let it stop us. We call it the Pride Community Club because there are a lot of GSAs and we wanted to be cool and call it something different. Our teachers are all supportive as well, helping us educate students in the school that being queer is okay.

What is cool about our club is having the support from our teacher to make it happen. I am also the cofounder of the club. I was shocked to see how supportive the staff at our school was about it all, especially being in a right-wing state. I always put a Pride flag on my locker. The first time it was taken down after a day. The second time it took about a month and the third time it took about a week. I didn't let it stop me and I kept putting it up along with other things that represent me. My school was very supportive of it and even helped me keep it up. I hope in the years to come they aren't taken down and people can just express themselves.

Thinking about it, even though we are a small town you'd be surprised how supportive people are up here in the far north. As I get older I start to see more LGBTQ people like me who all carry confidence and don't care what anyone thinks, which helps me find more confidence in myself. I hope to be an inspiration to the younger people as the older generation was to me. As I write this I am exactly six months on hormones today. I wonder what I'll be like when this book is out. It is weird to think about but makes me excited.

I've started to find more representation in the media and music. All of these people in the movies I love and the music I listen to help

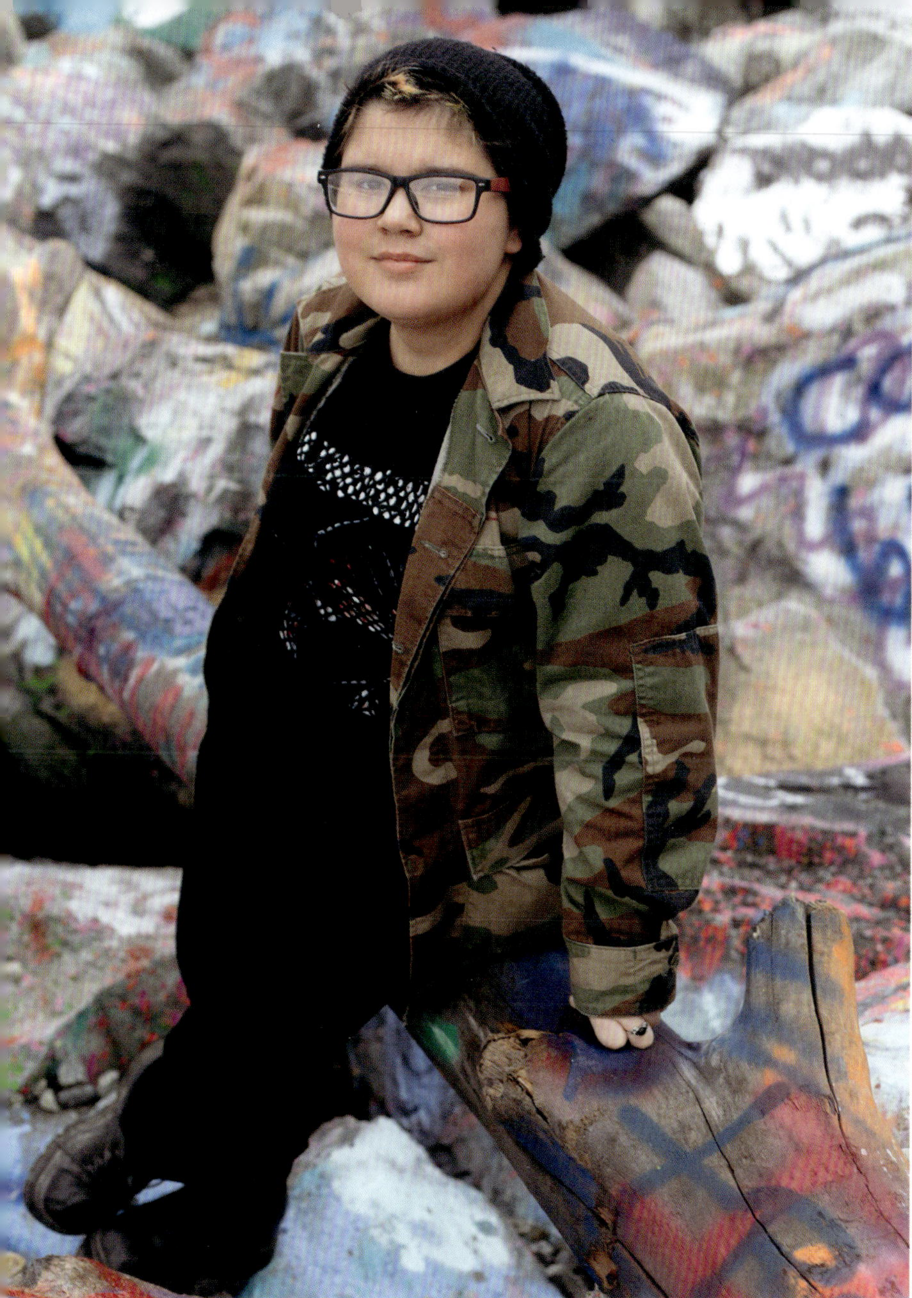

me learn more about myself. It makes me happy. It's also cool to see how much better representation has gotten throughout the years

My advice to LGBTQ youth like me is don't change yourself for anyone and don't do anything dumb to fit in. Fitting in is boring. I understand what it is like to feel alone, but use that time to discover you and who you want to be. Even if it means you won't have friends for a while, you will eventually find friends who love you for you, and not someone they think you are or want you to be.

Jo

17 years old, they/them, Wyoming

Hi, my name is Jo, I am Two-Spirit/Transgender FTM, and I go by They/Them pronouns. I am seventeen years old and currently live on the Wind River Indian Reservation in Wyoming.

Growing up on the reservation wasn't and isn't the easiest at all. It has a lot of hardships, like coming from a community and place where being queer isn't and hasn't always been accepted. But the irony in it is that there are a lot of queer people who live here. People on the reservation don't seem to care about anyone being LGBTQ unless it has something to do with them, and they don't care who other people love and who they're with. Well, some people do, but doesn't everyone at some point? This experience, being part of this book, has made me want to open up more. Not a lot of people know about me being Two-Spirit. I feel like this could help people in many more ways than one.

Being queer and trans in Wyoming isn't the easiest thing. A lot of traditional people live here, meaning they are not really comfortable with LGBTQ+ members. We had a really controversial case here in Wyoming that took place in Laramie, the Matthew Shepard case. Actually, last year I came out as Bi, and that case was what inspired me to do so. But in the back of my mind I worry about being discriminated against, not only for being queer but for being a Native American as well. I honestly have come out only once and, as I said above, it was coming out as being Bi.

I'm coming out more—honestly, it feels as if I have to again—but this time around I really don't have a problem doing so. My family knows and are supportive, and I recently came out to my school, meaning my teachers and the principal and a couple of my friends. They're all supportive, and I haven't seen much change, but they mistake my pronouns and my name, which at first did not bother me so much because deep down I knew it was going to be something to get used to, you know? I haven't really wanted to fully come out as Two-Spirit until I was ready, and now I think I am just scared of the judgment of others. But after a while it gets tiring not being who you are, truly. I feel as if this book will help me with that—being able to show people who I really want to be.

I came out to my mom first. When I was first questioning, which was about a year ago now, she was the one I wanted to go

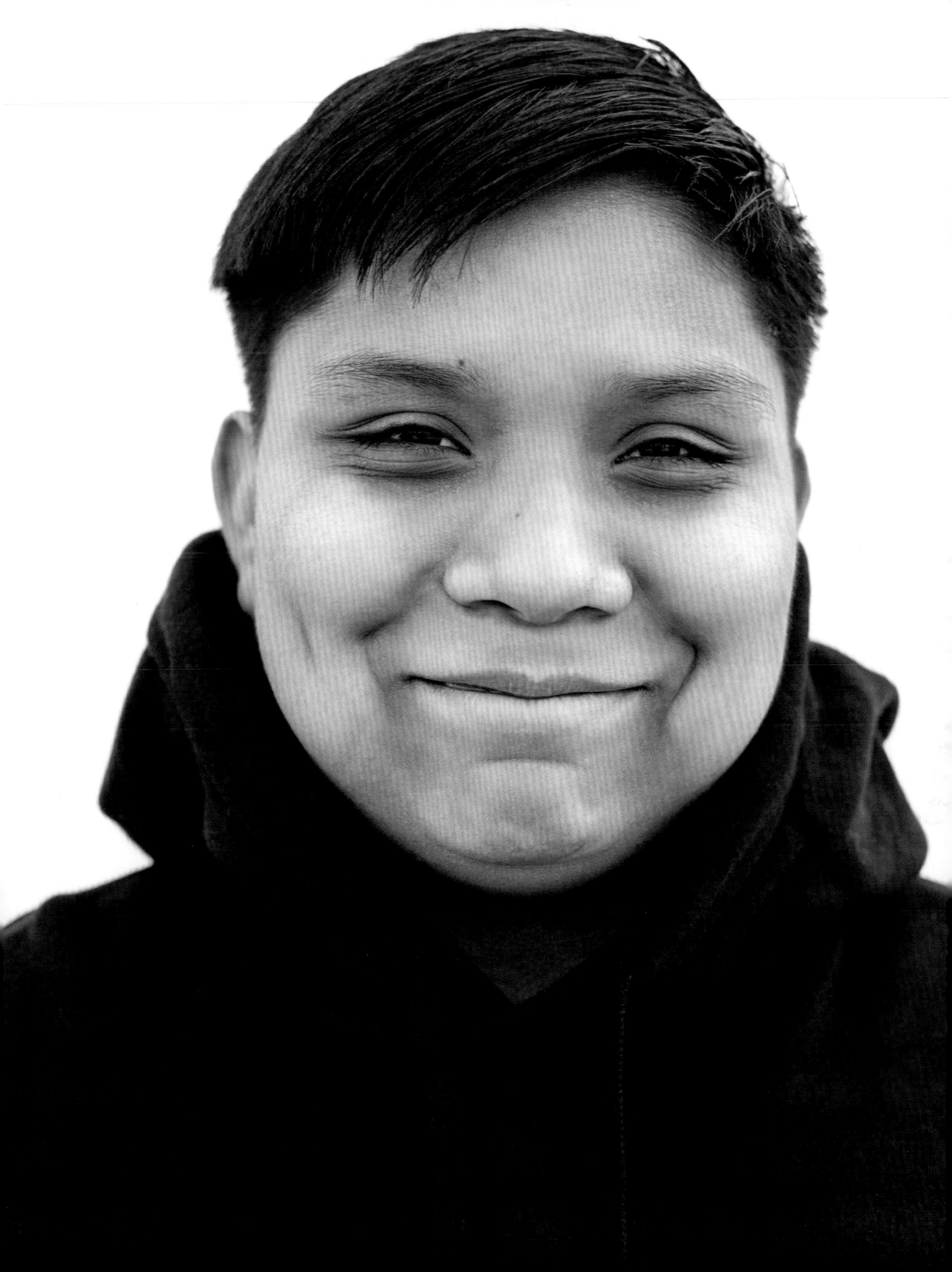

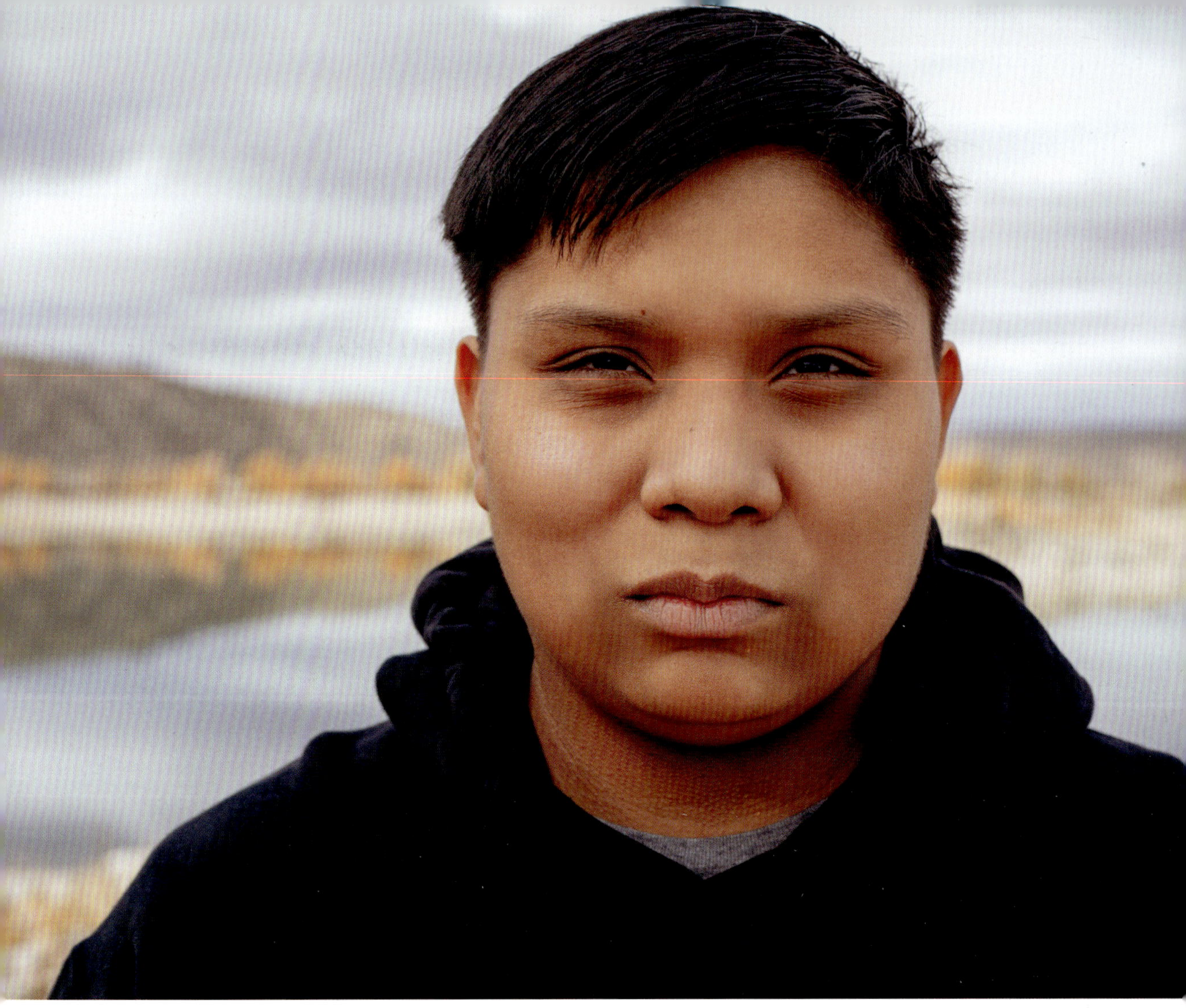

to. But I was scared, and at this point it was weighing heavy on my mental health. Actually, a couple years before that, when I was in the eighth and ninth grade maybe, I googled and YouTubed it, and at the time I thought it was bad and wrong. I thought something was wrong with me. Like, I wanted to go into talking and thinking about it more, but I was scared. I didn't know what to do, so I left it and pushed it back into my mind, far into my mind. I never thought I would be dealing with it again, but I'm glad I am because it's teaching me something.

My mom was the one who brought up the word *Two-Spirit* to me, and I looked into it. Honestly, I never thought I could have such a connection with a word. Two-Spirit, as far as I understand, is

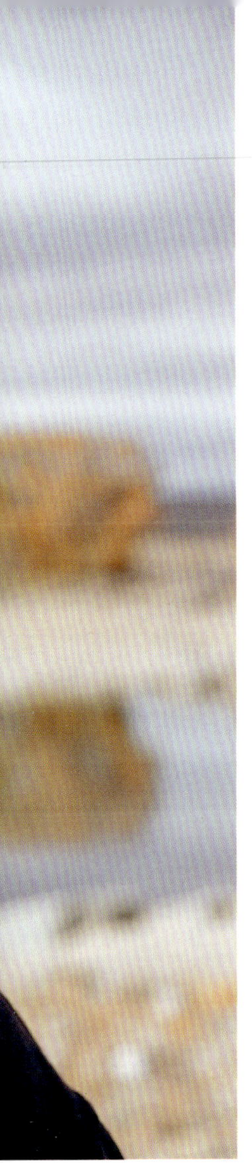

being able to walk both paths, meaning being able to see the world from both a woman's and a man's point of view. In the old days, Two-Spirit people were held up because they were in a higher connection with the spirit world. They were usually medicine people and were able to do many different things within the tribes.

At first, when I started questioning my identity, I didn't go to anyone except my mom for a really long time. The journey was really dark, and honestly one of the hardest things I've been through in my seventeen years of life—hard and confusing, if I'm being honest, but also one of the most fulfilling. I had tried talking to people about it but never asked for help when the dysphoria got real bad.

I'm going to start counseling soon so I'm hoping my journey can continue. I'm pre-T as of now, and I'm still questioning whether or not I want to go on to the next step. It's one of the biggest steps I believe, but the whole journey itself is a very big thing and I'm still so new to it. I know I've come so far from even a couple months ago. Right now I can actually say I feel proud of myself for coming as far as I have. I'm glad we have social media now because it's helped me figure out so much more. It's helped with researching and watching videos on YouTube, and even things like TikTok.

Something I would tell others like me is that no matter how much you are struggling, no one else's happiness is worth you being miserable—you deserve the world. I went through being alone for so long and not realizing that it could be so much easier, and in the end it's so worth it. I struggled for a really long time accepting who I really was. I really put it off in the beginning, which was the darkest moment throughout this whole journey. I wasn't talking to anyone. If you have been or ever go through this, *you are not alone.* You are accepted, and loved, and cared for. We've all been through it as a community. It gets dark, but in the end it's so worth it.

What I want you to take from this is it can be quite a journey, tough and dark, but there's a light at the end of the tunnel, a very beautiful one, one of being one's true self. Find your way back to yourself after going through this journey. Whether it's good or bad, you can always find your way back.

All of us who have been through this thing called life, queer or not, have had some really hard times, but I promise it gets better. Being free and being who you really are is an amazing feeling, and I hope one day you get to feel it too! Everything will work out; it'll go the way you want it to. If it doesn't feel like it now, hang on. For me, for your family and friends (new and old), for the great things that you'll accomplish—for the life you'll live truly being you. I love you!

Jose

18 years old, he/him, Oklahoma

Hello, my name is Jose! I am an eighteen-year-old male that goes by the pronouns He/Him, and I currently reside in Oklahoma. Ever since I was a teen, I've always wanted to tell my story to hopefully help others who are in similar situations as I was. I hope if you're reading this my story helps you.

My mother raised me as a single parent, so our bond was very close. I never really knew my biological father. He was in and out of my life. This would later cause distrust with male figures. My mother later met my stepfather, and after some time I started trusting him. They would later have my sister. Everything seemed perfect, and I would love to stop the story there, but, unfortunately, not everybody's fairy tale comes so easily. Around the age of ten I was picked on because I was a bit more feminine and had a higher-pitched voice than other boys my age. This didn't happen when I was at school, but rather at home by my stepfather. This was strange to me because I had never felt ashamed for acting the way I did until this started.

As the years went on my relationship with my mother would start to decline, but not as much as my relationship with my stepfather. There was a lot of "joking," which was actually emotional abuse with constant insults about my weight and acting feminine.

When I was in sixth grade, I finally learned the true meaning of being gay, but due to hearing so much negativity associated with the word, I linked "gay" to having a negative connotation. This is also when the thought entered my head, "What if I was gay?" I always felt this certain attraction toward males. I would just constantly push it to the back of my head. I mean, I had a girlfriend during fifth and sixth grades and I had a few others before that. This would eventually lead me into stumbling onto the definition of "bisexual." I thought, "Yes, this is who you are!" (Wow, I hate labels now that I think about it.) I figured being bisexual was better than being gay. Since I liked males and had dated females, it must have meant that I would be somewhat still "normal." So, toward the end of sixth grade, I identified as bisexual. Eventually, I told my best friend at the time that I was bi and she seemed so unfazed. This would start to chip away at those negative thoughts about being gay.

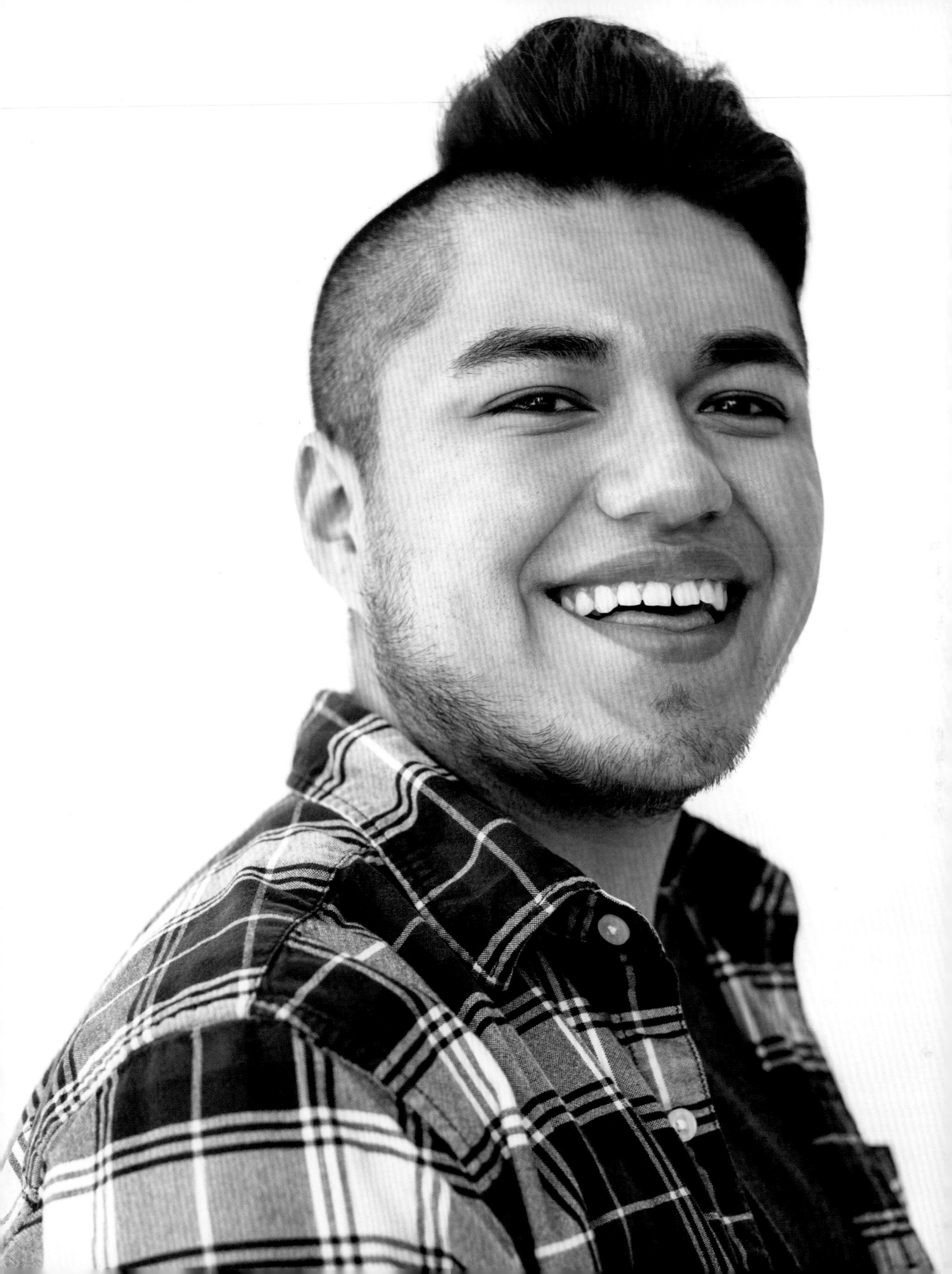

When I was in middle school, I thought Oklahoma was a horrible state to come out. I just figured since it is a conservative state it wouldn't go too well. I attended school in Jones, which is in the country. As I got older, I noticed Oklahoma was a loving state, and not only that, but Jones was also a town that accepted anybody with open arms. I blame myself for falling for those stereotypes, but I was young. The summer before my seventh year in school, after constantly trying to push the idea down, I finally opened up to the question, "Was I gay?" At this point in my life, I had already removed most negative connotations from the word, but I couldn't help but still feel like there was something wrong with being gay. I finally came to terms and accepted that I was only attracted to males. I felt instant relief, but more challenges were up ahead, coming out not only to my family but also to my friends again.

I decided to come out fully when I went to seventh grade. I was no longer ashamed. It was certainly liberating. I had such a strong support system at school that it helped me be content with myself. I wish I could say this was the end of my story, but unfortunately, like I said earlier, fairy tales don't come as fast for everybody. I felt like I could be myself when I was at school, but at home it was a different story. At home, it was almost as if I felt like I was trapped. It was such a strange feeling to pretend I was someone else at home. It's weird because most of the time kids don't want to go to school, but I looked forward to it every day. It was the one place I felt relief. The tension between my stepfather and me started to increase. There was a lot of speculation about whether I was gay or not, but the emotional abuse increased. I also still felt that something must be wrong with me. I also noticed that my relationship with my mother started taking a toll as well during this time. Even though things were bad at home, I still just kept my head held high. Little did I know that soon after I turned fifteen a lot would change.

When I was fifteen I came out to my parents, though not in the way I wanted to. I would have to leave my phone on the counter so I couldn't use it when I went to bed on school nights. One night this led to my stepfather going through my phone and finding messages to a guy I was talking to at the time in another state. (I would highly recommend being safe on the Internet. I frankly wish I had been more educated on this.) This invasion of privacy would create distrust and problems for my family, but not only that, there was now tension because they knew I was gay.

After this news broke, I instantly felt like I'd disappointed my mother. It also didn't help that our relationship felt more strained

each year. At this point my stepfather and I didn't have a relationship. It felt like he was a stranger living with us who I despised. The
emotional abuse only amplified after I came out. I would constantly
get picked on for being gay. Not only that, at times he would say
things that put me and my mother against each other. I felt almost
replaced by him with my mother. Unfortunately, things only wors-
ened as time went on. As I was reaching the age of sixteen, there was
one moment that things escalated and changed my life drastically.

One night, when my mother was at work, he commented to me,
"You know, you make your mother depressed." This was a thought
I had had plenty of times but never wanted to believe. I didn't want
to believe that I caused my mother's depression because I was gay.
I quickly yelled at him and told him "No, I don't! Stop lying!" He
struck me and continued. I would later attempt to tell my mother,
but it seemed as if she didn't take me seriously. This was the
moment I felt as if I lost my mother.

There would be two more incidents after that, but that was
the one that shook my core; it was the lowest I had ever been in
my life. I felt stuck because I didn't feel like I could seek help. Not
only that, but after dealing with emotional abuse for so long, you
start to lose yourself. You begin to believe this is how your life is
going to be. I could feel myself slipping, but I would just constantly
tell myself, "Just a few more years and you can leave." Luckily, I
still had a huge supportive system at school. My friends certainly
helped at the time (especially you, Neely!). When I turned seventeen, my mindset of being alone and my belief that my life was
always going to be hell started changing. My relationship with
my parents started to change for the better. As time went on they
started accepting who I am. My teen years were a hellish chapter of
my life, but they started getting better. The chapters that felt long
started to end. The ending of these chapters has led me to forgive
my parents. I love you, Mom and Dad. I also want to say thank you
to my friends for being there for me throughout these years.

The one thing I tell anybody I tell my story to is that it's a blessing and a curse. I was hurt in the past, but I learned a lot. I wouldn't
be the man I am today without those chapters of my life. That goes
the same for *you*. Each chapter of your life doesn't determine how
your fairy tale will end, but how you respond to it. Keep your head
up high and remember there is more to your story. I wish you the
best, and, of course, sending love and light.

Kamron

17 years old, he/him, Utah

Hello, my name is Kamron. I am seventeen years old and I am gay. At least I think so anyway. Sexuality is a strange topic. I use he/him pronouns, I am from Kearns, Utah, and have relocated to Saratoga Springs, Utah.

I love music. It has been my life for years, and if I put my mind to anything I will do it no matter what. I always loved music, art, and dance growing up but never really dove deep until I got to high school. I have eleven siblings and I love every single one of them to death. I love baking and I am neurodivergent—specifically, I have autism spectrum disorder (ASD).

From a young age I always knew that I was different. I never really talked or got along with the boys. I used to take my jacket and wear it as a skirt. I used to take my mom's high heels from the closet and run down the stairs in them. I would dress up as mermaids and fairies for Halloween. Young life is kind of a blur for me. Some things flash out here and there—high emotion parts in my life.

I always knew I was a little fruity, but the day I knew for sure was in the fifth grade. I was going through a rough patch at this age. My mom was in an abusive relationship, and I was struggling with an identity crisis and having to make the decision to stay with my mom and protect her, or move in with my dad and live a safer life. I was eleven, and in fifth grade I had a teacher named Mr. Mottl. He made such an impact that year. I went into class one day and I was doing work when he came up to me and gave me a bag full of school supplies. He helped me so much with that one little gesture. He was very attractive as well. With this newfound attraction, I figured out maybe I didn't like girls. A year later I would come out to one of my best friends. She said she already knew and, looking back on it now, it makes sense.

After that I got up the courage to confront a boy and tell him that I liked him. He had helped me through a lot in my life and I had developed feelings for him that were new. He was the first boy I ever had a crush on. Sadly, he was straight and didn't return those feelings.

But rejection followed after with a second boy. Then a third and fourth. It felt like I wasn't wanted. I never felt wanted in school and felt like if I disappeared no one would notice.

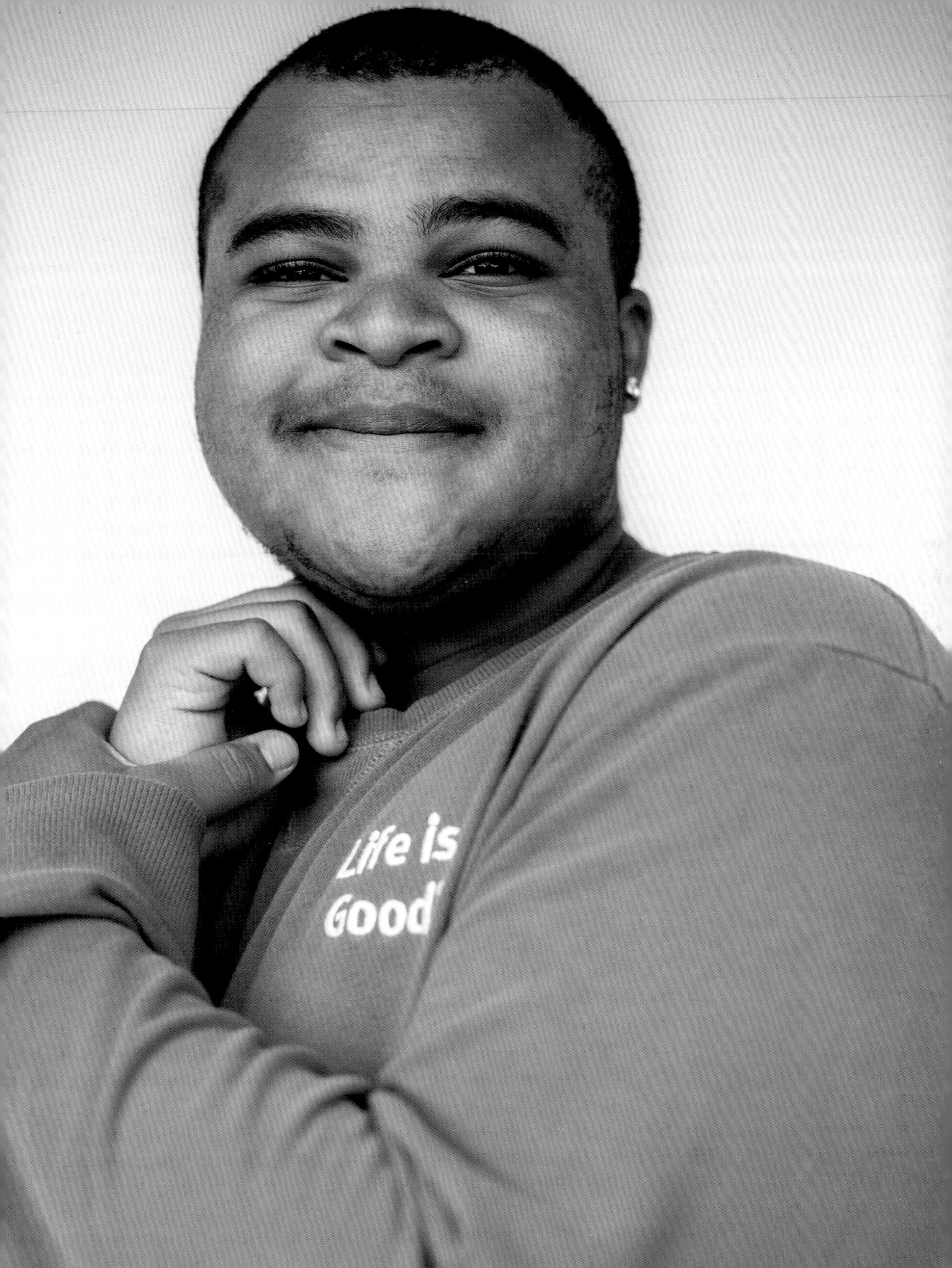
Life is
Good

Dealing with that kind of rejection throughout junior high and high school was rough, and it still is. Never getting asked out on dates or having my first kiss is hard. People make it seem so easy. Being African American in the gay community is difficult. Especially being bigger as well.

I always felt out of place—within the gay community, the Black community, and everywhere else. I was never bullied to my face about my sexuality, but I have heard words thrown across the classroom that are rather distasteful. I once introduced myself as a part of the school's GSA and was laughed at by football players during a diversity meeting. How cliché. And I personally know people who have been bullied to the point where they don't want to live anymore.

I can say, though, that I was lucky to be blessed with such an amazing family and support system of friends. I know that kids out there have families that treat them in cruel ways, but I am so grateful and lucky to have a family that didn't. My oldest brother is the one that started it off, being trans and all, so from a young age I understood gender and sexuality. After that my second-oldest brother came out as gay, and my fourth-oldest brother is gay as well. And then there was me—little old Kamron—the last straight boy on my mom's side. I felt an enormous pressure to stay straight for some odd reason, even though everyone knew I was queer. It was still nerve-racking. I still to this day haven't physically spoken the words "I am gay" to an adult in my life.

Getting past the hardships and the struggles of having identity problems, and my mess of a family dynamic, I am still pushing on. I have my rough days where I cry and miss being a part of my family. We moved away from each other after we lost our house, and I ended up moving in with a friend. Another difficult part of my identity is dealing with homophobia, knowing that if I say "You have pretty eyes" to a boy that it could ruin our entire friendship. Never knowing what teenage romance is like and getting that experience that so many of my peers have. I still have a smile on my face as I walk down the hallways of my high school knowing I always have my family and my friends to support me.

The thing I would like to leave you with is that love will find its way to your heart; all you need to do is give it time. The number of days I have spent crying and being sad are countless, but no matter what I kept pushing—like you should. You will never see the light of day if you follow the dark around the world, so start walking toward that warm glow of light that is looking for you. I may know you, I may not—but I love you. More than the words on this page can describe.

I was also asked to give you advice. The advice I would like to leave you with is this: The tears you shed today become the space you leave in your heart for the love you will receive tomorrow. There will always be a second opportunity for you. No matter how hard life gets there is always someone out there thinking about you or wondering how you are. I had to learn that the hard way. At one of the lowest points of my life I felt like I couldn't turn to anyone, but I waited just a little longer and there it was: a gentle hand there to help me out of that dark place. It could come from your family or your friends or a rando that you just met in the lunch line at Costa Vida.

You are loved. And I don't say that lightly. I hope reading through this has given you—or anyone who reads this—some light into living your life as a queer youth. Some days are harder than others, but past all the slurs that get tossed in the hallway and the mean folks, there is always a community of queer kids that will be your safety net when you fall. Make me a promise. Keep hope until you can see the end of the tunnel. You'll never find the light if you stop halfway. And may love always find you.

Keaton

17 years old, he/him, South Dakota

My name's Keaton and I'm seventeen. I identify as gay and use he/him pronouns. I live in Rapid City, South Dakota. I participate in track and love to hike in the local Black Hills. I'm a senior in high school and plan to study physics in college. In my spare time I read poetry, listen to music, and do everything with my friends, from cooking to garage sale shopping.

I grew up in a large family with four siblings and a dog. I feel like they always had a hunch that I was gay. It could have been Princess Peach being my favorite Mario Kart character or my love of Disney's *The Little Mermaid*, but who knows. I think I knew I was gay when I was about nine, and I finally accepted it when I came out on my fourteenth birthday. A friend of mine had suggested that we go to the movie *Love, Simon* in theaters. I had secretly read the book and was excited to watch it. After the movie I decided to come out to my friends and then to my parents that night. One thing people don't tell you is that you will have a *lot* of talks with your family when you come out (or at least I did). My parents wanted to check in on how I was feeling and were open to who I was. It was pretty awkward at first, but they were just showing they cared about me.

When I came out, only a few people knew. I was pretty alright with that. In my experience, no one really batted an eye at someone who was gay. Still, I only told people if it came up in conversation or when a girl asked me out. I reached out to a couple gay upperclassmen I looked up to for advice. It was nice to form a community and try to understand my new life. Now being gay is sort of second nature to me. It's still funny to surprise new people with it or to say, "What about it?" when some a-hole at the gym calls someone gay.

I know that this is not everyone's experience though. I was quite fortunate to feel so accepted by everyone around me. Other queer youth, even in other situations in my same area, face lots of struggles. Parents can invalidate their children's identities or even kick them out of their homes. Being a white, gay male, I did not have to face some of the troubles that less accepted queer youth (including transgender youth and queer people of color) do.

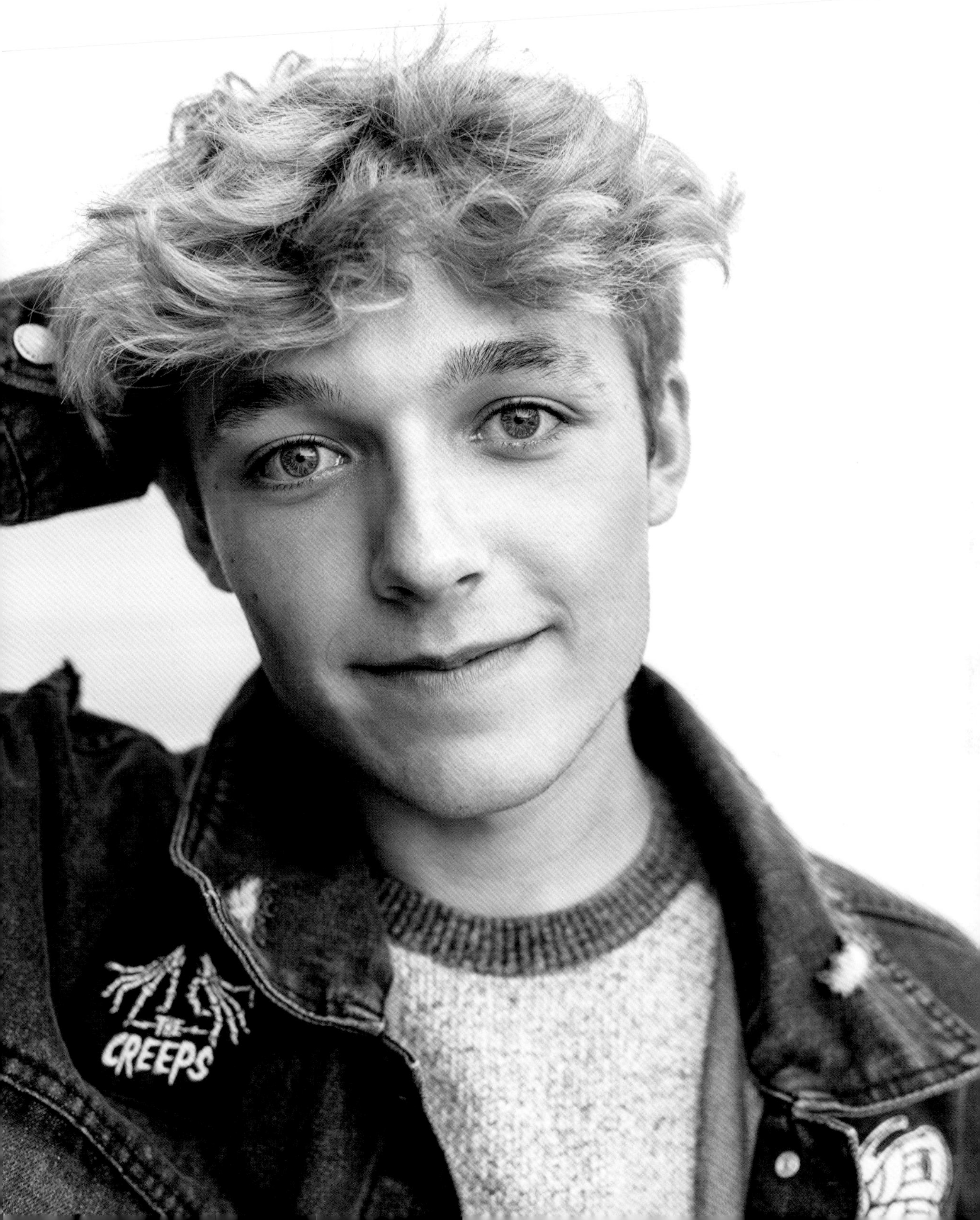

THE
CREEPS

I know my story isn't like a lot of people's. I have a family that accepts me. I have friends that are there no matter what. I have a community that I feel safe being myself in. I guess the message I want to share is that it doesn't have to be a big deal if you don't want it to be. Coming out can be as simple as mentioning a guy you like is cute. You can casually introduce your best friend to your new boyfriend at a party. Rainbow doesn't have to be your favorite color scheme and Pride parades don't have to be your thing (but I do recommend going to one; they're a blast). You'll still be you after all.

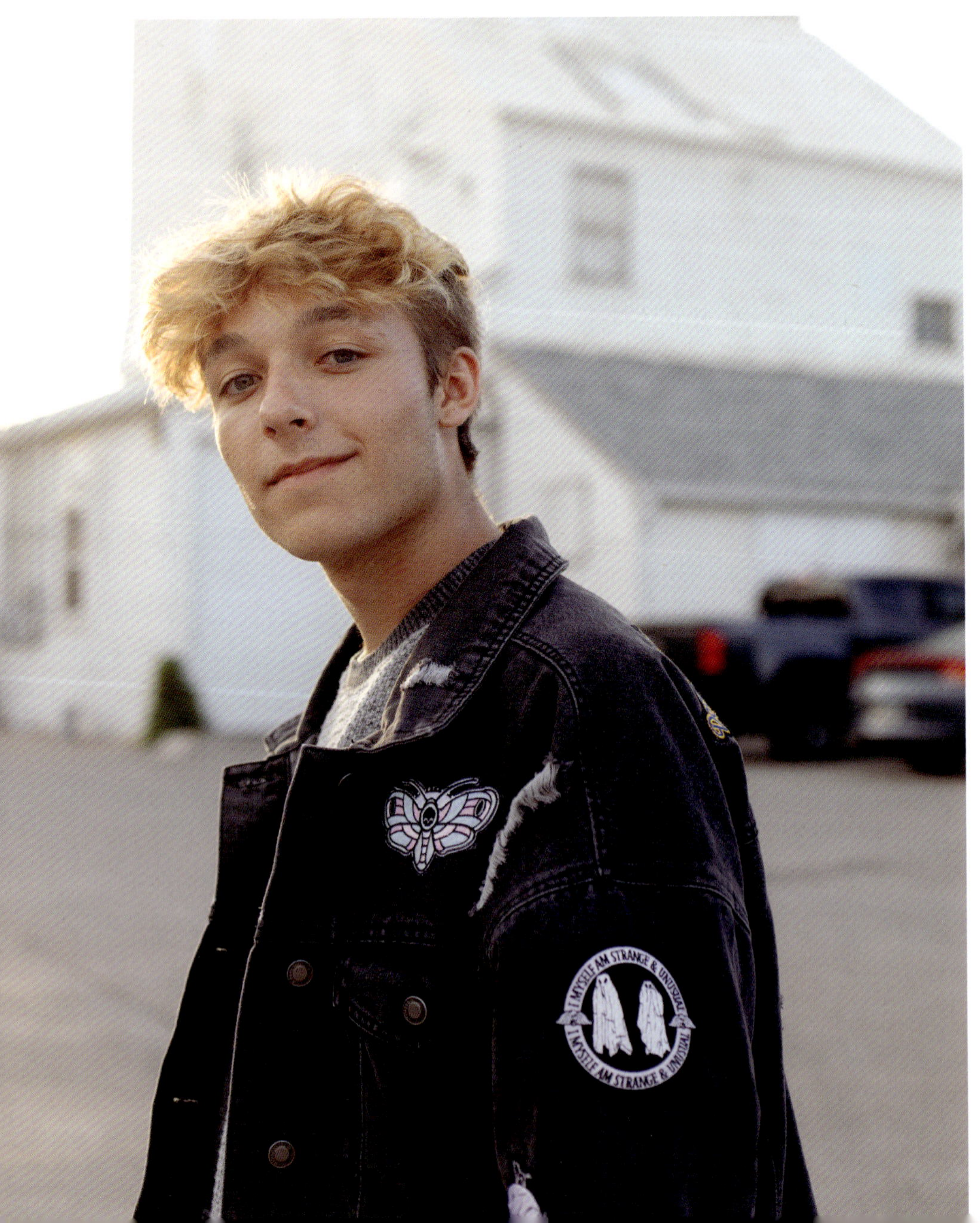

Kyler

18 years old, they/he, New York

Greetings, my name is Kyler. I'm deaf since birth. I'm eighteen years old, gender-fluid, and demisexual. Furthermore, I do accept all pronouns, although mainly I use They/Them.

I was born in Brooklyn, New York. I grew up with good and bad experiences in NYC. Ever since I was a kid, I learned to be independent, busy, and cautious. The environment I grew up in was very difficult for me. I was in the closet until I was almost eighteen. I knew I liked girls when I was eight. Not only that, but I wasn't sure about my feelings due to the taboo of being gay. My family is deaf, and we are from Puerto Rico, and being Hispanic has had a big effect on my family's perspective on homosexuality and gay rights. Also, we often don't have proper access to information due to our deafness. In my time growing up, the sources of information (for instance, videos without closed captions or a sign language interpreter) weren't very accessible. The deaf and hearing communities were very divided in the early years of my growing up. I wasn't able to come out until I was fifteen, when I came out as a bisexual person. At that time I only knew that gay, lesbian, and bisexual people existed. My parents were shocked when I came out to them. They were very ashamed that I was gay because of the stigma they were taught about the LGBTQIA+ community. The fifteen-year-old me just wanted to be loved again, so I returned to the closet for a few more years. I endured many crises throughout those years. Lying to other people and myself did a lot of damage to my mental health. I coped by talking to other safe people to try to understand myself more, researching about LGBTQIA+ issues, and asking LGBTQIA+ people questions. I learned to experiment with clothing, makeup, and hanging out with LGBTQIA+ people.

Later on, at seventeen years old, I was slowly learning about the LGBTQIA+ community through a friend who is my partner now. They were very educated in that area because of their better accessibility to the LGBTQIA+ resources and very supportive parents. I had a gender identity and sexuality crisis for a while to sort myself out. Eventually I came out to my partner as demisexual, and then I discovered my gender-fluid identity a few months later on.

I came out to my mom first. She has known I was gay since I was a little girl. She is doing good and trying to be progressive with

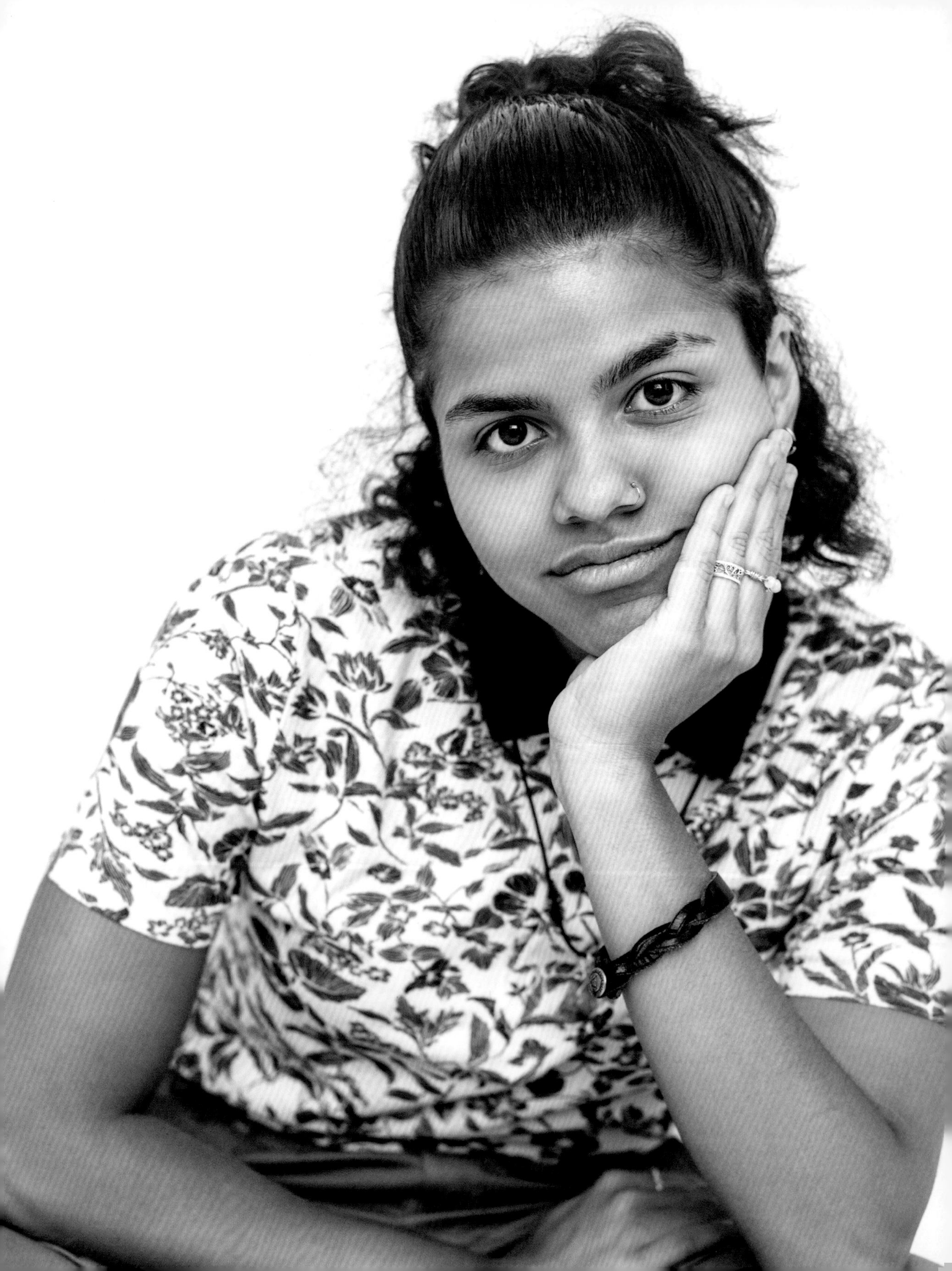

my sexuality and gender identities now. Then I came out to my dad. It was very hard on us for several months since my dad wasn't properly educated about LGBTQIA+ due to his limited access to information about the community. My relationship with my dad is getting better at a very slow pace. We are slowly reconnecting with each other over time.

Since I am the oldest child and the only daughter out of three siblings, I carry the burden of being the rebellious one. So I can make a big difference and hopefully make it easier for my brothers to grow. My dad, he's trying his best to love my partner as his own. I'm proud of my parents for trying to process the big changes and learning more about being LGBTQIA+.

My advice for LGBTQIA+ youths? Only you can keep moving forward even if your supporters aren't there for you at every step; you are your own biggest supporter. I'm so much happier being out and I'm so in love with being authentic, living my life exactly how I want, for myself. You do you: Trust me, you know yourself better than anyone. Don't let anyone tell you any different.

Lexy

18 years old, she/her, Alabama
CW: This story contains references to self-harm, suicide, drug use, and sexual assault.

Hey y'all, my name is Alexia, but I also go by Lexy. I'm an eighteen-year-old lesbian Muslim girl who uses she/her pronouns. I now live in Portland, Oregon, starting my second year in college, but I spent most of my life in Prattville, Alabama, in the heart of conservative America.

I was born to a military family in Camp Lejeune, North Carolina. I wasn't raised by my biological father. I grew up with my half-brother's dad, who has always just been "Dad" to me. He took on raising me, a strong and independent woman who rejects societal rules. My biological mom, who is my best friend, divorced my dad when I was young.

From a young age I was always pretty outspoken and a little bit of a rebel child. When I was younger, I lived in a few different places due to my dad being in the Marine Corps. He and my stepmom were pretty conservative parents. My mom, on the other hand, is a super-liberal feminist activist. Growing up my parents let us make our own choices for the most part. Something changed, though, when we moved to a conservative town in Alabama in 2009. I'm a mixed child and have always experienced some form of racism and prejudice. Add being lesbian and disabled on top of it and you got yourself a world of discrimination, especially in conservative Alabama. I always kinda knew I was different. I had to force myself to like boys growing up because my dad has pretty conservative views.

I didn't officially come out to my dad till I was around sixteen because I was scared due to his conservative Christian views. I came out to my mom first because she is my best friend. I also knew she'd be accepting of me. My dad wasn't completely accepting and told me that he still loved me but didn't want me to talk about it or outwardly display it. It took a huge toll on my mental health. I had already struggled with my mental health and had received four previous diagnoses shortly after I lost my grandmother; I was also diagnosed with type 1 diabetes.

Sometime later I'd fall into the wrong crowd. I was lacking a good support system—my world was on a downhill spiral. My dad would tell my psychiatrist at the time he thought my sexuality was a phase, and she agreed with him, which hit me even harder in the gut. I started self-harming and even turned to drugs, and by the time

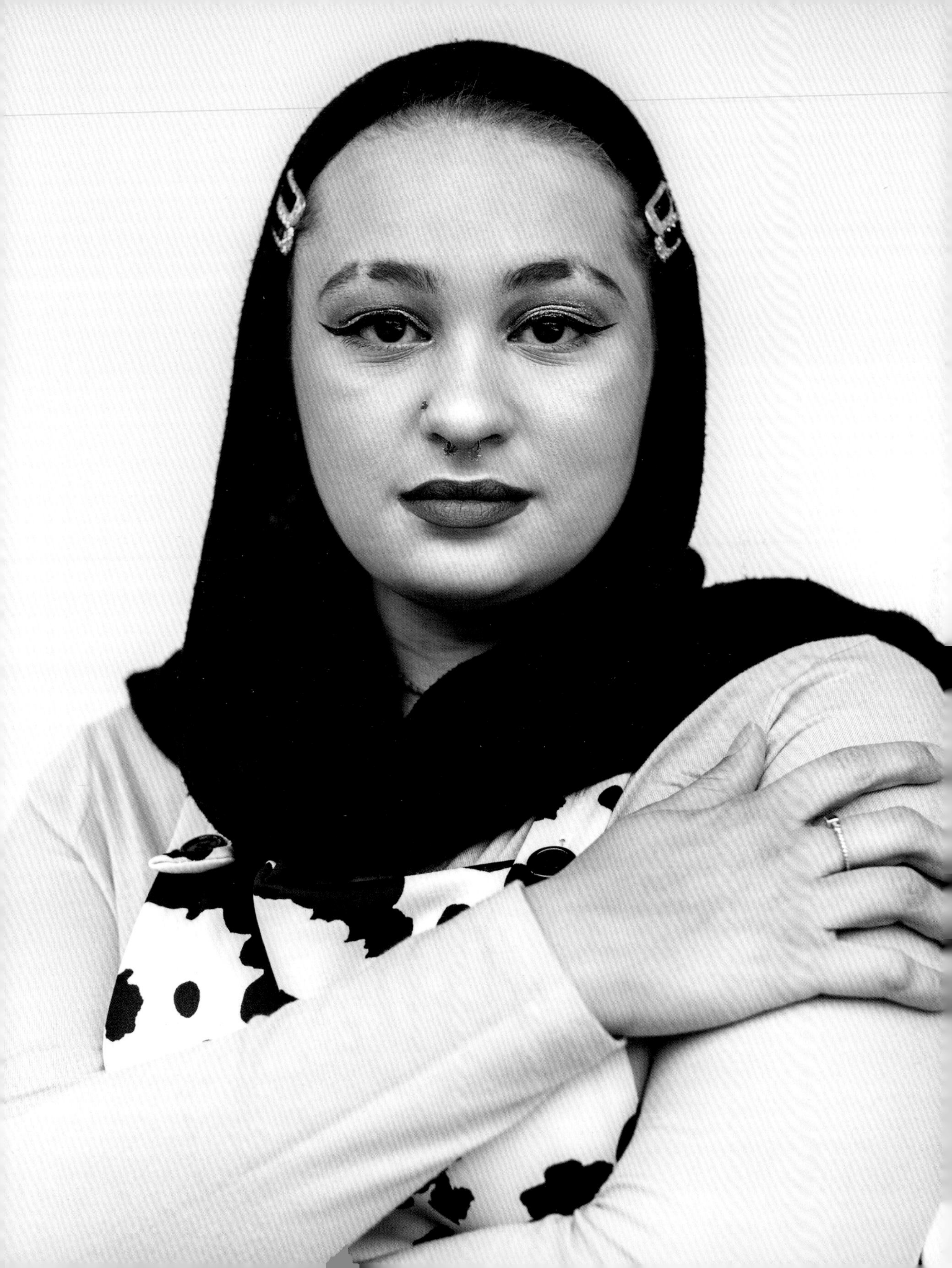

I hit seventeen I had already attempted suicide seven times. I had been hospitalized in a psych unit a total of four times, the longest being six months. I was addicted to pills and cocaine, my grades slipped, and I received three more psychiatric diagnoses for a total of seven mental illnesses, the hardest being bipolar, borderline personality disorder (BPD), and PTSD, most of it stemming from emotional trauma, sexual assault trauma, and just bad relationships at home.

I took a hard look at what I was doing and how I was living. I fell far from Allah and my religion. I ended up graduating high school and went to college at the age of seventeen at the University of South Alabama in Mobile, Alabama. I fell into the wrong crowd yet again and failed my first semester. Right when I got to college I felt pressured to identify as bisexual and not lesbian, not by my family but by my peers. I was also getting discriminated against by my college for being Muslim, Queer, and disabled.

My mental health went on an even bigger downhill spiral. At the end of my first semester, in December, I was raped by the fourth person in my life because he "wanted to turn me straight." My school did nothing. They brushed it off. I felt disgusting and hated myself. I thought, "All this because I like women?" I couldn't understand what was so wrong with that. I couldn't understand why people thought I was "sick" or an "abomination."

One day my brother dropped me back off at my college dorm and sat with me and talked. He wanted me to know he still loved and supported me and that he would always fight for me. He gave me hope. If it wasn't for my brother, I wouldn't have made it through that night. I decided I was gonna get clean, go to treatment, and find an accepting group of friends. I was on a mission.

I later met my three best friends in the world, Taylor, Serena, and Ginger. They were so accepting of me and supported me through recovery. They showed me I was valid and that I was loved. I got clean shortly after and started my treatments again. I started showing up to class and even finding an LGBTQ+-friendly mosque. I finally found myself. I soon got offered a once-in-a-lifetime research opportunity in Oregon. I also got a scholarship to the University of Oregon, where I am currently studying virtually. I returned home for the summer and told my parents the news. They were surprisingly happy for me. My dad had also slowly changed over the years and became more accepting and understanding. I was finally breaking free from my conservative town in Alabama. I still got called slurs by strangers and old friends, but to me that didn't matter because I knew who I was.

I still stay in touch with everyone back home. It does get better. Keep your head up and don't let your crown fall: Y'all are all kings, queens, and nonbinary royalty. I decided to share my story because I know it's hard, especially for LGBTQ+ youth.

You are stronger than you'll ever know, so when you feel like your world is over, keep pushing. Dig deep; you have it in you. I'm cheering each one of y'all on. You are brave, strong, intelligent, beautiful, handsome, and—most of all—loved. People are filled with hate but y'all can be the light, the hope, and even just the smile that gets someone through their day. To anyone struggling right now, keep your head up, love whoever you want to love, and just be you! Thank you for reading my story. I hope it provides some inspiration and some comfort that someone—even me, a stranger—loves each and every one of y'all.

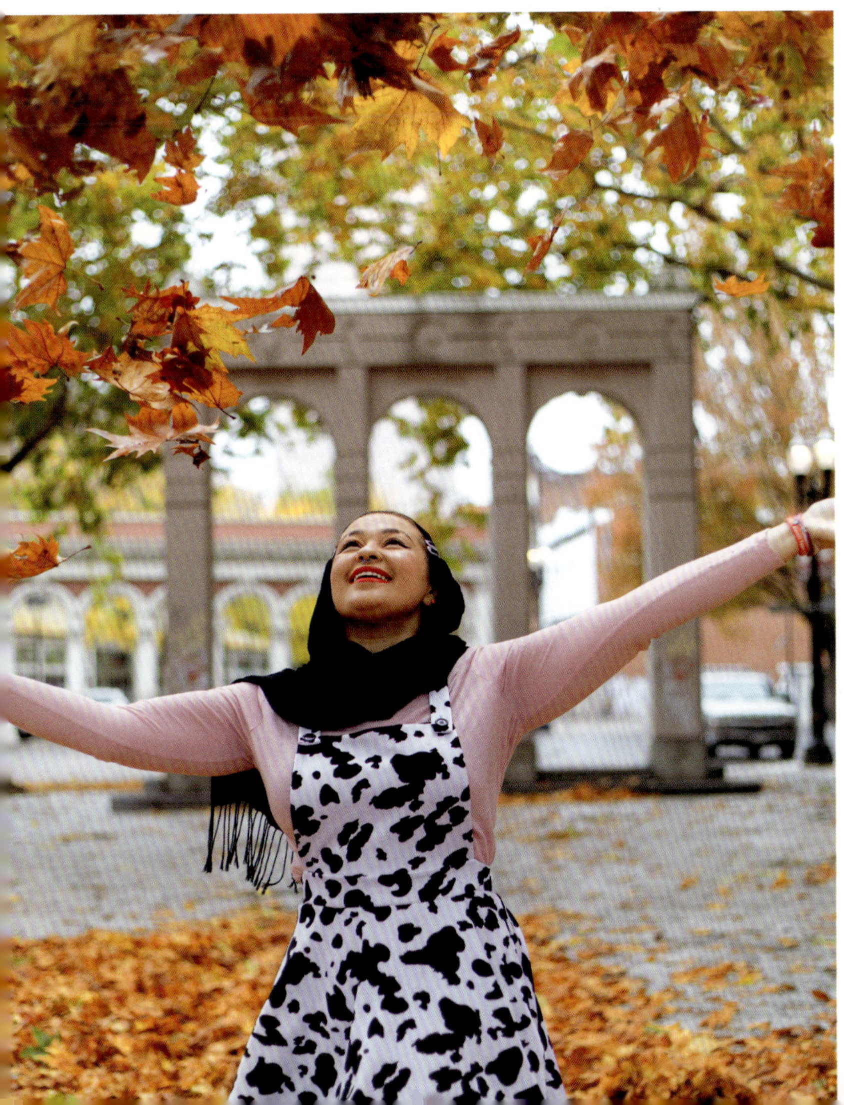

Lilli

15 years old, she/her, Louisiana

Hello world, my name is Lilli! I was born and raised in Louisiana. I am female and I am an asexual lesbian! What does that mean? It means I do not feel any sexual feelings at all, but I still have romantic feelings toward women and nonbinary people.

I am a real human! I hope that you find comfort in the fact that I live in a very red state but am still very loved by my family and my chosen family.

Where I live in Louisiana, being queer is usually widely accepted and normalized, but when I go outside my little bubble it is very hard to tell if someone is going to judge me for being queer or not. It isn't a stereotype if it's true: There are a lot of tight-knit religious communities throughout Louisiana, and you can really see and hear queer people there struggle to find acceptance and community. I don't know a ton of kids outside Louisiana, but I have one friend who moved out of our city and I hear how vastly different and alien they feel there.

It's hard knowing you're different, but sometimes it's even harder when other people assume you're different. I had a rough time in school. I was considered weird and therefore judged. In the third grade I had issues doing what the teacher told me to do. I felt like an outcast and unlovable. I started to doubt myself and my identity and wonder if I really wanted to be myself in front of others. I was scared that they would make fun of me or not accept me. I don't know where or quite when the fear began to sink in, but it did. I felt so afraid of what others would think. If I was different, that meant I was an outcast, worthless.

The next three years were a little weird for me as I was trying to figure out my identity and deal with my middle school life. In the sixth grade I realized that I liked girls. I was a big swimmer at the time, so you'd think being in a locker room filled with other girls would make me have stronger feelings toward them. It didn't. Then I realized that while I loved the idea of a romantic relationship, I don't feel anything sexually.

This was a weird awakening for my friends, who were mostly straight. They didn't understand that I didn't get crushes or butterflies by looking at someone. They also didn't understand my preference for females. Most of my friends were at least very nice

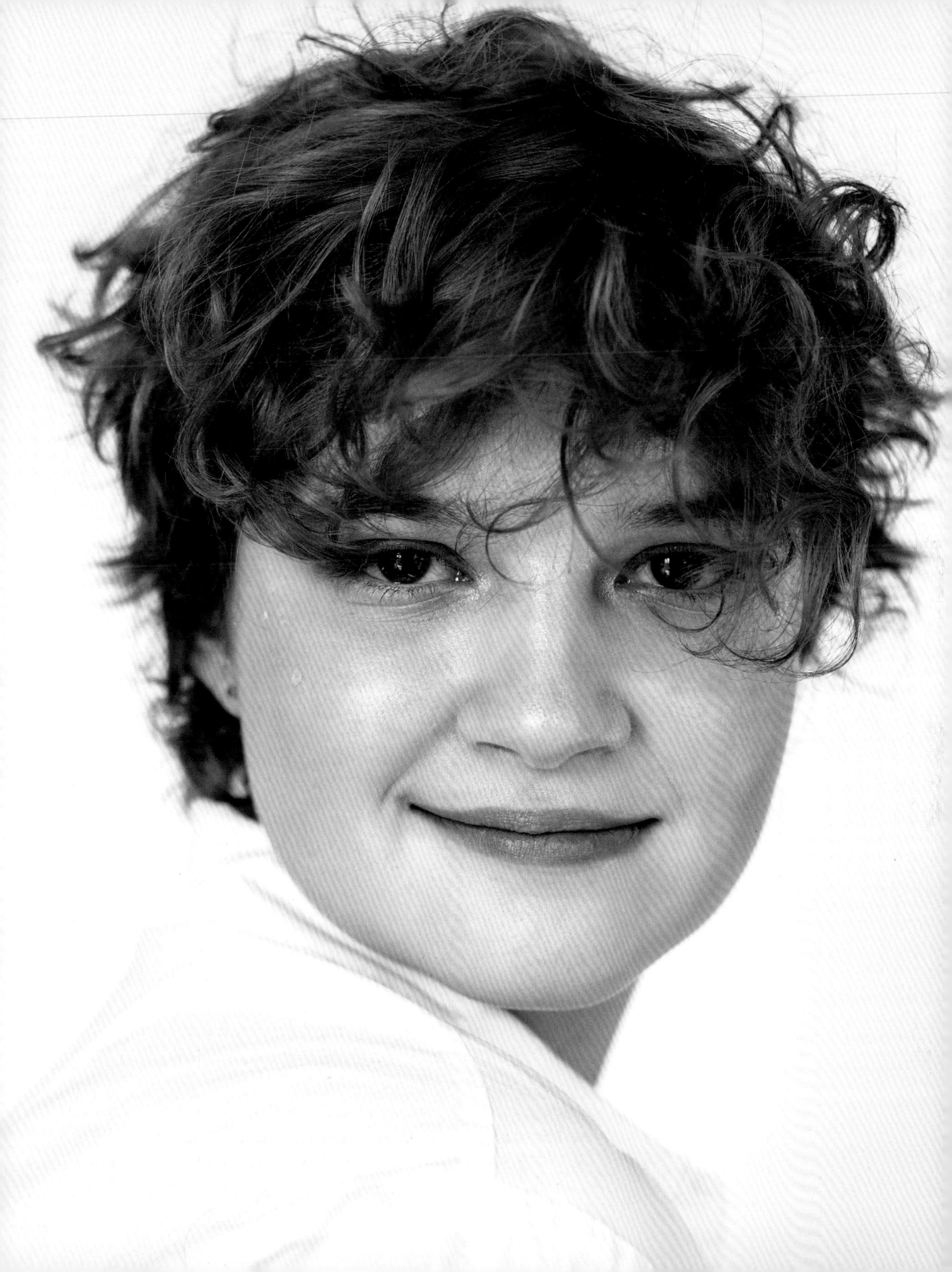

about it. There were some who didn't understand that just because I like girls didn't mean I liked all girls. I had some girls think that I was looking at them when I wasn't and I really didn't like them.

One day one of my friends outed me to everyone. This really hurt my feelings and it was not a nice experience, but most of my friends didn't care. The first friend that really accepted me is still my best friend today. We go to different schools now but we talk almost every week. They understood what I was going through at the time, and years later they have come out as nonbinary. I was the first person they came out to. My friend called me on Christmas day crying, worried about what people would think and how their family would react. I simply told them that I would always be there for them because they are my chosen family and my safe space.

When I reached high school I realized that I had no interest in guys. Up to that point I had thought that I could form a romantic relationship with a masculine-presenting person. Some of my deepest friendships are with guys and masc-presenting people. Although they are great friends, I cannot see myself in a romantic relationship with them. I have found that when I think of myself in a relationship it is always with a female or nonbinary person.

There is really a mix of people being accepted by their families here in Louisiana. Sometimes it's pretty evident some kids are accepted by their families. On the other hand, there are a lot of kids who struggle at home, including my best friend, who struggles with being accepted by their parents. Some of my friends' parents accept them being trans but then think it is weird they are bi. There are also some parents who are okay with them being gay but then struggle with their kids transitioning and using different pronouns.

While my parents are very accepting and open to trying new things, most of my chosen family struggle with their relationships with their parents, and so I have built up a family that is not blood related but one I would always go to the ends of the earth for. I try to make sure that they know they are heard and loved, because that's what chosen families do.

Making relationships, platonic or not, is hard. When I make friends I never come out to them outright anymore, but I am always afraid that when it comes up it will destroy the bond we have made and they will leave because they don't accept me for who I am. When I was younger it would have hurt me deeply to lose a friend. Now that I am older, I know that the best thing for me is to let go of that relationship. I know now it is not healthy for me to stay in a relationship where friends are constantly berating me for something that is totally acceptable, and I encourage you to do the same.

My best advice to anyone who relates to me in some way, or who is searching for comfort in this book, is to be kind to yourself and to those who support you. If you are in a bad situation, know that one day you can get out.

Remember, I am a real person who is still on my own journey of self-love and discovering my self-identity. It is okay to reach out of your comfort zone and change your identity, even if you're older. I am young, and I could decide that I may have a male partner one day. Even as I write my story, I know it doesn't mean my journey is set in stone.

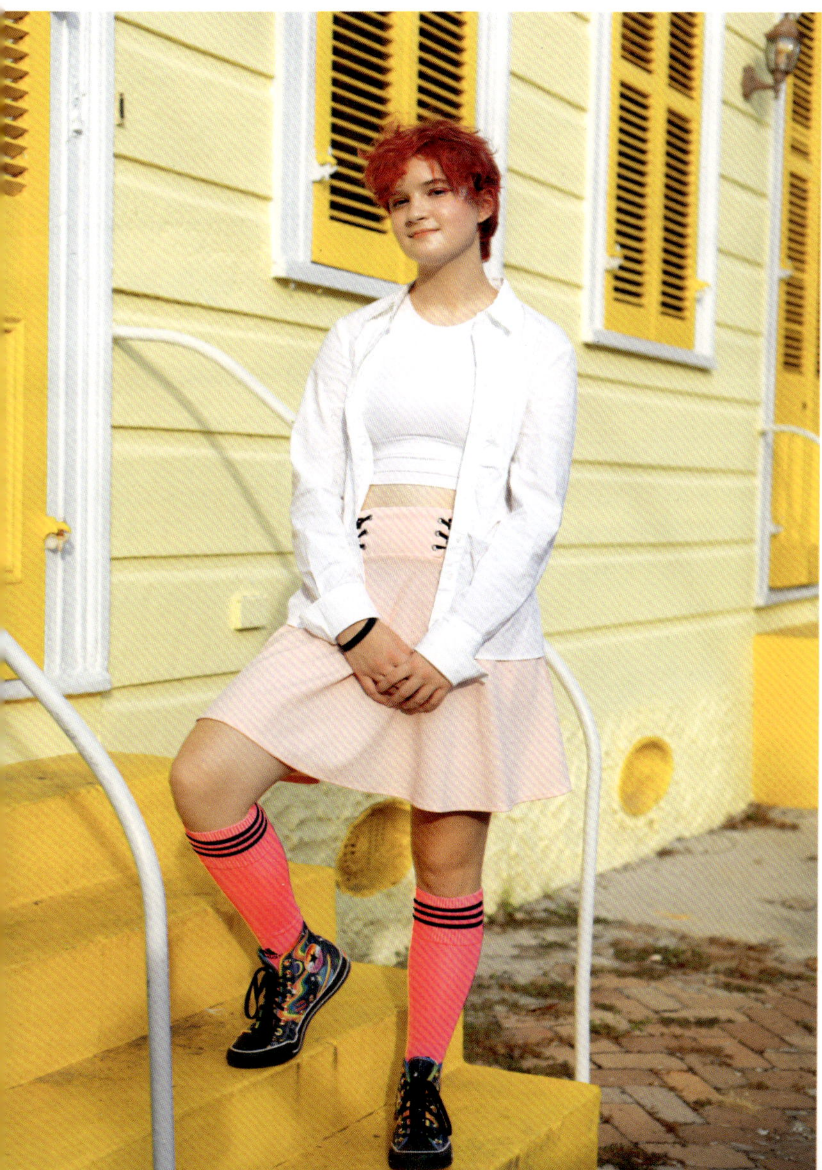

Luke

14 years old, he/him, Utah

What can I say to start? I am Luke. I am fourteen years old. I like math, learning new things, and Dinamita Doritos. I am also transgender. I realized that I was transgender when I was eight years old and the toys and the clothes I was wearing—they just didn't suit me. So one day I decided to talk with my parents about how I felt. I was unsure how they'd react to the conversation. I can't remember exactly what was said, but I do remember them giving me boy clothes and helping box up all the feminine stuff in my room. A neighbor donated clothes that her boys had outgrown, and me and my brother were the same size back then, so we shared. I remember how included I felt in that moment, knowing that my neighbors accepted me. My parents reacted in the best way I could have imagined. As I've gotten older and heard of others' experiences I realize how lucky I am in that department.

As I've gotten older, the challenges I face daily at school have gotten worse. The violence that I see from other students and on TV makes me feel sad. At times I feel guilty knowing how good my home life is compared to others. I have received threats to my safety and threats about telling "my secret." Even though I am "out" I don't yell it from the rooftops, so there are people that don't know and I want it to stay that way. I don't think that everyone deserves to know all about me. I am proud of being transgender but also want to blend in. It is difficult at times knowing who I can trust as a teenager. It's hard to know who the good ones are that will respect you and support you. The GSA club has helped me a little bit with that, and so have the Pride activities in the community. There are still things that could be so much better.

If you're one of the "good ones," reach out to kids that might be struggling and let them know that you are a safe place for them. If you are someone that is struggling, seek out positive people who will help uplift you. If your home environment isn't supportive, find a community that will give you a space where you can be yourself so you can have a break. If you have friends who have parents that are supportive, reach out to them when you are struggling.

It is so important to remember that the things that are difficult today won't always be there.

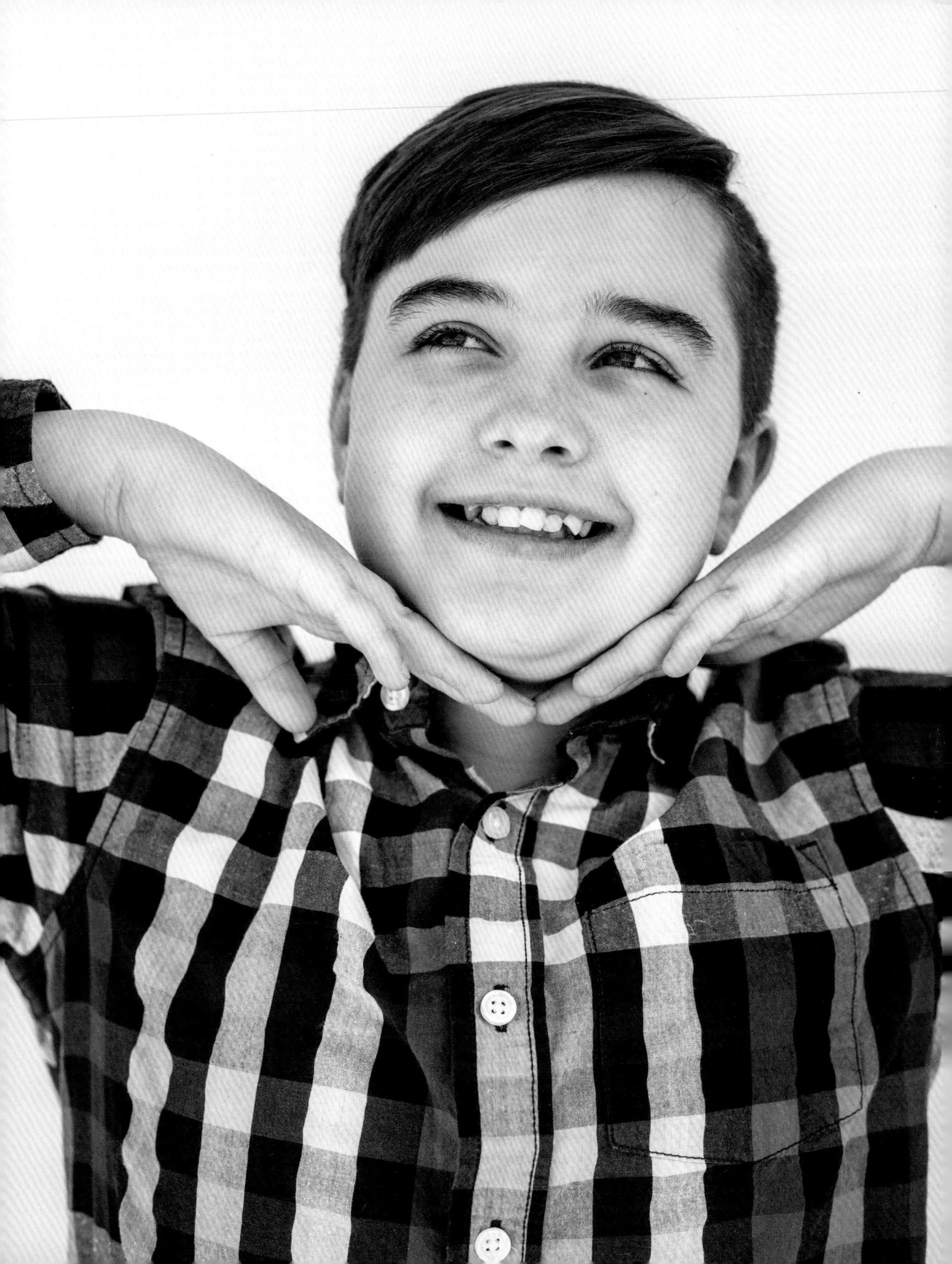

Maisy

16 years old, she/her, Kansas

My name is Maisy. I'm sixteen, I live in Kansas, I use she/her pronouns, and I identify as pansexual. I don't think I've ever written that down before. I've known from a young age that I was not very straight. At first I thought it was completely normal to imagine yourself with people of any gender, but as I got older I started to realize I didn't identify with what regular kids were assumed to be. One could argue it started with Shakira's *Hips Don't Lie* music video, or even just my strong crush-like attachments to both my male and female friends in elementary school; on the other hand, I think I've just always known. Being raised in a traditional Christian family while being queer wasn't the most comfortable environment sometimes. While it wasn't nearly as bad for me as it is for countless others, I did feel the undertones of homophobia from certain members of my family and church.

It took me a long time to admit to myself that I wasn't straight. Back then, I had no idea what pansexuality was. In my mind there were three possibilities: you were either straight, gay, or bisexual. While bisexuality seemed like the best fit then, I came to realize that pansexuality fit me much better: I like people regardless of their gender identity, and I feel that gender doesn't really factor into my attraction to others. By that time I had already come out to many of my friends and family members, so I just sort of decided that it was too late to make another announcement and it was just something I should keep to myself for the time being. Surprise!

Coming out was definitely nerve-racking. The first person I ever told was my friend Carly. We were sitting in the lunchroom, and I dramatically-yet-discreetly whispered across the table that I was bisexual. My first coming out experience was positive, albeit somewhat silly. It's such a vulnerable experience to lay bare such a big part of you and not know how someone is going to respond. While it is scary, it can also be extremely rewarding. On more than one occasion I've come to realize that I have just gravitated toward friends who were like me without even realizing. I've also discovered that I was surrounded my whole life by people in my family who have gone through similar experiences to me. I was extremely surprised that, when coming out, I found out some of my siblings were also queer. In hindsight it was glaringly obvious, but

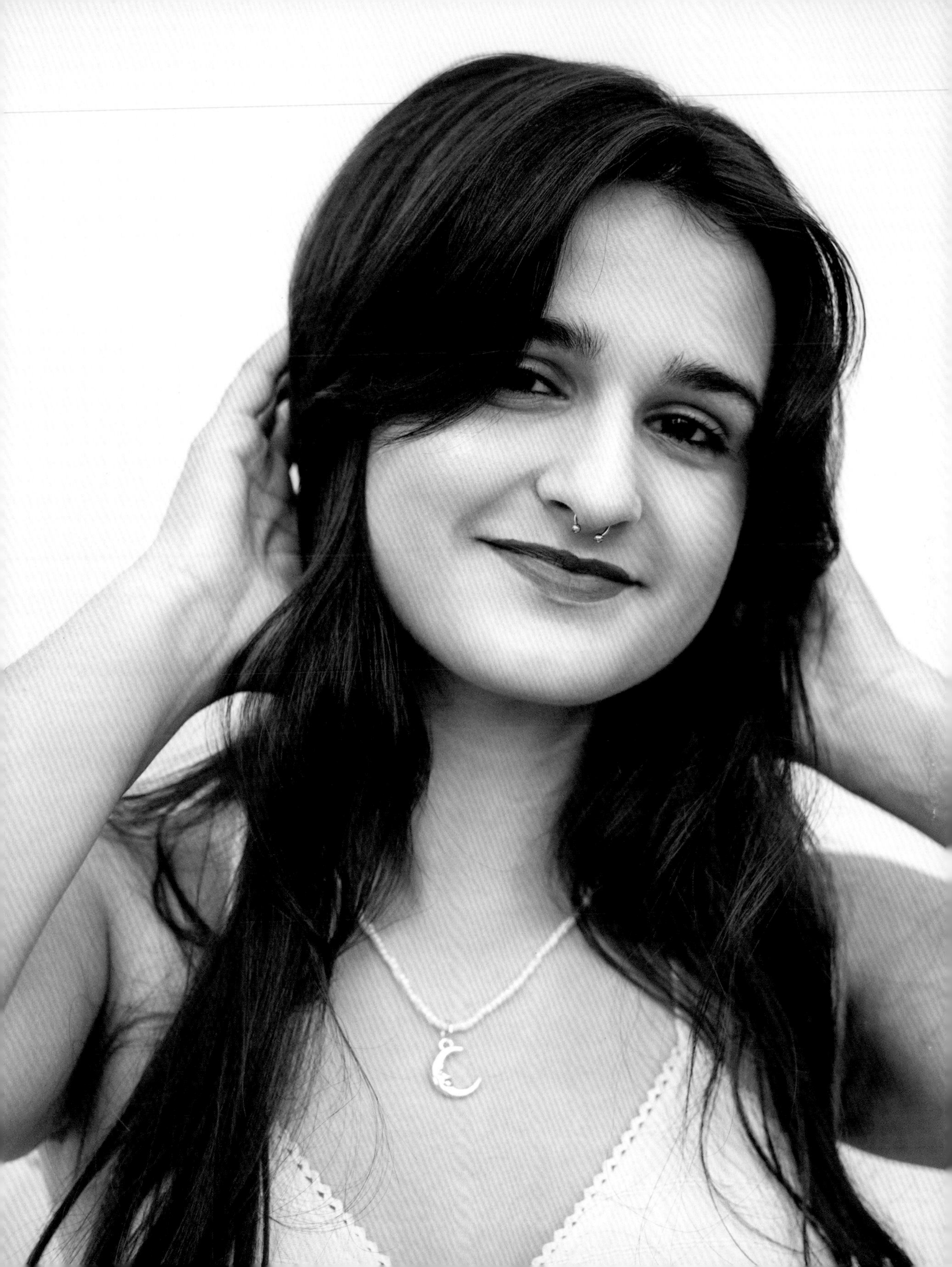

it's interesting to think about how we probably all thought we were alone in that regard.

While I've had mostly positive experiences coming out within my own community, it's certainly challenging to be a queer teen in Kansas. There are definitely accepting people at my school, but it's not uncommon for people to be neutral or homophobic regarding the LGBTQ+ community and their rights. It's completely normal for people to use *gay* as a derogatory term, laugh and judge gay relationships, and even say slurs without being reprimanded or acknowledged by adults. While I call people out whenever I see that behavior, it's tiring when you're the only one in the room who speaks up about it. In my town and school, a completely normalized stigma exists around gay relationships, even among teachers and authority figures. I could count on one hand the number of times teachers have mentioned being accepting of all sexualities or proclaimed a no-tolerance policy for bullying of that sort; when a teacher does do that, I don't think they know how meaningful it really is. When it comes to sex education, I have no experiences of teachers talking about safe sex for same-sex relationships or anything related to gender and sexuality identity. My mother did a presentation to the school board about the lack of inclusive sex education in the school system using my school health textbook as an example.

Although being out comes with its hardships and trials, it has made my life all the more fruitful. I've come to find out that the people who really love you will still love you after you tell them, and anyone who doesn't is not worthy of your time or energy. It is also okay to not be okay when someone you value does not respond to or accept you how you thought they would. We've all been there, and although we shouldn't be used to it, you're not alone in that experience. You are not a sin, or a stereotype, or a phase. If you haven't heard it already (or you haven't heard it enough): you are valid, you are loved, you are brave, and I'm glad you're here.

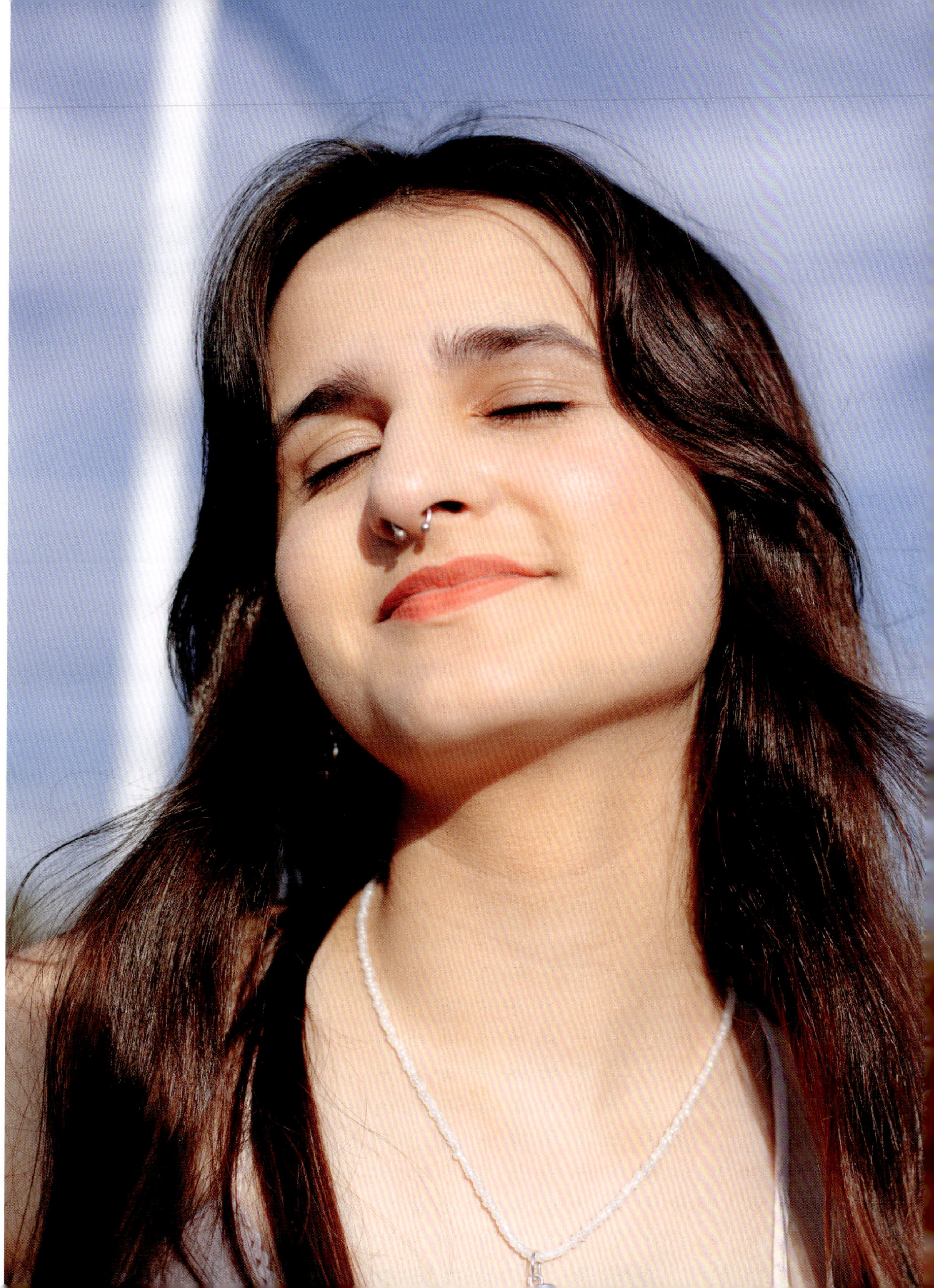

Malachi

16 years old, he/they and she/her, Wyoming
CW: This story contains brief references to suicide ideation.

Hello, my name is Malachi—many call me Mal. I am a sixteen-year-old gay student who is currently in high school. My pronouns are He/They and, when I'm in drag, She/Her. I am from Riverton, Wyoming, living on the Wind River Reservation. I am Native American and have been raised through our teachings. Growing up in my community you are taught in many different ways. You can be raised a Christian or Mormon, or if you're born Native American, you might have teachings that are passed down to you. Most are taught to see only male and female, and never two of the same gender in one person. Meaning, no matter what religion or community you come from, we are all taught a simple binary with no complex thoughts as to what gender could actually mean, no weight given to the thought of a gender spectrum.

For so long I suspected that I wasn't going to be the same as other boys, and I knew that I wouldn't be living up to the expectations of certain people in my life. Starting at the early age of eleven, I could tell I wasn't having the same normal feelings that a boy would at that age toward a girl. I would be minding my own business, seeing others around me liking girls, but I wasn't interested, only confused. At first I thought it was just that I didn't find them attractive at the time since I was still young, but that wasn't the case.

A year went by and I was still very much not into girls. One day, while in class in middle school, I heard that someone I knew liked people of the same gender. Being young and still learning about different things and not knowing about sexuality, I was curious to know more. Later, after talking to them, I had a better understanding about what gay was. My heart was confused, and I was questioning myself, "Am I like them? Am I gay?" I noticed I liked boys a lot. Still questioning myself, I went on trying to decide who I was and how to identify myself. I began seeing a change in how people treated me. They acted as if I was disturbing them because I had told them about my confusion.

Being scared of what people thought of me was normal, but once I began accepting myself it got worse. I started dabbling in makeup. Putting it on in school was the easiest—I could be who I was in school—but I would get caught coming home and forgetting

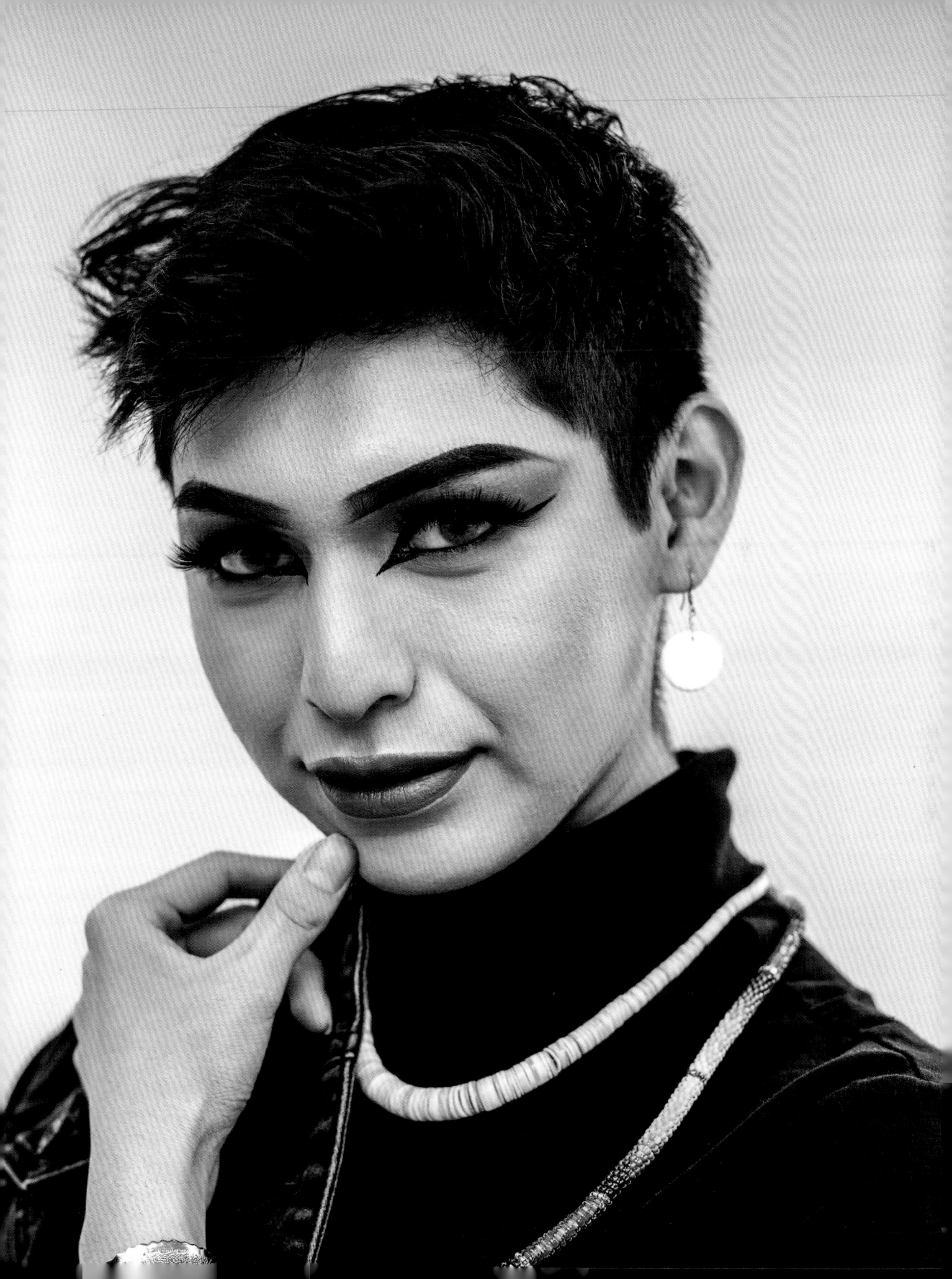

I had makeup on. My parents very quickly started catching on that I might be gay. Seeing my mother cry and tell me I'm not her son and that I was possessed hurt me. Her repeating over and over that I wasn't her son and to bring "him" back made me feel unwanted, like I didn't matter, making me hate who I was becoming. I began going into depression, feeling like a disappointment and like I wasn't meant to be living. I cried and cried, trying to tell myself to stop and to "grow up," but I never did.

I spent most of my first year in high school crying on the bus in the morning, or even in the locker room to hide my tears. I had fully realized that I liked boys. I began trying to show love for myself and taking all those hurtful words as fuel to lift my head high. My safety was becoming a concern to my friends and many staff in the district because I was coming to school so depressed. I began trying to find my safety in myself, and I did. I began showing my ability to do makeup more, and although it wasn't good, I practiced over and over. I felt safe and calm. The more I showed myself self-love, the more impact it had on my health. More people started supporting me and helping me grow, showing me the love that was withheld from me by the people I thought would be accepting in my life. I told myself loudly in my head, "I am gay and proud to be me."

Although things started going a little more smoothly and I began getting more comfortable with who I was and with my friends at school, the people I called my family began falling apart. My parents told me they accepted me, throwing the blame at each other to hide that they didn't accept me, until they had broken further from each other due to their personal problems. My parents' relationship came to an end. I sat by wondering if it was all my fault, but it wasn't. We sat, talked, and cried knowing that things wouldn't be the same as they used to be. At the end of that talk they had told me they loved me and who I was going to grow up to be. Hearing them both say they cared gave me happiness. I cried tears of joy because the close bond we had lost started to mend once they saw me for me.

Bigger opportunities began coming to light; hardship always has light. Life was never meant to be easy. People are made to be unique in their own ways, not to be the same completely. I was not choosing to be gay. I was born who I was. At a young age I had an idea who I was, but I didn't listen. Waiting helped me see me more, and today I make myself and others proud.

My plans in life, now that my life has begun with its spark, are to continue school, graduate, and go to college for business. So,

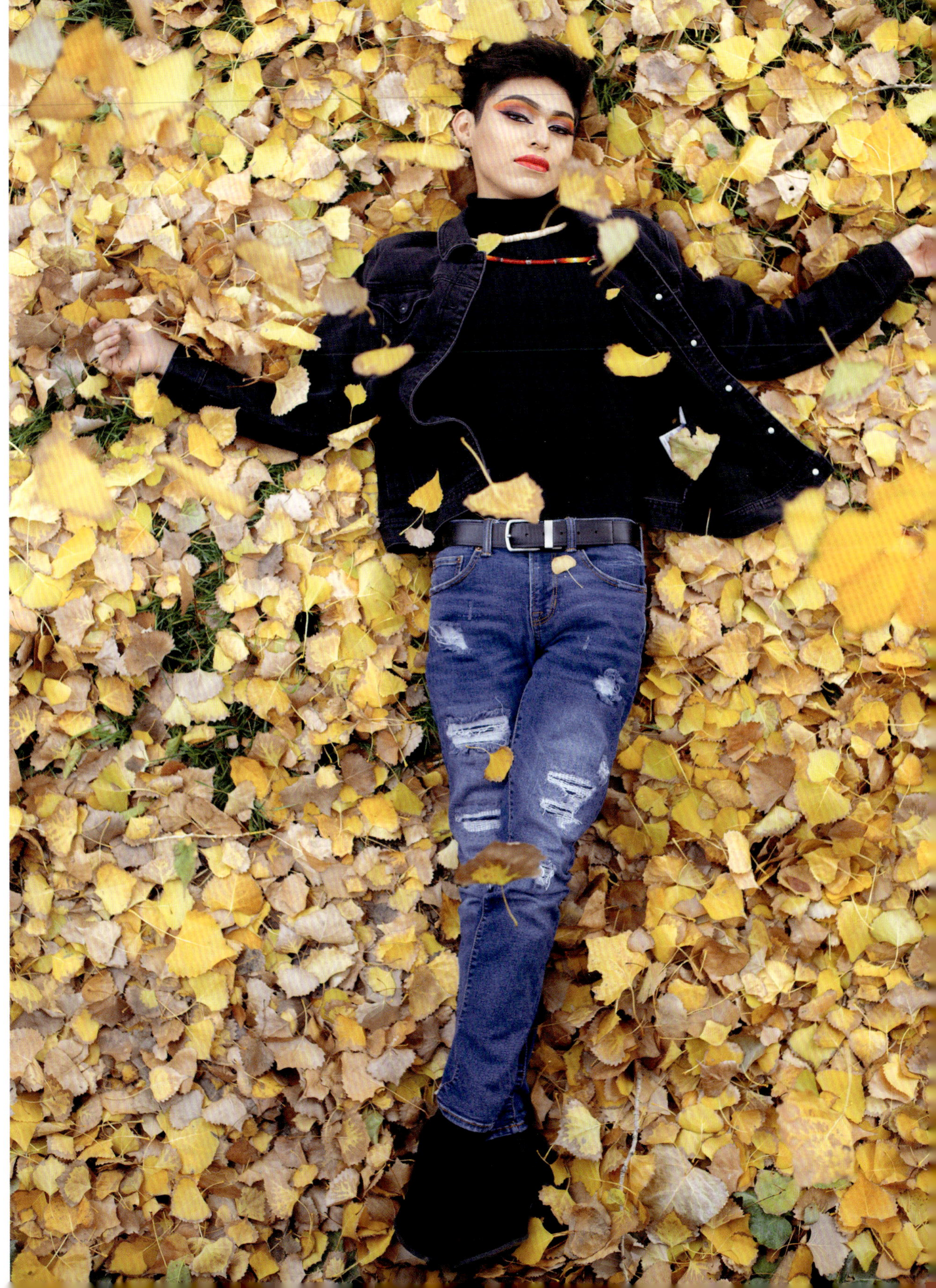

when the time is right, I will be able to begin my own beauty line and become an influencer to all ages because my biggest strength is depicting myself through art and makeup. I am inspired by others and wish to inspire as well. I have had many problems, many falls, and many breakthroughs, but they all paid off. Don't be afraid to stand out in your small community. It may seem hard, but the world changes every day, and we have to as well or we will be left behind. Seize your moment! Native American, Mexican, African American, Asian, European—all races are loved, and if you can't see it now, you will soon.

We are never alone. If you feel that you are, it's okay, but you must see that you're born to be you and to stand out. Although some people may struggle with accepting you, there will be others that will. Hold your head high, my sweet darling, for you are connected to yourself and your mind. You have the riches that are most valuable: strength, intellect, love, happiness, sadness, and more. Rise above, feel your spirit—we are all here for you.

If you are struggling with coming out, don't rush it. Take your time, start slow, and make sure you know who you are. Confusion is strong, but you can overcome it. Things take time, and it's not meant to be easy. The friends you have will love you. The ones that don't? Just remember they lost a beautiful and amazing person. Don't feel rushed and don't feel lonely. You are loved and it will all unfold for you.

Maleah

17 years old, they/them, Utah

I'm Maleah. Nice to meet you. I am seventeen years old and living in St. George, Utah. My pronouns are they/them, and I identify myself as a lesbian.

I grew up in California and moved around a lot. I lived in a very conservative area with my grandpa, and I attended a school that didn't have a lot of diversity. In about second grade I discovered that I liked girls. There were two cute girls in my class that I had crushes on, but I knew it wasn't okay and we didn't ever talk about it. I kept it to myself and never told anyone. In third grade I was in Girl Scouts. We were at a park and playing a game that involved getting married. We pretended to get married and the other kids dared us to kiss. I didn't think there was anything wrong with it, so we did, but the other girl got scared and told her mom, and her mom got upset. My mom asked me about it and was obviously not okay with it. It made me feel bad and like something was wrong with me.

In eighth grade some of my friends were talking openly about their sexuality. I didn't realize you could actually do that. When they asked me, I told them I was bisexual. There was a lesbian couple at school who dated on and off. I thought one of them was pretty and we became friends. They had gotten back together, and since I was friends with the one girl, the other got jealous. We had a math class together and she began to bully me. They followed me, took photos of me, and gave me dirty looks. It got bad enough that I didn't want to go to school. My mom asked me why, and I told her without telling her the exact reason. She asked if it was because I liked one of them. I started crying because we hadn't talked about things like that before. I told her that I did like girls and came out as bisexual. She asked why I was crying, and I told her I was scared because I didn't know how she was going to react. She said as long as I was happy, she didn't care who I liked. She was super support-ive, which was really nice. She was the first person I told, and I felt so relieved knowing that my mom, who I'm the closest with, accepted me for who I am and loved me unconditionally.

My freshman year there was this boy, and he was the sweetest kid ever. He walked me to all my classes and gave me gifts, food,

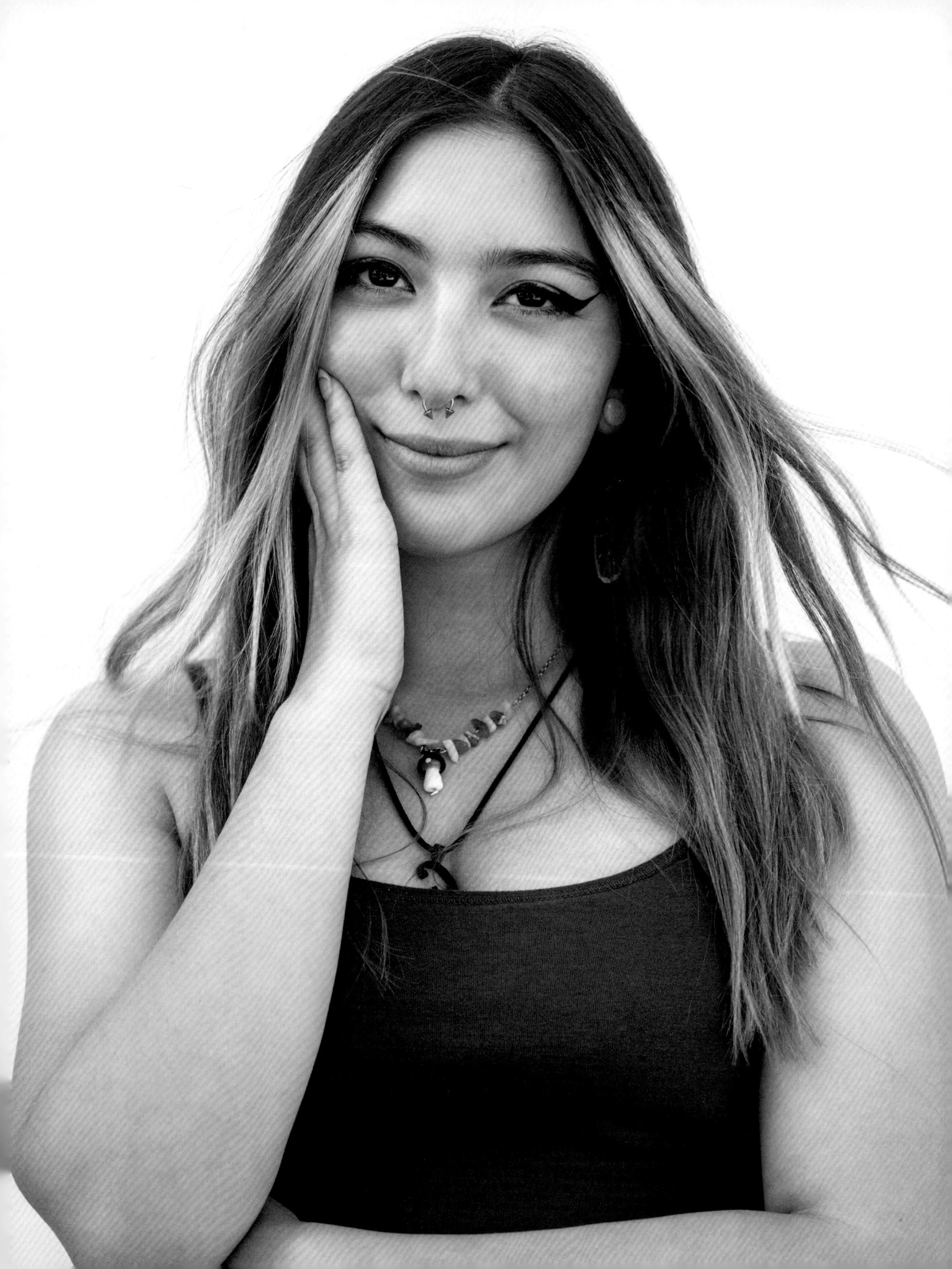

and his jacket if I was cold. We moved to Utah, but I still kept in touch with him. When we visited California he took me on a date. He asked me to be his girlfriend and he tried to kiss me, but I refused. I wasn't attracted to him like that. I just liked him as a friend, but he wanted more. My mom asked me if we kissed, and I told her, "Definitely not!" I kinda had a feeling that maybe he just wasn't my type. When we got back to Utah, I called and told him we couldn't be together because of the distance and that I just wasn't attracted to men. We never spoke again and I felt so bad. After that I told my mom and stepdad that I was only attracted to women and they were very supportive. I didn't come out to my dad until I was sixteen because he's more traditional and I was afraid of how he would react. When I did come out to him, it took me like twenty minutes. He asked if I was gay and when I said yes, he said he already knew. He was okay with it and told me I didn't need to be scared to tell him. I felt like it made our relationship stronger for him to know that about me. I'm not afraid of telling people anymore. I just want to be happy and myself.

I understand that coming out can be a scary thing because you don't know how people are going to react. Come out when you feel safe and to the people you're comfortable telling. You'll know when the time is right.

A friend of mine sent me a text that said, "I think I've already shared this with you before, but this Pride Month is just making me emotional right now. So, in case I haven't, I wanted to thank you. You and Syd really inspired me to be comfortable to come out and really be comfortable with myself and my girlfriend. I have never been around a queer couple my age before, and just seeing you two be so brave made me feel like I could be brave, and it really did change my life. I don't know where I would be if I didn't know you two. Thank you so much for just being you."

I responded to her by saying, "Awww, that really means so much, and even more coming from you. It has taken me a very long time to even be this comfortable, and I will say that Syd has a lot to do with it. At first we didn't know if it was okay for us to just be open about us being together and be affectionate, but it just got to a point where we weren't going to hide our happiness for other people's comfort. I'm so glad that our bravery helped you. It just makes me so happy that we have been able to make such an impact by simply just being our queer selves. If you ever have hard times with your identity or in literally any way at all, please reach out to me or Syd. Don't ever stop being unapologetically you."

It made me feel really happy that my relationship could have an impact on somebody else and make them more comfortable being themselves. And I hope that reading about my experience inspires you to be brave and live an authentic life.

Syd

16 years old, they/them, Utah

My name is Sydney, or Syd for short. I am sixteen years old living at the bottom of Utah in a town called St. George. I identify as a lesbian and my pronouns are they/them.

Growing up in Utah I didn't learn much about the LGBTQ+ community. I was raised in the Mormon/LDS Church and was a very strong believer when I was young. I shared my testimony every opportunity I had. I followed all the rules and went to church every Sunday. Around the age of twelve we had a lesson on homosexuality and it was the first time I didn't agree with what was being taught. I felt uncomfortable and embarrassed because my younger brother was in the room and I didn't want him to agree with what they were saying. I think that's when I began not wanting to attend church on Sunday. I would do everything I could to not go, from faking sick, to sleeping in, to sitting in the car or bathroom during church. I just didn't want to be there. I stopped participating in class. I would distract myself by drawing, looking at my phone, or passing notes to my friends. When my dad stopped attending church and lost his belief, I grew even more frustrated. Why did I have to go if he didn't? Eventually I just stopped showing up to class and would sit in the bathroom the whole time or leave with my friend.

In early 2019 I started spending time with a boy. We had similar interests and both enjoyed art. He was sweet, but something didn't feel right. I got a weird feeling whenever he complimented me or flirted with me. I didn't know why. I tried to force myself to like him because he was nice to me. One day I went over to his house and, when I was leaving, he went in for a kiss and I hugged him instead. I didn't understand why I didn't want to kiss him. I had been wanting to have my first kiss for years now.

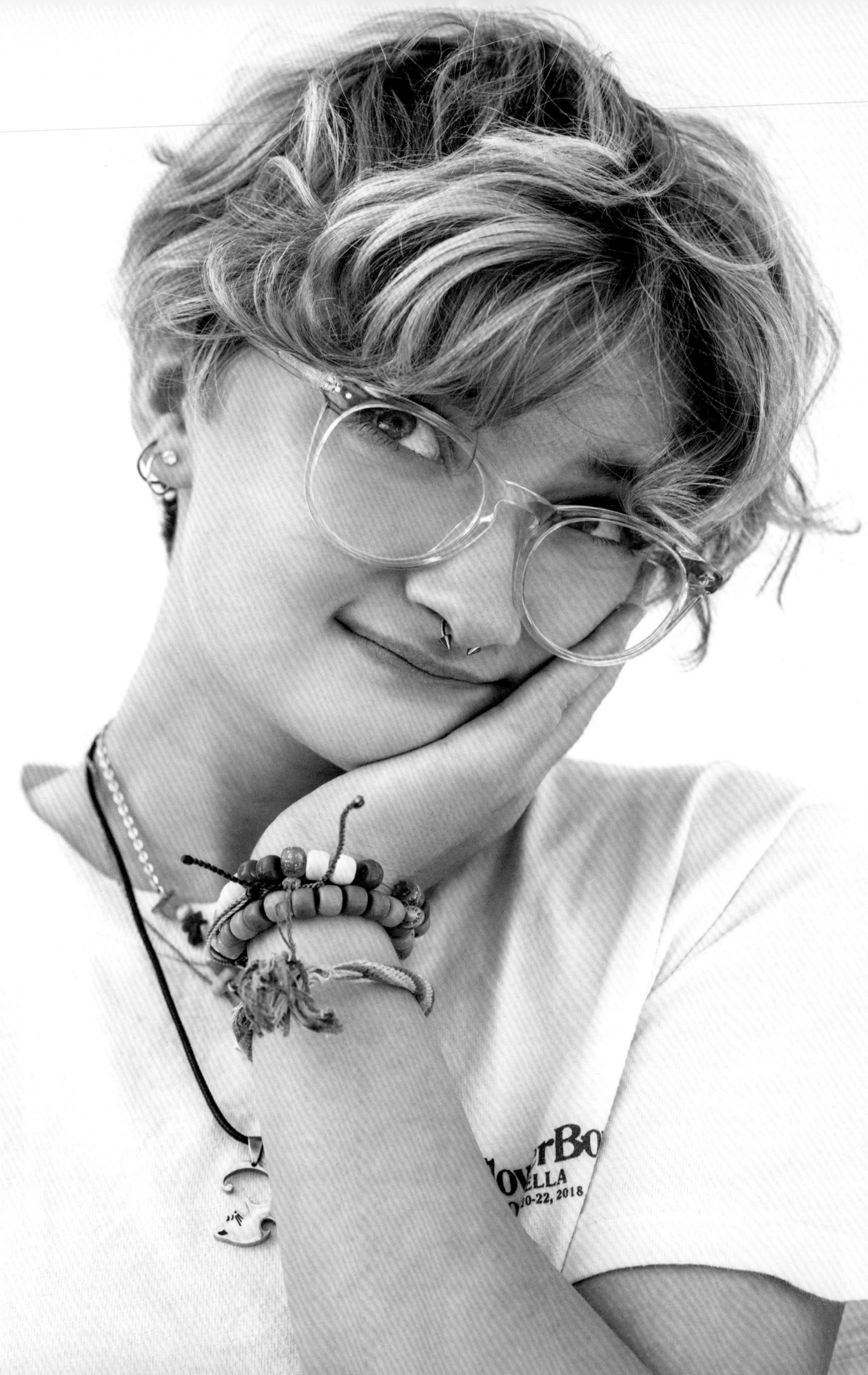

verBoy
OVELLA
70-22, 2018

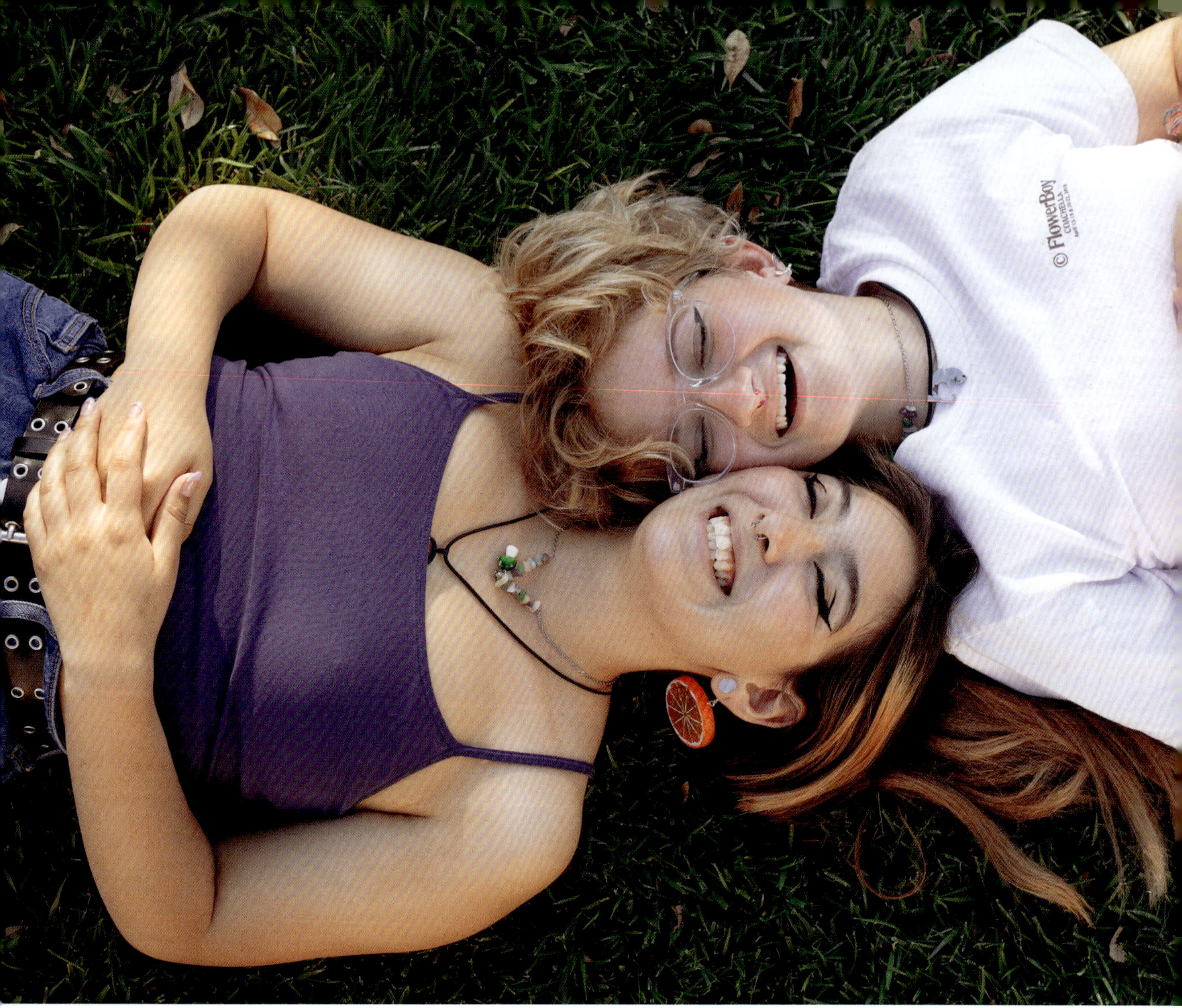

One day we were walking together in my PE class and I was looking at the freshmen. I saw this pretty girl and I stared at her for like twenty seconds. My face got all hot and I completely forgot that I was standing next to the boy I was supposed to like. I went into the locker room and sat on the toilet for five minutes thinking about why I felt that way. And it hit me . . . I like girls. I kept it a secret but eventually ghosted my "boyfriend." I felt bad, but I didn't like him and didn't know how to tell him. In my mind, telling him would make things worse.

Summer of 2019 I had a lot of time to myself to think about my orientation. I came out as bi to my mom through a letter. Of course she was kind and supportive of me. I went through seven drafts of the letter before giving it to my mom. I was so nervous because we had never really talked about it, and I wasn't sure how she felt

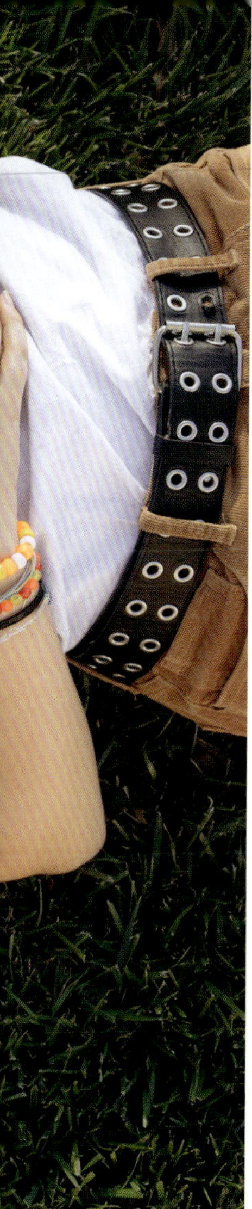

about the LGBTQ+ community or if she would say it's a phase. I felt relieved to know that she was super supportive and didn't think of me any differently.

For my freshman year I transferred to Tuacahn High School for the Arts in hopes of further developing my art skills and for a fresh start. I quickly made friends and started comfortably having crushes on girls. This time it felt right! When my mom was driving me to school, she asked out of the blue if I was really attracted to both men and women. I responded by saying, "Nah, I'm pretty sure I'm just gay."

My first time being public about my sexuality was National Lesbian Day, but most people already knew by then. I felt comfortable coming out at Tuacahn since around half of the student body identifies as part of the LGBTQ+ community.

After I had been out for about a year, I was walking to get coffee with friends when a truck full of four boys drove past and screamed, "F*** you, gay motherf***er!" I instantly felt sick and scared and uncomfortable. I was stunned and started shaking while my friends comforted me. We walked back to my friend's house, and every time we would walk to get coffee, I would feel anxious and in danger.

Around summer of 2020 I started talking to a very pretty girl from my previous art class. We started texting every day and I invited them to join me at the cat shelter that I volunteer at each week. It was a blast and I enjoyed every second with them. We started hanging out more often after that, and on June 30 they were at my house and I finally asked them to be my girlfriend. I have never been so happy! I love every second I spend with them and I'm so lucky to have them in my life; they make me so happy! I have learned so much from them. It feels so good to finally get to be my true self and love who I love.

My message and advice to you is be yourself. Don't let anyone tell you what you should or shouldn't be. That's for you to decide. If you aren't feeling supported at home, there are so many opportunities to connect to the LGBTQ+ community. Reach out to people who love you no matter what. I promise someone is always there for you. You are never alone.

Syd

Markus

17 years old, he/they, Alaska
CW: This story contains references to self-harm and suicide.

Hello. My name is Markus. I am nonbinary/transmasc. My pronouns are he/they and I am eighteen years old. I've lived in Anchorage my whole life; I've never called anywhere else my home. When they hear "Alaska," most people think about the beautiful views, the nature, the wildlife, and the outdoor activities. Of course no one can deny that those are the defining features of this state, but, as a minority, I have a couple more important things to add to that list. The words that I put onto these pages don't belong to me alone. These are things that every single person like me has thought or wanted to say. I want you to understand that everything you've been told is wrong, because I know what happens in this small community better than most.

To help you understand my point of view, I'll take you back to the very beginning of my life. I'm African American and Alaska Native; however, I was adopted into a white family at birth. I really couldn't ask for better parents, and I don't like to think about what my life would be like if I hadn't been adopted. But this hasn't necessarily made my life easier; if anything, it's given me the unfortunate responsibility of teaching myself what it's like to be a minority.

My mom and dad never forced anything on me, such as religion or different beliefs. They taught me the importance of education and maturity but always encouraged me to make my own decisions. I was in seventh grade when I came out to my parents as bisexual. I wasn't nervous or afraid to tell them because I knew that they supported me either way. We had already been through so much together. They accepted me of course, which is something I'm very thankful for because I know that many people my age have struggled with coming out to their parents. I wish that everyone put in as much effort to be good parents as mine did.

In middle school all the problems I was born with really hit me at the same time. Hitting puberty was the main reason, but I had experienced bullying and hard times even before them. For about two years I struggled with self-harm and suicidal ideation. I was in and out of therapy, tried different medications, and visited the ER quite regularly because I was a threat to my own safety. Eventually, on one of my visits to the hospital I was admitted to inpatient therapy.

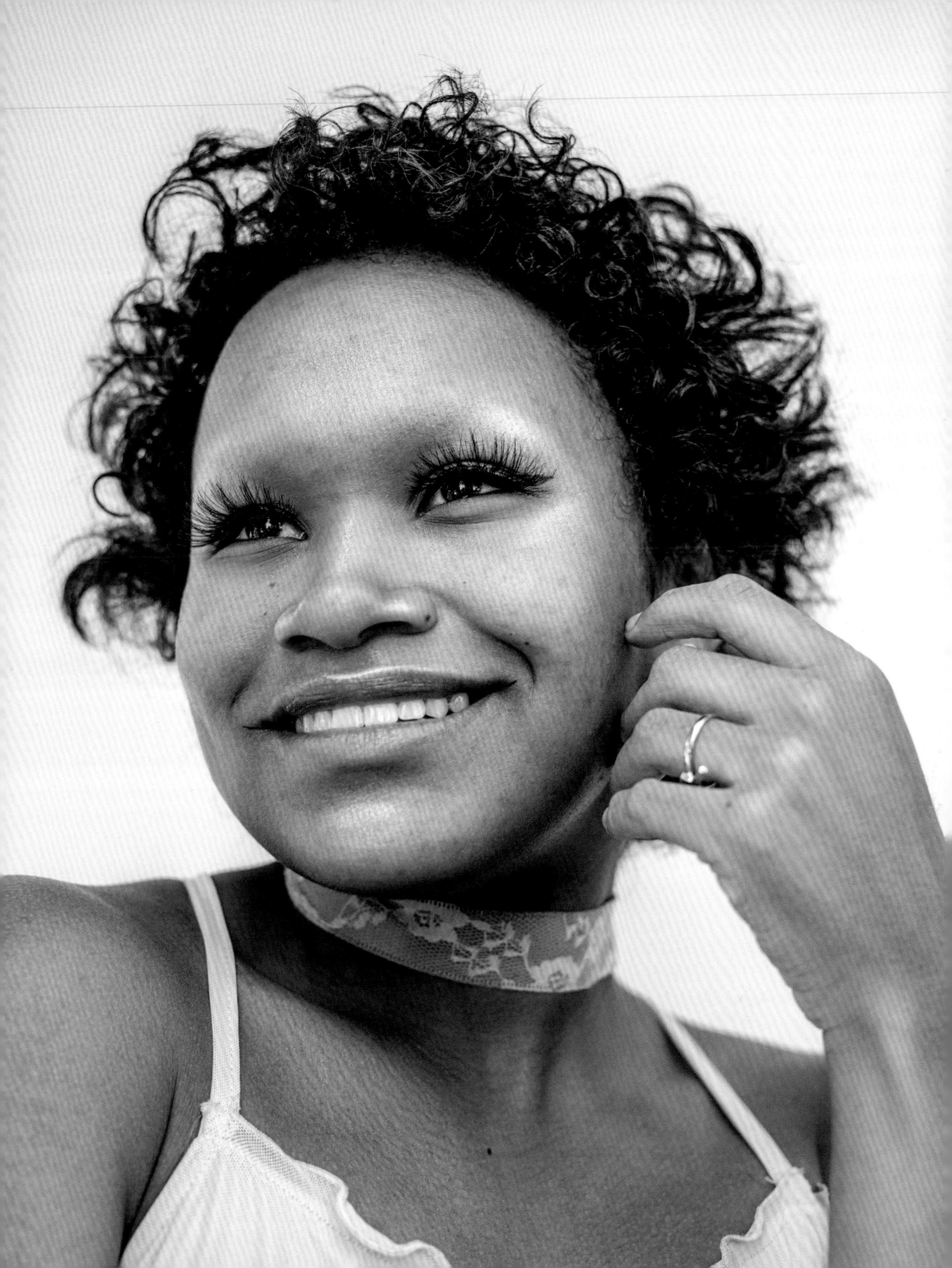

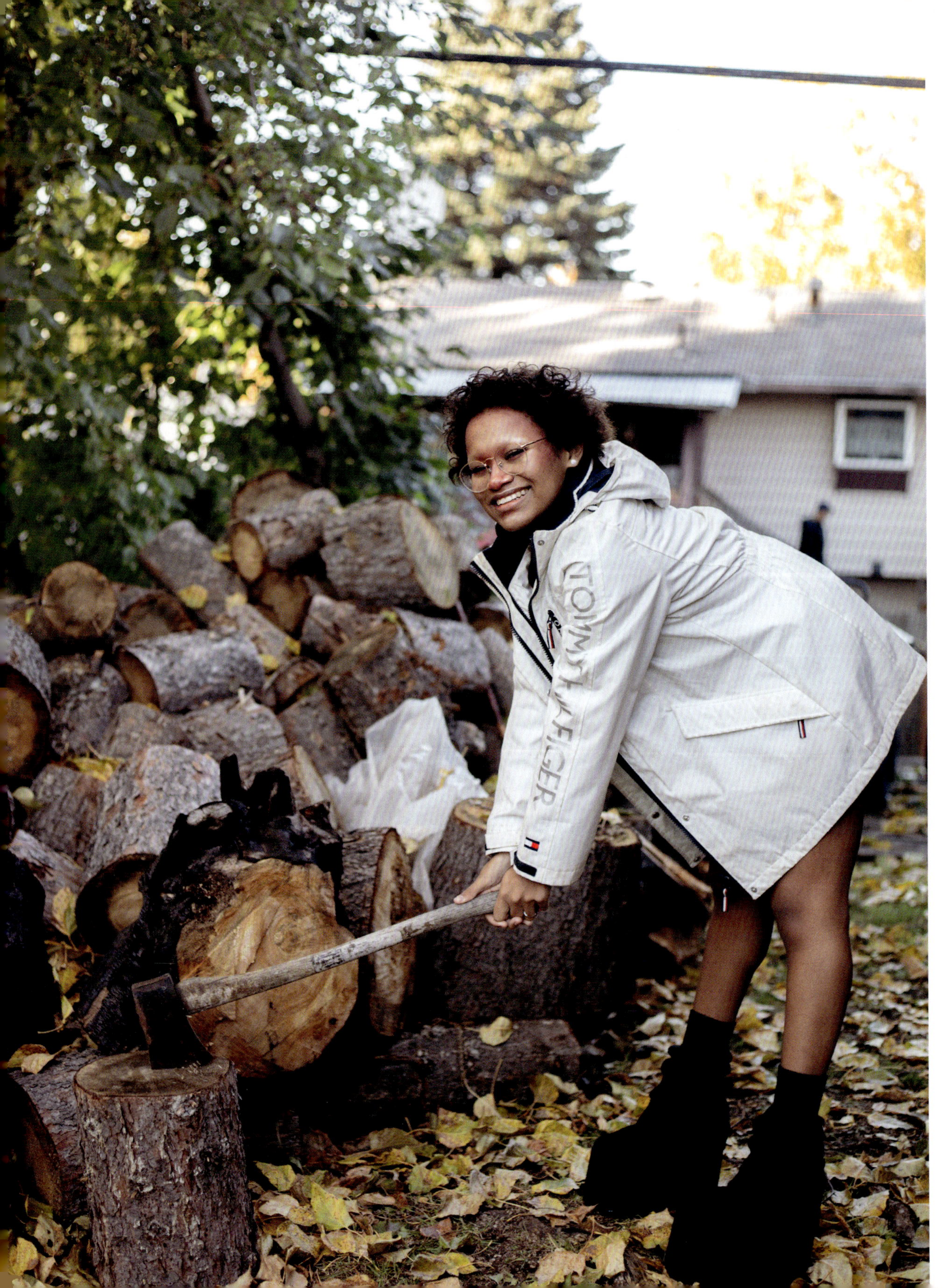

My second time being admitted was less than a year later. I spent about a month there, and luckily I was able to make it—barely—to October of 2018. It was right before my fifteenth birthday when I went into a residential behavioral treatment facility. At this point I thought that I was beyond help. I had been trying to get better for years and nothing seemed to work.

During my stay at this facility I really started to question my gender. I knew for sure that I was bisexual, maybe panromantic. My gender was always a weird thing for me to think about. I hadn't shown any "signs" of being transgender as a child, but I started to realize that feminine and female are not the same thing, so I tried out different gender identities.

It was clear to me then that I had never been female. To me, being feminine was a performance, sort of like being a drag queen. Female just wasn't a label I was comfortable with. Being trans was perfect: I could identify the way I wanted while still being able to be myself. Being a trans man who still presents very feminine was, and still is, very confusing to most people. The best way I can explain it is that I'm just a feminine male. I do wish I was cisgendered sometimes, but being trans is such a large part of my life, and it's not something that I want to hide.

I stopped caring about what other people thought about me when I started high school. I had already been bullied and survived the hardest part of my life so I had nothing to be afraid of. Coming out to my friends was easy, and so comforting. Many of my friends had been out in the LGBTQ+ community for years. Having a group of people who genuinely care about you, even when you don't care about yourself, is so important. It makes the experience of being yourself that much more special.

May 2020 was a turning point in my life. My greatest achievement was leading the very first Black Lives Matter protest in Alaska. It was a beautiful moment and it touched my soul to see so many people actually care about what minorities had to say. It was the first time I had seen something like that in my community. After the killing of George Floyd, I was enraged that people in my state weren't reacting, but I realized that if no one was going to do it, I wanted to do it myself. I had never participated in a protest, and having my first experience being in one as the leader was electrifying. There were a couple hundred people, which is an amazing turnout for only a couple days' notice. It was the first time I had acknowledged my identity as a Black indigenous trans male in public. It was the best moment of my life. I felt accepted and loved by everyone there. It felt exactly how I imagined it would, and it was what I needed to do to begin to accept myself.

Being an activist in my community is so important to me because I was given this body and this mind for a reason. I have faced racism, homophobia, ableism, sexism as a female, and transphobia as a male. I've been treated terribly by those who I thought cared about me. I've fought my own mind. I've been called every name in the book. I've even been sent death threats. But, at the end of the day, it has all been worth it. Being able to protect others and stand up for them, being an inspiration to my peers and a support to my friends, and being able to do literally anything I work for makes all my struggles worth something. It wasn't all for nothing.

I know how hard it can be to imagine the future when the present is so dark, but pushing through it all is so important. Because who knows, maybe someone can benefit from hearing your story too. There are people who love you and are waiting for you in your beautiful future.

I have been to the darkest part of my life and came out on the other side. Sure, I have mental and physical scars to show for it, but they remind me of my own strength. I just turned eighteen years old and, as I'm writing this, I am only a couple days away from moving into an apartment with my partner. I have a stable job and decent grades. And, most importantly, I have dreams and hopes for the future, which is something I never had before. My life hasn't come to an end just because it settled down.

I am beginning my story. This is just the foreword.

Marshall

18 years old, he/him or ze/hir, New York

My name is Marshall and I am a transsexual gay man. My pronouns are he/him or ze/hir, I am eighteen years old, and I live in Buffalo but grew up in Lancaster, New York.

Lancaster is a suburban town around fifteen minutes from Buffalo. It was so, so isolating for a plethora of reasons: I was low-income for most of my childhood, I grew up as a child with an undiagnosed learning disability, and I was the "fat kid." Now add being gay and transgender to that fun mix and you've got the perfect storm for a weird kid who didn't have a group of friends until high school. It was very, very traumatic for me, and I didn't have much support until I got to high school and began going to our school's GSA, where I met my first out-and-proud trans man. His success and ability to thrive as a trans man showed me that I didn't need to restart my life when I graduate, and that coming out wasn't a guaranteed failure. Meeting him literally changed my life, and I am so eternally grateful for everything he's done for me and for having the honor to be his friend.

But a few years before that I first came out as transgender to my cousin, basically to test the waters. We're both the same age and we have always been close, so it wasn't too nerve-racking. I told her that I was trans and was trying to pick a name. She told me that I reminded her of a character from a cartoon we both loved, so for probably seven or eight years now I've gone by Marshall, which is that character's name. I really was out only to her for a while after that. She was my first true ally.

When I felt ready to come out to my parents, it was the summer between my freshman and sophomore years of high school. At this point I had met my trans friend who inspired me to come out. Me and my guidance counselor had a meeting with my parents, and she helped me advocate for myself and explain my identity to my parents. While they didn't fully "get it," it at least opened their minds to learning about trans identity. They let my teachers know I was trans and used he/him pronouns, I changed my name at school, and I started to live and dress as male. It took a little while, but with some elbow grease (and a lot of hard conversations) my parents and I were able to really begin to be on the same page. I never used to be comfortable with my parents (or family

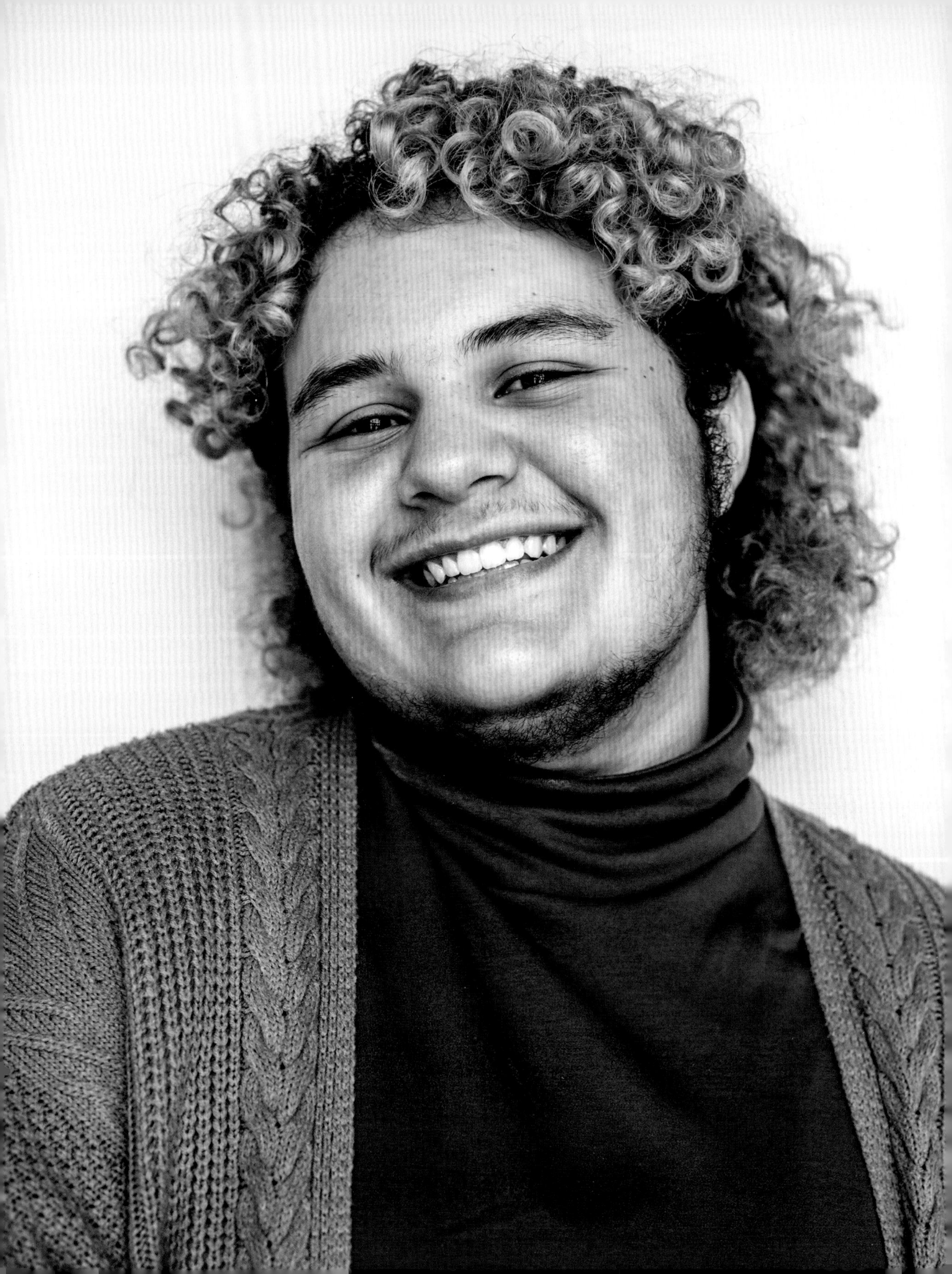

in general), but once I was able to show them the real and true
Marshall, our relationship grew. I am closer with my family, both
extended and immediate, than I have ever been before.

Speaking of family, the name I was given at birth was my pater-
nal grandmother's name. It's an honor in my family's culture to be
a namesake, so my *yiayia* (grandmother in Greek) and I always had
a special bond, but when I first chose my name I was still under
the impression that I wanted nothing to do with my family when I
was older, so I just continued to go by Marshall despite it not being
Greek. When I was finally ready to change my name, my parents
were very supportive and wanted to help me transition legally. We
began to fill out the paperwork, and then I realized I have a middle
name! I ended up making the masculine form of her name, Isaiah,
my new middle name. It was a turning point for me, embracing and
wanting to be a part of my family, as opposed to running away in
fear of conflict. I'm still close with Yiayia, and I don't know if she'll
understand, but I'm okay with that. I still love her, and she still
loves me.

Now to talk about Buffalo: I didn't really participate in the gay
community until I was around sixteen or seventeen, when I began
working at Leaving Our Legacy. They're a youth-led group that
works under a state grant that allows youth to teach their peers
about HIV/AIDS and other STIs. This group is primarily focused
on the city of Buffalo, and I was the only youth in the group who
didn't live in the city. The other members at least sort of knew each
other and went to different community events together (which I
never really got to experience beforehand). I began to go to these
events and then, of course, the pandemic began! So it really feels
like I was robbed of an immersive gay experience in so many
different ways. However, many events in Buffalo are resuming! In
June of 2022 I will be marching with my friends in Buffalo's Pride
parade, and for many of us it will be either our first Pride, or first
Pride being over eighteen.

For every and any queer kid out there who feels like they don't
have a place in the world where people understand, I just want to
tell you that you will find your people. There are spaces that have
people of every sexuality, gender, race, religion, nationality, eth-
nicity, heritage . . . the list goes on. So get in your community and
find your allies and fellow queers! My recommendation for you if
you live in an unaccepting area is to make an Instagram account to
find some other closeted peers, and don't be afraid to jump out of
your comfort zone! Not only will you find your people, but you will

also have the ability to continue the inspiration and help another person who could be in a situation just like yours.

And for all the trans youth: When you finally come out and people use your name and pronouns, it's going to feel like a euphoria you've never felt before. If you decide to go on hormones, you're going to feel incredible that you're finally making that step, but you have to be patient to really see the effects. It is a second puberty after all; think about how long it takes for "regular" puberty. It happens quicker for some, slower for others, and that's normal! Don't compare yourself to your cis peers, because being trans is something beautiful and sacred that we get to cherish. Being transgender, trans, transsexual, nonbinary, genderqueer, transneutral, none of the above, or all of the above is to be celebrated and it's special.

Milo

14 years old, they/them and it/its, Texas
CW: This story contains brief references to self-harm, suicide, and sexual abuse.

My name is Milo. I am nonbinary and I'm queer. I am fourteen and my pronouns are they/them and it/its. I live in the desert (literally) in Midland, Texas. It is a place known for tumbleweed and pump jacks. We moved here a year ago from the Dallas-Fort Worth area.

I lived in the same city my entire life before we moved here. I grew up with the same kids, the same schools—all the things around me were familiar. That's where I came out and where my journey started. It's a more liberal area for Texas. There were the typical shitty kids, and I had my fair share of harassment when I started middle school, but I always knew I had support from friends and principals. Bullies might call me names, but I wasn't going to get really hurt. I felt safe. I was beginning to experience what they call "living my best life" in the middle of seventh grade when the pandemic hit. I left for spring break and never went back. It was horrible. Isolation while you are going through your gender journey is suffocating. So I did what every teenager would do and hid in my room and googled anything I could find on LGBTQN+ topics . . . and cats. Lots of cat videos.

I had already done a lot of research as I was coming out and started to really dig in on my gender identity. I didn't really know who I was or where I fell on the gender spectrum (I am more androgynous now), but I knew who I was not. I didn't fit into the social norms of girls or boys. My body dysphoria told me that without any research.

When we moved, I hated the thought of losing my friends and everything that was normal to me. I was freaked out over moving to a very conservative and non-affirming city in the middle of the desert. I know my parents were worried too.

Right after we moved, my mom found Pride Center West Texas (PCWT). It was exactly what we needed, a community with open arms. I found my tribe: a group of misfit kids that didn't fit into society's standards but came together and could be their true selves. I see leaders in the LGBTQN+ community and the allies that stand with us and it makes me stronger.

I have been in dark places during my journey. I am a survivor of sexual abuse, depression, high anxiety, PTSD, suicidal ideation, and self-harm. Add in dyslexia and neurodivergence and I'm a bit of a

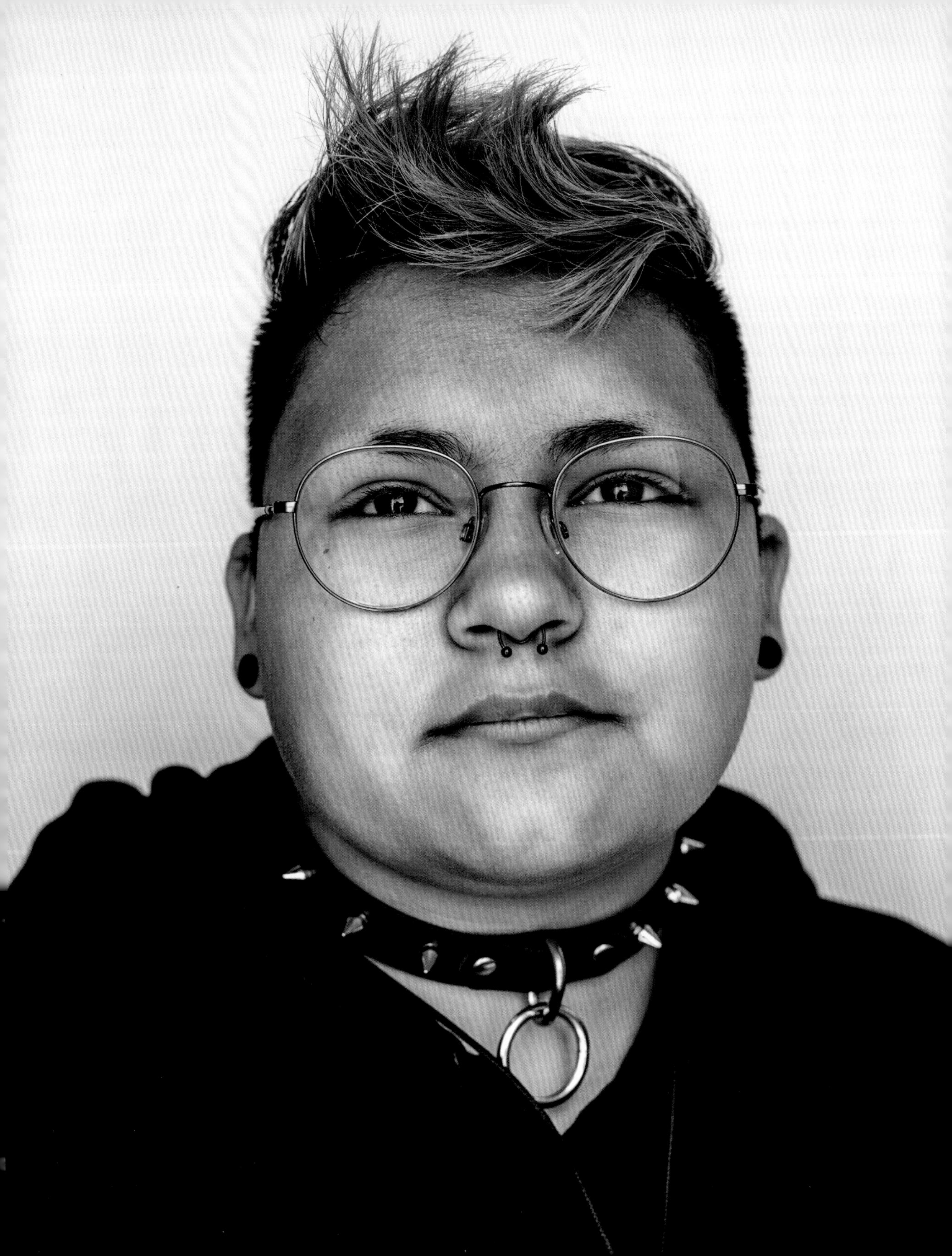

mess. I'm a work in progress. What I have learned in the past year has lit a flame in me that is helping me heal. I want to advocate for those who don't have a voice. I want to fight for not only my rights, but your rights too. I want to help create a world where equality is *truly* equal.

So what would I tell the younger version of myself? What would I tell the thousands of young teens hiding in their rooms for days on end? What would I tell the kid wanting to tell the world who they truly are?

Advocate for yourself. Don't hide yourself. You will know who stands with you and who doesn't. Focus on the ones that stand with you. Don't worry about the ones that don't. They aren't your people. The worst thing that can happen is you *not* being your true self. It is suffocating and it will eat at you every day.

Give yourself grace. Your journey is yours and you are still growing and finding your way. It is fluid and ever changing. Allow it to take you where it does. Some days are hard . . . really hard. Some days are empowering. Listen to yourself . . . your true self.

Give grace to your immediate family as you come out. Most of their pause is out of fear for your safety and a lack of education. They need the time to process, and they need to educate themselves. They will mess up your pronouns. Give them grace. If they choose not to be your advocate over time, remember that *you* are your number one advocate.

Find your tribe. We are out there, whether you live in a big city or the middle of nowhere. Start looking up local or regional nonprofits in your area. If you need help, send a message to www.pridecenterwt.org.

Stay away from things (and people) that are not healthy for you. Substance abuse does not help and is a negative coping mechanism. It is a temporary fix that will have long-lasting consequences. It will not lead you to being your true self or your best self. If you have any thoughts of self-harm or suicidal thoughts, get an adult involved ASAP. I have been there many times. Don't hide it. It will only get worse.

Heal yourself by helping and advocating for others. Find a cause you are passionate about and get behind it. See the bigger picture, not just what's in front of you. It will spark a fire and give you purpose.

Be patient: This one is hard. Change takes time. People take time. Society takes even longer. You need time. Give yourself the time.

So that's me. Me right now. I am not done. I know I am just beginning. I know what it feels like to not see a future for myself. Little by little I am seeing it form. I'm embracing the journey. I hope you will embrace yours . . . fiercely. Find your space. Take up that space. Own that space. You won't regret it.

Nathaniel

18 years old, he/him, Texas
CW: This story contains references to physical abuse.

Black. Queer. *Black! Queer!* I can finally say those words aloud with no shame. In fact, I am an unashamed black, queer male!

Growing up wasn't the easiest for me. Being from one of the only Black families in Boling, Texas, was one thing, but being Black and queer was another. I remember mostly emotional abuse from my dad. Some physical. For me it wasn't easy at all. Some may think they wouldn't have made it in my shoes back then.

Growing up I always felt that I stood out, whether I was speaking or not. I still feel this way today. My body language, facial expressions, one wrong eye roll—it all set me apart from the others. It also didn't help that I was the only open Black, queer male in little ol' Boling.

Ever since I could remember I have always had predominantly female friends. I never remember it being a problem for me. For other little snotty-nose kids, though, it was. I'd get questioned on why I didn't sit with any guys or if I had a girlfriend. I remember feeling ashamed, shy, humiliated, angry. I felt angry not only with the ones asking the questions but also with my friends. In my young mind I felt as though they were obligated to try and derail the topic in my favor. Meaning if someone were to question me about my queerness, or anything related to it, I expected my friends to interfere or change the conversation—but they just let it happen. I was shy. I felt embarrassed. I didn't want to talk about it with anyone at that age or time.

I grew up in a Christian family. At fifteen I'd come out to my parents, not knowing how big a deal it might have been and even ignorant of their feelings about being gay. I had expected them to accept me with open arms, not knowing that would not be the case. I remember always feeling as if I was being picked on and belittled by my dad because I wasn't interested in what he liked, or because I didn't do the things my younger brother did. I didn't do the things he thought a "real" son should do. When I told my parents, their exact words to me were, "You can be whatever you choose to be, but you will not act it under this roof or bring any partners around. *Ever.*"

They were sure to be clear on that. They wanted me to be this person I wasn't. Sweep everything under the rug, which is exactly

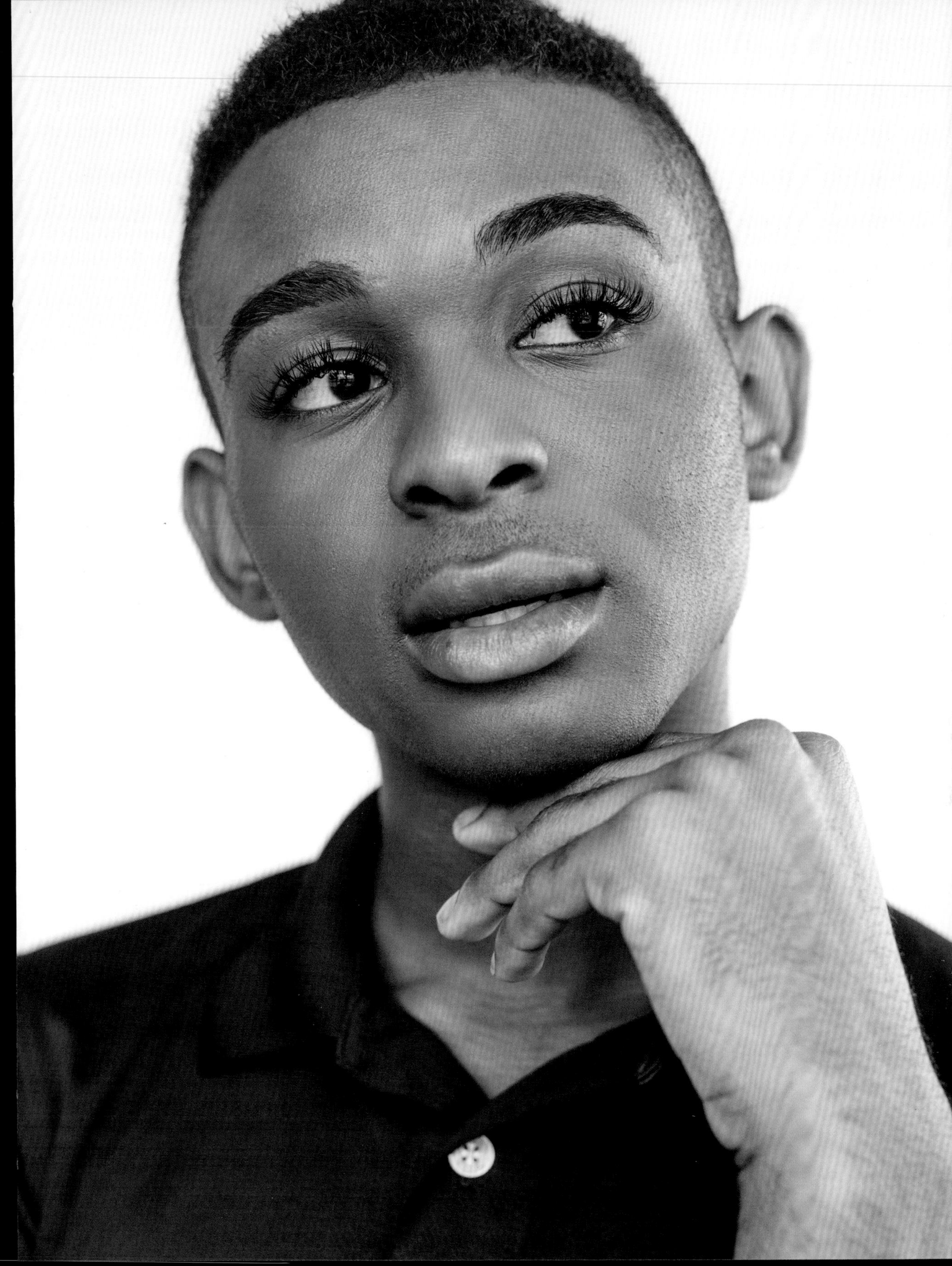

what they did. Swept me under the rug. I was expected to act in a specific way not only at home, but everywhere else too.

After that I did exactly what they told me to do. I acted and dressed accordingly in front of family and friends, and I kept my head down trying to reach eighteen years old. That wasn't enough. By sixteen my dad had started getting violent with me. I was raised getting spankings, but this was pure violence done out of anger. One small thing would set him off, whether it was talking back or looking the wrong way or even my subtle "feminine" eye rolls. One time my cousins from Houston were in town staying with us at our house. I'm close with one of my cousins, a girl. She had no clue what I had started enduring in that house and I had no plans on telling her.

So there me and my dad were, getting into it yet again. By this time it had started getting very repetitive. I remember I had done something wrong. I can't remember exactly what, but I rubbed him the wrong way. I remember he was yelling at me. My normal and instinctive reaction was to put my hand on my hip. That was a total mistake and it set him off. My grandmother, his mom, came running into the room trying to simmer him down and sending my cousins outside. I thought that was my cue to leave. As I began to walk away my dad picked up a trash can and hit me on my head and then my back as I fell to the ground. As I got up my dad began to fight me. As I tried to get away, he ripped my shirt off.

I remember it was pouring rain that day and, regardless, all I could do was run out the door. With no shirt and only one shoe, I ran to my teacher's house nearby. She already knew I was having trouble at home because the school had gotten involved before and informed Child Protective Services (CPS). She always said I could come to her if there were any problems. I spent that night with her. I had no clothes, so she and her daughter bought me two outfits and a pair of shoes. I will always remember that because no one had ever done that for me before.

The next day I went to school and my teacher had to inform the principal and CPS. They told me I had to go back home because there was no other option. Since I was a minor, my teacher could have been charged with harboring a runaway.

After the meetings with CPS I was offered therapy because I was the only gay child. Since I was involved with CPS, they told me I had free therapy for life. They interviewed me and my brother, and after that I never saw them again.

I didn't know how to answer any of their questions. I didn't want to get anyone in trouble. My parents were treating me nicely for the first time in a while, and to be honest they were only ever mean to me. They never treated my other siblings badly, so I didn't want to get them in trouble because I didn't want my siblings to have their parents taken away.

After all of this my grandma decided it was best I go live in Katy, Texas, with my aunt. That was the last time I ever spoke to my parents. I had realized the only reason they were being nice was because they were being watched and monitored by CPS.

As the months went by and I finally left home, I was expecting things to get better for me. Things were starting to look up. I had just graduated from high school. I was preparing for and taking college classes, and I even found myself a job at the local grocery store. I had finally turned eighteen when things began to spiral.

I had quickly realized that living with my aunt was not ideal whatsoever. I lived with her for about eight months before things went sour. Shortly after an incident there I lived with a coworker, Claudia. After two and a half weeks and thanks to a GoFundMe started by my friends, I was able to get enough money to rent a room. Now that I have overcome these situations and have continued to prosper and grow, I hold control of my future. I am currently attending college and still working at the grocery store. I have many goals I wish to accomplish and I can't wait to keep climbing.

I want to share my message to hopefully help someone who is going through a similar situation understand that they can overcome the worst. Growing up I have always been very flamboyant. I may not have known what the feelings or actions meant then, but I knew I was "different."

As I have gotten older and my story has continued, I have realized that being different is unique. I grew up in a place where being Black was different and being queer was different. Now I am gaining back my happiness more and more each day being a *Black queer* Texan.

Nidhi

16 years old, she/her, Texas

I didn't have the most orthodox introduction to the LGBTQ+ community: I didn't know what being "gay" was until I was ten years old, and I had never heard the words *lesbian, bisexual,* or *transgender.* My first exposure to the LGBTQ+ community was the Percy Jackson series, in which (spoilers for an eight-year-old book, I guess?) one of the main characters comes out as gay. That was the first time I realized boys can like other boys and girls can like other girls, a shocking revelation for someone who'd believed since the age of five that to be a girl you had to date a boy at some point in your life. Because of that, I was quite oblivious to the fact that the girls I'd really, really wanted to be friends with throughout elementary school were probably crushes, and the crushes on boys I chose to have were a product of my internalized heteronormativity. But, through fiction and the Internet, I figured those things out.

I still don't know what my identity is; I have mini-crises every few weeks, but in the end, it's too much work for something so intrinsic to me. I go by queer because it's the most welcoming to me, and it fits me well. I've been asked why I chose queer, because it also means strange and unusual, but those are words I'd use to describe myself too. And the queer community has made me feel like I can be as weird as I want to be without judgment or fear, so I embrace that in my label.

The feeling of community is what's most valuable to me about my identity, and I've always wanted to make sure other LGBTQ+ teenagers have that too. That's why I, along with my best friend, decided to start a Gender-Sexuality Alliance (GSA) at our high school. I'd read about GSAs in my search for my identity, and I'd already created a small queer family just with my friend group at school. It is true what they say, that the LGBTQ+ kids find each other, one way or another. I wanted to make it even easier for us to find one another and give us a space where we could be ourselves unapologetically. It was fairly easy for us since there had been a GSA at our school before that just needed a little extra attention to get restarted. Our GSA, though small at first, was one of the most wonderful experiences of my high school career. We did school-wide events, like our Kindness Week, where we had all students post notes on a wall to send encouragement to each other, and

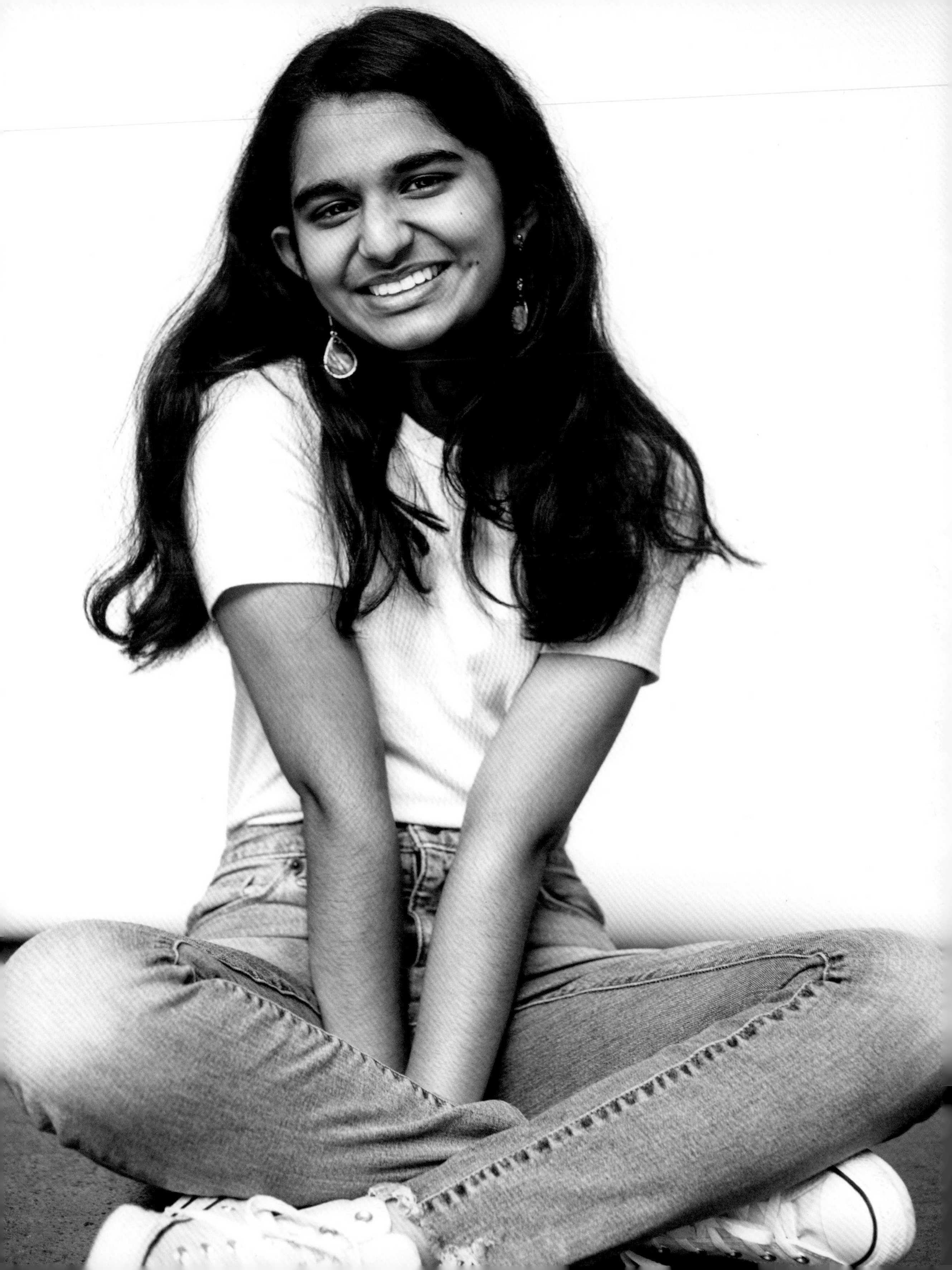

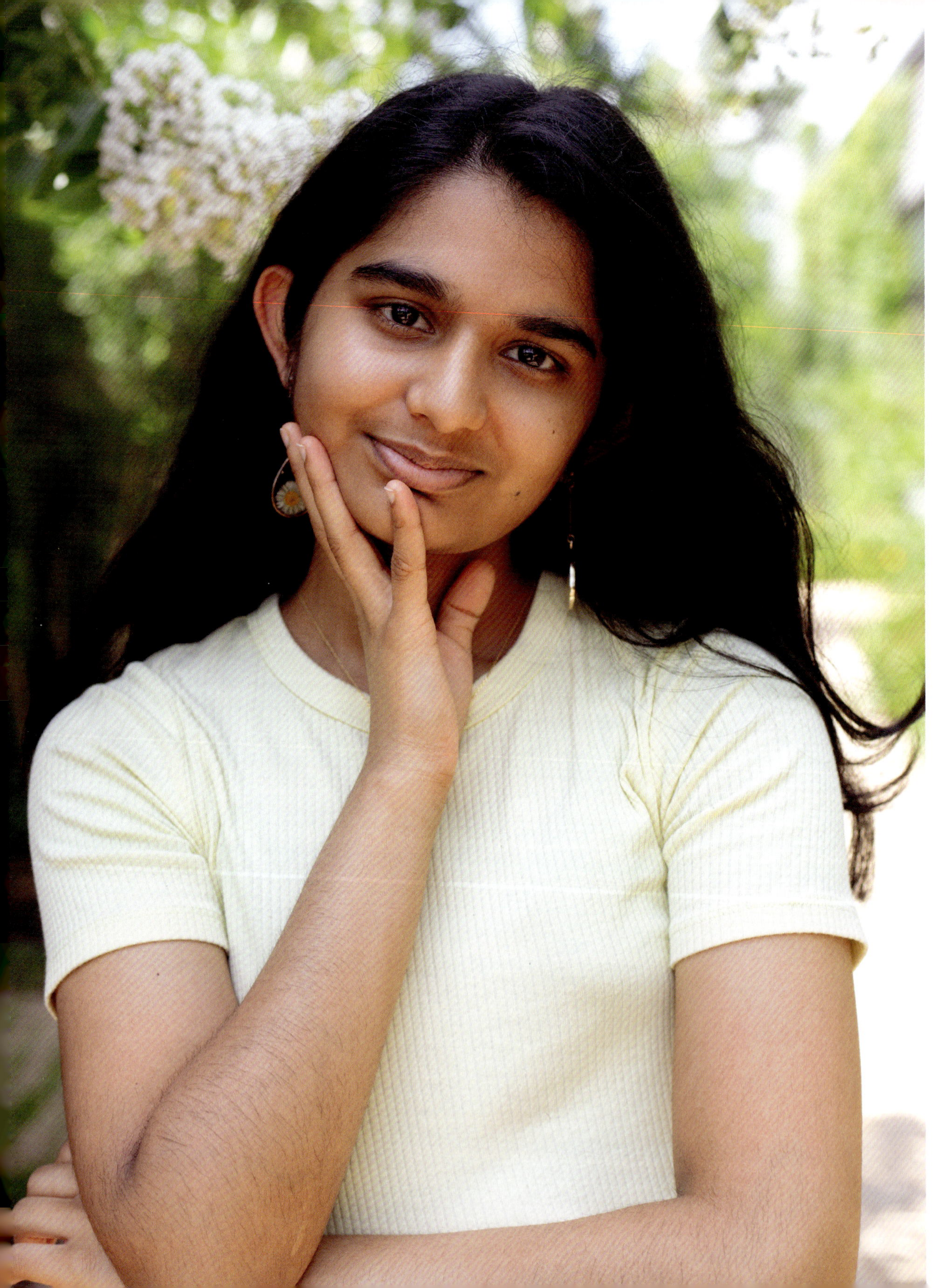

LGBTQ+ History Hall, which was a timeline of important LGBTQ+ figures and events throughout history. Even more fun were the meetings we had: We gave our favorite queer media recommendations, did LGBTQ+ history lessons, had discussions over queer issues, and just hung out and talked about the struggles of having feelings for your best friends, straight and not. In one memorable, ridiculous meeting, we played Shuffle Your Buns, also known as Aggressive Musical Chairs—not queer-themed or anything, just for fun. The most difficult thing was making sure it kept up, even as we went to senior high after our tenth grade.

So we created the Plano GSA, an organization that would connect GSAs across our school district, and we founded new GSAs at schools that didn't have them. So far we have GSAs at all high schools in Plano, a huge improvement in just the past two years. We've taken that to the regional scale now with the North Texas GSA Coalition, and I've gotten to meet GSA leaders across the state so we can work to improve conditions for queer youth in Texas. From a group of a dozen queer kids at a lunch table to a statewide network, my community has grown so much, and it's made me feel more and more like I belong to something bigger.

I haven't had the struggles most queer youth have had. I'm endlessly grateful that my parents are always there for me and that my school, while not necessarily accepting, is far more tolerant than many. It's only because I've had the space and support to do this work that I've even been able to accomplish what I have with our GSAs. If I hadn't had such wonderful parents and friends, I'd still be blindly going along with my heteronormative life. What I can say is this: The queer community is joyous, and I hope every one of you reading this can have some part in it. But always, no matter what, make sure you are safe.

If you want to find your community, here are some things you can do: If you're able, find a GSA at your school. There is no better place to meet people who understand even a little of what you've been through or what you're going through right now. If GSAs aren't a possibility, look for other events, like a local Pride, or a Gay and Lesbian Alliance (GALA) for your area. And, if all else fails, the Internet won't. Whether by watching queer YouTubers or following activists online, find other LGBTQ+ people and remember that you are not alone. You have a community, a family, of people who will accept you and love you for who you are. If we can't be with you right now, we'll be right here waiting for you when you can join us!

Nyx

16 years old, she/they, Michigan

Hi, my name is Nyx, I'm sixteen years old, and I go by she/they. I am also autistic and am proud to be autistic. I live in a house where being autistic is the majority, and have other family members who are too—but one thing that they are not that I am is queer!

The first time I figured out I was part of the queer community was when my family was driving back from Disney World and I asked myself if I was straight or not. Sitting in the car, I tried to figure it out, and at the end I figured out I wasn't straight. I kept it to myself because I wasn't sure how anyone would react. When I realized I was queer it made me a little nervous.

I did tell a few of my friends that I wasn't straight. Before I figured it out my friend came out and was proud of who she was, so I came out to her first. It made me feel happy, but my childhood friend is uncomfortable with some parts of LGBTQ+, so that's why I kept it a secret, and still keep it a secret, from her.

I did know of the LGBTQ+ community before my friend came out, and I would always see everyone's reactions when someone talked about it. Everyone around me would either react in a bad way or they just didn't care.

It wasn't that hard to come out since I am still attracted to boys, so besides the friends I told, no one else got any hints of my queerness. This all took place in the seventh grade. I started coming out to my core group of friends about a year after I realized I was queer. They all accepted me. There was no negative thing about it.

Around the same time my family and I were together around Christmas. My aunt had mentioned something about the LGBTQ+ community in conversation. It wasn't anything bad, just something in passing. My mom then mentioned how we are all allies, then my family told everyone that they were allies too. Then I told everyone, "I'm not an ally." My mom turned her head around and looked me up and down, stating, "Um . . . we are allies." I was adamant that I was not an ally. This started to make my family confused. When my mom repeated, "*We* are allies," I said, "I am not an ally, I'm a member of the LGBTQ+ community." That's when my mom said "Oh! Well, then, why didn't you just say so?" Then everyone was fine with it. It made a funny story when I came out to everyone else.

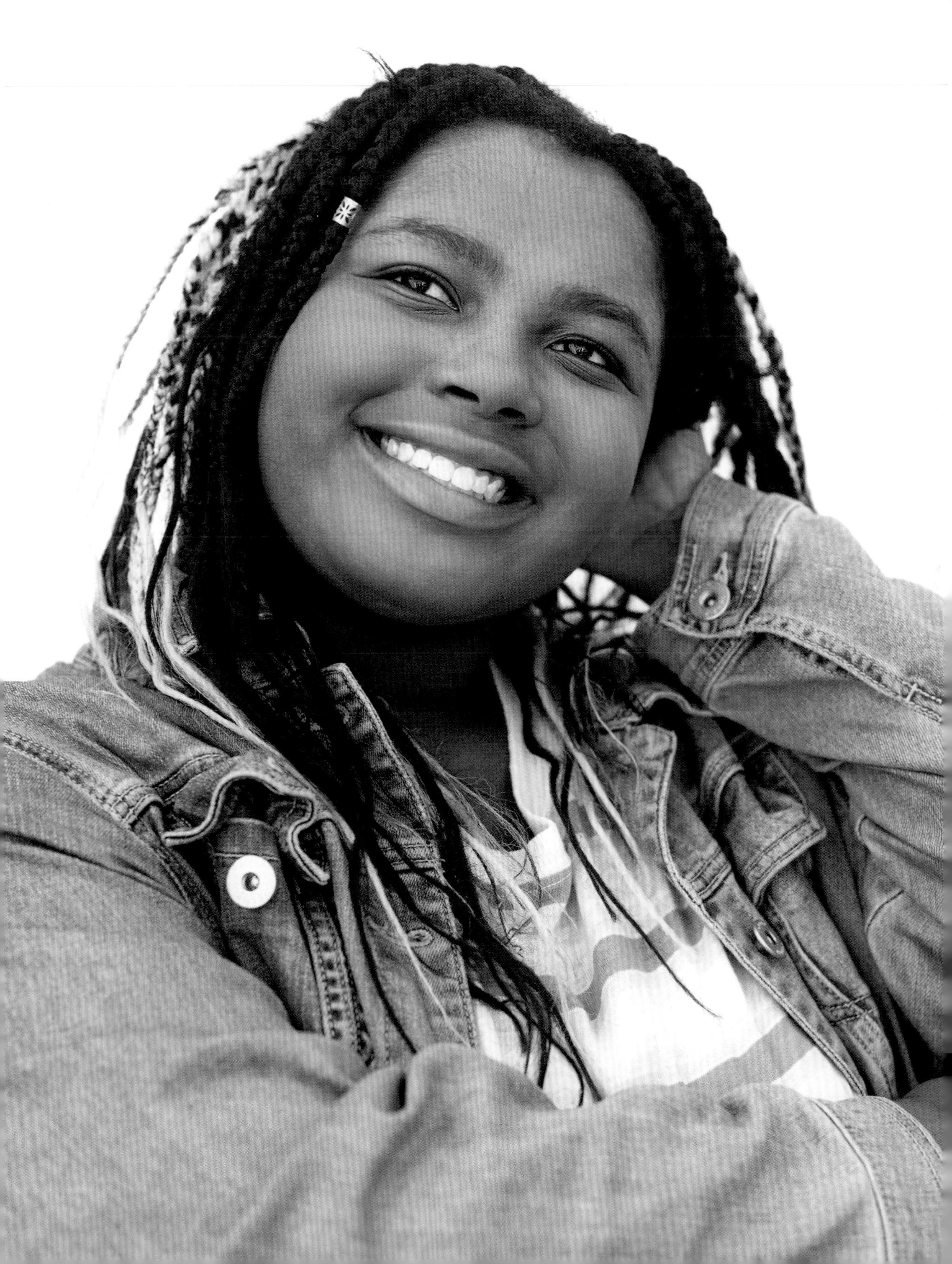

It wasn't a big deal coming out to my family. Afterward, my mom contacted Affirmations in Ferndale and started to help me spend more time with my community at their drop-in center. My mom was already an LGBTQ+ advocate working in our community. She was going to attend a one-day queer summit called BAMM Pride Summit. This summit was a place to help LGBTQ+ people and allies, but more importantly to connect people to youth groups, spaces where I could learn more about myself, make friends, and have fun. Being there was nice. I liked learning more about my community and affirming our lives.

Not long after the BAMM Pride Summit, one of my friends who I'd come out to started a GSA. This was the first GSA in our middle school. Our principal was excited for us to start this. He was hoping it would help more students and said, "I don't know why we didn't do this before." I joined the GSA and it made me prouder of myself.

Growing up in Michigan I had first heard about the LGBTQ+ community on the news when the Supreme Court said queer people could get married. I thought everyone could already get married. I thought it was legal when my grandfather was born and when his grandfather was born, but when it finally happened I saw my community celebrate—even though it should already have taken place many, many years ago! I see some people in Michigan, mainly in Ferndale, who are like me. Where I live it is nice to be queer, and I feel safe.

My journey to discover who I am was like a Cedar Point roller coaster. Wild and scary, but fun. Or like the Disney World ride, The Seven Dwarfs Mine Train. At first it takes off fast and you're taken aback! Then you enter a beautiful room filled with gemstones of different colors. It was sparkly and gorgeous. Then you get *snatched* backward! Life starts throwing you around. It was crazy! Eventually you finally slow down and see more beautiful things, laughing hard and having a roller coaster of a time. That is what it was like discovering who I am as a queer person. It was scary at times, and sometimes you didn't know which way you'd be pulled, but it ended up being beautiful. There are a lot of queer kids still riding this roller coaster, with a lot of different obstacles in their way.

My exceptionalities as an autistic person are only one part of me that makes me unique in this queer community, and I want to be a voice for other queer autistic people like me. My advice to other queer kids would be to take time to learn who you are and love yourself. I will always walk around the house and tell my mom how much I love who I am, and now it's your turn.

Ollie

12 years old, he/him, Indiana

Hi, I'm Oliver. I'm a twelve-year-old trans kid in the seventh grade. I am just trying to get through life. Sometimes it's not easy, and that's the lightest way to put it. Having to go through life as a trans person isn't the easiest. It'll get better if you meet and greet people who inspire you and understand the community. Those are the people who you should stay around. Yes, you'll always have people who think you're different, and there is no nice way to put it: We're a tad bit different than "normal people," but that doesn't change that we're all still human. There are things in life that may be hard, but we must push through.

I decided to come out to my stepsister in fourth grade when I was still figuring myself out. I went by the name Lynx at the time, and I chose her because she was the one I thought I could trust. Later in life I noticed how bad of a role model she was, and I fixed who I looked up to and figured myself out more.

Later, in sixth grade, I noticed how wrong I was about my name, so I chose my current name, Oliver. I've gone through many changes about myself, pronouns and more. It's normal to change and figure yourself out. It takes a while to figure out how you feel as a person. Being a young trans kid always takes a while for people to get used to and understand. It'll be like that, but you and I will get over any problems we have. Trans people are some of the strongest people I know. We are all different and unique. None of us are the same, but we are all beautiful.

Some people view your coming out differently, like my mother. My mother was accepting, and she's one of the reasons why I was happy to come out. I thought it was a good idea to move in with my mom since she is very supportive about the community, and it's a choice I'd make every day, repeatedly. Yes, me and my mom have times where it's not so good, but we fix it every time, and that's all I could ask for.

My father, on the other hand, wasn't supportive and protested this. I don't know why he would protest when my mother said he has had LGBTQ+ friends before, but I didn't want to have to live in a toxic environment, so I moved away with my mother.

I've been here in South Bend, Indiana, full time for over eight months now, and I'd like to stay here. In my old town there were

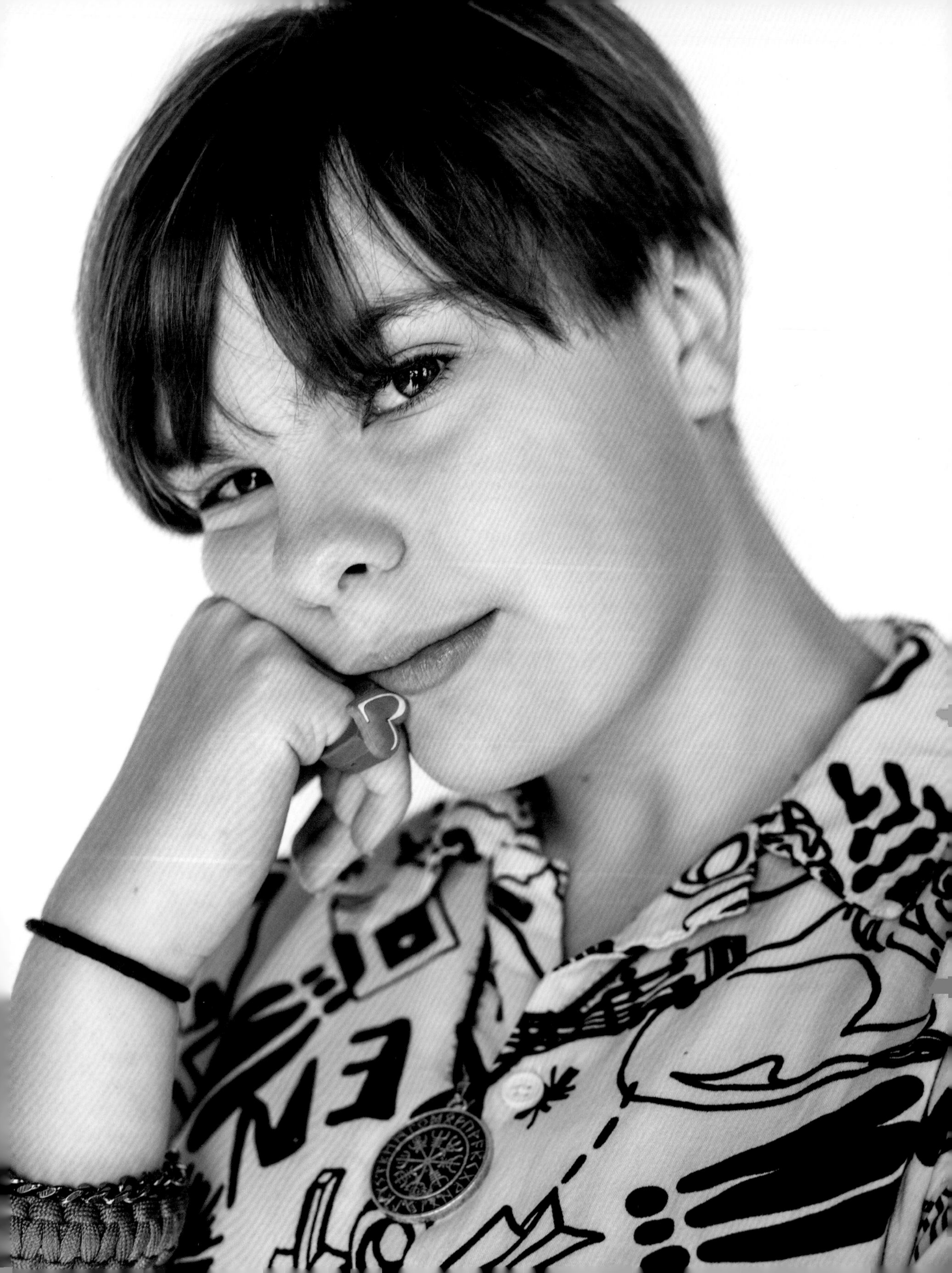

no support clubs or anything like that. Being out here and having a small community and support system has been great, especially getting to meet and bond with other people just like myself. South Bend, Indiana, had an openly gay mayor who ran for president, which is really inspiring. It says a lot about our town and how safe this place is.

Being open about my truth was very scary, and I know there are a lot of people out there who would rather hide, but I hope you are reading my story and others and know you're not alone. We may struggle and we may fall, but it is how we rise above each time that makes us beautiful.

Omar

16 years old, they/them, California
CW: This story contains references to self-harm and suicide.

My name is Omar, I'm sixteen years old, and I'm a nonbinary (agender) and pansexual young adult residing in Adelanto, California. I use they/them pronouns.

Through most of my youth I've lived with my mom and grandparents in a small town in the middle of the Mojave Desert called Adelanto. Despite there being nothing out here, I wanted to make the most out of however much time I would be spending here. Throughout every school period I went through, I made new friends, respected and befriended the teachers, and always got my work done on time. Being a straight A student didn't stop me from dealing with straight assholes, unfortunately. I always got asked by random straight kids if I was a girl, if I was gay, or if I was on drugs. I always denied the former two because, at the time, I told myself that I would always like women. Fortunately, I wasn't close-minded enough to be against queerness as a whole. So, as I got older, I started meeting new people and learning new things about myself, others, and the world. But it wasn't until I saw Billy Unger as Chase Davenport on Disney's *Lab Rats* that I truly started to question my sexuality and gender identity.

Yes. You read that correctly. Chase. The nerdy bionic boy who was a combat expert, had the world's knowledge at the touch of his temple, and could move things with his mind. His charming looks and scripted intellect managed to move their way into my heart. But after that fling (or, more specifically, after Disney XD canceled the show and stopped airing reruns), I thought nothing of it. Then I started truly overthinking it when I was watching a gay sex scene in *Empire* with my mom one night. I asked her, "Mom, is it wrong for me to think that that guy is cute?" She paused for a moment as a light switch went off in her mind, alerting her that the gay had begun to consume me. She proceeded to calmly tell me, "No, sweetie. I sometimes think that some ladies are cute, but that doesn't make it wrong." Smooth thinking, Mom. My mom is way too smart. Even when I gave her the most wild mental curveballs, she still managed to find an insightful way to answer.

I was in seventh grade when I realized that there was a smidgen of a chance that I might be queer. I was in a computer science class

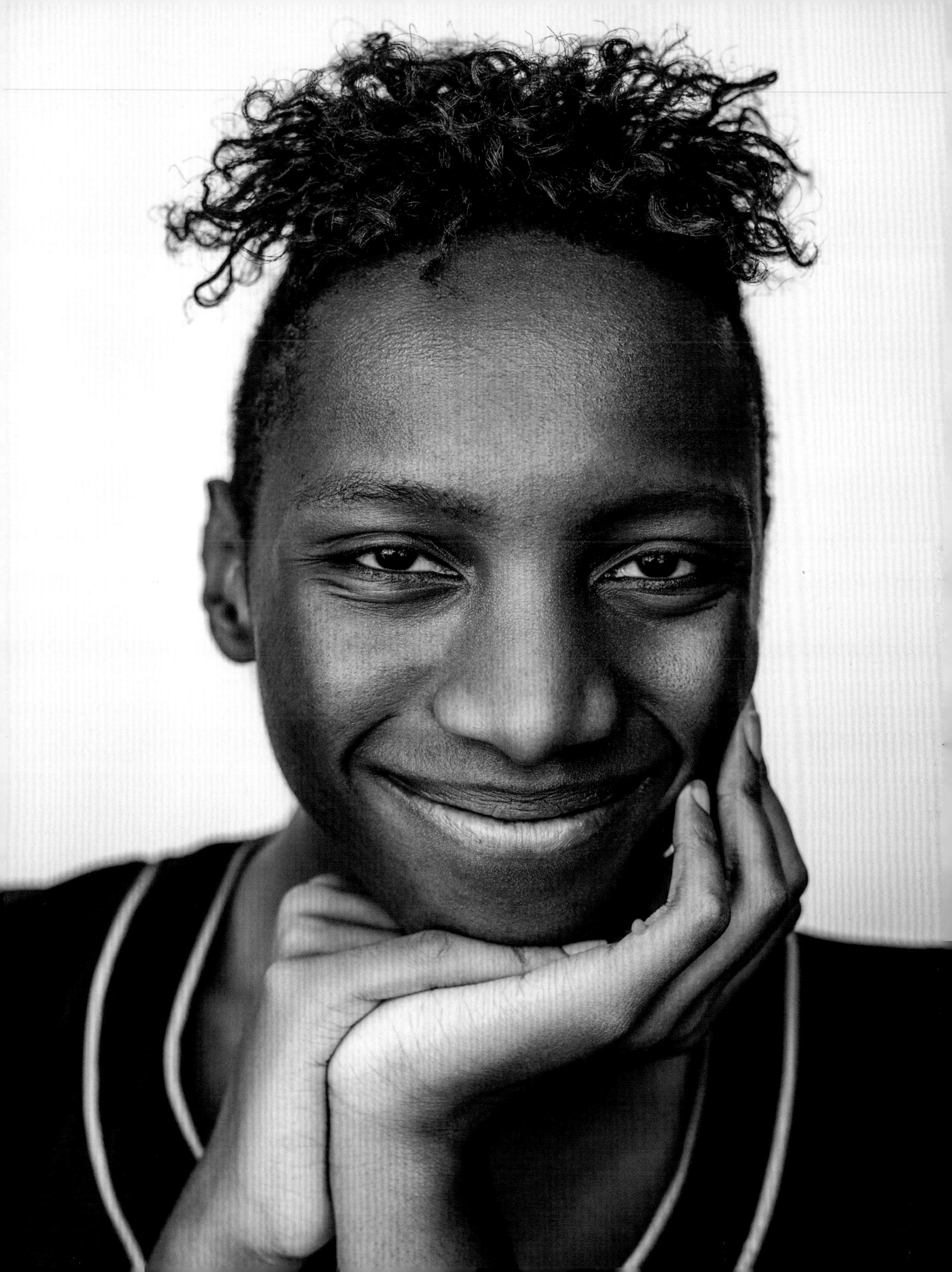

on the first day of school on a campus I didn't feel comfortable on yet. The first thing our teacher did was have us sit in a circle and go around the room introducing ourselves. I sat next to this smart, tall gay boy we'll call Jimmy. Pretty much everything we said in our intros was identical. We geeked out over our shared interests and decided that we would find each other at lunch later. When lunch came around and we sat down together, he asked me, "Not to be rude or anything, but are you gay?" In that moment I was briefly disappointed to have been catapulted back into that old position of unconscious denial, but after that brief moment, I told him, "Uhhh, I think so. I don't have a label for what I am yet."

Throughout the course of my friendship with Jimmy, I cycled through different labels based on what felt right to me. When I entered high school, I realized that my gender identity needed to go through that same cycle. I never acted the way my parents expected me to act. I was always me, though I could never pinpoint what "me" was when I was younger. I always enjoyed wearing my mom's clothes and pretending I was walking down a runway. I loved tying my blankets around my waist and acting like they were trains. It never dawned on me then, but I knew I wasn't a man or a woman. I was stuck in an in-between that my mind was incapable of finding comfort in.

The first time I tried to come out to my mom, she assumed it was merely a phase and that I was just metrosexual. For those unaware of what that means, it is essentially a straight man with the stereotypical mannerisms and interests of a queer person. And for some time, I went along with it. However, I knew that wasn't true and I shouldn't keep lying to myself or the people I loved about it, so, a few months following that I came out to her again while we were going to the movies. I was super scared because, like a lot of Black parents, she was raised in a church community where being queer was frowned upon due to misconstrued Bible passages. I was so relieved when she embraced me and all that I am with open arms. That day solidified our relationship entirely. Later on I started experimenting with labels again, but I fully came to terms with my gender identity during the pandemic.

I started wearing clothes I felt more comfortable with that most view as "feminine" or "unmanly" on a guy, and I began to experiment with pronouns to see how comfortable I felt with the change. For a lot of trans people in the LGBTQ+ community, their definitions of transitioning may vary depending on their situation. Everyone's transition is different. No one person's experience is the same as someone else's. Whatever you want and need to do to become the version of yourself that you can see thriving ten years from now is the best thing you can ever do for yourself. The one thing we all do have in common is a beautiful community.

The LGBTQ+ community has been such a beautiful space for me to learn in. The version of Omar in this book is not the same as the four-year-old Omar who was catwalking and voguing on the dance floor of a distant relative's wedding. Or the seven-year-old Omar who got called a faggot by their classmates on a near daily basis. Or the nine-year-old Omar that got pressed by their grandfather when they were strutting down the hall in a blue snowman blanket. The difference is that I no longer have to hide. I'm grateful to know that if I'm gonna get hate thrown at me for being me, that it's *actually* me, not the person they want me to be just to make them feel better.

When I was younger I used to be a theater kid. Being in theater gave me the ability to pretend to be whoever I wanted. An old man rocking on a wheelchair telling people scary stories, a sassy, pregnant purple kangaroo who was secretly a Karen, and a British spy who rambles more than I do. However, the most difficult role I've ever had to play was a version of myself that I didn't feel comfortable with. Being out and openly proud has been the most cathartic experience I could ever ask for. There has never been a day in my life since coming out that I've taken for granted. I know that for a lot of people coming out isn't an easy thing to do.

While most of my story probably doesn't make a lot of sense, I will say that one thing that people should take away from it is that you don't have to force yourself to be someone that you're not. Don't make the same mistake that I did and push away the parts of yourself that you love to make others comfortable. It is not your responsibility to cater to their warped norms. You will always matter. You are valid and loved in every way possible. And if you ever need any help, you have me and an entire community of people right behind you rallying for you all the way. You deserve that love and respect. We all deserve it because we're all meant to shine and grow with valiance. To paraphrase the words of the great Sparkle Cadet from *Craig of the Creek*, don't let anyone dull your sparkle. Stay safe, stay queer, stay educated, and stay loved.

Ophelia Peaches

16 years old, he/she, Colorado

I'm Ophelia Peaches, and I'm a sixteen-year-old drag queen. I hail from Denver, Colorado. I'd say that my pronouns are "fluid" as I'm gender-fluid. I unofficially started my drag career when I was six years old. My older sister had a huge box of dress-up clothes so I hosted lavish tea parties and runway shows in our living room. I have never looked at gender as being a way to define myself, I chose to wear "girl clothes" and "boy clothes" whenever I wanted. Having a supportive mother and sister helped me to be a very fashionable first grader.

The Dress of Choice

I was lucky enough to be enrolled in a theater school, but I still had trouble showing my real self since it was a religious school. Our school had a day called Dress of Choice Day where we didn't have to wear uniforms. I decided to take that literally and planned to wear my "*dress* of choice." So, with a skip in my step, off to Goodwill I went. Fortunately, a black, sequined Ann Taylor gown spoke to me, and I knew The Dress of Choice had chosen me.

I remember having a sinking feeling in my gut that morning. My backpack seemed to be on fire as my backup clothes were in there and I didn't want to have to resort to wearing them. All the way to school that hoodie and a pair of shorts were in that bag . . . taunting me.

When I arrived (fashionably late, of course) the staff were surprised, but my classmates started cheering as I entered. I was confused because I certainly didn't expect a standing ovation! My teacher admired my courage and gave me extra credit for my courage. The morning was finished and I had more confidence than ever. Next thing I knew, it was lunchtime. I had just sat down with my friends, and as quickly as my bag hit the table my friends disappeared. I tried to hide my confusion, but that sparked a really terrible afternoon. My theater teacher had much to say about my dress, all of it negative. I remember asking to leave for the restroom and brought my bag with me. I hesitated in the stall for a while just staring at it, hating it with all my will. Then I reflected on my morning, filled with standing ovations and extra credit. I told

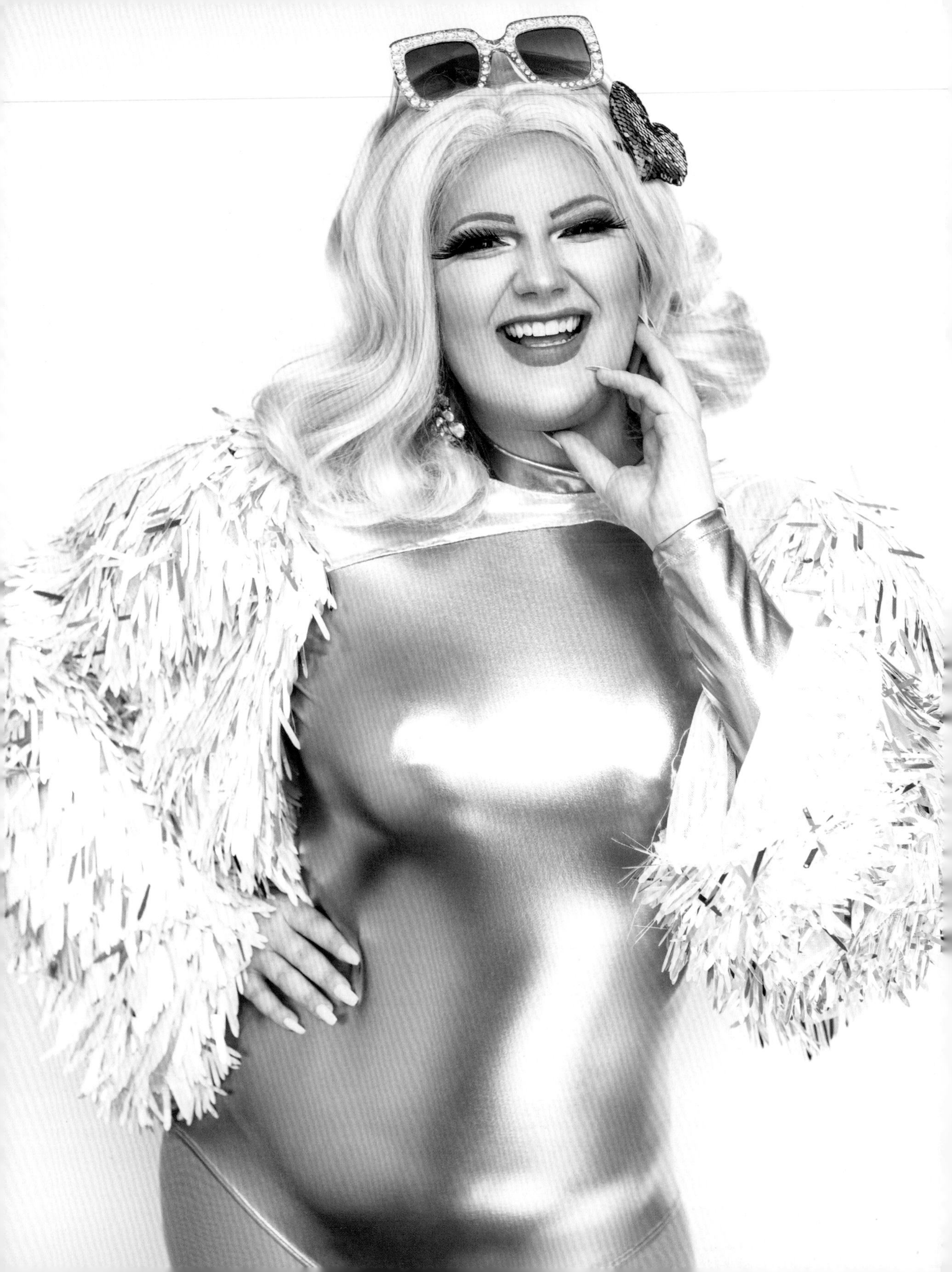

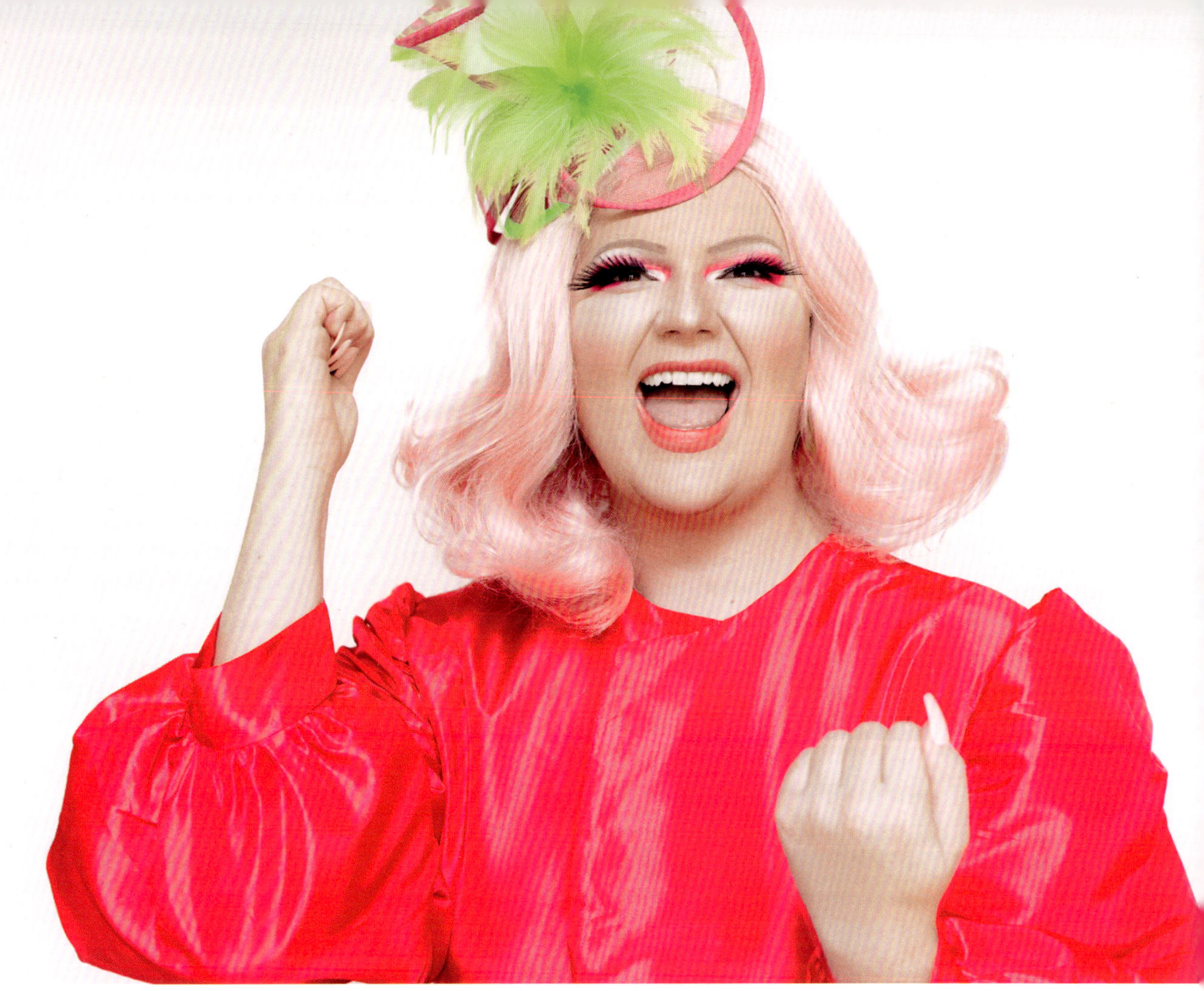

myself that I couldn't let them determine my mood, so Ann Taylor and I emerged from the stall and confidently marched back into the theater. Before I knew it, the end of the day had arrived and I had found friends that appreciated my courage and taste. I knew that I didn't need the people who gave me odd looks and snide comments. I vowed to never change myself for others. I would surround myself with people like me and people that loved me.

Becoming Ophelia

On my thirteenth birthday I asked for a drag queen party. Luckily, my mom loved the idea! She found a makeup artist who applied my new face. I donned a wig, a thrifted pink satin dress, and some sparkly silver sandals. I remember that when I was spun around in the mirror, I fell in love with myself for the first time. Face to face with my drag self, I felt more *me* than I had ever before.

I was greeted by friends at Hamburger Mary's and I spent the rest of that evening talking to . . . real queens! It was phenomenal because I was meeting people that had the same feelings as me, seeing them as their true selves, speaking to me about how they also felt the way I did, and how impressed they were that I had the courage to do drag at my age; it was praise, yes, but it was also the validation I needed. The crowning jewel of the birthday celebration was a backstage pass to Drag Nation. I was absolutely stunned by all the beautiful performers who were dancing and who were there because they all accepted each other. After the show I was invited backstage. There were seven-foot-tall glamazons adorned with the sparkliest jewelry I had ever seen. I expected them to act like celebrities, but they genuinely engaged in conversation. I realized that they were as human as I was. I met my (now) drag mom there as well, the gorgeous Ginger Douglas, who embraced me and told me that whatever I was doing, whether it be drag or just being an LGBTQ+ teen, that I was valid in doing so. Those words still embolden me today, and I will be forever grateful to my drag mom and bio mom for a night I will never forget.

Dragutante

I was ending my year in seventh grade with my newfound passion for drag, and I was entering the summer with a plethora of ambition. I made plans to attend that year's Pride and maybe even do some drag shows along the way. My mom and I had talked about creating a group for kids that shared the same interest in drag as I did, so we invited local drag performers and makeup artists to do a drag photo shoot so that I could meet people like me and they could meet people like them. As my mom was explaining this whole shoot to the makeup artists, they gasped, "You can't simply get into drag for just a photo shoot. We *have* to have a ball!" We were new to this scene and had no idea what a ball was (in my mind I would be a Disney princess), but we quickly learned that it was *way* more than that.

As we planned the show, local queens heard about our event and contacted my mother. Working together, my soon-to-be drag mom Ginger Douglas and my bio mom became soul sisters. I have two supportive moms now.

During the walkthrough, my mind was overloaded with nerves. This room would become the very spot where I would finally share my true self with the world. When the day finally came, backstage was hectically beautiful. I could hear the crowd outside. I remember not being scared to go out on stage, I wasn't worried because I knew that everyone who was there was supporting us all. As I emerged from the black curtains, I was blinded by the stage lights and my eardrums were flooded with noise from the song and the cheering crowd. I had made it: I was strutting down that runway lip-synching to *Born This Way* by Gaga, and I was *living*. I felt as if I was floating—weightless from the cheers and screams of the crowd—for a moment. After the show I asked to speak on the mic to thank everyone for coming. My mom didn't know I was going to speak and was shocked that they gave shy Jameson a mic, but at that moment I was not Jameson or Ophelia, I was both. I was me.

I'd like to end with a bit of advice for gender-fluid/genderqueer teens. Sometimes I feel like it's the hardest place to be on the Pride flag, because you're the opposite of transgender or nonbinary . . . you're *both*.

Explaining to people that sometimes you're male but other days you're female is exhausting. Just remember that you're confident enough in your own body to not deny both aspects of your personality. You're not in conflict with your fluidity, you're in harmony. And in the words of Noxeema Jackson, "If you have way too much fashion sense for one gender, you're a drag queen."

Rae

15 years old, she/they/he, South Dakota
CW: This story contains references to self-harm.

Hello, my name is Rae and I identify as nonbinary. My pronouns are any of them, and I am fifteen years old from Rapid City, South Dakota. I am Native American, Hispanic, and Black.

Growing up in my community has been a roller coaster all my life. My family has always struggled financially, so it was hard for me to fit in everywhere we went and hard for me to call a place home because my sisters and I have been homeless almost every year since 2014. I was always the outcast at school because I constantly had to make new friends since we were always on the move.

My childhood was the hardest for me and my identity. I didn't know who I was or what I was doing. Looking back, it just feels like a fever dream. I wasn't sure why I was feeling this way because I hated everything about my life at the time. It was a difficult crossroads because I was struggling with my day-to-day life while simultaneously struggling with self-harm and body dysmorphia.

When I was younger my aunt would always tell me not to put scars on my arm. I never knew what she meant by that because I didn't understand why I was even doing it. I wasn't self-aware. Now I can see what she truly meant. Not to self-harm emotionally and physically, because every time I went back to it, it always brought me back to a dark place and I didn't like that. I personally didn't want to do it anymore and be in that mindset.

It was hard for me to start seeing the truth of the world and my world around me. I started to realize that my mom was mean and was only there physically, meaning she was just literally there in front of us. She wasn't there for us mentally and emotionally. It took my mom a while to realize what she was doing because most of the time she was on drugs. In the past she acted like she was our sister and not our mother, and she acted like she could do whatever she wanted, even telling me what I was going through was a "phase." Because of this my older sister became my motherly figure and guardian for me and my other sister, along with my aunt.

When this happened I guess you could say I was living some true parts of my life. As I grew closer to understanding my identity as nonbinary, I started overthinking everything. I started to think heavily on my future and how my life was going at the time.

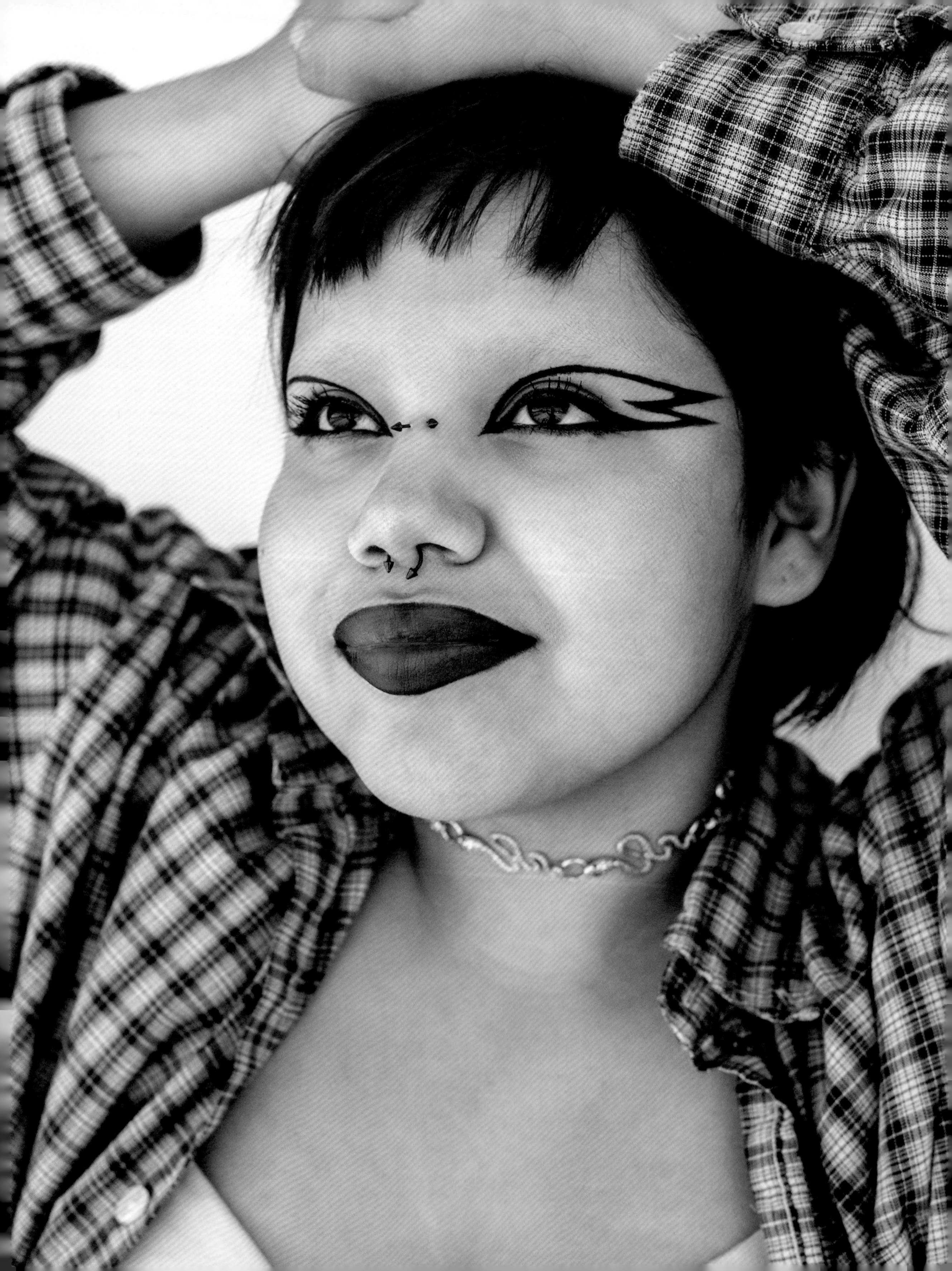

Being nonbinary was scary for me at first. I didn't know who I was going to be. I thought there were only two genders until I educated myself more. Finding this out started to help me see myself in a whole new way. I was excited to learn about this because I didn't have to worry about being a male or a female.

For a while it felt like I was gender-fluid, but in the end that didn't feel right to me. I didn't identify as any gender. When I was in the fourth grade I shaved the side of my head, giving me a short look! When I was thirteen I had long hair and looked more female. Back then I would always dye my hair. My hair was a big part of helping me discover my identity, a tool I used to help my comfort . . . and so was glitter and eyeliner! It was funny. I looked like a child who didn't know how to wear makeup, but I would always wear it on my eyelids or cheeks. It was important to me. I have one picture of me with a lot of glitter on and seeing that photo helps me see me!

As I always say, "Living isn't the same as surviving in this world." It has been a struggle for me to find happiness, even though it is within me. I've struggled with homelessness, losing parents, gender dysphoria, and my family's acceptance. Even through all of these experiences I found myself by doing what felt right for me. Last year I started to cut my hair shorter. At first I was comfortable with just being gender-fluid, and once I realized this feeling was going to be a part of my life forever I began to accept that and understand that I am nonbinary.

In sixth grade I came out to someone, and since then she has been one of my greatest friends and support systems. She was the first person I came out to who accepted me for who I was. We are still friends today. Whenever I had a crush I could go to her and talk about it, and it helped me feel like I was important and the "main character" of my story. I always struggled with seeing myself that way, even in my own life. I also had one person come out to me after I came out. They told me they liked me! The feeling isn't mutual but now we are friends, and they even helped me find the words for this story.

I have always loved school very much because I love being an outcast. I don't care if I look different or dress differently than other people as long as I am just myself. If I am, I am happy with that. Because being yourself is what makes you stand out the most.

Find people who make you feel comfortable inside and outside, and who make you feel like you are worth everything, 'cause when I was discovering myself I started to realize I was never myself hanging out with the ones who didn't accept me. I totally lost myself. It was horrible.

Finding myself has helped me find happiness. My scars are now covered by a tattoo. It's an image of a mushroom head with a human body. It symbolizes that I should always feel comfortable with myself.

My advice to anyone out there who can relate in similar ways is just fucking be yourself, because the only opinion that matters is yours. Not nobody else's. There are going to be haters and bullies, but you should never doubt yourself, because the LGBTQ+ community are the most beautiful people ever. They always have really kind souls and I am so grateful to be a part of this community.

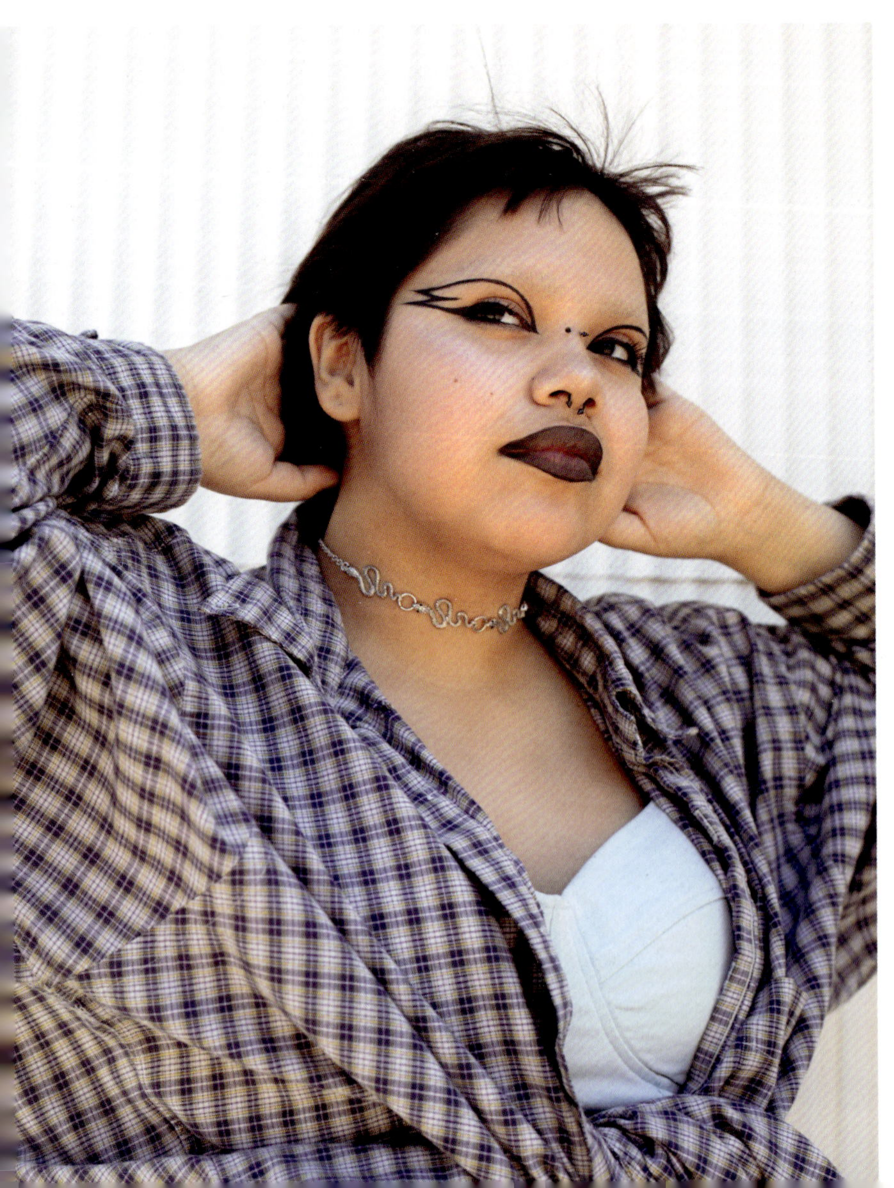

Ray

13 years old, she/they, Colorado

Being me is an interesting thing. It's hard living knowing that every ten minutes I might want to be a man with big fluffy hair that all the girls would stare at in bookshops. Maybe being a boy might help me finally look good in eyeliner and I could feel good in skirts with a flat chest and no worries. Then it might hit me like a wall. Boom. Suddenly, being a man is gross. I wish to have long beautiful hair, and get into pants that look good, feel good, in a full face of makeup. I'd be a girl who guys would talk to their friends about, a girl people would write songs about. Her lips are full, and her hands are soft. And yet I am still stuck in the middle. Man jeans. Eyeliner. Some three-day-old T-shirt I found on my bedroom floor because it's the only thing that seems to make me feel like a strange mix of this dumb teenage boy and a girl who's being herself. At this point my eyeliner is my best friend.

I came out when I was seven years old. I was living in New Mexico at the time, sitting in the kitchen crying my eyes out, the same old yellow cabinets looking back at me because it was hard to look at my mom and explain that I wasn't what I was assigned at birth. It's an interesting memory I'll hold close to me forever. My parents are divorced, so I did call my dad that night and explained what had gone down thirty minutes before—and, just like that, they listened and were there for me, and I'm so grateful they were. But coming out was like a whole new door opened; it was fun and exciting but could also be hard and frustrating. I had to find my community and find my people and it was hard, but it got me to where I am now. I've learned a lot and seen people's true colors because of it. It's hard to think about it, but I lost family. Like when people tried to tell me it was all for attention, or it was some stupid trend that I'd grow out of because they didn't understand or want to see me as who I was. There was the time when my aunt sat with me in the car and told me she'd never respect me. Before I came out I'd always been her little girl. I had family members in Florida that I couldn't even call family now because of the things they said to me. It's hard seeing the people you love and admire treat you so badly. But it was the little things that got me closer to being who I am right now. I took small steps forward with the people who are

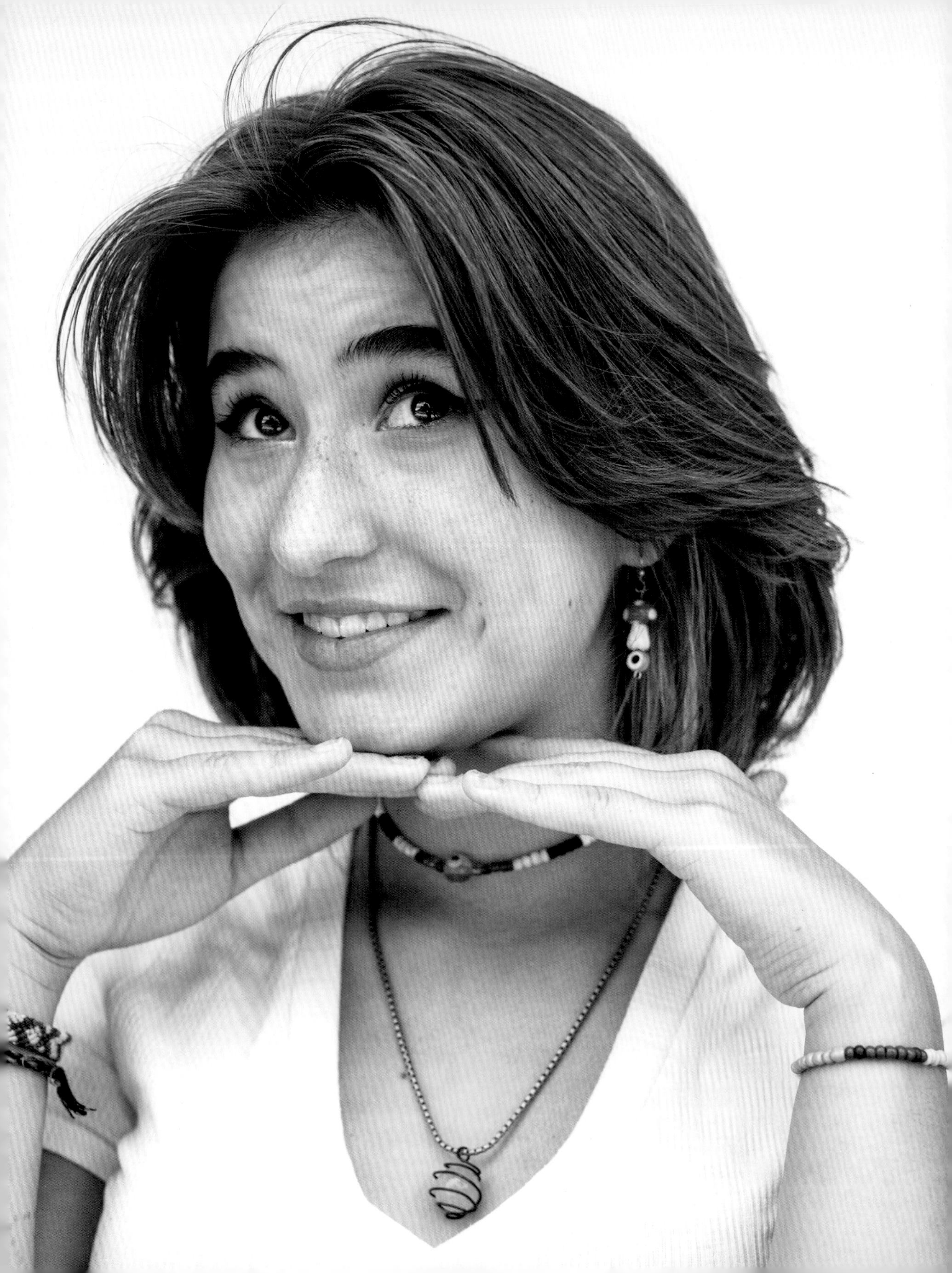

family. Sometimes family isn't just about blood. I made my family, and I am still making my family.

Then a process began. I wanted to be comfortable in my skin, so first it was off with the hair. It was the best haircut I think I've ever had. Chopping it all off held something so satisfying—if only I knew cutting my hair once would lead to probably fifty more hairstyle changes throughout my years. Now my hair is a different color every two weeks. Then I started going through my clothes. I've gone through more style changes than I can count. The most important and somehow annoying thing was the many times I'd have to say "Ray, my name is Ray," before people would get it right. And trust me, it was hard for a while, but I did it and I'm proud. It all paid off because a few months ago I got my name legally changed—and boy, it was one of the best days of my life.

School was a whole new ball game though. Having a spin with the mean office people and the many things I had to change so it would actually be correct was insane. Sitting and thinking to myself, "What bathroom do I use?" isn't the best feeling either. I think people overlook the small challenges that come with being a part of the LGBTQ+ community, like not being confident in going to the bathroom, or worried you won't get down a hallway without someone using your deadname. To this day I still have problems with it, but what came along with the problems were new beginnings, new friends, and new opportunities. Hell, if I didn't go through it all I don't think you'd be reading this—and all of it saved me. I built a community and found my people. It was no easy ride, but I'm glad I took it. When life got hard I just had to remember I'm me, and bloody hell I'm lucky I am. Sure, random waves of dysphoria did feel like a living hell and I'd wish to be anyone but me; but somehow, on days I couldn't even look in the mirror, I stayed strong and stood my ground as myself. In spite of all the mean nicknames, and all the hardship, it's worth it.

Even though there are ups and downs, I cherish every moment and I know in the future I'll get to where I want to be and I'll be proud of myself. I'll have my friends, I'll have my people, and I'll get to be who I've always wanted to be. I'll get to be myself and be happy with just that.

You will too. As you read this, look around you. Think about who you are. Are you who you want to be, or do you think you're a version of yourself that society wants? It took me a really long time to think of myself highly. It was hard to understand that I shouldn't care what others want if it's not what I'm comfortable with. If I'm not being who I want to be, then I'm doing something wrong. I had to learn that I didn't need people's validation. Even if people didn't like it, I was confident in who I was and the right people came my way. They understood who I was because I was being myself and they liked that. I'm happy to have made friends and helped people who helped me. I'm happy I have them all and they are all so important to me.

So within it all this is just one story, about how a kid possibly like you is just trying to be themselves in their environments, and I guess that all you really need to hold onto is who you are and how you are in the world as yourself. Because you are important. You are valued and heard. You aren't alone, and when you feel like you are, just know: You are special. You are loved. No matter how many people let you down or think they can walk over you, you will never be alone.

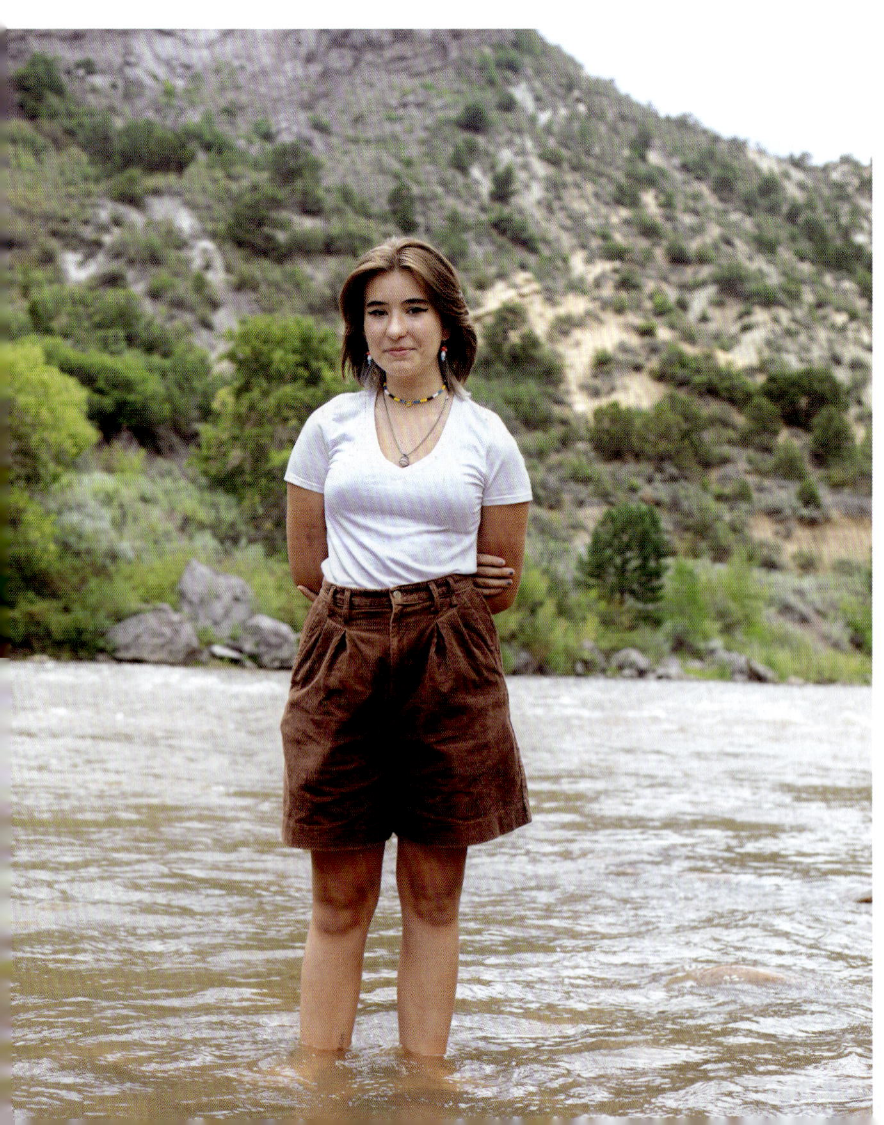

Reece

17 years old, he/him, Indiana

My story is not one of peril or strife. My story is one of success. Nonetheless, I feel like I have a very important story to tell. I cannot tell you exactly when I first realized my true self—that part of my life is a haze. I don't remember much of it, but I do remember my journey.

It was around eighth grade that I started questioning my sexuality, and after some time I came out as bisexual to myself and close friends, At first I didn't know what it meant, but I was happy and content knowing that at last I had a term to define myself. I didn't know exactly what it meant to be bisexual; I just knew that I had some sort of attraction to both guys and girls. Then I met Elijah. He was my first boyfriend, and he made me so comfortable with myself. He made me come to realize new things about my sexuality, and it was during my time with him that I came out fully as gay.

During that time with Elijah I became much more confident. I stoppcd hiding as much, and I made no secret at school that I was gay and proud of it. It was also during my relationship with him that I came out to my parents. I had avoided coming out to them for such a long time not because I knew that they would disown me—I knew that they would love and accept me. I just never came out because I didn't know how to talk about it, I didn't know what to say. I didn't know how to sit down and say, "Mom, Dad, this is my boyfriend. I'm gay."

I don't want this story to be a tell-all on how to come out. There is no one way to come out: Everybody has their own story, and everybody is going to come out differently. I don't remember much of the conversation, but I do know that they were both so loving and supportive of me. They didn't judge me; they accepted me. I cannot be more thankful. I remember us having a conversation after I came out about exactly what it meant, and what it meant to me; that, to me, was really, really heartwarming because it showed me that they had an interest in who I was. I was not just their child they thought they knew everything about. I was also a person they wanted to learn more about.

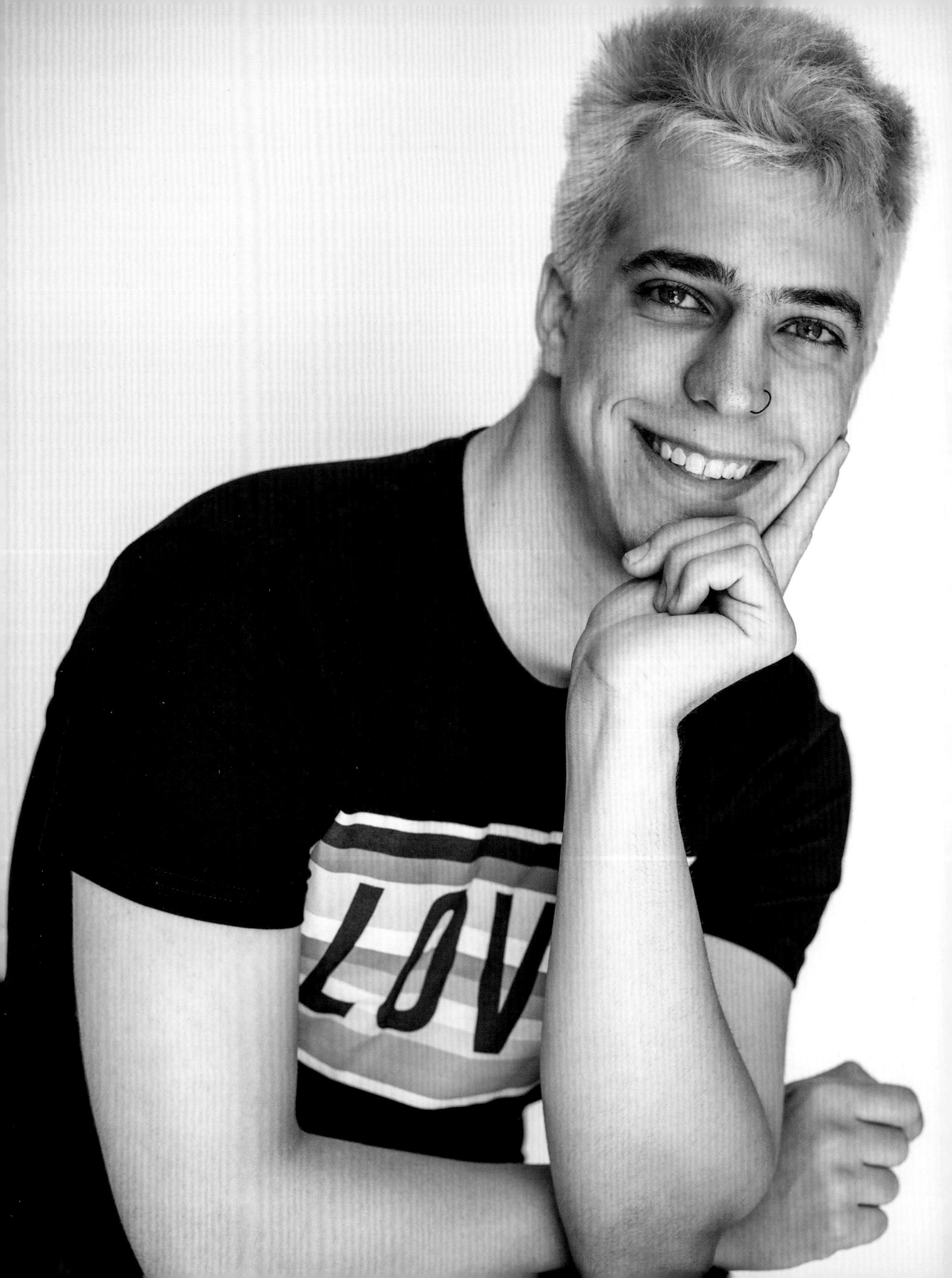

Unfortunately, my relationship with Elijah ended in strife, and at the same time COVID hit. During those months of lockdown I reflected on myself—and most importantly on my sexuality—a lot. I questioned it so many times. I wondered if being gay was just a phase, if I was just doing this to seek attention or to be different. There were times when I thought I'd never love again, times when I questioned what's the point of it all. Through those rough times I had an amazing support group to keep me going, and somehow, someway, I made it to my junior year.

That year I decided I'm going to be who I am. That year I finally felt like I was living as my true, authentic self. I made absolutely no point to hide who I was. In fact, I made it part of my personality. I made it part of me, and I embraced my queerness. I was confident, I was comfortable, and I was happy for the first time in a long time, happy with myself. The biggest thing that changed who I was in my junior year was that close to the end of the year the school told teachers to take their Pride flags down from their classrooms. When I first heard about that it made me so mad; I turned that anger and frustration into a voice, and I campaigned for the reinstatement of the Pride flags.

I started a petition on Change.org that garnered more than 4,200 signatures from around the world. I spoke at school board meetings about how important that symbol was, and how remaining viewpoint neutral was wrong in this case. I made a name for myself. Unfortunately we ended up losing, and to this day the viewpoint neutrality stance still stands. Then it was finally time for my senior year. I went back to school uncertain how I would be treated, uncertain what sort of divide I would see the school go through—and let me tell you, I have seen that divide only grow. I have fought tirelessly for LGBTQ student rights in my school, and there has been so much to fight for. My pride and joy is the GSA. Ever since the Pride flags were ordered to come down, I knew that it was time to re-form the GSA at our school—and then we were denied the ability to promote the GSA. This was a huge blow. Once again I challenged the school and once again the school stood firm. I fought this tirelessly, but they would not budge. I was not alone in the fighting—I had the support of students and community members as well as my parents—and after what seemed like hundreds of phone calls we finally caught the attention of the ACLU.

After months of struggle and rejection and being denied by the school board, our saving grace came in the form of Ken Falk, the legal director of the ACLU of Indiana. After we explained our case to him he said he would take it, and the following Wednesday a lawsuit was filed against our school for discrimination against the GSA. As I'm writing this, the lawsuit is still in process, but we have high hopes.

No matter how many times people may judge you, criticize you, bully you, deny you, you must keep fighting, you must keep your head up. Do not lose faith, because eventually you're going to start winning. You're going to start changing people's minds, and you're going to start being accepted for who you are. Don't give up. One of the biggest things that I learned from all of this is that no matter how bleak things might seem, you have people who love you, who support you, who care about you, and are willing to fight for you and help you.

Update: A bit after I had finished writing this, we got some amazing news: *We won the case!* After months of hard work and so many rejections, we finally did it, we finally made change. I want this to be an inspiration to everyone out there who is facing similar challenges. Don't give up, don't ever lose faith: There are people out there who will fight for you, who will fight for what's right. Maybe someday that person might even be you.

Riley

18 years old, he/him, Wyoming

The journey that a transgender person takes will happen over a lifetime. No matter how far they decide to transition medically, socially transitioning never stops. Just like everyone else, we are constantly changing and growing as people. I've grown as a person by joining this project. But even with how far I've come medically, socially, and most of all emotionally, I am often still afraid and—I hate to admit it—even ashamed to share with people who I truly am. I have let fear control me and force me into a life of stealth. I hide the fact that I am transgender from everyone, unless for some reason it becomes necessary for them to know. But recently I have been stepping out of my shell, being true to who I am and no longer hiding.

Being my authentic self has opened so many doors for me. I just turned eighteen and recently started my own upholstery business with two wonderful ladies who don't think any different of me since I came out to them. We call it Peak Custom Crafted—"peak" like a mountaintop since I love to backpack, as well as top, or "peak," quality. This is just another step in my lifelong journey of becoming the man that I want to be.

For the most part, my journey has been great. I came out at thirteen and slowly started to tell my family, friends, and eventually my classmates about my being transgender. The most opposition I faced was from the adults who ran the school board. My fellow classmates never gave me a hard time, but instead they were inquisitive. Occasionally kids would make rude remarks or comments, but they were few and far between. They had no idea what being transgender truly meant, and they were genuinely curious about it. I find when talking to most people that it is a general lack of education that fuels their misguided thoughts toward members of the LGBTQ+ community, especially transgender individuals.

This has a large part to do with growing up in Wyoming. Here in Wyoming we tend to pride ourselves on being *tough*.

What's tough is refusing to leave a bus seat because you won't let society define you by the color of your skin. What's tough is continuing to stand up for women's rights to an education after surviving a Taliban bullet to the head. Tough is continuing to fight for equal rights after your son was brutally beaten and left to die

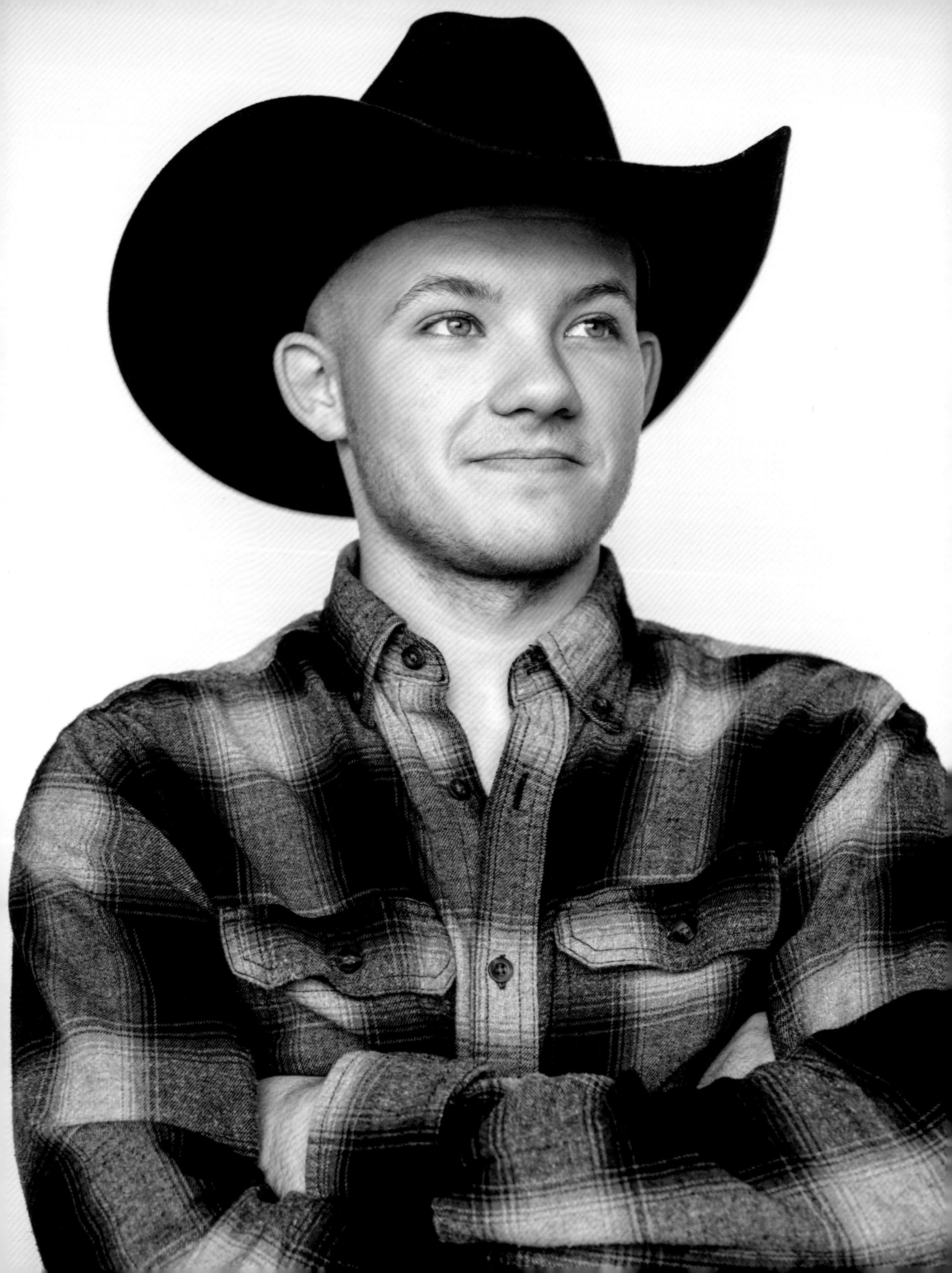

because of his sexual orientation. Tough is still believing that people are really good at heart while hiding in an attic as millions who share your religious beliefs are being killed for simply that. Tough. Tough is choosing to stand up and fight for the rights and safety of others.

Despite being called the "Equality State," Wyoming does not have a great reputation for treating everyone as equals. It seems as though many Wyomingites in the past felt that in order to look tough they must straighten out anything that bends, so to speak, but recently Wyomingites have truly taken on the challenge of being *tough*.

My hometown of Casper has created an LGBTQ+ Advisory Committee for the city council, and we are currently working on passing a nondiscrimination ordinance. I have been asked to speak at multiple LGBTQ+ rallies and events in my community aimed to increase education and end discrimination. When I began my transition in middle school, there were few procedures in place in order to help with my transition. Since then the schools in my area have started to create a "safety plan'" in order to ensure a smooth transition for students. The climate in Wyoming is changing. All it takes is a few brave people to stand up to create change.

Just be yourself and don't let others change who you are. Be proud of who you are and what you do. Stand up for yourself and for others. Your voice matters! You will be heard! Do your research and help to educate others in the LGBTQ+ community. Keep being *tough*!

Ryleigh

11 years old, he/him, Louisiana

My name is Ryleigh. I am eleven years old and I am transgender living in Louisiana.

I've always felt like a boy even though I was raised as a girl. I have always been pretty masculine, or tried to be. Then I got the name "tomboy," but it never really made me feel confident. I always preferred masculine things and I always wanted the "boy" toy in my McDonald's Happy Meal.

Discovering who I am was hard at first. I've never really had a strong father figure in my life, so looking up to a guy who I wanted to be like wasn't always easy. I was adopted and never really knew my bio dad. My adoptive dad moved away and then he passed away. The next boy figure in my life is my older brother, but he also moved away and works a lot, so it was and is hard for me to find someone to look up to. Instead I try to look up to the people who encourage me to be myself, like my family and my counselor Felicia. Unlike my family, Felicia is also queer and gender-fluid. I have always felt like she was a person I could tell my problems to. She has always been really nice to me.

When I started to hear the word "trans" I began to look online. I was on the Internet one day and I saw that it was very normal to be like this. My parents never talked about the queer community, so I had never really heard it before. For some reason I thought they were trying to hide it from me so I wouldn't become trans, but I was completely wrong.

I texted my Mom that I felt like a boy. She first thought it was a phase, bringing up the word *tomboy* once again. Later, after she saw how hurt I was, she realized it wasn't a phase at all. I was ten when I came out to my mom. She was and is very supportive. When she realized that me being trans is not a phase she took me to get a haircut and new clothes immediately. So, shout-out to my mom for that. I am very lucky most of my family has always been supportive of me being trans.

School can be a little different. I try to not talk about it at school because everyone there doesn't feel the same way as they do at home. The other students at school are homophobic. I do have a lot of friends, and most of my friends know that I am trans now, but I make sure I trust my friends before I tell them.

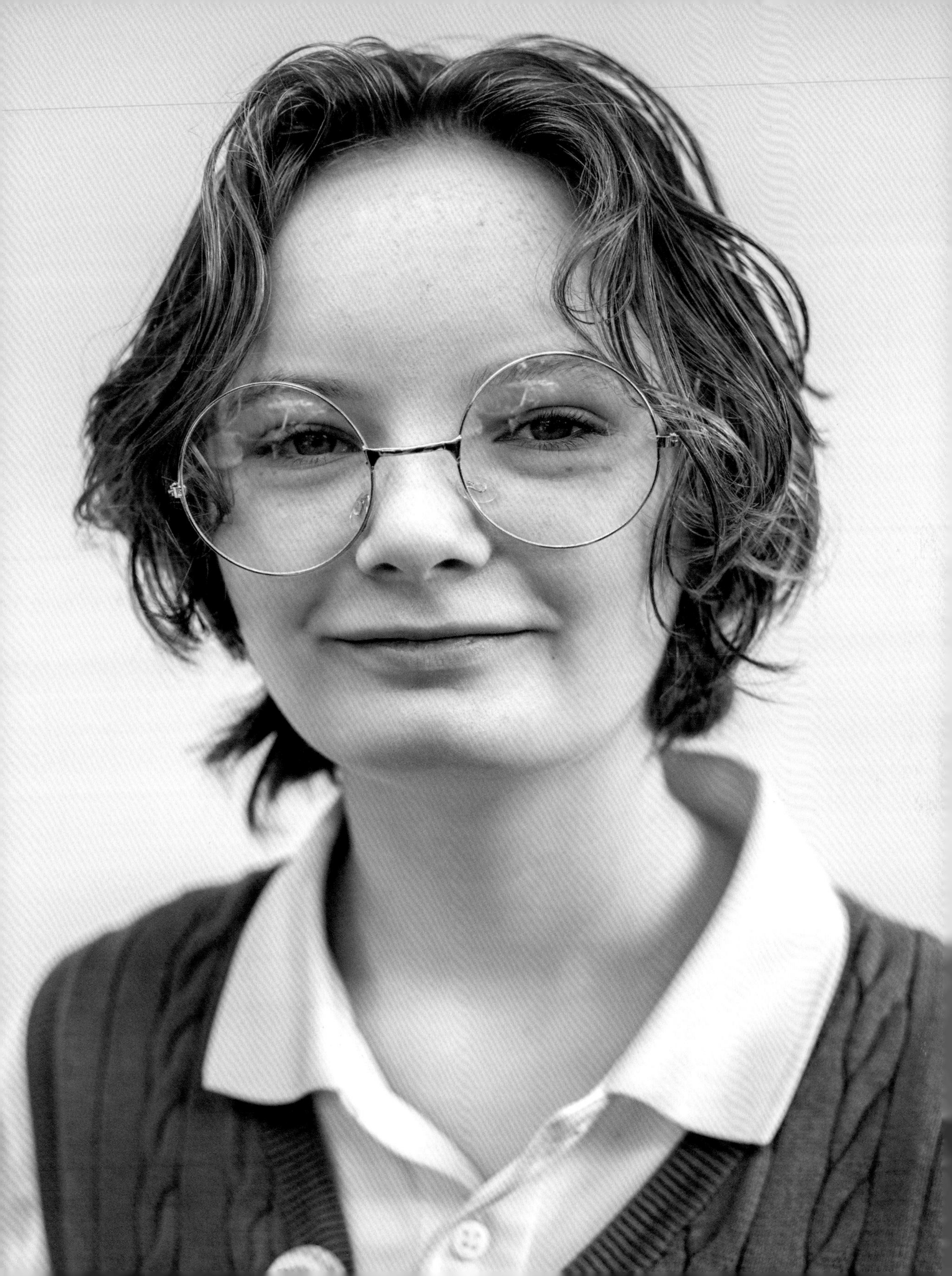

Kids will always say "you're gay" or use the F slur. It makes me feel not accepted. If I were to tell them who I was, they would immediately start yelling at me and calling me the same slurs they jokingly call their friends. It isn't like I want to talk to them anyways due to their humor. They think it is all funny, but I'm sitting here not laughing at all.

The school I am going to now is also new. I moved schools and towns last year, which made me sad. My old friends in my old neighborhood were always very accepting of me. When I came out it also helped a few of them realize they were queer too. It helped my friends come out and find themselves. But as soon as all this happiness and group self-discovery took flight I had to move away; I lost contact with all of them. I still cry about that when I go to bed. I miss them a lot and they made me feel so happy. I know that if they saw me doing what I am doing now they would be super proud of me. I know I will see them again one day.

Making new friends is hard because people in my old town were more accepting. In my new town, there are not as many people who are queer or LGBTQ+ allies, so it is slim pickings, but that doesn't bother me because I make a lot of friends online. They make me feel awesome and they are really nice, always helping me realize that I fit in and have a place in this world.

Art also helps. I am an artist. I love to draw. It is a part of my therapy and self-discovery. When you live in a place like my town, where trans kids are not so common, making art can help you feel more like yourself. I draw and create queer characters and I show them to all the people I know. I create these characters and stories in my mind and on paper to help me feel like I, too, am living in their world, a world with more people like me. I have been drawing my entire life. It makes me feel good about myself and I am pretty good at it!

This isn't a very supportive part of Louisiana, but I have made friends, and I know you will find your people too.

It also helps to look toward my future. I see myself in the future as a confident artist. I want to use my art to create something beautiful and meaningful for people like me.

My advice to other kids like me is to just try to be yourself. That doesn't mean go around telling everyone, and if your family doesn't support you, try to be safe. Don't feel like you're alone, and know that you are always supported by me and other people like you. You are loved.

Saber

17 years old, they/them, Louisiana

Hi! My name is Saber, I am queer and nonbinary, and I use they/them pronouns. Currently I live in Louisiana, and I am seventeen years old. I came out to myself, as pansexual at the time, in June 2020, after months of questioning whether the feelings I had been having were real or if I was making them up.

Growing up in church in a small Louisiana town, we never spoke about the queer community. It was a topic that was pretty much ignored, and I wasn't aware that people used any pronouns other than she/her and he/him until my freshman year in high school. Even then, there was one nonbinary person out in my high school, but I didn't yet understand what it meant to be nonbinary. My sophomore year I was accepted into a residential high school with a large queer community. I made friends who were constantly educating me about their identities and sexualities, and I became an ally for the queer community. During my sophomore year I also formed my first crush on a girl. I remember telling my best friend that me and that girl had kissed, and being so happy thinking it was the most incredible experience, and all she said was, "I thought you were straight." I instantly felt very judged and confused.

After that I tried to ignore any feelings I had that made me question my sexuality, until I was speaking with a friend of mine who had just come out as bisexual. They encouraged me to really listen to the feelings I was having and expand my horizons. In some ways I tried to water down my feelings out of desperation. Identifying as a woman at the time, I had watched women give in to the male gaze my whole life. In a way, I felt like I was just desperate for attention, not really attracted to women or nonbinary people. In the midst of discovering my sexuality I forgot entirely about how the next step in my journey should be to come out to the people I am close to in my life.

My coming out story is kind of funny because I intended to come out to my dad first, and then accidentally told my mom. After I told her, and she didn't say anything, I panicked and said, "Well, now that that's out, when it comes to really loving someone for who they are, I don't care what their gender is." I was so scared standing there waiting for an answer because I had heard sad stories of queer teens coming out to their parents, and I wasn't entirely

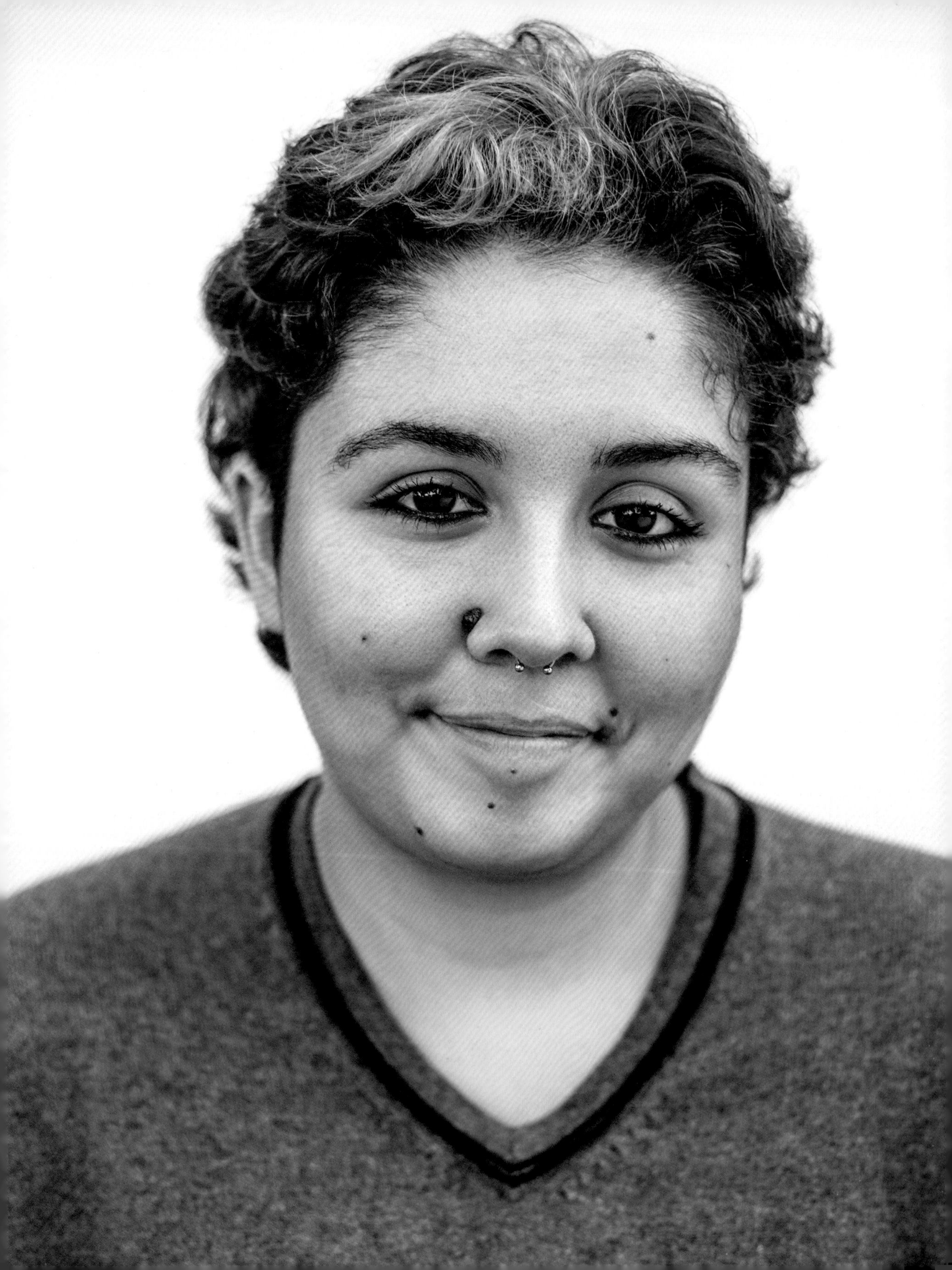

certain of her views on the queer community. After a moment of my mom realizing that I was waiting for her to say something, she told me that she figured I wouldn't let something like gender stand in the way of loving someone, and that was the security I needed in that moment. Then I came out to my dad by telling him I accidentally came out to my mom, and he was instantly supportive, just as I knew he would be.

That summer, with the help of my dad's partner, I organized a queer youth hangout during Pride Month that was a big success. I met some really cool people, and even met some allies that had shown up to support their friend. This was also around the time when I started to question which pronouns I was comfortable with and began to consider that maybe I was nonbinary. It took many months before I discovered how comfortable they/them pronouns made me feel, but it was worth it because I learned so much about myself in the process. Being hit with the double whammy of questioning first my sexuality and then my gender just a month later was really tough at some points, but continuing to listen to my feelings and what I needed to feel comfortable in my own skin helped me through those journeys.

Looking back to those months when I was trying to figure everything out, I realize there are two things that I wish someone would have said to me: 1) you don't owe your coming out to anyone, and 2) everyone's journey is different, and for that reason you shouldn't compare yours to anyone else's.

I wish someone would have told me. I doubted myself and my feelings a lot when I would hear about other people's experiences as they discovered their identity. The friends in my life that were supporting me had already labeled their sexuality in some way, and because I wasn't aware of their journey, and the work they put in to feel confident in themselves, I felt the need to rush mine. There were many times where I would think to myself, "It's not that hard" or "You should know this about yourself." Your timeline is not going to look the same as others', and you deserve the opportunity to grow as you see fit and as you are comfortable. It is still important to get help from the people you trust in your life, but don't feel like you should be doing something differently just because they did. Your journey is your own, your feelings are your own, and you are valid through all of it.

As sort of a closing remark, I want to emphasize to whoever reads this how important you are. It can be very scary and confusing to spend your whole life learning that society wants you to be one way, and then discover you aren't like that at all. Even though you might face trouble throughout your life because of your identity, know that you are so incredibly important. You never know how your story, and your wisdom from those experiences, might help someone in the future. I want to encourage you to take full advantage of the people in your life who you trust to support you through this journey, and don't ever feel like you are a burden by confiding in them. You have made it this far and I am extremely confident that you will continue to push through your struggles. And I am so proud of you! I want to thank you for taking the time out of your day to read my story, and I hope that you can take something from this that will help you in the long run. Stay safe and stay cool!

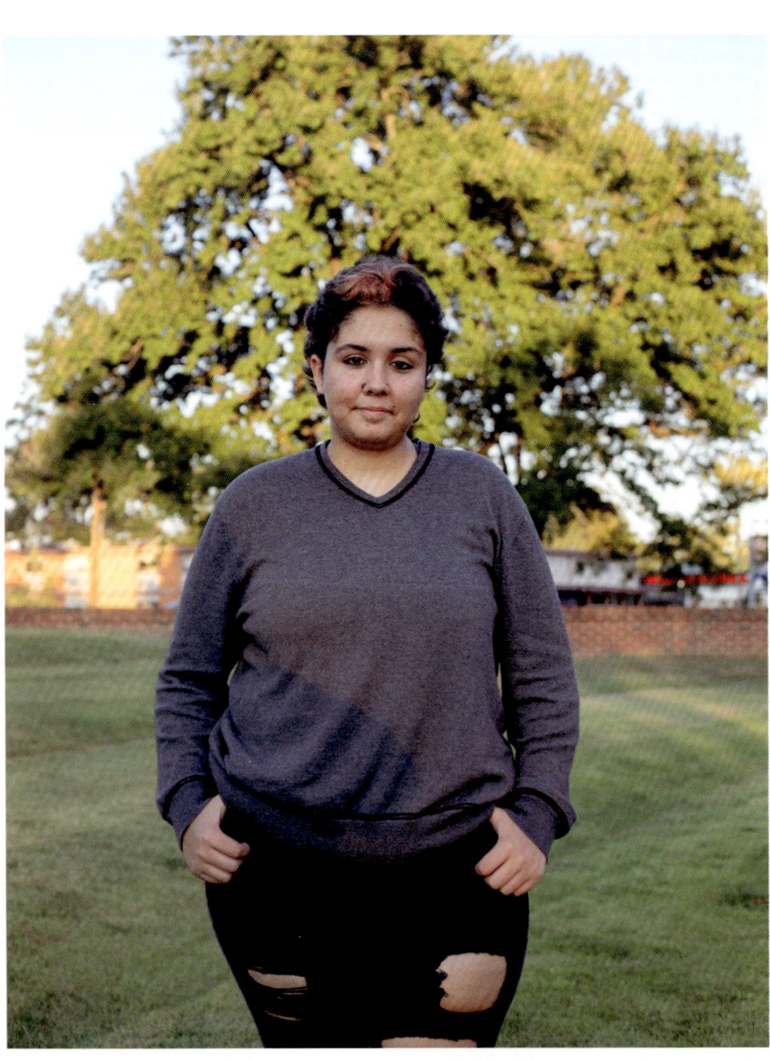

Samuel

10 years old, he/him, Arkansas
CW: This story contains references to bullying and physical violence.

Hello, my name is Samuel. I am ten years old. My pronouns are he/him/his and I identify as pansexual.

I was different from the moment I was born. Not only am I pan, but I was also born with a cleft lip. I don't have a father, really. He wasn't around when I was born, and he told my mom he didn't want a child just yet. When he heard my mom was pregnant with me, he told her to get an abortion or he was going to leave. It was a risky birth. The doctors told my mom I'd be born a vegetable and that they should abort me. My mom didn't know if I would live or die before I was born. The doctor told her I had a rare disease and told her to consider my options. She went to the hospital not even knowing if she'd be taking me home, but instead I was the perfect gift, born on Christmas day after an emergency C-section.

When I was first born into this world my mom struggled being a single mom, so I was left with my super conservative grandparents a lot. When my mom came out as a lesbian, my grandparents filed lawsuits and child abuse charges on my mom to "keep me from evil." At first my grandparents tried to teach me homophobia. My mom would come home and I would scream, "You're a lesbian and are going to hell!" It took time and psychiatric therapy for me to finally feel safe with my mom and accept her. Soon I realized that I am a part of her world.

I never liked boy things. My mom would often walk into my room and find makeup smeared all over my face. I used to beg to do makeup and do other things boys shouldn't do. I always wanted teddy bears that were soft and comforting. Then eventually everything "boyish" got discarded into a pile.

Growing up in Arkansas as pansexual has been challenging, and it can be hard. Being different has caused me to be bullied a lot, not only because I'm pan but because of my cleft lip. The bus is where I feel least safe. It is where most of the bullying happens. People will call me gay because they don't really care about the other labels. They will make fun of me, and I have even gotten a death threat. Last year I was bullied so bad they broke my arm and leg. I was scared of getting beaten or worse. I spent the entire summer in a

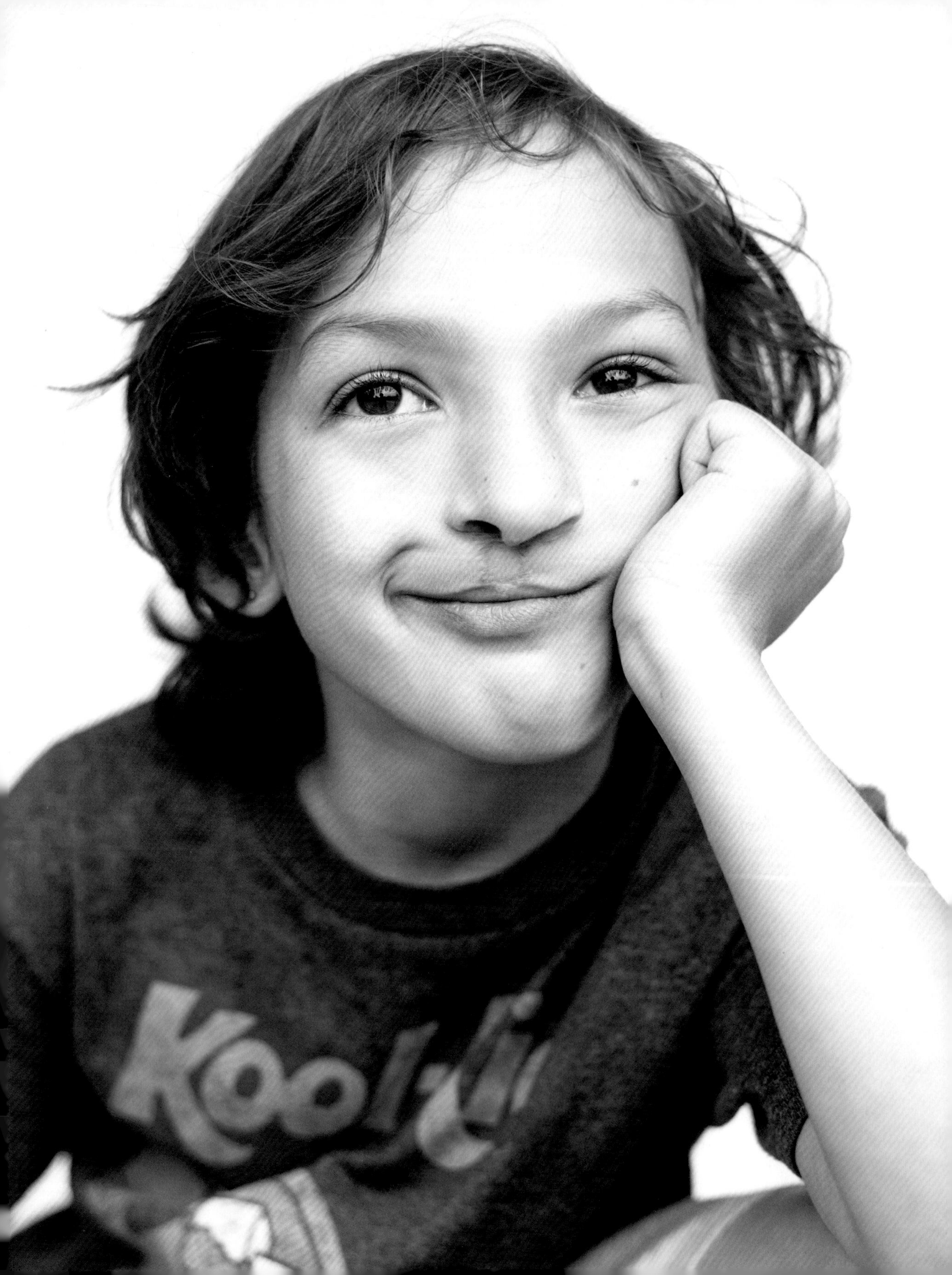

cast. My school didn't really do anything about it. All they did was keep the bully away from me on the bus and put us in different classes. Even the cops didn't do anything. It's funny how school adults let you down more than lift you up in conservative places like Arkansas. They sometimes remind me of bullies too.

I realized I was pansexual when I got my first best friend. As we got closer I began to realize I had feelings for him. I tried to hide it for a while because I knew he wasn't gay or anything. Then he found out I liked him and started to tell people.

There are a lot of people on the bus and at school I see every day who are not straight. So, because of them, every day on my way to school I would ask questions and learn more about labels and who I might be. My friends made me feel happy and more confident in who I am. They also help me feel safe. As I began to discover what that feeling was for my friend, I realized that I was pansexual. I used to think I was bisexual or gay, but then I realized that when I would hang with my crush I liked him for his personality. I thought, "Well, I like his personality, and others' personalities, so I must be pan!"

I feel lucky and grateful to have not only one mom but two moms who both love me and accept me for who I am. I met my dad three months ago and I still hide who I am from him because I am afraid of the repercussions. It helps to have queer parents like my moms. They met because they worked together and they fell in love. Being home is nice. We have lots of animals, one being my pet parrot. I have siblings that make me happy, I am lucky to have a great place to call home, and it's getting better now that I am making more friends at school.

Living in Arkansas, I don't go to a lot of things outside my house because I wanna be home and not at anyone else's house. I haven't even been to a birthday party before. It makes me nervous because I like to be home where I feel safe and happy. You'd think I'd wanna get out of the house more to be with friends, but I am quite happy at home.

I have a lot of friends at school who are queer, and being with them helps me find confidence and pride within myself. I like to get my nails painted, do photo shoots with my mom, and dress up for them. These are all things that make me feel 100 percent myself. I also love the drag scene and I even want to perform one day!

My advice to other kids like me is to ignore the haters and be yourself because it is important to be who you are and not live in the shadows of others. I was born on Christmas day, so I am a gift to the world, and so are you!

Sasha

17 years old, he/him, California
CW: This story contains references to rape and abuse.

"I hate you, you ruined my life, and I wish you were dead."

My bones are still strung together in the proper place, my skin is not broken. Yet I can't forget that from the time I was tiny and four, all the way to being filthy and thirteen, I often thought that my body would be more cared for buried under the skin of Earth. This taught me to accept abuse, sabotage my happiness, and devalue myself.

I don't think anyone understands social constructs made with the unjust power of blood-soaked pale hands long before we were alive. Not from birth certainly; even far along in life many follow the logic blindly for fear of losing the benefits of life and liberty. My neurodivergent traits were never noticeable to others, with their shallow understanding. I was deemed argumentative and whorish. At a young age I had perfected masking out of necessity, altering my natural behaviors to be safe from the consequences of not following neurotypical expectations. If only I could not feel worse—I was in pain the first moment I woke up with what I did not know was a physical disability. I'm too pretty to be disabled in any way, that is what they told me. I gathered that adults are very concerned about prettiness, especially in little girls. They gave me self-image issues disguised as compliments to make me take up less space.

In terms of fitting in, I was extremely well liked and cute. This was not without struggle; I'm a Mexican Asian American and I often wished I was mixed with white, like the mixed kids who were empathized with were. I knew that if I expressed wanting to be like boys in my class I would not be treated with care like the kids in my class who belonged to a specific cultural group were. I felt excluded and wanted acceptance, a found family. The only person I resembled physically was one of my parents, who was abusive to my primary parent for over a decade and did not have full custody. My primary parent saw this and was constantly extremely abusive to me. My primary parent had never learned to be emotionally independent, leading me to sacrifice my emotional sanity in place of a gift resembling my unconditional love. I could be beaten horribly to the point of dissociation yet be loved and doted on the next minute.

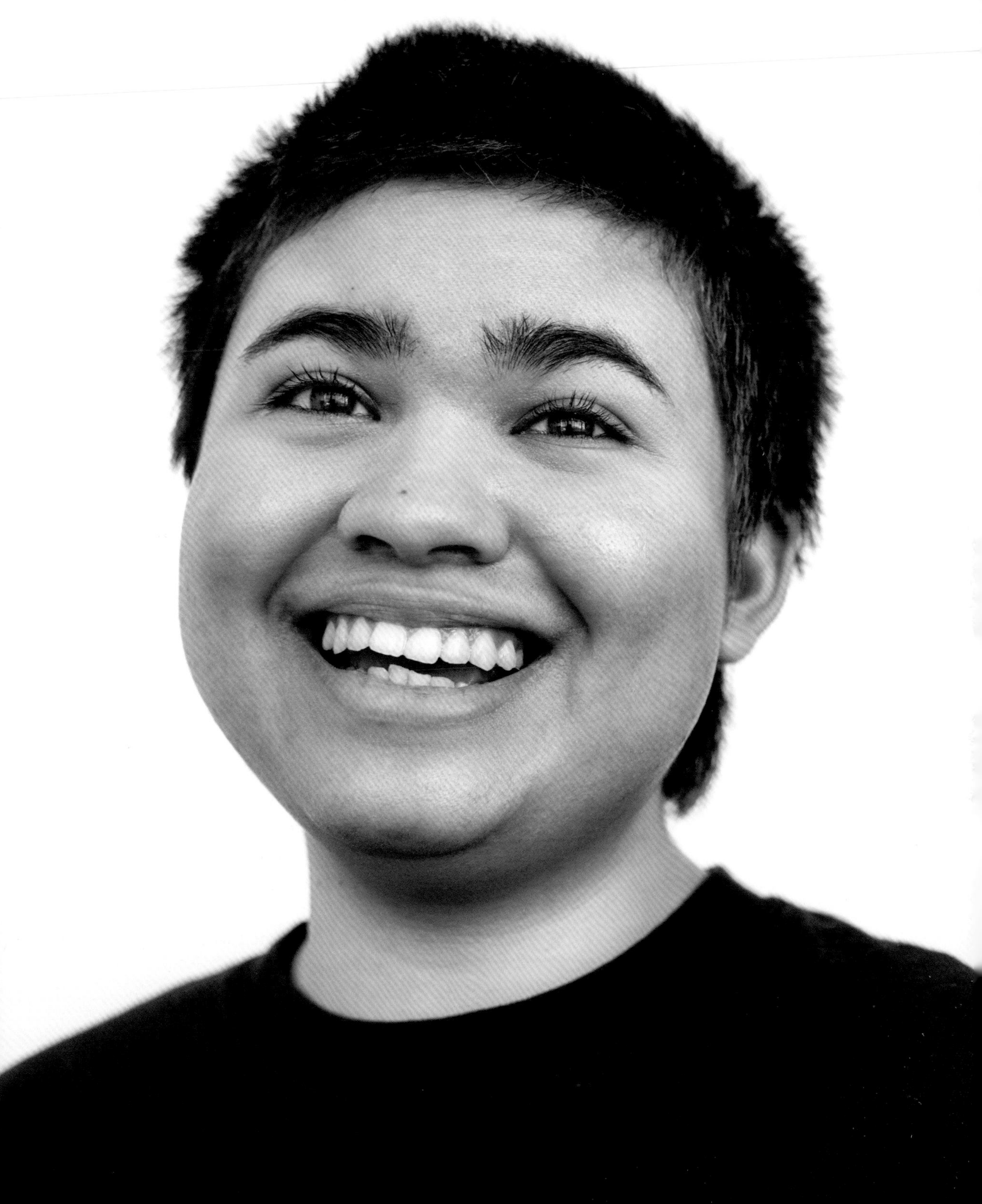

I gave everything to be loved and was guilted for existing, perceived to be an enviable blank canvas with no worries. "I would not do this to you if you were like me." I was seen as ungrateful for openly objecting to dresses, feminine shoes, and pigtails, which is how I expressed my gender nonconformity at the time. Many people blind themselves to make you appear red, an enemy. My queerness has always been seen as a rebellion from a proper and successful life. Many will try to convince you that's what being queer is, even saying what was said to me—"You know you can do boy things and be pretty, right?"—under the guise of caring concern, as if I can't be as pretty or prettier as a boy. Or, like being handsome would be wrong for me. As I write this from my disabled body with wrists that are sore naturally, not just from writing, my heart aches when I remember that my identity has always been seen as a deliberate act to be irresponsible, foolish, and incapable of receiving love.

This trauma led to very low boundaries and made me a love-hungry child. I was raped at thirteen, when I was staying with my estranged parent as part of a mandatory court decision; I excused it as my mind playing storyteller. At my new school I met a boy with extremely large and anger-filled eyes. When you looked at him, he felt like pure malice and forced choking—smelled like it too. Perfect for all the lack of love I had ever known. He love bombed me, giving me gifts, attentively following me everywhere, and slowly poking holes in my boundaries while texting me every second. Did he even sleep? He confessed to liking me romantically. I wasn't feeling mutual. Being grey-romantic, it takes a lot for me to like someone romantically at all, and although being asexual certainly does not mean abstinence, I felt uncomfortable expressing sexuality as it wouldn't be genuine from me. He got handsier and more forceful. I couldn't tell the difference between what I had always known and this behavior I excused as devotion, which made me feel stupid when I realized it years later, blaming myself. I couldn't tell why my flesh felt like it was crawling off of me, down into the drain. My genitals felt like wounds with salt. He was soon expelled for premeditated murder, wanting to stab and murder me out of jealousy for how my peers found me lovable without trying, while they found him creepy and off-putting no matter how much he lied to be liked.

My estranged parent had said to the school faculty that it was partly my fault since I latched onto him, smiling like that was just common sense. My understimulated and depressed brain felt that my rapist's intensity in his pursuit of either murdering or loving me suited my needs. I was addicted to the adrenaline that I felt I could not have from a healthy relationship. I needed support; one of the first steps to finding strength is noticing that. I came out as trans after these events, feeling tired of feeling wrong in myself and wanting to have just one thing for myself despite how I would be seen as ugly.

I am not stupid, I don't deserve abuse. I'm trans, I'm autistic, I have grown to be handsome and pretty, I am called a boyfriend by my long-term love who loves me so deeply. I am asexual, I know exactly how I feel about sexuality, and even if you're confused on what you want, you deserve a place in the world to be celebrated. I, like many of you, have worked damn hard to even exist. I have worked hard to even gain the courage to know my feelings are based on reality. So many people will try hard to convince you that expressing your identity is something ugly. Believe me, they will be tricky. It won't always be flat-out insults. It will be subtle boundary pushing, half apologizing and half blaming, it will be making you feel guilty through tears and holding puppies up to your face while regarding you as inconsiderate for bringing up your own feelings. Gaslighting is rampant, victims are not delusional, and being a victim doesn't excuse someone from becoming an abuser.

I know what I'm good at; I'm exceptionally talented at many things, and one of those things is finding out the truths of people. I can see they are blinded by hatred, part victim but now abuser, open-minded about one thing but not another. I'm queer and I'm dangerously hot, extremely attractive and intelligent, and I can't wait for all my fellow queer youth to realize this about themselves as well. For now, trust my eyes and know that I know the truth: Being queer is not an ugly thing. You're going to love this feeling, and on days I'm feeling burnt up, you'll raise me back up too.

Savannah

15 years old, she/her, Michigan
CW: This story contains references to self-harm.

Hi! My name is Savannah. I am fifteen and I come from Waterford, Michigan. My pronouns are she/her and I identify as lesbian. This is my story!

One happy summer day my girlfriend and I went to a water park. We were having so much fun enjoying each other's company. Then, surprisingly, I saw my grandma coming toward us. As she made her way to us she instantly smiled and began telling me how happy she was for my girlfriend and me. She made me feel like I was free. Like I could be myself and be proud of my relationship. However, when I woke up that wasn't the case.

My parents have been split since I can remember, and things haven't always been easy. My grandma, though, she always had my back. She and I were best friends. The only downfall was that she was very homophobic. She was religious in a sense, and also very traditional. Every time she saw a "queer" she would complain about how they are an abomination. One day I even heard her say that if any of her kids were gay she would disown them. Yes, even her own kids. This really took a toll on my life, and we'll get back to that later on.

Growing up I never really heard of the LGBTQ+ community. So in fourth grade, when I realized I had my first crush and it was on a girl, I was really just confused. I didn't know if it was natural, or if the feelings that I had were even valid. I came home from school one day and told my dad I thought I liked girls, and to my surprise he was cool with it, but even after that conversation I stayed closeted. I never really confronted my feelings for women again until the sixth grade. I developed another crush on my best friend at the time—we'll call her J. We started dating at one point but kind of just kept it to ourselves. I had never felt more myself than when I was with her. However, finding interest in a straight girl did me no justice. She ended up calling things off with me and started dating a boy soon after. This is what started my depression. I felt betrayed and humiliated. I felt like I could never come out. After that J and I still talked, and she had taken notice of my behavior and mental health. I was very suicidal at the time, dealing with attention issues and some internal homophobia. Because of this J went to my school counselor. My counselor, obviously concerned, called

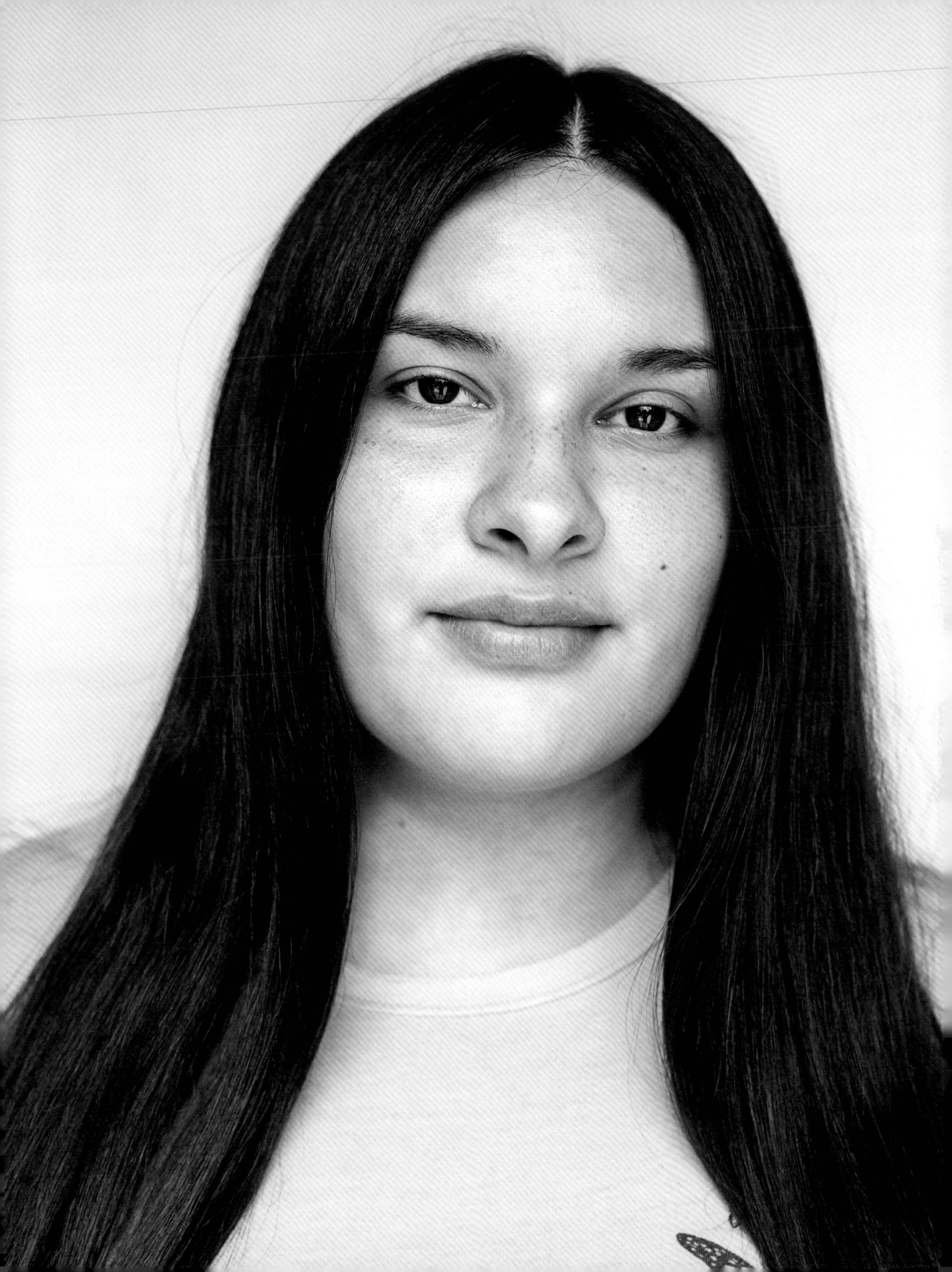

my mom and told her everything that had happened between J and me. When I got home that day my mom sat me down and found self-harm marks on my arms. I was terrified of how she would react. She ended up just laying with me in my bed and just listening. That's when I came out to her. She told me that no matter what she would love me and that all she wants is for me to be happy. This really opened my eyes and made my fear of being rejected diminish.

Some time passed after coming out to my mom, and I continued to feel better about myself. I was more confident and I embraced my sexuality around the people I felt most comfortable with. Then just one night ruined all of that. Out of anger my aunt told my homophobic grandma I was a lesbian. This set off an explosion. My grandma called me that night and expressed to me that she believed I was "sick" and that I needed "help." She told me she wished for me to never find happiness if it had to be with a woman and that I would go to hell. Then she ended with those four words, "It's just a phase." This absolutely broke me because, as I said before, my grandma was my best friend. This made all my anger toward myself come back. I tried so hard to push every gay feeling out of me. Because of that I ended up dating a boy for about a year. I was never interested in this boy, but it was my only escape from myself. I would tell myself, "You can't like girls! You have a boyfriend." Saying that to myself didn't work though. I knew I was attracted to women, and I knew it was just going to get harder to push that away, so I finally ended things with that boy and haven't dated a boy since. Anyway, back to my grandma. She recently passed away about a year ago, and the beginning of my story was just a dream I had since her passing. That dream gave me closure; it made me hopeful that she was no longer hateful, and that she accepted me.

Since her passing I have managed to be in a committed relationship, and I want people to know that, no matter what life throws your way, you can still find love. Being with someone who truly loves you for you is so powerful. You should always keep people around you that give you those positive feelings. Along with my relationship there have been challenges. I'm not talking about challenges with each other but challenges between us and society. In her town we get stares when we hold hands in public and rude comments when we kiss. Being a woman, openly lesbian, and Nicaraguan has definitely had its not-so-good moments. Luckily, in the Waterford/ Clarkston area it is more diverse. Kids don't judge you for being in the LGBTQ+ community, being a person of color, being a different sex, etc. Most adults don't either. People are more open-minded and just see past all the religious and traditional stuff. However, I know everyone can relate to the bad experiences of being openly a part of the LGBTQ+ community. When I'm in my girlfriend's city, which is more traditional, it feels like I have to hide who I am for my own safety. I wish my love was considered normal to everyone, but all that matters is that my love is accepted by someone. That's what you always have to remember, that someone looks at you and doesn't see a transgender individual, a gay individual, a bisexual individual, a pansexual individual, etc. They see a human—someone who is loving, smart, kind, and funny—and that's what I see.

For a while I never told anyone I liked girls; only my close friends and parents knew. I didn't know how my older family would react so I just never tried to be myself around them. One day my mom posted homecoming pictures of my girlfriend and me, and to my surprise all of them were accepting. I never gave my family a chance, and that was one of my worst mistakes. Sometimes you need to just trust your family. I am appreciative of how supportive my parents and family are. It has gotten me through the worst times.

I hope you know that there is always room for growth and change. People can develop different mindsets, especially if you show them there's no reason to hate. Always go through life open-minded because someone will likely learn that from you. Also, try to spread love to the world because everyone needs it just as much as you do. There is always light at the end of the tunnel. If you feel like you've hit rock bottom, there is only one way to go from there and it's up. Love yourself, beautiful human, because that's what's going to matter most when it comes to getting through every day. Let your soul shine!

Seba

13 years old, he/him, Indiana

Hi, I'm Sebastian. I'm a thirteen-year-old Indigenous trans boy from the Indiana state border. I use the pronouns he/him/his, and this is my story.

I started transitioning in the first grade, but it was a slow and confusing process in the beginning. I felt like I was born in the wrong body, but it was hard to explain because I didn't really know about trans life or what it meant. As I got older I felt more sure of who I was. Ever since I can remember my mom and siblings have been my safe place. The first person I came out to was my mom. She's always talked to me about how I felt and supported me.

Growing up in my community has been difficult at times because there's a lack of support and acceptance for LGBTQ+ youth in my area. In school it was always the same questions or comments: if I was a boy or girl, if I liked girls or not, down to what bathroom I should be using. I felt my peers were more interested in my gender than who I was. By fifth grade I had a few good friends, and my stepdad came into my life. He has also been very supportive and protective of me.

Middle school is when my life kinda got flipped upside down. At school one day during lunch I was told that I had to be straight to sit at a certain table, and it was in front of people who I thought were my friends. Nobody stood up for me or said that it wasn't okay to say that—they just laughed—and even though it hurt me, I stood up for myself. After that I felt like I had no friends and that nobody wanted to hang out with me. My parents advocated for me at school, but I felt that nothing had changed there. My opinion about the school had changed because I felt that I wasn't validated and that something that I was proud to tell other people about and trust them with had been betrayed.

Then the pandemic happened and everything went to online school, which was very nice because I didn't have to worry about being bullied. I have chosen to stay with online school. I feel that it helps me stay focused on my education without being picked on or wondering what others think of me.

My parents and siblings have been very supportive and are a big part of my life. My mom got in contact with the LGBTQ center in Southbend. I started doing the trans youth Zoom meetings,

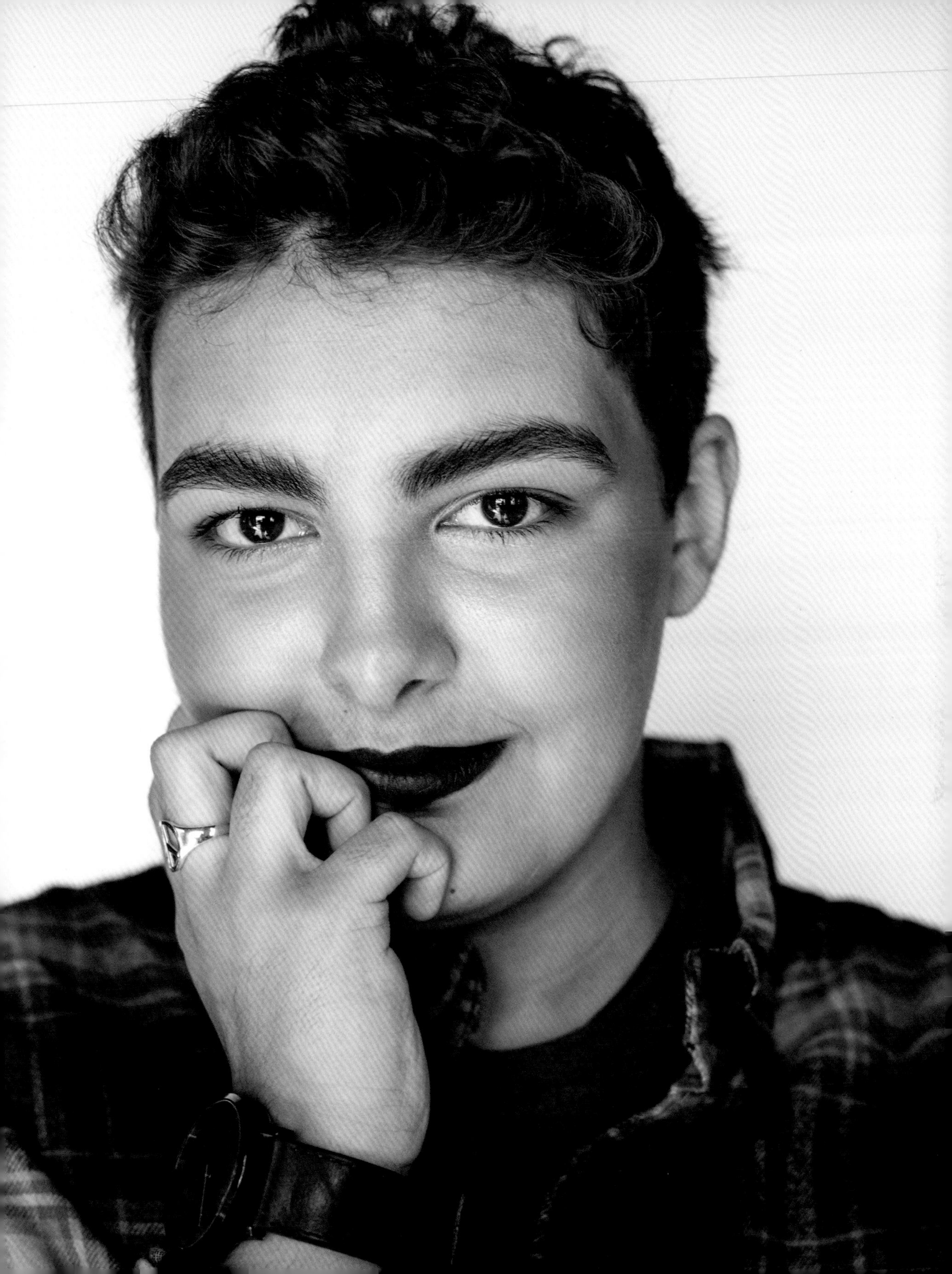

and in the summer of 2021 I started going to their youth drop-ins. Everyone has been nice and welcoming. I am already creating great memories there and look forward to going to drop-ins in person. This past year has been great because I haven't been bullied, but I know it won't always be like this. I have a great support system, and that's important.

My hope for other queer youth who are having a difficult time and who don't have someone to lean on is that they find their local LGBTQ center. Don't be nervous to get in contact with them. I'm glad I did.

Today I love myself and I have confidence in who I am. I use art to express my pride and who I am as a trans youth. I dress in what makes me comfortable and I am free to be me.

If you are reading my story, please don't allow others to back you into a corner to where they make you feel like you aren't cared about or don't belong, because there are a lot of people who support and care about you. You just have to find them. And don't be afraid to stand up for yourself. You are gorgeous!

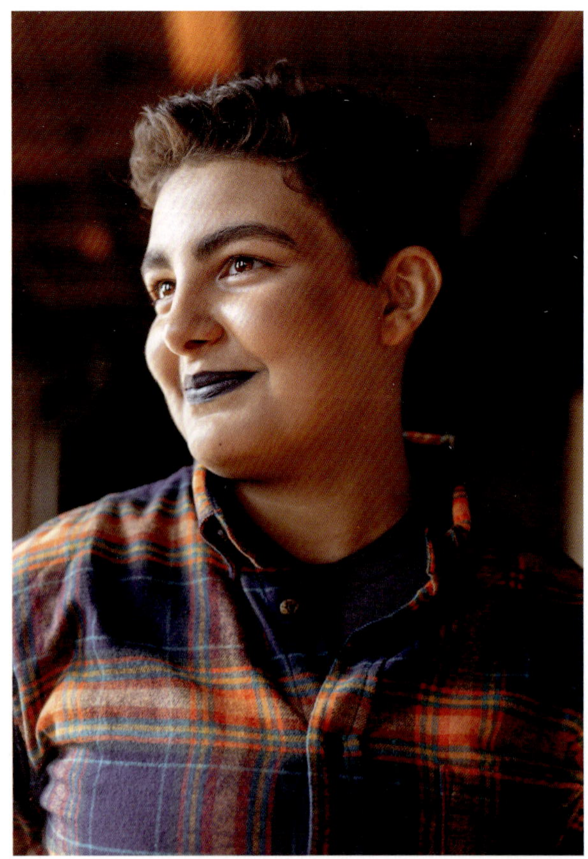

Skyler

16 years old, they/them, Utah
CW: This story contains references to sexual assault.

"Always remember where you are going and never forget where you have been."

It might not surprise you, but I got this quote from a Panda Express fortune cookie. Regardless of its origin, I regularly dwell on those words and how much they apply to my own experiences. While on my journey to the ripe old age of sixteen years old, I have had the honor to be myself: I can be a nonbinary, neurodivergent lesbian. But I wasn't always so confident and understanding about every part of my identity, and that is the story I want to share with you today.

Not only was I raised as a member of the LDS Church, but I was also raised in Utah, which meant that as a child I never saw an authentic representation of myself. Whenever anything remotely queer was brought up in Sunday school, my religion was quick to encourage mixed-orientation marriage or lifelong celibacy as a solution. Because of these religious policies, the Family Proclamation, and the teachings against LGBTQ+ individuals, I grew up believing that the queer community was impure and unnatural.

Like most impressionable children, I used things like baptism, sacrament, and getting sealed to my family to feel validated by my parents, bishop, and God. It was because of that very affirmation that I didn't even realize the dangerous situations I was placed in as a kid. An example was when I was required to meet alone with my bishop before my baptism. I sat down with him, and he interrogated me like any other child, but this meeting quickly changed as soon as he asked me if I was still chaste.

As an eight-year-old, I asked for elaboration on the topic, which led to him asking and explaining wildly inappropriate questions regarding virginity, masturbation, and porn. Unfortunately, a few months prior to this meeting I had just gone through a very traumatic sexual abuse experience. Despite how unprofessional and disgusting those questions were, I trusted this man, so ultimately this line of questioning led to my bishop being the first person to learn about my rape.

His immediate response was silence, but after some time he explained to me that all this had occurred because of my own doing. He continued by telling me how I was impure, that baptism would clear away this "sin," and that I should never share this

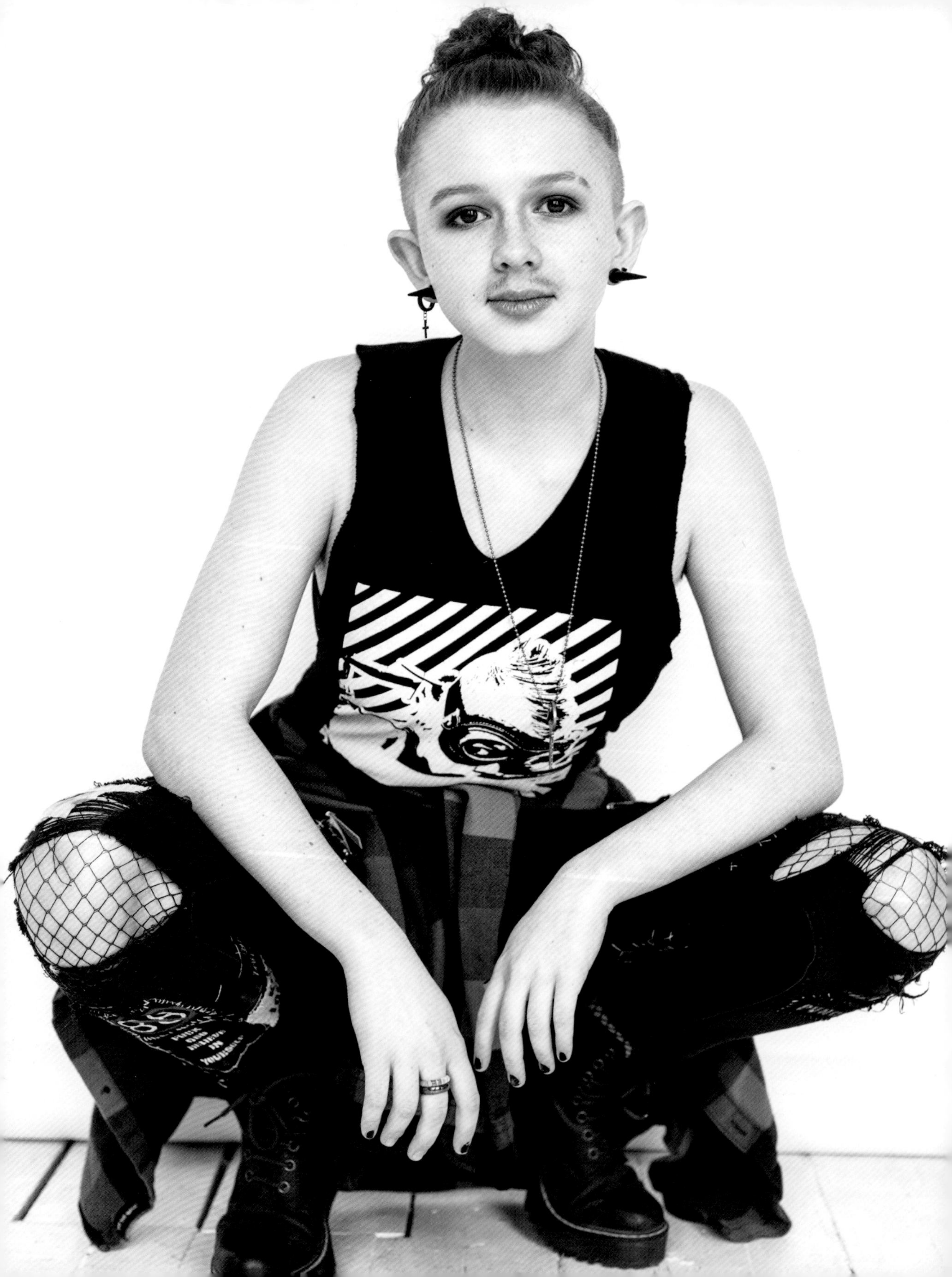

secret with anyone else. Because of these words I was silent on this subject for almost nine years.

Later on in my life, when I started realizing my sexuality, I even blamed my queer feelings on my rape; ultimately, it made me feel like God didn't forgive me for this "sin." The self-doubt grew to a point where I truly believed it was my fault and that my cousin's sexual advances were a thing of normalcy in families.

I carried this burden throughout my academic career, causing me to deal poorly with my depression and queerness through secrecy. I would feel discouraged when my friends talked about the cute boys they held feelings for or when they joked about queer identities. But, through the darkness, I remember the very first time I truly felt validated for my sexuality and, without knowing it yet, my gender identity too.

I was in sixth grade, and I would often play basketball at recess with those supposed "cute boys" my friends would gush about. After a particularly long game, we all sat down in a circle and ate lunch together making normal back-and-forth banter. The boys started acting giddy when the topic of crushes came around; weirdly, I felt understood when the boys around me described their feelings toward my female peers. As they described their experiences, my mind ventured off to the times I would get butterflies when a girl would grab my hand, play with my hair, say I looked cute, or even prolong a goodbye hug. It was because I liked girls the same way my bashful male peers did.

I felt liberated from a false sense of myself until one of my peers looked at me and loudly stated, "Hey, we should stop talking about this with a girl around. She's one of them." At this moment, before I could interject, my friend spoke up saying, "It's okay. She's one of us." Other members of the circle were quick to agree and continued their conversation. I was absolutely dumbfounded by how validating a few simple words and head nods made me feel; since then, I've tried my best to be myself.

That motivation led to me coming out through a testimony meeting.

During my testimony everything abruptly ceased. I tapped on the microphone and felt confused as to why my words were now muted. I quickly turned to inform my bishop about the faulty microphone, only to be met with a disgusted look and stern tone, "Please sit down."

Yet again a few simple words had changed my entire perspective on life. The man I grew up putting on a pedestal and respected just as much as I do my parents wore a look of disappointment. This same man had told me the most awful things about my rape and silenced my voice, but he still thought of himself as holier than me.

After coming out at church I got bullied for being a lesbian, both in person and online. This was not only from strangers but also from the people that I trusted most, including friends, family, church members, and neighbors. Now that I'm older I have some advice for others who are going through this: Ignore them, because their opinions can't change who you know you are. It's your life to live, and only you can know what that truly means. There is nothing wrong with you. You are beautiful, wanted, and perfect just as you are.

Overall, LGBTQ+ people deserve change, love, and support from our society, and that is the bare minimum to being treated as human beings. Fundamental human rights have never been, and will never be, a want, for they are a necessity. As a young LGBTQ activist I strive to bring equity and awareness to our community, because without equity for those who are less fortunate we will never truly be equal. Going into the future, we need to collectively use our voices and support those within our own communities— especially our trans women of color. Just as said by Marsha P. Johnson, the Black trans woman who is one of the many pillars who holds the queer community's platform high, "No pride for some of us without liberation for all of us."

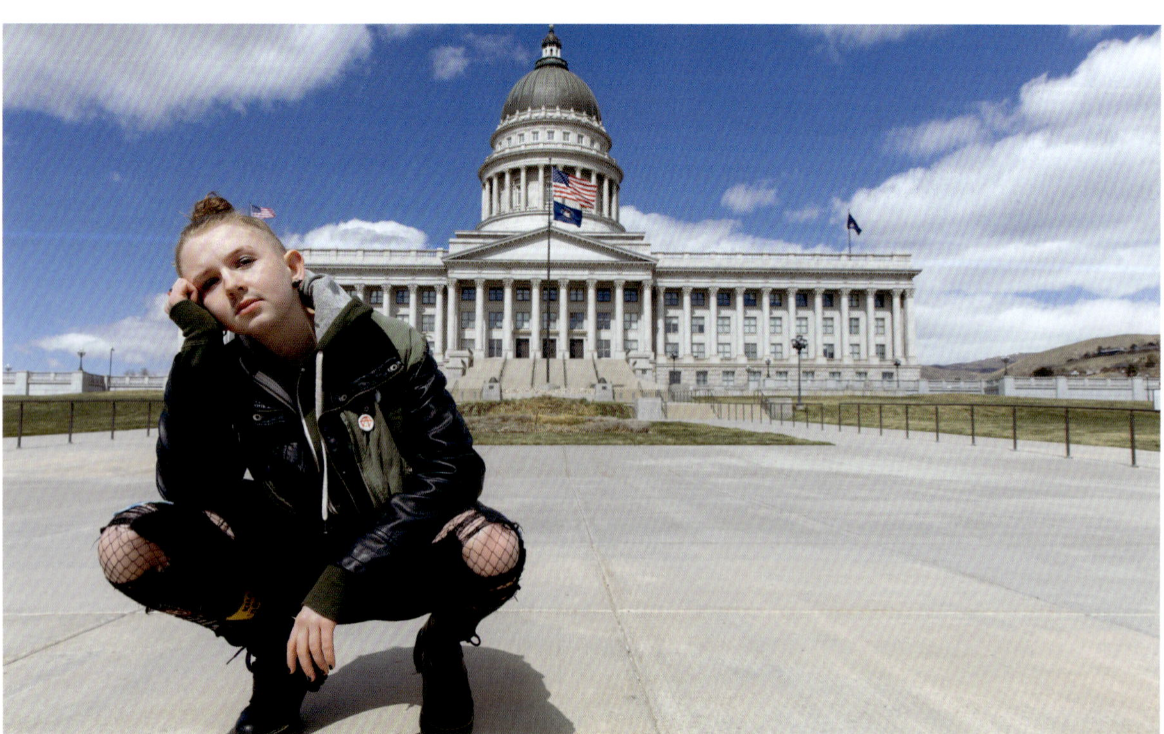

Theo

17 years old, he/him, Alaska

Hello, my name is Theo, I use he/him pronouns, I am seventeen, I am queer, and I am disabled. I like to write poetry. I am bilingual (German and English), attend a dual enrollment program (high school and college), I am a major in my JROTC battalion, and I am a Christian. I live in Anchorage, Alaska. I love *Star Trek* and I like to collect trading cards from popular media.

Back in 2018, when I first participated in Project Contrast, there were a lot of unknown reasons why I did certain things. Why I held a pencil like that, why I talked like that, and many other whys. I knew I was queer, but I identified a bit differently. I now use the term *queer* for my overall sexuality and *transmasculine* for my gender identity. I am not sure if I will still use those terms in the future, and that's okay! You should never feel the need to be 100 percent sure of what labels you use.

As a disabled person I get looked at differently when I use my crutches, especially because I didn't use to need them. I get asked why I don't use them all of the time, or why I need them at all. I get stared at, especially if I am also having tics. However, when I first came out, things were similar. "Why didn't you know/tell me earlier?" was a common phrase. It became striking to me later on that things are never concrete, whether it be gender, sexuality, or disability. Everything changes over time, and that is okay.

Living in Alaska is isolating, but I am lucky enough to live in the biggest city in Alaska, so I have access to more resources than others. I still struggle with finding others like me, but I have found other ways to connect with a community. Alaska has a rough history, and our history is filled with harming the Indigenous people who live here. I live on Dena'ina land, which is important to acknowledge, especially since I am white. My school district includes 100+ different spoken languages. I have friends who come from different places and different cultures, and that's important to have. Alaska may be isolated from other parts of the United States, but we connect in our own way.

At age thirteen I wrote, "When I was twelve years old I started to question my sexuality. I had just turned thirteen when I began questioning my gender. At first I didn't know of any terms to describe myself, but by using the Internet I was able to find out more words

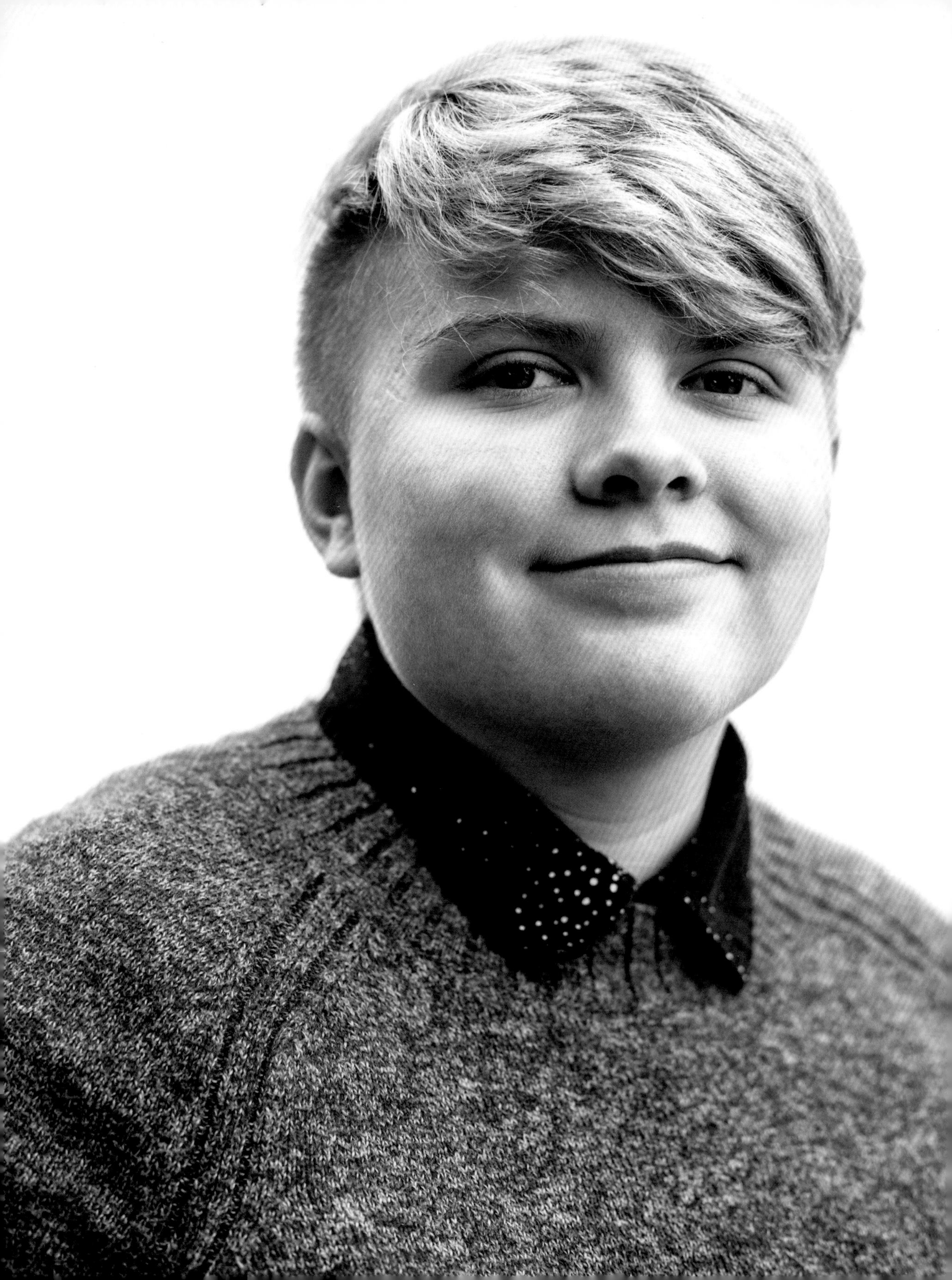

that fit. The Internet is one of the most common ways that LGBTQ+ people can explore, find terms, and connect with one another quickly. It even helped me to find myself." Now I'd like to say to thirteen-year-old me, "You will learn that you treasure the ways you can find others like you through the Internet, and the Internet will let you know that it is okay to be you, and you will grow confident in yourself in all your queer, disabled, trans, strange ways."

I wrote a short speech, a sermon you could call it, for Pride Sunday. I talked about how God created me to be a queer person, and how I was not a sinner for living up to how God created me. I was made to be loved by them and all of her people. I am his creation, and I am proud of that, no matter what some may say. He created me to learn, to help, to create, and most of all to love.

I think that I will wrap this up by highlighting a few things: You are allowed to change. In fact, you should change so that you can become a better person. You are allowed to, and should, find your people. You are allowed to be who you are, and if you believe in a creator/creators, they made you to be you. You are allowed to be you.

Tia

15 years old, she/her, Michigan

Hello, my name is Tia and I am fifteen. I go by she/her. I am a
pansexual person of color. I live in a suburb near Detroit. I'd like
to tell you how and when I figured out I also liked girls, and how I
came out.

Not a lot of people acknowledge that I am queer. I barely have
any queer friends, and to be honest it can get pretty homophobic
here. But I am a confident queer woman and here's how it started.

When I was in sixth grade I had a physical education class. And
I hated it. I didn't do much. I played a few games, but for the most
part I just sat around. There was a girl in my class who also didn't
want to play any of the sports and games we did in PE. Because we
were both extremely lazy and didn't participate in the class activities, we started to talk every day in that class. She was very nice
and had a lot of the same interests as me. And I thought she was so
incredibly gorgeous. We soon started to talk outside of that class,
and I realized I got the same butterflies in my stomach that I did
when I talked to a boy that I liked. And that really confused me. I
constantly asked myself if something was wrong with me and why
I was feeling this way. I chalked it up to me just really wanting to
be friends with her. Then she came out as bisexual—it was a game
changer, and she told me all about it—and I started to wonder if I
was bisexual too. I watched a lot of videos on sexuality and coming
out. I was still really confused if I liked girls or not, but I just didn't
bring it up to anyone. One day my friend from PE started dating a
girl, and I didn't like that at all. I wondered how she was so comfortable in her sexuality, and what that other girl had that I didn't. I
realized I liked her as more than a friend. I told another friend who
was also in my PE class and who I knew was a closeted lesbian.
Because of this I was sure I could trust her.

Eventually the girls broke up and part of me was glad, even
though my friend/crush seemed to be really upset about it. One
day during PE we were playing kickball outside. Like usual, me
and my friend didn't participate. We played in the grass and talked
about classes, teachers, and classmates. Then the topic of crushes
came up. My heart was racing and I was scared; I wasn't ready to
come out. And then the only friend I had told came up to us and
asked what we were talking about. I felt like I was safe, like no one

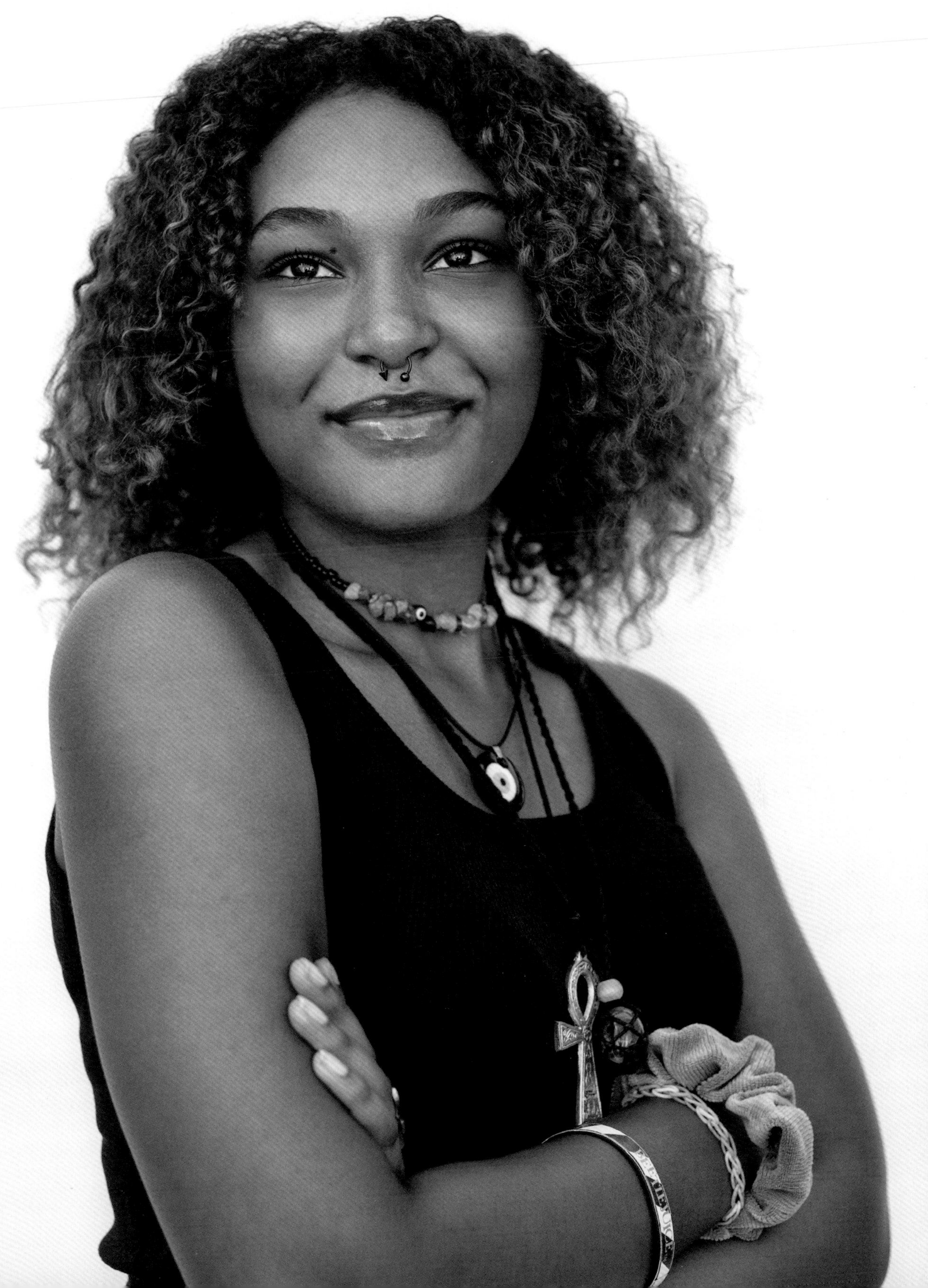

would find out—until my crush told this friend what our conversation was about. And my friend said, "I know who your crush is!" and looked at my crush. I was so scared that she'd run away and never talk to me again. But we all just ignored it, pretended it never happened, until later, after class, my crush looked at me and said, "It's me, isn't it?" I was shocked and scared, but to my excitement she told me she liked me too. But she was moving away, and we wouldn't be able to hang out or see each other. I was so sad, but I was happy she still cared about me.

That was three years ago, and I still think about her. I thank her every chance I get, because without her I don't know when I would have figured out my sexuality. She's helped me be comfortable in my own skin and I'm so grateful. I'll never forget her because within my community there aren't a lot of people to help you figure out the feelings you're having.

After doing nothing in PE for quite some time, how did I come out, you say? A year later I was sitting in the car with my mom. She was talking about one of her friends who is gay. I was like, "Mom, do you know what pansexual is?"

She goes, "Yeah." I told her I was pansexual and she said, "Okay." That was much easier than gym class.

Sometimes it's hard being a queer person of color (POC) because discrimination comes from both sides. A lot of black households are very religious, and this can cause a lot of homophobia. Because of the homophobia rooted in ethnic households, POC are less likely to come out, so the LGBTQ+ community has a lack of POC representation.

That brings me to my next issue, racism in the LGBTQ+ community. The queer community is mostly white people. And despite all the protests, movements, and hashtags, racism against POC is still a very large issue.

Our community is so rooted in homophobia that I felt like I didn't belong in my own community because I was different. People constantly putting me down for who I was made me want to find the confidence I knew I had. I found my confidence being a queer person of color through social media platforms, videos, TikToks, and anything I could find. And by doing so I found a community like me. I saw they were comfortable, beautiful, and looked like me. They were truly themselves. Then I asked myself, "How can I be like these women and men? So open in their sexuality and so comfortable with themselves?" I looked at myself and said, "I look like that. I can do things like that too." The LGBTQ+ community is for all of us, and I had to realize that I belong there too.

So if I'm not accepted in the POC community or the LGBTQ+ community, where do I fit? Well, thanks to the Internet it's a lot easier to find allies from both sides. You can do things like join safe LGBTQ+ chat rooms, make your own LGBTQ+ chat rooms, or post videos to find and help other queer teens find allies. If we all work together and support each other we can help all queer kids, especially queer POC, find allies and safe places. With love, Tia.

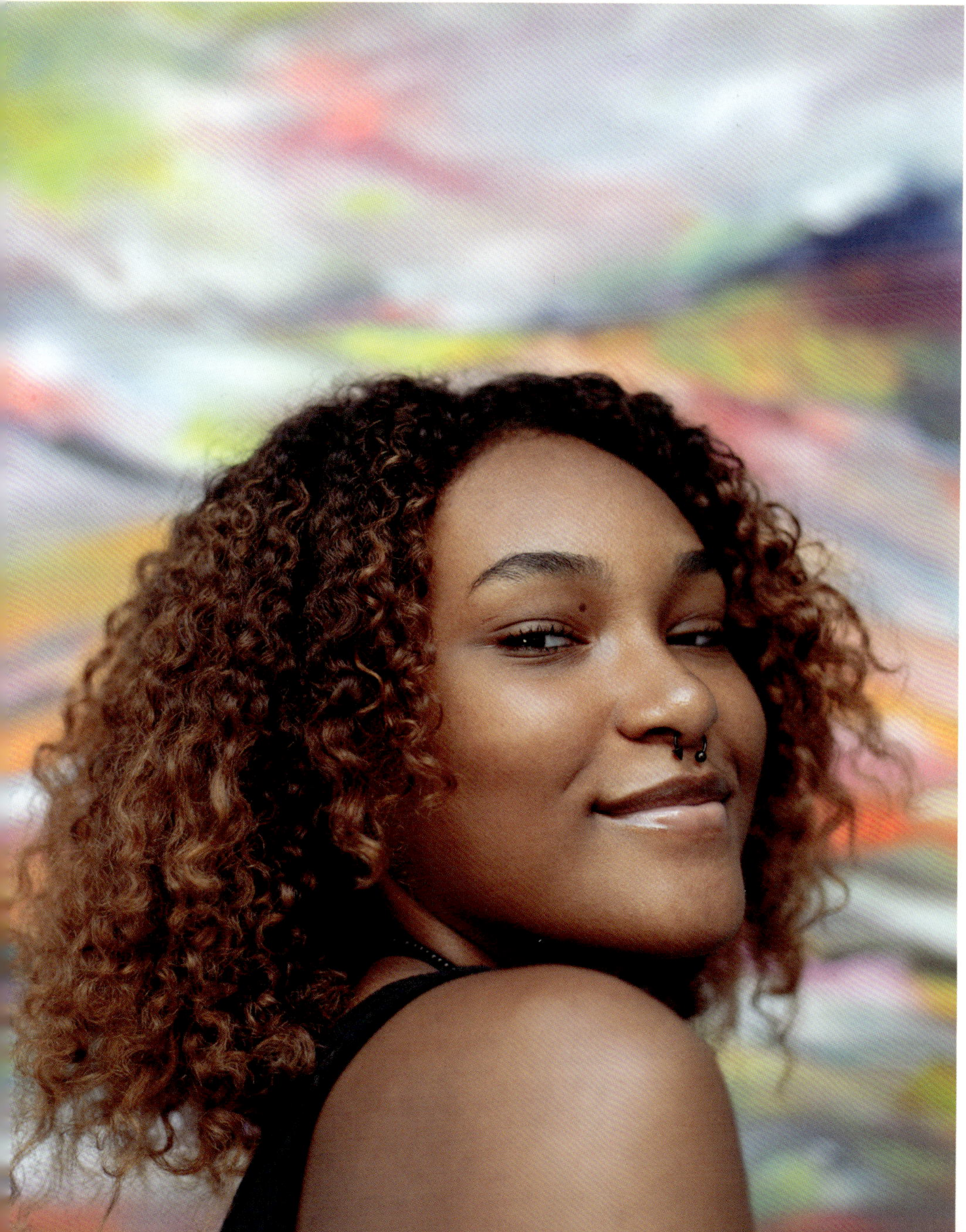

Tia

Trevor

17 years old, he/him, Texas

Hello, my name is Trevor, my pronouns are he/him, and I'm here to share my story and experience of being gay in the South. Most people know me as the "nail boy," but my story is much deeper than that. My story is about defying the odds and the growth that has come from being a gay male in the Bible belt of Texas.

I live in a decently sized, overly conservative town in West Texas called Abilene. I realized I was gay in seventh grade, but because of where I live, this isn't a "good thing" to the close-minded people here. I was fortunate enough that I got to live in Minnesota for three years, and that is where I fully came to terms within myself. I realized that this world is an ugly place and I should never let anyone degrade or belittle me in any way. I came out the summer of sophomore year and my life turned upside down. I started to see how far back in history my town is. I lost a lot of friends, I made new ones, I sometimes got bullied for my sexual orientation, and I slowly started drowning. That was until I found my forever friends and never looked back. Being gay in West Texas hasn't been easy, but if I had the chance to change my experience I wouldn't. I realized that I am amazing and there is nothing wrong with me, or anyone else who is queer in this world. I started to educate myself and become a person who advocates for others, who sticks up for what's right, and who refuses to let close-minded people get to me. That is how I got here.

At the end of November last year, I finally took a stand at my cruel and unethical school. I got suspended for a week for wearing nail polish—yes, nail polish. It was a defining moment for me, and I couldn't take it anymore, so I cried out for help and posted a Snapchat, not knowing that the whole world would soon hear my story. It was a complete roller coaster of emotions, but it was also the best experience of my life. I soon found out that I am not alone in this world, and there are so many people who understand how I felt. The media, people from all over the world, my family and friends—all of them supported me in every way. Through a bunch of trials and tribulations I got the school dress code to be gender neutral in all ways! It was an experience I will never forget, and through it I found a passion that I could work with for the rest of my life. I plan on being a civil rights lawyer and crushing

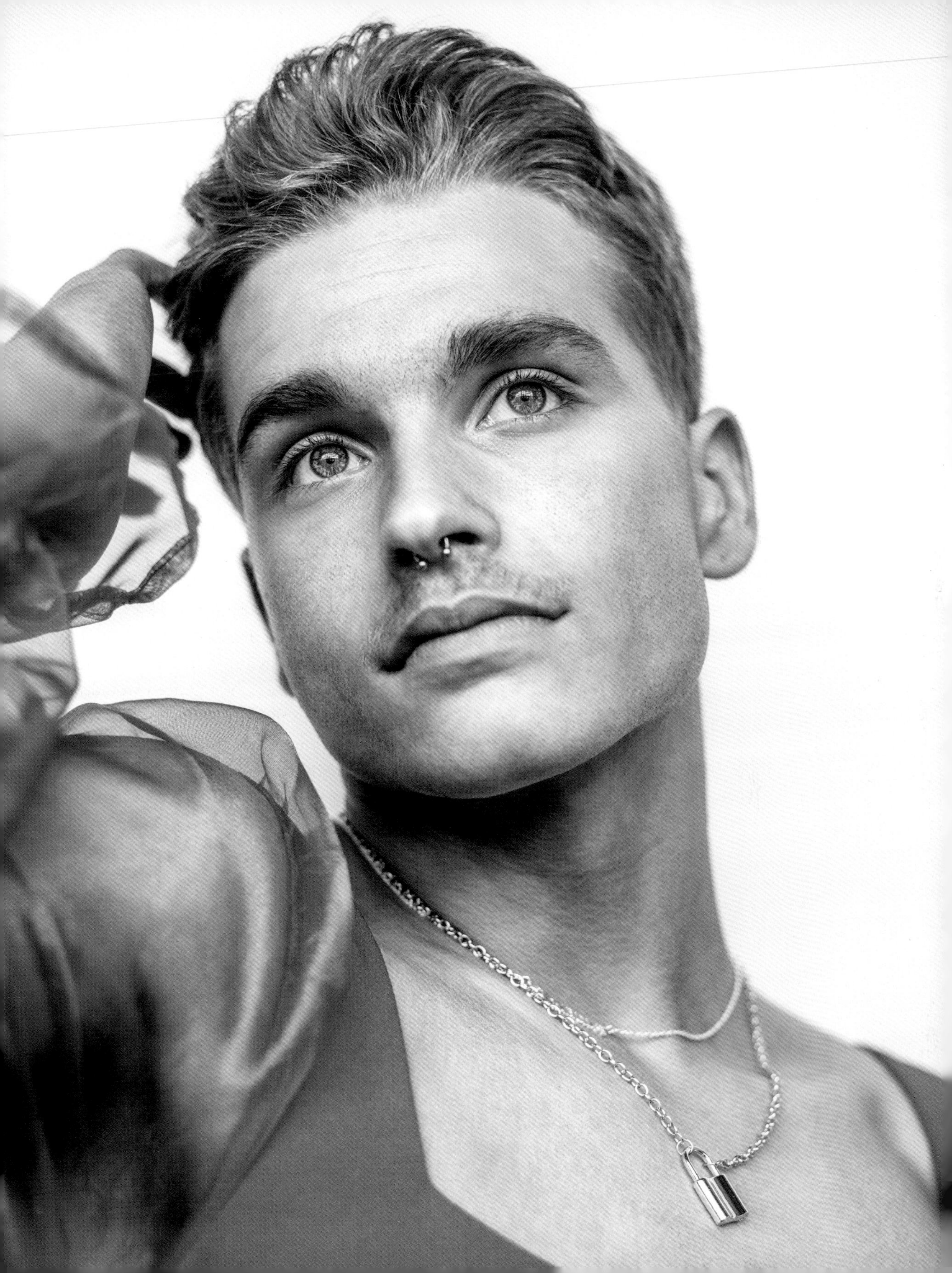

gender norms, discrimination, and homophobia for as long as I can. Living in Texas, I have always been so afraid of who I am, but—excuse my French—fuck this world. I am a gay male and I am beyond proud. I love myself in every way and wouldn't change who I am for the world.

I know that so many people have felt and still feel the pain I once felt. If anyone reading this feels this way, please listen. You are amazing, you are loved, and you are beautiful inside and out. There is not a single thing wrong with being gay; if anything, I think it personally adds flavor :) It sounds so cliché, but pain is only temporary—you will make it out of there. I would encourage you to find people like you and people you can relate to. You have a whole community behind you! We all support you from all over the world, so just know you're not alone. This world is an ugly, cruel place and, regardless if you're gay, straight, trans, or anything for that matter, someone is going have something negative to say. So why waste time trying to please everyone else? Be *you*, and stunt on these old, close-minded people! Lastly, know that I am proud of you for waking up every day and trying to keep a smile. You are loved, you are amazing, and, most importantly, you are you.

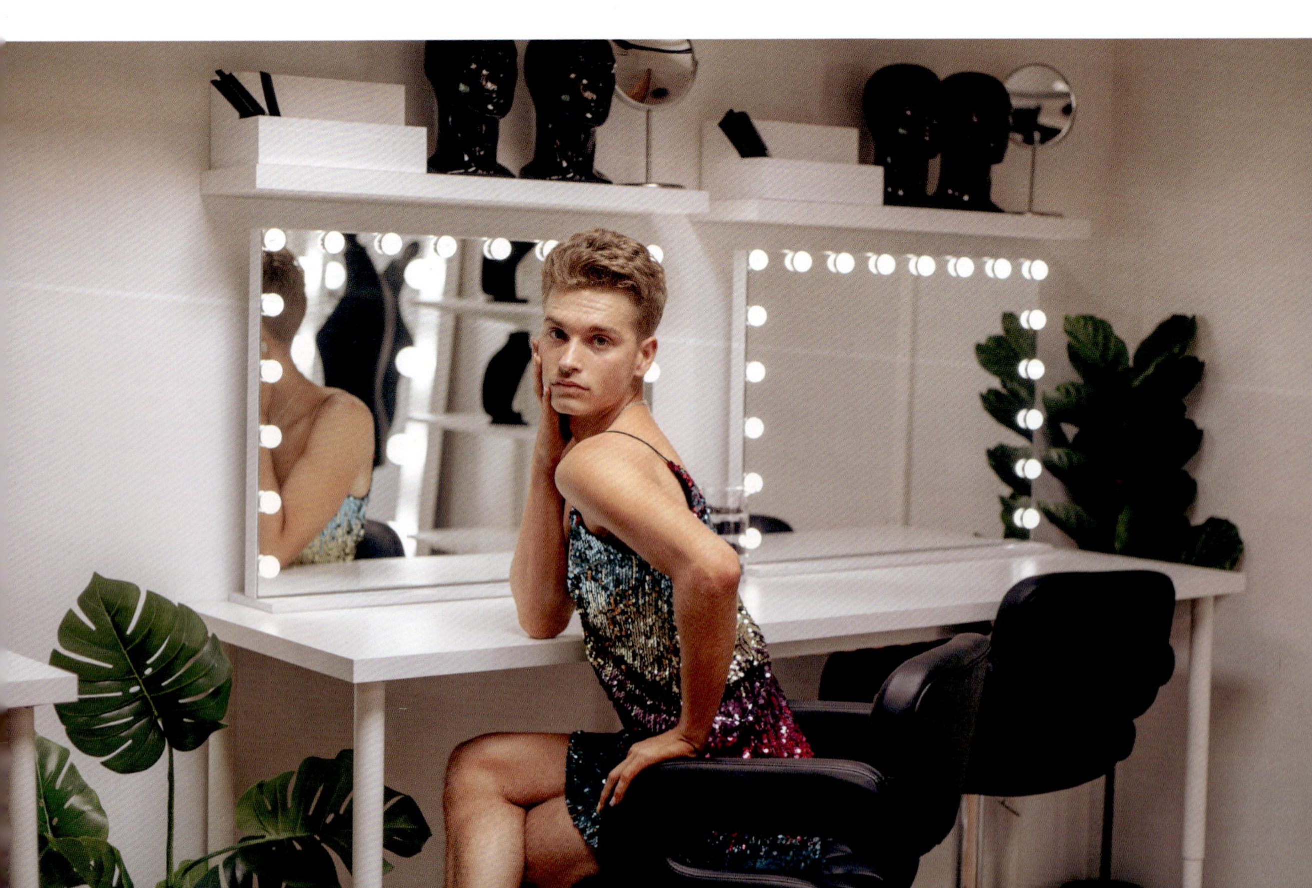

Tristen

18 years old, he/him, California
CW: This story contains brief references to self-harm.

Hello, I'm Tristen, my pronouns are he/him, and I am a trans man who is currently eighteen years old living in Visalia, California.

Tranny, butch, tomboy, transvestite, and all the like have been said to me growing up. Ever since I was a kid in elementary school I've struggled with my identity and who I identified as. It was difficult grasping that at the age of eight. I always thought it must've been a tomboy thing, or that I was simply into more boy things than the average girl. But as time kept passing by, every time I looked in the mirror the image I saw grew more unfamiliar. All the dresses and girly things felt disgusting on me, and I would tear them off just to throw on baggy clothes. Every time I got mistaken for a boy my self-esteem would rise and I would feel a sense of joy. However, growing up in my community was a struggle. My family and the people surrounding my family held traditional beliefs, so I still found myself growing distant every day because of my identity.

It was not only my family but the town I lived in as well that held traditional beliefs. It's ironic because you would think any part of California would be accepting since it's a blue state, but people forget about the Central Valley of California: Fresno, Bakersfield, Visalia, etc. The red cities. I mainly kept to myself growing up, still figuring out my identity while hiding my overall alternative beliefs. It was tough, being in a small town where practically everyone knew each other; I never felt lonelier in my entire life. I never had anyone to turn to for LGBT advice because I never knew anybody who was out, and I didn't come to terms with my identity until middle school. I relied solely on the Internet for comfort and looked for support in the art community by pretending to be a man online.

In middle school I realized my depression kept getting worse for whatever reason, and I finally learned what being trans was by browsing and having discussions on the Internet. I panicked at first, coming to terms with it. My diehard Christian family definitely wouldn't accept me for this, so why was this on my mind, I would ask myself repeatedly. I kept denying and denying until I finally was able to cut my hair short. Simple things like that made me passable and filled me with an overwhelming sense of joy. I

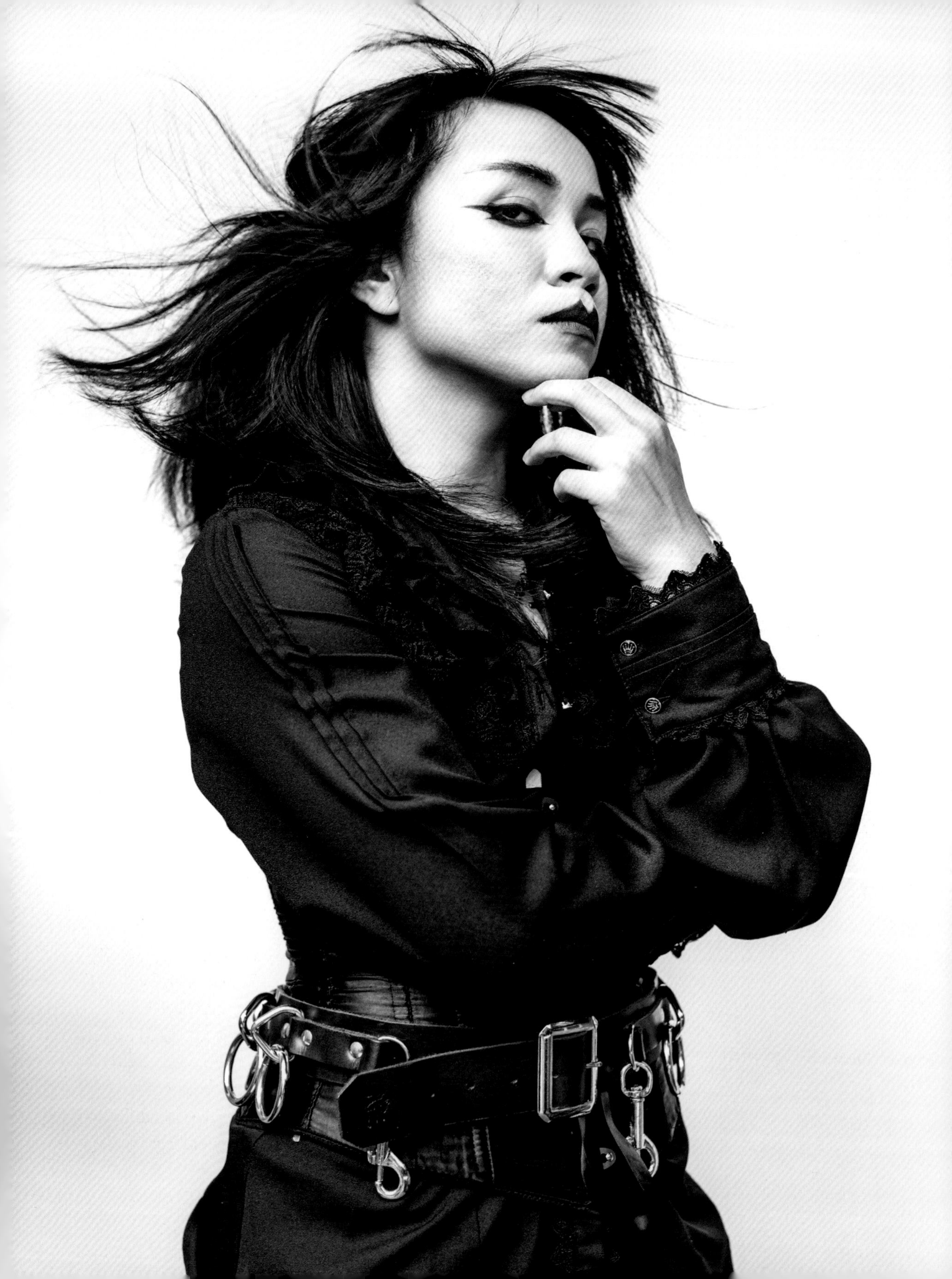

finally requested a therapist to help me with my ongoing problem and to start my journey of self-realization.

I never came out to anyone and kept my discussions with my therapists to myself and away from my family. I remember asking my grandparents a hypothetical question like, "What would you do if I brought my friend over who was trans?" to which their answer simply was, "I don't want them here. If I ever found out you were trans I would wait until you were eighteen to kick you out." At that point I knew my family couldn't be the support system I needed to better myself in life. I remember I came out to my friend in middle school first. I remember how terrified I was telling her, my hands shaking and stuttering all over the place. I had only experienced having to hide myself and just dealing with rejection at that point. However, my friend welcomed me with open arms and comforted me. That was the first time in my life I ever felt safe. We parted ways when high school started.

As time went on in high school, I still struggled with my identity and even came to the point in life where I rejected the LGBT community and refused to be a part of it. I distanced myself from my friends and family and hung out with the wrong type of crowd, which just encouraged my path of self-destruction. The self-hatred lingered in freshman year of high school until my depression came to its tipping point. My wake-up call? Waking up in a hospital bed with a doctor giving me papers and numbers to call for suicide hotlines.

Sophomore year I began to find my way back, speaking with my therapist more in depth and finally coming out to my friends and family. There were friends I lost but also friends I've had where our bonds grew closer because of it. I joined groups and organizations to support local LGBT folks and tried my best to get involved with the LGBT community. Coming out to my family was rough at the start, but my therapists helped me through it and eventually my family came around to accepting me.

It's been a rocky road to get where I am today, but I can proudly say I am a trans man—a trans man who loves himself and can happily be out and proud. Once you finally come to that point of acceptance in life you start to cherish those memories and hardships you faced. You start discovering the people you can trust the most and how fulfilling life can be. It does get better; just take it one step at a time. Once you get over that hump in life you start to realize the better and bigger things you can do. Stay strong: You're doing amazing just being here today.

Tyre

17 years old, he/him, Oklahoma

My name is Tyre and this is my story. I was born and raised in Tulsa, Oklahoma, with my dad up until the age of nine years old. Then I was placed with the Department of Human Services because he was abusive. They put me in foster homes across the city. A year later I was put back with my dad and he started abusing my step-mom. One day I finally had enough and I had to leave. I was put back into the system at age fourteen.

Growing up in an abusive home and being gay wasn't easy. I couldn't tell anybody, 1) because I got picked on a lot, so I didn't have friends because of the way I talked and walked and the way I acted, and 2) the adult figures in my life weren't helping either, because being gay was considered a sin. My family thought that if I was gay and if I wanted to talk about my problems, they wouldn't help me or care because they were trying to make me something that I wasn't: straight.

I decided to come out in the sixth grade, but I wasn't truly myself. I came out as bisexual because I thought that if I still liked girls I wouldn't get picked on, but that wasn't the case. So one day I finally decided that I wasn't going to be afraid anymore. I didn't care what people thought of me. I got to a point where I realized that I can't be whatever everyone wants me to be. I didn't feel truly comfortable in my own skin, so I thought that if I came out truly as me that people would see me for who I truly was.

When I went back into the system at fourteen is when I came out as gay. I felt scared and alone, but I wasn't alone. What I didn't realize at the time was that there is a whole community full of people who love and accept me for who I am.

I began to meet other young queer people in the shelters I would go to. They would ask me questions about my coming out story and how I overcame telling my parents who I was, or telling my friends who I was. They asked me for advice on how to come out and be comfortable with who they are. It made me feel happy knowing that I could help other people come out because I didn't have that support system during my journey of acceptance.

I came out because I wasn't scared of what people would say about me, and because being who you are isn't a bad thing. That is

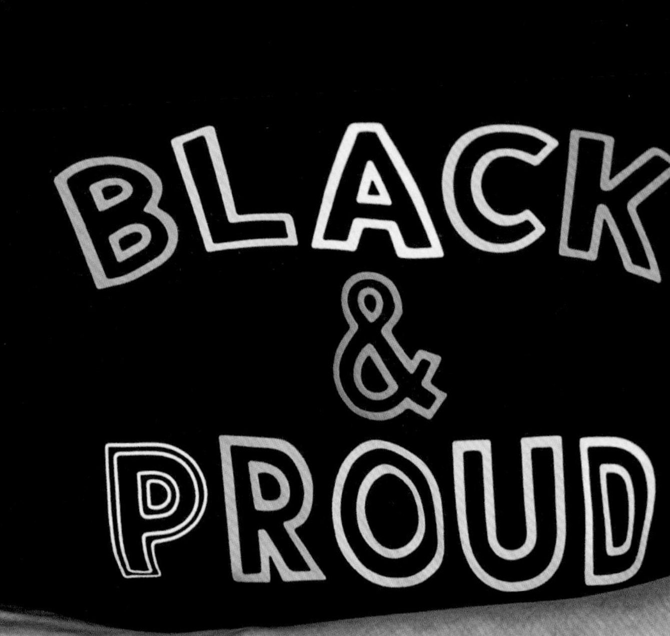

BLACK
&
PROUD

why the kids felt comfortable coming to me for so many questions and advice.

People who don't see queer people as human beings label us as monsters or not regular, but the truth is they're afraid of what isn't considered the "regular." That is why it is important to have our voices heard now, because we couldn't speak up in the past.

Our community has fought for decades to have the freedom of being ourselves without someone bashing us for being who we truly are. That's why a lot of people in our community are scared to come out, because we're taught that being something other than normal is a bad thing. Especially in the Black community, being gay with an abusive parent is hard, because Black people have always been bashed on. Not only am I Black, but I am also gay, so it made me more terrified to try to be who I was.

But the truth is you don't have to be afraid anymore. I am Black and proud! I wish someone was there for me when I was struggling to figure out who I was, but I want to continue to be that person for others, just like I did in the past.

I want you to know that you don't have to pretend to be something you're not. You're allowed to find yourself, and to know that you're not alone. There are people out there who are here for you, so don't be afraid to be yourself and love yourself. As long as you are true to yourself, nobody can tell you who you are and what you are.

I am proud to call myself gay now because not only do I have a community who loves me and is there for me, but I also have an adoptive family who accept me for exactly who I am and don't ask me to be anything less.

I love each and every person who can be themselves without worrying what other people think or say, so my last thing is don't give up on yourself. You're not alone. You're way stronger than what people say, and you are free to be whoever or whatever you want to be. So don't forget it, and don't forget there are people who are here for you and they love you, just like me.

Vinny

16 years old, he/him, Oklahoma

My story starts, as all of ours do, as a small child. I think a lot of queer people say, "I have always known I was [insert queer identity here]." I don't doubt that that is true for some, but it definitely was not for me. I was much like any other girl as a child. I liked playing with any toy that didn't require an imagination, really. Nothing was ever "off" or inherently queer about me, but I was also never really able to fully grasp the actual idea of what was "off" or queer, not until I was much older, at about the age of eleven.

I was enrolled at a homeschool co-op and in about fifth grade I overheard my peers talking about a girl who had just come out as pansexual and making fun of her. This was basically the first time in my life I had ever heard any animosity toward a queer person, and I realized that not everyone was accepting. It was really just the little comments, the inadvertent disgust from everyone in my life toward gay people, that cemented the idea that I couldn't be myself—or express that part of me, at the very least.

When I was around twelve I thought I was a lesbian, but I think I just thought that with the term *lesbian* I would feel more able to express myself in a masculine way. I felt extremely uncomfortable being associated with the traits or roles of a girl or woman, but when I expressed my vague discomfort, everyone attributed it to puberty. I came out to my mom at this time, and it didn't necessarily go badly, but I do remember her saying, "Is there anything else? Are you sure?," which is pretty funny now, considering. When I was thirteen I started attending an LGBTQ youth group, where I got my first binder. It changed everything. It was amazing. I felt so much more comfortable than I ever had. I watched video after video about testosterone and its effects, and top surgery, and just everything I could learn. I was so excited for my future. I had talked to my mom about it at some point, but she wanted me to be eighteen before I did anything. I also started going by the name Vinny at this time. I came out as transgender, but my family had basically already known. It wasn't very hard, and I am very, very, very grateful for that.

I think my experience with gender now versus when I came out is very different. The online trans community was very insistent on gender conformity at the time, and it really affected the way I saw myself and my dysphoria. I think that as a neurodivergent

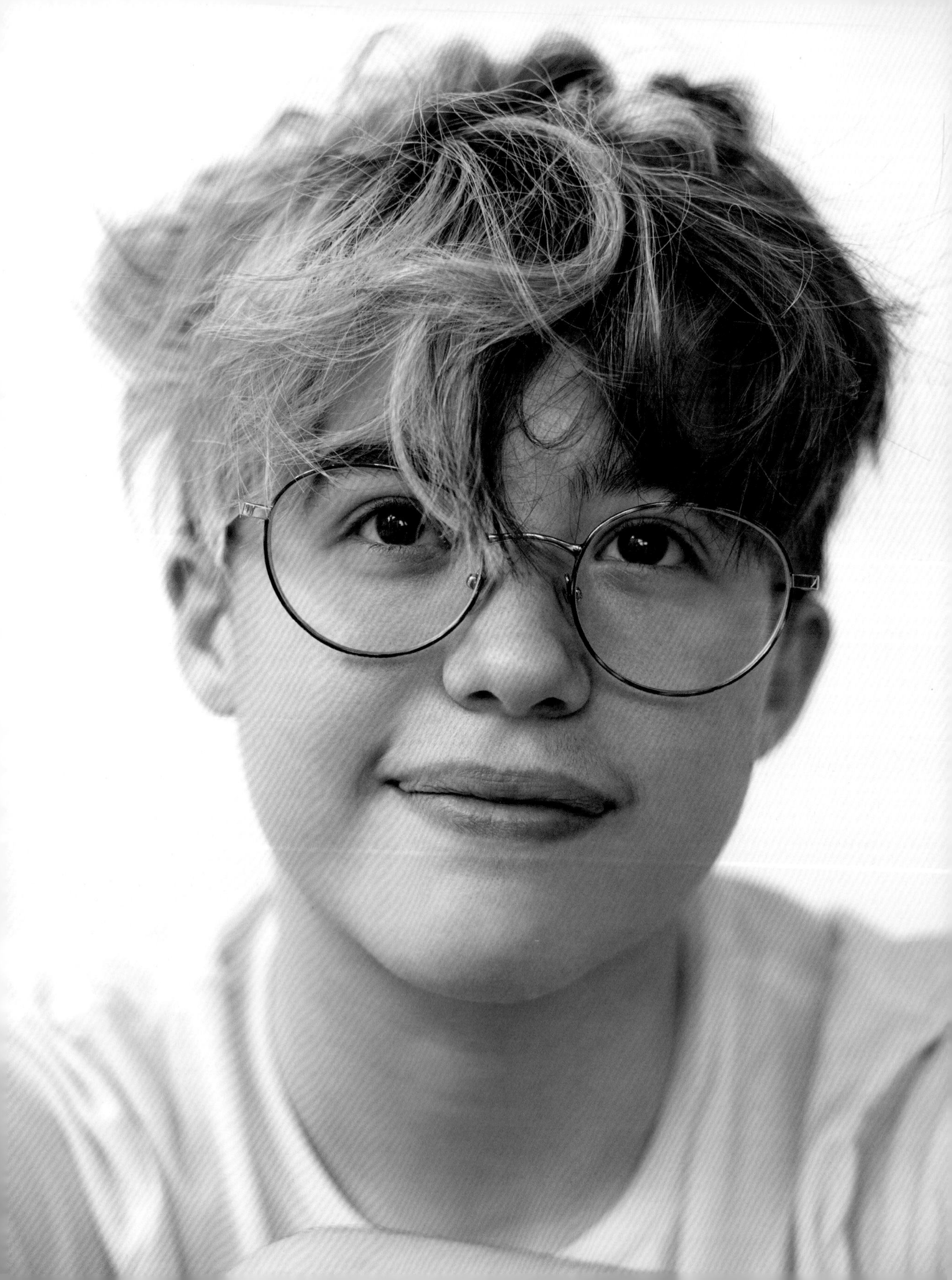

individual, things like conformity and rules for how I was supposed to present my gender came with many positives, such as not having to figure out myself and my expression as much, but they also come with negatives. Many people in the community were very quick to shame other transmasculine people if they expressed themselves in any nonconforming or feminine way. I can only imagine this was done out of a want for cisgender approval. They policed others out of fear that the outside world would not take individuals who express themselves outside of the binary seriously.

This made for one of the most confusing times for me. On one hand, I wanted to fit in with my newly found community. But on the other hand, presenting and identifying as completely masculine also made me dysphoric. I mistook this for maybe not truly being trans, which of course I was very scared about as a trans child who had just come out. I didn't realize this until much later, but the definition of being trans was becoming warped by binary expectations. When I started testosterone I had a similar experience. I liked most changes going on with me, but some I felt were too masculine. Luckily these were all cosmetic and easily taken care of. I realized that I value my androgyny greatly.

As people, we are constantly growing and changing. This is something to be embraced and celebrated, especially with sexuality and gender. Allow yourself compassion when it comes to yourself. That compassion is something I never allowed myself in my first years of gender discovery. I thought I was supposed to be one thing and one thing only, when gender, to me, is complex and beautiful. It's fun to explore what makes you comfortable and euphoric, and even that may change over time.

I'm lucky to have a wonderful group of people around me to support me through an ever-changing exploration of myself. I've learned that it is much better to be myself than to live a lie. I'm sure that many have said the same words before, but that just means it's tried and true in my eyes. Be authentically, unapologetically yourself and all the right people for you will follow. To show confidence in yourself is to invite others to be confident in themselves as well. I never thought someone like me would be able to empower, inspire, and educate others with my unique perspectives and experiences. For that I am so grateful and lucky. I had to learn that I had to accept myself and all my complexities before it seemed possible that anyone would do the same. It takes time and lots and lots of practice, but it is infinitely fulfilling, beautiful, and inspiring and will lead to many great opportunities and people.

Wilbur

14 years old, he/they, New York
CW: This story contains references to self-harm.

My name is Wilbur. I am currently fourteen years old and I live in New York. It's a more conservative part of New York, and most people here aren't supportive. I hear people constantly misgender people behind their backs and talk badly about the people who identify as queer. It's a challenge to even go to the bathroom. I feel unsafe, and I'm constantly on edge out of fear of being outed. I live with my two sisters, my brother, my parents, and my dogs. I'm trans and bisexual, I use he/him pronouns, and my friends call me Fan or Pigeon. I am so excited to share my story, and I hope to inspire others!

One conflict I had growing up with gender dysphoria was the way I dressed. I felt uncomfortable with traditionally feminine clothes. When I first experienced discomfort with wearing feminine clothes I was confused and tried to deny my feelings about it. I liked wearing boys' clothes and roughhousing and playing in the mud. Everyone thought it was just a phase I was going through, a phase that almost every girl goes through, but that wasn't the case. I felt so confused about everything; I didn't know why everything I did felt so wrong. I felt like I was just overreacting. Maybe there was nothing wrong and I was just going through a weird phase that everyone has when they're younger, but I was scared because it felt like more than just that.

My grades were slipping, I had no friends, and I wasn't sure how to interact with people. The only thing I could focus on was my interests. I felt alone, and I had a hard time talking to people because I hated my voice and I hated the way I looked. I was seeing my school counselor, but she didn't help much. I began to skip appointments she would make to see me because I felt like she wasn't helping. And that's when I began cutting. It started out as an easy way to make myself feel better, a way to relieve stress and make myself feel grounded and more connected to my body and reality. It helped for a bit—it made me feel like I was real and like everything else around me was real—but I never really learned how to stop. I tried so many times, and each time it felt like my world was falling apart. I felt like I wasn't real, and it felt like the things around me and the things I was doing weren't real. I thank myself

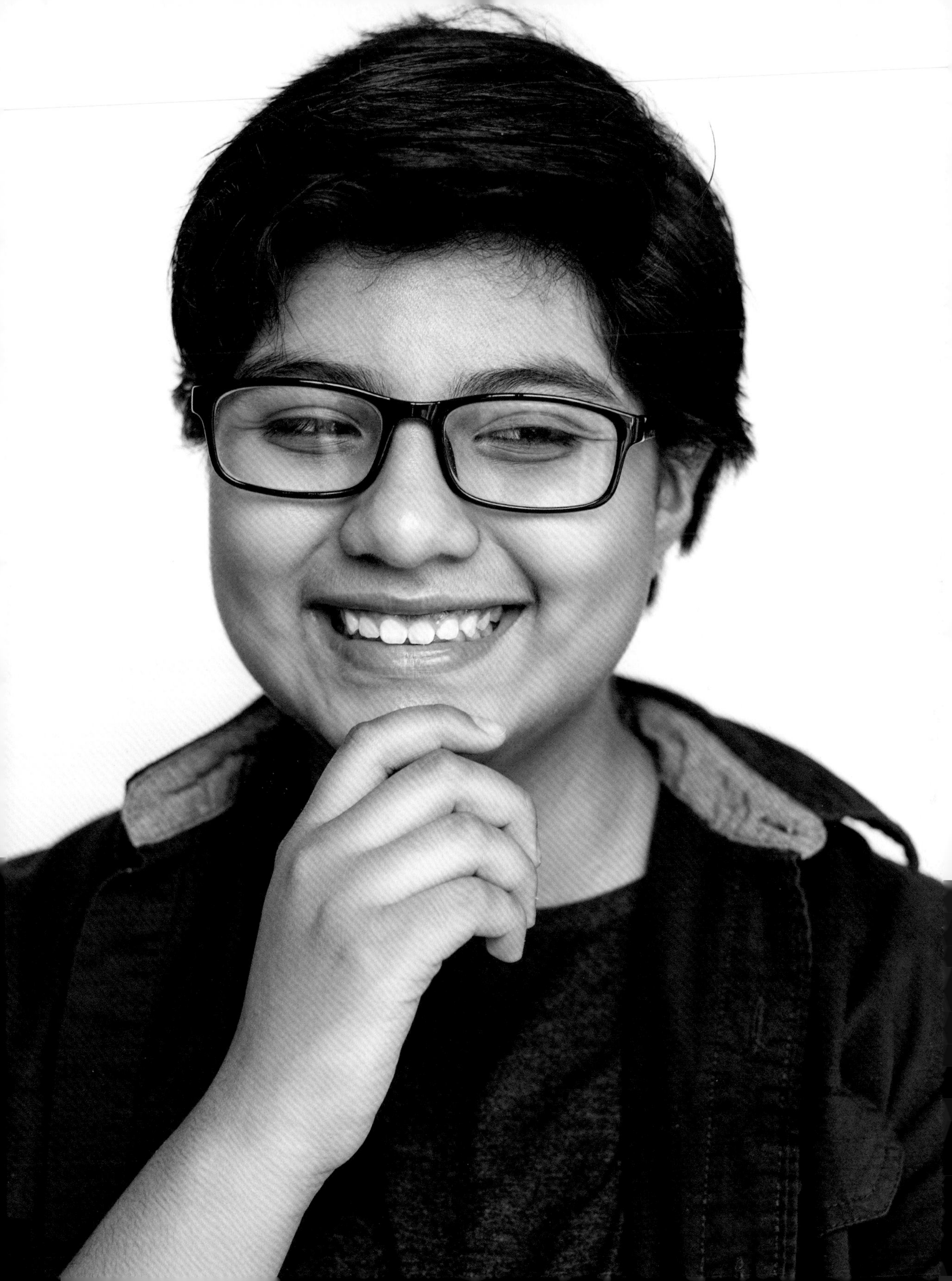

for making it through the year, because I couldn't see myself making it to high school around that time.

I came to terms with being trans when I was in sixth grade going into seventh. The first person I told was my sister, who was in tenth grade at the time, and she was extremely supportive. She told me that she would support me no matter what, and for the first time in such a long time I felt good about myself. With her supportive response I had finally built up the courage to come out to my parents. I first came out as trans to my parents about a week after coming out to my sister. I felt confident about myself and I was confident about my identity, so I was finally going to tell them. It felt like one of the biggest mistakes I made at the time. I was sitting on the couch hearing both of my parents explain that "women can be masculine!" and "I acted masculine when I was your age," and, the worst one, "Oh, well, you're too young to know and it's probably because of your phone." Those things hurt me. I felt as if they had completely ignored my feelings and tried to preserve their own by denying my identity. Every day between then and now was a struggle. I made attempts to avoid them by joining clubs and being on my phone constantly; online friends came and went. I was in eighth grade, and I felt like I was trapped. My parents' denial made me question my identity, and I didn't want them to lecture me about it again, so I decided I wouldn't change how I dress. I thought maybe they were right. Maybe I really wasn't trans and I just wanted to dress differently. Eighth grade wasn't that bad. I had good grades, I had friends, I was in clubs, and I was generally happy. But dysphoria wouldn't let me fully enjoy anything. I was insecure about the way I looked and dressed and the way I spoke. I was embarrassed of myself and I was insecure about everything. I began talking to my parents more, and it helped more than I initially thought it would. Although I still got lectured about identifying as trans on a regular basis, I was able to cut my hair and I started going by the name Pigeon to compensate for my lack of a new name.

Ninth grade was a blur. Every day was the same. I would wake up late and go to my Google Meets and maybe skip a few every now and then. My school counselor would occasionally call to tell me my grades were dropping and I would stay up late to catch up on missing work. I somehow managed to refrain from self-harm the first couple of months, but around the end of the year and the summer I just couldn't hold it in anymore. I lost motivation to do anything, and everything felt like a huge mess. I couldn't keep myself together, so how was I supposed to keep my work together? My parents made it seem like it was so easy, but I had nobody—no friends, no phone, and no reason to continue with my work. I still passed, I started going by the name Wilbur in school, and I was finally starting to look how I wanted. It wasn't what I considered a good year, but I felt like I was changing.

I've changed a lot over the summer and over the course of coming out. My entire family supports me and they started calling me Wilbur. My grades have improved so much, and I finally feel safe. I still don't like my voice, and HRT is a bit of a sensitive subject with my parents, but I feel a little bit better when talking to people. I feel so much more confident, and even though I'm still confused, I'm finally content with myself and I don't feel alone, and for the first time I'm genuinely happy with who I am!

Sometimes you just gotta believe! I know it's hard, but you can't give up on yourself. Things get better and nothing will stay the same forever, no matter how bad a situation is. Everything changes—people and situations change—and you can't give up no matter how bad things are. You need to believe in yourself, and you need to believe that things will change, and you need to put in the effort if you want change. It's easier said than done, but my situation has improved a ton because I put in the effort to take care of myself and meet people who support me, and you can do the same!

Zelda

11 years old, she/her, Colorado

Hi, my name is Zelda! I am an eleven-year-old transgender sixth grader! I love to do things like art, coding, gaming, and sports. One thing I wish right now is that I was in the seventh grade, because sixth grade is too easy except for my double accelerated math class. I am taking blockers right now and will soon be taking estrogen. My pronouns are she/he/they. The reason I say that is because I think it is too much to worry about what pronouns I have because I feel comfortable with all three and I even feel like I am all three!

I am from a small town in New Mexico, which is where I met Maxwell, but I moved to Colorado two years ago, when I was nine years old. Now me and my family are living in Colorado Springs!

My life has been filled with many people who have helped me along the way, and also ones who have not. When I was four I started to realize that I liked the things girls did, and I also felt like a girl. At first, my parents did *not* want me to wear a dress. This was solely because they didn't want me to experience bullying at such a young age, so they said no until they learned that this was called being transgender.

Once this happened they let me be myself. They let me buy the dresses I wanted and they let me grow out my hair and do other things to make me feel more me. I finally felt free! And as I grew, I slowly started to be open about it to those that were not in my family.

Around a year later I started to think, "I want a new name. I don't wanna be called 'Kenny.'" So one night, around my bedtime, I started to think of names, and after some deep thought I decided on the name Zelda. Then I talked to my parents about it. They liked it and decided to call me Zelda at home, but it was not public yet. This was because my parents wanted me to see if I truly liked the name, and as you can see, I did.

After a bit my parents decided to get my name and gender legally changed, so after this my name and gender went from Kenny/boy to Zelda/girl. This brought up some problems school-wise. My school in New Mexico would not change my gender, and to this day they have not changed my name on the school tests and attendance. It also brought up many bullies who would purpose-fully call me a boy, and that is my reason for now being he/she/

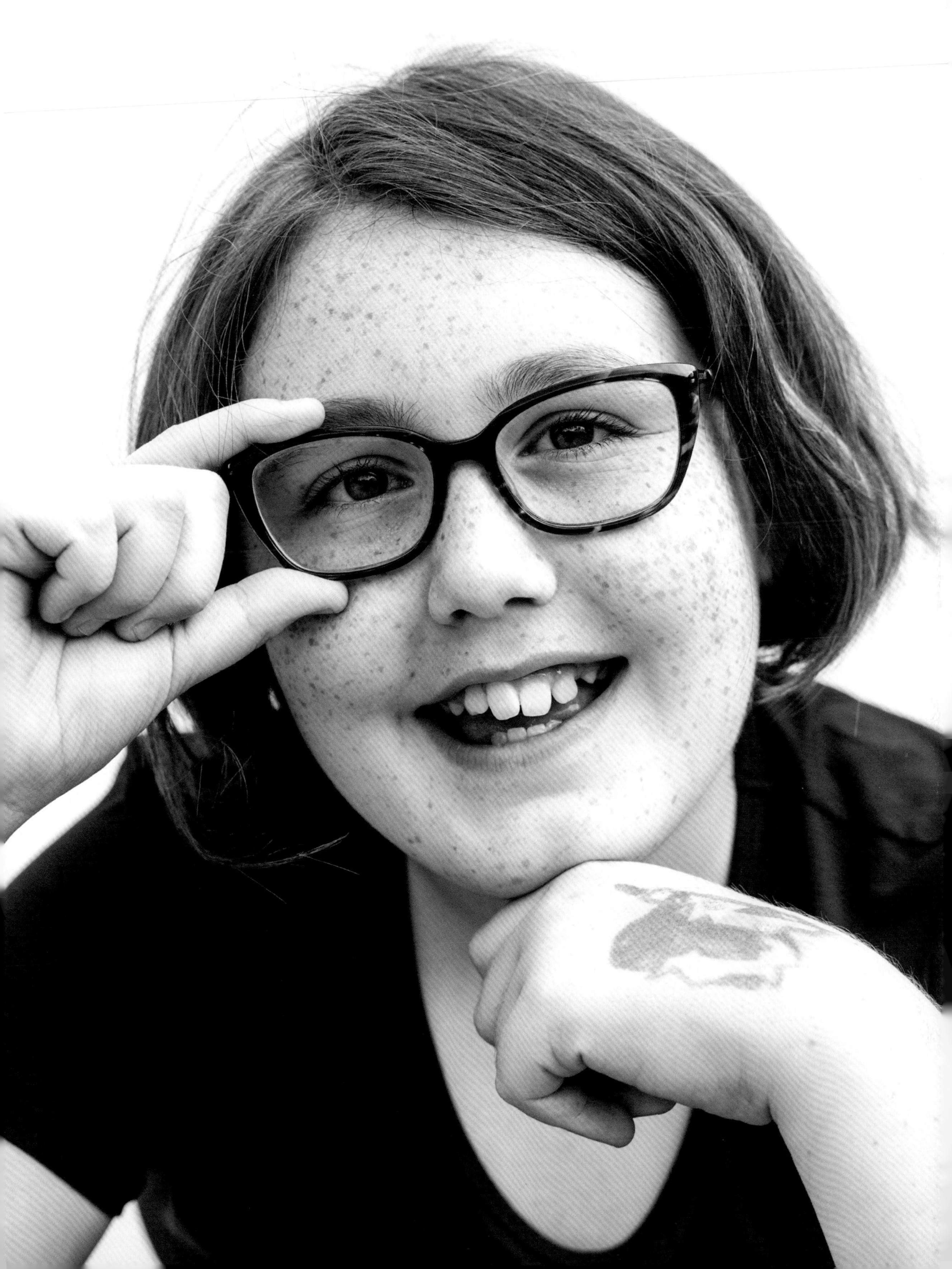

they. Another form of bullying that came my way was being called Kenny, even though they knew very well that my name was Zelda.

I have only had one small incident in my new home of Colorado Springs. One day my brother was outside with our neighbor friends and I was inside. Later, one of my friends asked me, "You are trans, right?" I asked where he heard that, and he said that my brother told him. They didn't really seem to care about it, but then after some thought my neighbor told me I shouldn't be trans. It made me feel sad, but I didn't let him get me down. I was in a new place and with new friends and I am *Zelda*.

There were also some people in support. And I want to point out that my entire cheer team was very supportive and accepting of me and my name change. When I arrived for practice one day they surprised me with a gift bag to celebrate my name change. Another supportive group I was in was my LGBTQ+ group. That was also my first encounter with other people who were in the LBGTQ+ community. It made me feel like I fit in. Another person who helped me was my counselor, Wendy. Every day I went to see her, and it was amazing. One last thing that was amazing was when I went to do Project Contrast. It was really fun to talk about my story and have it publicly shared. And now, I'm in this book!

These events of people supporting me and not supporting me continued almost all the way until I moved to Colorado Springs. It was nice to be somewhere new. It felt good to be at a new school where nobody knew that I was trans. I was known as just "Zelda," not "Zelda who used to be a boy and used to be named Kenny." Since I moved here I haven't really had anyone who has been supportive (just because no one knows I am trans) or anyone who has been not supportive.

The times where people were mean to me or told me I shouldn't be trans made me sad or angry, because I don't trust those people, but regardless I am proud and happy to be me, Zelda.

In the near future I am planning to go to UCCS. At the moment I do not know what I will go there for academically, but that will come to me when the right time comes.

Some advice to anyone, LGBTQ+ or not, is to never listen to those who hurt you, physically or mentally. And also, always stay positive.

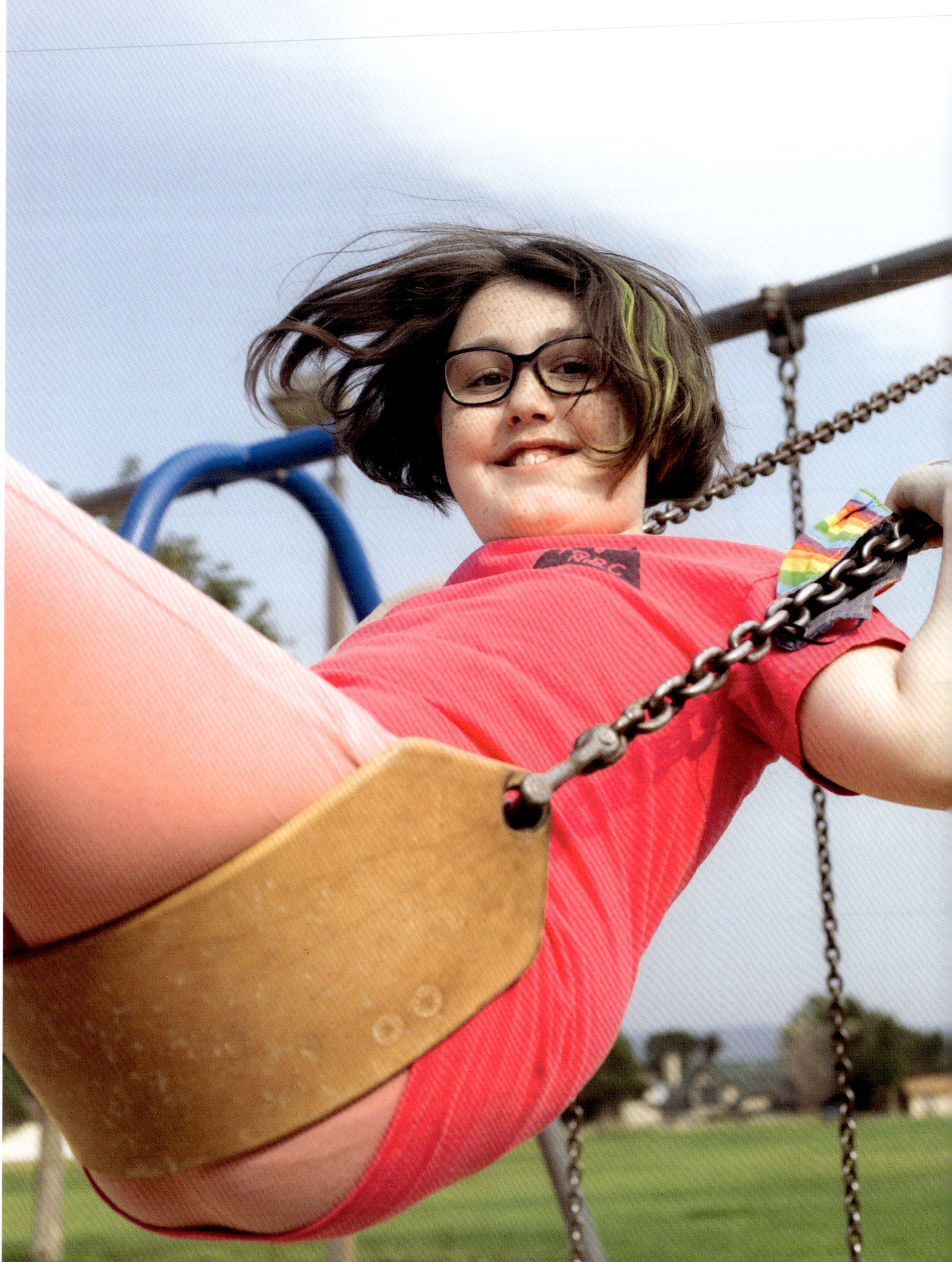

Alyson

Our son Stockton was a long-awaited gift in our home: He was adopted and was adored by us and his two doting sisters. He was always a light in the home, with lots of love and character. For as long as I can remember he was a hugger and loved to give kisses. I often told him he was born in my heart—a heart that I knew had the capacity to love without conditions. Little did I know that this beautiful baby boy was about to stretch my heart in ways I didn't think were possible. This was the beginning of my personal transformation, and that of our family.

At the age of thirteen Stockton came to us and told us that he was gay. Not fully understanding what that meant, his dad and I started looking for any and all resources available to help our son on his journey. Unfortunately, there weren't many available, nor was this topic one that anyone in our community seemed comfortable talking about. We were desperate for information and resources to help him navigate his life in a healthy way. These formative years are hard on teens as they try to find their way among their peers. This was a time where we saw our son's light start to fade. He began to experience depression, and with the help of his doctors he was being treated with medications. We desperately tried to find something that he could connect with, and to find others who would love him for the person he was. It seemed at every turn there was another roadblock telling our son he did not belong. It felt like we were fighting an uphill battle, and Stockton had no place where he felt safe outside of his family.

My son would reach for those in need and was always looking for the outsider while silently suffering himself. Stockton was and will always be the one who taught our family to love more freely and without judgment. We had the opportunity to become involved in the LGBT community in Utah, and there Stockton found his tribe. But, in spite of this, my son felt a great deal of pain losing his community and wanting to feel a part of the things he had known all of his life—his church, neighborhood, and peer group at school. It wasn't the mean words or occasional bullying that hurt him as much as it was being ignored, being left out or not being acknowledged. I believe with all of these situations there is a layering effect; our lives are a culmination of experiences. Knowing my son as I do, I believe his pain must have been immense for him to ultimately take his life. This is where my life has been changed forever. We lost Stockton to suicide on June 27, 2016.

It has been so difficult for our family to be without our son, and the heartbreak we experience has been life-altering. My son did not feel loved by his peers, his community, or his church. It seemed as if we had forgotten the one while serving the ninety and nine. I hope to honor my son by helping bridge the gap that often occurs between LDS members and their LGBT brothers and sisters.

I certainly believe with all my heart that we as parents would do anything for our children, and that we love them with a depth that only a parent understands. So often in the work that I do with kids in the LGBT community, that is not the message these kids are hearing and feeling. We are here for a purpose, and that purpose is *not* to inflict more pain on these kids.

I myself had to learn that it wasn't my job to impose my beliefs on my child, but to allow him to experience life and to provide him with a soft place to land. To be a haven from the storm and teach his siblings and other family members that we will continue to love and support. Oh, how thankful I am that my son left this life knowing he was loved just the way he was. I love this quote by Thomas Merton: "The beginning of love is the will to let those we love be perfectly themselves, the resolution not to twist them to fit our own image. If in loving them we do not love what they are, but only their potential likeness to ourselves, then we do not love them: we love only the reflection of ourselves we find in them."

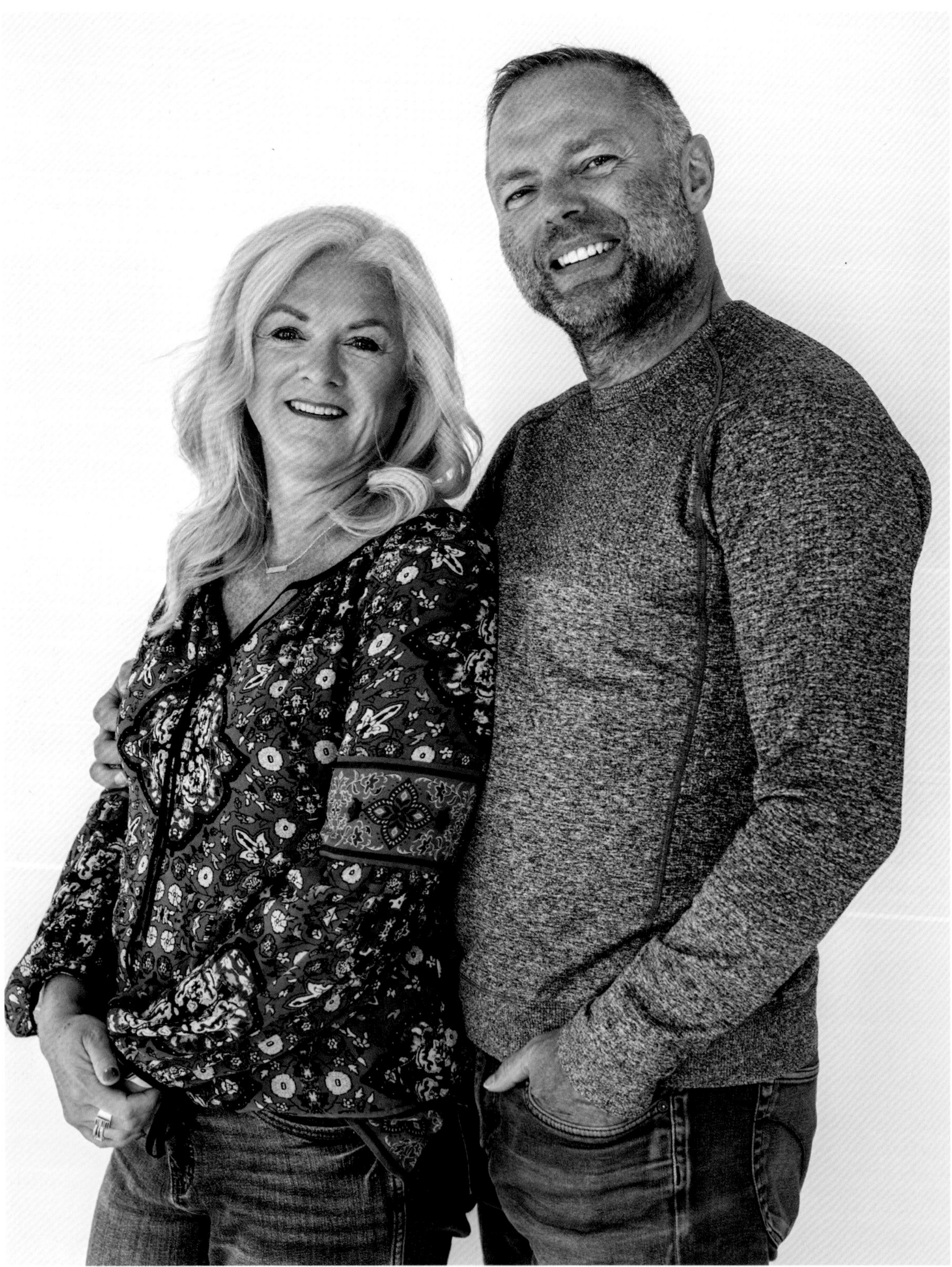

I, for one, know that I can show more compassion. Compassion
for those cast on the side of the road whom the Levite and priest
passed by. I can share our covenant to bear one another's burdens,
to mourn with those who mourn, and comfort those who stand in
need of comfort.

After the shock and numbness wear off comes a pain indescrib-
able. Feelings of guilt, anger, sadness, and helplessness mercilessly
pile on the survivor with only brief periods of relief. At such a
point there are two choices: withdraw in bitterness, or find a way
to bring some good out of the devastation.

And so my son's legacy is about what I think he would want me
to do. If you are experiencing life after death, be kind and patient
with yourself. Choose light over withdrawal and grief. For myself, I
have chosen to be a voice and to take a stand for Stockton.

George

*If you love someone, you are always joined with them—in joy, in
absence, in solitude, in strife.* —Rumi

From the moment I set my eyes on my son, I fell in love with
him. His infectious smile, laugh, and mischievousness were an
instant hit with me. His precious hugs and endearing gaze would
melt any frustration and would heal any sadness. His light was
powerful. His light continues to be powerful.

My son didn't always feel accepted and appreciated by others.
My religious community treated him in a way that left him asking
questions about what might be wrong with him. As I watched and
felt the pain of these experiences I realized how vital it is to create
safe spaces in our homes and in our communities. Safe places are
places where our family, friends, and others feel that they don't
need to hide themselves from the potential harm of others.

On June 27, 2016, my world changed in a most significant way.
It was the day that my son took his life.

As a father, I felt a great need to not only deeply love my child
and all of my children, but also to protect them. The grief I feel
includes the struggle of wondering why I needed to protect my son
from people who should have treated him with kindness. I also feel
the loss of a community that I thought was going to support me
and bear my burdens with me.

Many years ago my wife approached me and wanted to pur-
chase flower baskets to be placed around our home to add color

and beauty. At first I was a bit resistant when she told me the cost, but, as is usual in our home, I relented and quickly appreciated them for many reasons. It became my responsibility to care for these flowers and ensure that they received the water they needed. One day my wife asked that I remember to water the edges of the baskets. She said, "George, please remember to water the edges of the baskets. If you don't, the flowers will die." Little did I know how profoundly her comment would affect me after Stockton's passing.

Just after his funeral I was out in our yard watering those same flowers and her words came to me with such force that I began to cry. Those precious flowers on the edge of the flower basket were my son, along with other members of LGBTQ community—put on the edges, marginalized, and even abandoned. They weren't put there by the Creator. They were put there by fellow travelers.

As I composed myself and took a deep breath, I thought more about the significance of the flower basket. It was beautiful—all of it. It was filled with many colors, all adding to the beauty of the whole. I began to think how often we—myself included—believe that others must change to be more like us. I thought how drab the flower basket would be if all the flowers were green, or the same color, having no variation and difference. Just like my flower baskets, we all need water, nourishment, love, kindness, and appreciation for our divine design. And just as with my flower baskets, there is great beauty and benefit in differences. We are created with differences for a grand and divine purpose.

As much as this is incredibly difficult, I have gained an understanding through my son's experiences of how vital the community can be and needs to be. This experience has moved, motivated, and inspired me to reach out to the community and to look at each one as I would look at my own child.

The loss of my son has ultimately provided fuel to raise my words and deeds, seeking to create a safe place, encouraging a community of deep love.

CONCLUSION

I never gave up hope of making this book a reality. As I write this paragraph I am sitting on my last flight of the project, back to Los Angeles. I've traveled to sixteen states and visited forty-six cities, towns, and rural areas. I've taken thirty-eight flights and a dozen road trips, all within four months. It took me an entire year to find seventy-three queer youth across the nation during a global pandemic. Sitting at my desk in my own home. Connecting via Zoom for months. Interviewing each kid multiple times and getting to know them and their families. Not being able to travel safely until vaccinations were widely distributed. This was exceptionally challenging since we find youth through LGBTQ+ youth centers, groups, GSAs, etc., but during the pandemic everything was put on hold. Local leaders and teachers were not meeting with these kids face-to-face. Attendance at meetings plummeted and connecting with the kids was difficult. What had once been in-person meetings became Zoom meetups and the youth lost interest. Centers closed down, clubs dissipated, and kids were stuck in their homes.

I've spent years documenting queer youth. Sharing what each one goes through on a daily basis while living in completely different geographical areas with completely different demographics, beliefs, and laws. Yet, despite all their differences, they find their similarities. Even if those similarities are the struggles that others put upon them, it makes them stronger. It is time to start changing those challenging moments that each queer youth has to endure and help them find the light within themselves. It is crucial that we keep our queer youth safe and make them feel loved and seen. We must because they are our future.

Thank you for reading this book and seeing the faces of all these beautiful young queer people across America. I will ask you only two things now that you've made it to the end.

1) Share this book with someone who needs it. Share it with struggling queer kids who need to find community. Share it with a struggling parent who needs help accepting their child. Give it to a local politician who has never met a transgender person yet fights to take away their rights. Share it with the world!

2) Always teach love. Always spread love and only receive love.

I believe this book will save lives and change the lives of others. Not because of me. It is these seventy-three stories from these amazing people who will change the course of someone's life forever and always remind you that you are loved.

State Resources

Alabama LGBTQ+ Resources:

Magic City Acceptance Center—Birmingham

Montgomery Pride United—Montgomery

Prism United—Mobile & Fairhope

Alaska LGBTQ+ Resources:

Alaska Pride Foundation—Anchorage

Identity, Inc.—Anchorage

Arkansas LGBTQ+ Resources:

Hot Springs LGBT Alliance—Hot Springs

Lucie's Place—Little Rock

NWA Equality—Northwest Arkansas Transgender Equality Coalition

California LGBTQ+ Resources:

The Center for Sexuality and Gender Diversity—Bakersfield

The Fresno Spectrum Center—Fresno

The LGBT Center of Long Beach—Long Beach

LGBTQ Center of Orange County—Santa Ana

Los Angeles LGBT Center—Los Angeles

NorCal Outreach Project—Redding

Oakland LGBTQ Community Center—Oakland

On The Move/LGBTQ Connection—Napa

The Outreach Center, Antelope Valley—Lancaster

Pacific Center for Human Growth—Berkeley

Pacific Pride Foundation—Santa Barbara

Pomona Pride Center, Inc.—Pomona

Rainbow Community Center of Contra Costa County—Concord

The San Diego Lesbian, Gay, Bisexual, Transgender Community Center—San Diego

San Francisco LGBT Community Center—San Francisco

The Source LGBT+ Center—Visalia

Stonewall Alliance Center of Chico—Chico

Trans Wellness Center—Los Angeles

Colorado LGBTQ+ Resources:

The Center On Colfax—Denver

Four Corners Rainbow Youth Center—Durango

Inside Out Youth Services—Colorado Springs

Out Boulder—Boulder

Youthzone/The Space—Glenwood Springs

Indiana LGBTQ+ Resources:

Damien Center—Indianapolis

GenderNexus—Indianapolis

Indiana Youth Group—Indianapolis

The LGBTQ Center—South Bend

Spencer Pride Community Center—Spencer

Kansas LGBTQ+ Resources:

The Center of Wichita, Inc.—Wichita

Haus of McCoy—Lawrence

Our Spot KC—Kansas City

Louisiana LGBTQ+ Resources:

LGBT Community Center of New Orleans—New Orleans

Out of The Box LGBT Center—Baton Rouge

PACE—Shreveport

Youth Oasis—Baton Rouge

Michigan LGBTQ+ Resources:

Affirmation—Ferndale

Grand Rapids Pride Center—Grand Rapids

Jim Toy Community Center—Ann Arbor

Out on the Lakeshore—Holland

Outcenter of Southwest Michigan—Benton Harbor

Outfront Kalamazoo—Kalamazoo

Transcend the Binary—Ferndale

New York LGBTQ+ Resources:

Brooklyn Community Pride Center—Brooklyn

The Center of Hauppauge—Hauppauge

Hudson Valley LGBTQ Center—Kingston

Identity Youth Center—Binghamton

In Our Own Voices, INC—Albany

The Lesbian, Gay, Bisexual & Transgender Community Center, NYC—New York

The LGBTQ Center of the Finger Lakes—Geneva

The Loft LGBTQ Community Center—White Plains

Pride Center of Western New York—Buffalo

Pride Center of Staten Island—Staten Island

Oklahoma LGBTQ+ Resources:

Dennis R. Neill Equality Center—Tulsa

Diversity Center of Oklahoma—Oklahoma City

South Dakota LGBTQ+ Resources:

Black Hills Center for Equality—Rapid City

LGBTQ+ Family Connections Center—Rapid City

The Transformation Project—Sioux Falls

Watertown Love—Watertown

Texas LGBTQ+ Resources:

Abilene Pride Alliance—Abilene

Austin Outpost—Austin

Borderland Rainbow Center—El Paso

The Center—Pride Center San Antonio—San Antonio

Coastal Bend Pride Center—Corpus Christi

FUSE, United Black Element (UBE) and Gender Brave —Dallas

LGBTQ Saves—Fort Worth

Maven Youth—San Antonio

The Montrose Center—Houston

Open Arms Rape Crisis Center & LGBT Services —San Angelo

OUT YOUTH—Austin

Pride Center West Texas—Odessa

Pride Community Center—College Station

Resource Center—Dallas

Utah LGBTQ+ Resources:

Encircle—Locations in Provo, Salt Lake City, Logan, Ogden, St. George, Heber

Equality Utah—Salt Lake City

Utah Pride Center—Salt Lake City

Wyoming LGBTQ+ Resources:

Casper Pride—Casper

Rainbow Resource Center—Laramie

Wyoming Equality—Cheyenne

Wyoming GSA Network—Cheyenne

If you wish to find LGBTQ+ centers, groups, or allies you can also use CenterLink, a community of LGBT Centers. Please visit www.lgbtcenters.org.

ACKNOWLEDGMENTS

It is safe to say that this book took an entire queer army to make, from my Project Contrast team to the dozens of LGBTQ+ advocates, leaders, parents, and allies throughout the country. You all helped me make this possible. My hat's off to you all.

Thank you to my Project Contrast team: Lisa, Wylie, Alex, and Yvoty. Without you I wouldn't have been able to complete this book or make it to these places while you kept Project Contrast afloat. You should all be so proud. I love you.

To my editor, Natalie Butterfield at Chronicle Books, I am truly grateful. Thank you for helping me amplify these stories. I couldn't picture making this book with anyone else but you and the Chronicle team.

Thank you to my agent, Jon Michael Darga. Words cannot express how happy I am that I met you that fine rainy day at a sushi restaurant in New York City, not knowing that you'd help guide me into making this book a reality. I look forward to so many more queer adventures with you.

Thank you to Jacob Dunford. Without your trust in me I wouldn't be here today. You are a big part of my life forever, and none of this would have happened without your early support.

To everyone who helped me in each state, there is not enough room in this book to express my love and gratitude for you all. (I also recently learned about how strict word counts are in book publishing, and boy did we go over!) I hope you know how much I mean it when I say thank you, from the bottom of my little gay heart.

Throughout the country: Deborah Levine, for creating CenterLink and helping me reach so many LGBT centers, advocates, and allies. In Alabama: Corey Harvard; in Alaska: Brooks Banker, Justin Dickens; in Arkansas: Justin Ray Rawls; in California: Melantha Hodge and Rani DeMesme-Anders at the Los Angeles LGBT Center, Rae, Justin, and Brian at It Gets Better, and Brian Poth; in Colorado: Cortny Stark, Jennifer Stucka-Benally, Jenna Howerton; in Indiana: Moe Smith, Lauren Grocock, H. R. Jung; in Kansas: Dawna Raehpour; in Louisiana: Hershey Krippendorf, Evan Stevens, Felicia Jessup, M'issa Fleming, Caleb Dufresne; in Michigan: Justin Bettcher; in New York: Faith Winship, Gi Swords; in Oklahoma: Shannon Fair and my love Kris Williams, the Mama Bear of Oklahoma City; in South Dakota: Amy Rambow, Susan Williams, Nancy and Jen Rosenbrahn (You have changed my life forever, Jen. May you rest in peace. I will always call you my family); in Texas: Frederick Heather, Hayden, Bryan and Clint Wilson; in Utah: Amber McMillan, Stephanie Larsen, Landon Creer, Justin Kwong, and my loving family; in Wyoming: Manuela at the Wind River Reservation, Debra East, Shannon O'Quinn, Mallory Pollock, Liz Hardwick, Jordan Cranch, and Wyn Wiley, better known as Pattie Gonia.

Most importantly, I want to thank each and every young queer person in this book who was brave enough to share their story with the world and show everyone what beautiful humans you all are.